Northern Fishes

Mary Lake, Itasca State Park. A typical Minnesota lake. Photo: William D. Schmid.

Northern
Fishes

With Special Reference to the

Upper Mississippi Valley

Third edition, revised
and expanded

SAMUEL EDDY

AND

JAMES C. UNDERHILL

UNIVERSITY OF MINNESOTA PRESS, MINNEAPOLIS

The contribution of the McKnight Foundation to the general program of the University of Minnesota Press, of which the publication of this book is a part, is gratefully acknowledged.

Preface

In the twenty-seven years since the second revised edition of this book was published, there have been significant changes in the distribution of Minnesota fishes and important additions to the list of species known from Minnesota waters. New species have been introduced, intentionally or accidentally (for example, the coho salmon and the alewife). Continued collecting and improved collecting techniques have revealed the presence of several species which were not thought to exist in the state and have provided further information on the abundance of several species which formerly were known from only a few localities. Although further changes will occur in the fish fauna, it seems appropriate at this point to bring the record up to date with a thorough revision of *Northern Fishes*.

Fishing is easily the favorite form of outdoor recreation in Minnesota. Statistics compiled in 1972 by W. J. Scidmore and Leonard Wroblewski of the Minnesota Department of Natural Resources indicate that of the 3.8 million residents in Minnesota approximately 36 percent are fishermen. In 1970 there were 1,425,800 "certified" fishermen in the state; this is the actual number of resident and nonresident licensed fishermen. By comparison there were only 377,384 "certified" hunters in the same year. A total of 654,155 resident fishing licenses were sold in 1971. The value of fishing to the resort industry becomes quite apparent from a casual perusal of outdoorsmen's magazines and an inspection of the displays at sportsmen's shows. Sport fishing is one of the more important economic resources of Minnesota and is particularly important to the economy of the central and northern parts of the state.

The state of Minnesota extends for 400 miles from north to south and 352 miles from east to west across the widest part. The state is unique in that its waters drain to the sea by three quite divergent routes — north to Hudson Bay, east to the gulf of the St. Lawrence and the Atlantic, and south to the Gulf of Mexico. The four major drainage systems are the Hudson Bay drainage (the Red and Rainy rivers); the Great Lakes drainage (the St. Louis

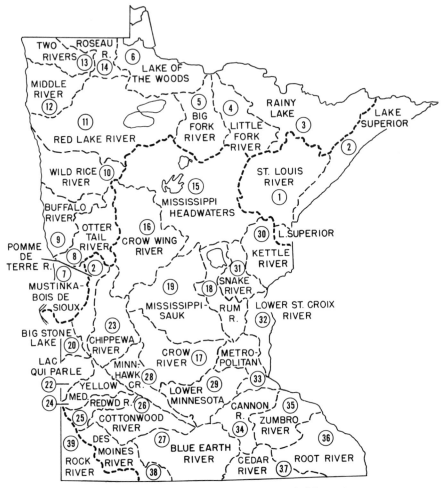

Map 1. Major drainage basins and stream systems in Minnesota

Key to Map 1

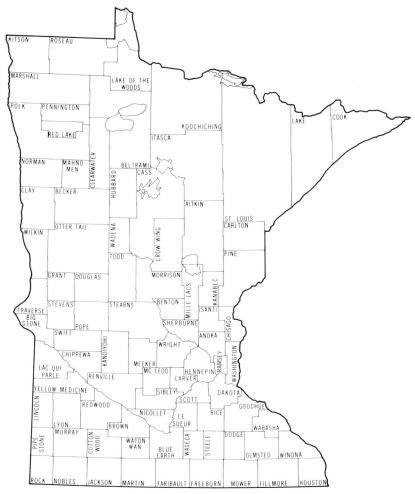

Map 2. Counties in Minnesota

River and the streams along the north shore of Lake Superior); the Mississippi River drainage (the Mississippi River, the Minnesota River, and the St. Croix River); and the Missouri River drainage (a few small streams in extreme southwestern Minnesota). The total area of the state is 84,068 square miles; approximately 59 percent of this area drains into the Mississippi River, 21 percent into the Red River, 13 percent into Lake of the Woods and the Rainy River, 7 percent into Lake Superior, and 2 percent into the Missouri River. Each of these drainage systems contains certain species of fish not found in the other systems. Map 1 shows the various streams and drainage systems in the state, and Map 2 identifies the counties in which certain lakes and streams are located.

The largest navigable rivers include the Mississippi, Minnesota, St. Croix, Rainy, St. Louis, Red, and Red Lake rivers. All but the St. Croix and Minnesota rivers have their sources within the state and are fed by thousands of lakes, smaller rivers, creeks, and brooks. Six percent of the area of the state, or 2.5 million acres, is water, not including the portion of Lake Superior that lies within the state's boundaries and covers another 1.4 million acres.

Brochures for visitors to the state frequently point out that Minnesota has more natural lakes than any of the other forty-nine states. At last count there were 15,291 lake basins in the state with an area greater than 10 acres, and of these approximately 12,000 were permanent bodies of water. Of the 5,100 lakes with areas of more than 40 acres, some 3,000 are recognized as good fishing lakes. The 10 largest lakes within the state are: Lower Red Lake (246 square miles), Mille Lacs (197 square miles), Upper Red Lake (184 square miles), Leech Lake (174 square miles), Lake Winnibigoshish (110 square miles), Lake Vermilion (58 square miles), Lake Kabetogama (31 square miles), Cass Lake (25 square miles), Otter Tail Lake (23 square miles), and Lake Minnetonka (23 square miles). Most of Minnesota's lakes are less than 90 feet deep, but a few are more than 200 feet deep: Lake Saganaga (240 feet), Gabimichigami Lake (226 feet), Mountain Lake (210 feet), Lower La Salle Lake (208 feet), and Loon Lake (202 feet). There are several large lakes in addition to Lake Superior that Minnesota shares with neighboring states or provinces: Lake Pepin and Lake St. Croix (Wisconsin); Big Stone Lake and the Lake Traverse Reservoir (North Dakota and South Dakota); Rainy Lake (Ontario); and Lake of the Woods (Ontario and Manitoba).

The conditions present in Minnesota waters have been changing rapidly and the rate of change seems to have accelerated in the past three decades. This has occurred as a result of several factors — all of which are related directly or indirectly to people. The population of the state has become more mobile and many Minnesota families now have two dwellings, one in a city or its suburbs and the other on a lake, a river, or a stream elsewhere in the state. The number of resorts, marinas, and lake developments has increased tremendously, and the figures for boat ownership have also risen. With the resulting steady increase in the need for power and the concurrent dwindling of our sources of economical hydrological power, we are finding it necessary to turn to various fossil fuels and nuclear energy to satisfy the demand for electricity. Utilization of these power sources creates problems of heat disposal, and the unique characteristics of water make it the least expensive medium of heat exchange. At the same time urban growth has increased the amount of water used for sanitation. Agricultural practices such as the drainage of wetlands to expand the tillable acreage and the irrigation of cultivated areas have also claimed a sizable share of the surface and underground water supplies. While Minnesota is blessed with abundant water, we hope it is apparent that these supplies are not unlimited. In addition to supplying man's needs the waters of the state support thousands of kinds of plants and animals besides the various species of fish. Their continued existence will depend on the wise management of our most important and abundant resource, water.

Drought has not been an important factor in the hydrological picture in Minnesota for the past three decades, but there are indications that it might become a serious problem in the future. Intensive agriculture has opened up to cultivation more and more land that was formerly considered marginal and was left in pastures or woodlots. The effects of this on the streams of the state are already evident — a number of springs have dried up, local flooding is more common, and some permanent streams have become intermittent. Sound land and water management of the watersheds seems to offer the only real solution to these problems. Unfortunately, the potential seriousness of the gradual changes (siltation, pollution, destruction of spawning and feeding beds) that occur in the smaller streams often is not recognized until it is too late and too expensive to repair the damage. Furthermore, no small streams have been selected by the state for preservation as natural areas. The St. Croix River is part of the "wild river" system, but it is now quite apparent that it is overused in certain sections. The Boundary Waters Canoe Area is another example; in 1937 it was regarded as virgin wilderness, by 1947 outdoorsmen were "discovering" the area, and today the number of visitors must be restricted to prevent overuse.

These problems are generated by people, and ultimately people must find the solutions because under the circumstances the problems can only become worse. The preface to the 1947 edition of this book pointed out that obviously conservation measures must be taken by all who are interested in conserving our fish resources. At present it is clear that the proper measures have *not* been taken despite the obviousness of the problems, and the same problems and additional ones face those who wish to conserve our aquatic resources. In this book, as in the preceding editions, we seek to provide information that will be helpful not only to the sportsman and the ichthyologist but also to the naturalist and others who are interested in conserving the fish and water resources of the state.

Acknowledgments

We wish to express our deep appreciation to the many individuals who have contributed to the present edition of *Northern Fishes*. We are particularly indebted to our good friend and associate David J. Merrell, who read the introductory chapters, provided us with constructive criticisms, and made many excellent suggestions. William D. Schmid, another close friend and associate in the field and in academic pursuits, supplied helpful suggestions on several chapters and made available to us his talent as a photographer. Miss Janet Thomas patiently and skillfully typed the preliminary drafts of the manuscript, and her dedication and good humor throughout the early going was especially gratifying. Mrs. Carolyn O'Brien assisted us in innumerable ways, and Miss Gayle Busack typed portions of the final manuscript. Mrs. Marilyn Sterre provided us with important counsel on the illustrations, prepared the original figure of the mouths of the redhorses (*Moxostoma*), and adapted the drawing of the drainage map. Anne Underhill, who read the preliminary drafts, provided useful lay criticisms of the text and served as a most considerate sounding board for ideas.

A book on fishes and fishing in Minnesota owes its existence to many workers, among them the early ichthyologists who first collected and wrote about the fishes of Minnesota waters: Ulysses O. Cox, Barton W. Evermann, Homer B. Latimer, Henry F. Nachtrieb, Thaddeus Surber, and Albert J. Woolman. The collections of Cox, Nachtrieb, and Surber formed the nucleus of the present collection of fishes in the James Ford Bell Museum of Natural History at the University of Minnesota; this collection was made available to us through the kind cooperation and assistance of Walter J. Breckenridge, director emeritus of the Museum, and Harrison B. Tordoff, the present director. Through the years we have also benefited from the advice and counsel of many professional ichthyologists, and we wish to acknowledge especially the contributions of Carl L. Hubbs and Reeve M. Bailey.

We are very much indebted to our close associates Edward Bellis, Thomas Collins, Joseph Eastman, David Etnier, Richard Forbes, John Hudson, Daniel Isaak, David J. Merrell, Peter Moyle, Darby Nelson, Frank Nordlie,

Gary Phillips, William D. Schmid, Richard Stasiak, and Roy Tasker for the many hours they spent in the field assisting us, for the continuing stimulation they provided, and above all for their pleasant companionship.

Over a period of almost half a century another group of people have contributed a great deal, directly and indirectly, to *Northern Fishes* — the personnel of the Fisheries section of the Minnesota Department of Natural Resources. (As a matter of fact, the first edition of *Northern Fishes* had its origins in the former Section of Research and Planning of the Division of Game and Fish in the 1930s.) In this connection we would like to thank the following individuals on the Fisheries staff: Charles R. Burrows, Merle W. Johnson, Howard F. Krosch, Jerome H. Kuehn, Donald E. Olson, Arthur R. Peterson, and W. J. Scidmore. Special mention should be made of the contributions of our friend John Dobie, retired fisheries biologist, who was always willing to search the department records for pertinent facts and figures and who also contributed illustrations to this and earlier editions of *Northern Fishes*. We are also deeply indebted to John B. Moyle, technical assistant to the director of the Minnesota Department of Natural Resources; a scientist and a naturalist for over forty years, he has been an unfailing source of information on fish, fisheries, and aquatic biology in Minnesota.

We are very grateful to Lloyd L. Smith, Jr., who made available to us his extensive collections from Lower Red Lake; to Don Olson for the use of his collections from the Rainy River and its tributaries; to Emory Anderson for specimens from western Lake Superior; to Howard F. Krosch for numerous specimens from Lake St. Croix; to Thomas F. Waters for his collections of sculpins; and to Hollie Collins for his records of eels collected in recent years from Lake Superior. In addition, we would like to thank all those who in the past have contributed specimens to the University of Minnesota's collections and to museum collections elsewhere.

Over the past forty years the Graduate School of the University of Minnesota has provided grants-in-aid that have enabled us to carry out the necessary fieldwork on the fishes of the state. We would be remiss if we did not express our deep appreciation to Professor Magnus Olson, head of the Department of Zoology at the University of Minnesota, for his understanding and encouragement.

Last but by no means least, we wish to acknowledge all the fellow anglers and naturalists who have anonymously contributed their knowledge of fish and fishing to the present book, and we treasure our sometimes fleeting conversations with them alongside a stream or in passing on a Minnesota lake.

Contents

Illustrations

Northern Fishes

Success in Fishing — Skill or Luck?

On what does success in fishing depend? Fishing is one of the oldest and most popular sports throughout the world and for all peoples. Ever since primitive man invented the fishhook, his descendants have been searching for a sure method to make fish take it. From the time of Izaak Walton, much has been written on the subject, but most fishermen are still blundering along. Their success depends partly on perseverance, partly on skill, and partly on luck, any one of which may predominate. Perseverance is a personal quality and can be cultivated. Skill can also be acquired. On the other hand, luck is an unknown factor.

It is indisputable that on some days fish do not bite as well as on other days. Censuses secured from many anglers on the number of fish caught per fishing hour prove this fact. Some people believe that the weather determines whether fish will bite or not, others believe that falling atmospheric pressure encourages fish to bite, while still others believe that fish bite according to the phases of the moon. None of these explanations has yet been proved. As far as we know, fish bite mainly because they are hungry or curious or because they are pugnacious. The male bass, for instance, strikes at any moving object near its nest; although it eats very little during the breeding season, it is highly pugnacious at this time. Then, too, fish must be capricious, for almost every fisherman can remember times when his wife at one end of the boat hauled in one fish after another while he at the other end could not get even a nibble. Such experiences as these leave little doubt that luck plays a part in fishing.

There are no fixed rules about baits or fishing methods, although some kinds of baits and certain general methods may apply more to one species of fish than to another. Some species will sometimes show a distinct preference for certain baits and then without advance notice will change their preference. One week the crappies in a certain lake may bite readily on grasshoppers and apparently be uninterested in anything else. The next week they may be satisfied with nothing less than live minnows. Still-fishing with

3

the time-honored bait of worms is largely relied on for catching sunfish, perch, and bullheads, but an occasional bass, crappie, walleye, or northern pike can also be caught by this method. Bass fishing, on the other hand, requires a specialized technique which differs from that for catching walleyes, northern pike, or trout.

Fishing for different species is generally done in different waters. Bass are usually found in the weeds, and three or four types of bait must be tried until a successful one is found. The largest sunfish and crappies often congregate out beyond the weeds where the bottoms drop off to deep water, but after sunset they may rise to the surface over shallow weed beds. Walleyes are usually in the deeper waters and respond to live and artificial minnows which are offered to them by still-fishing, trolling, or casting techniques. Sometimes, however, the bass may be in the deeper waters, and the walleyes, particularly in the evenings, in the shallow waters — all of which demonstrates that a single rule is of little value. The fisherman must use his judgment; when one method fails, he must try others, always keeping within the general class of baits and lures suitable for the particular fish he is trying to catch. Often enough every method will fail, and nothing will induce the fish to bite.

To improve his chances for success in finding and attracting fish, every fisherman should know something about their feeding habits. These habits vary greatly. For example, walleyes seem to prefer to feed after sunset, the time of day when northern pike sometimes stop feeding. This observation is corroborated by the catches taken in experimental nets; these catches usually show that walleyes come into shallow water after sunset and that northern pike move out into deeper waters.

Fishes such as bass, sunfish, crappies, and bullheads eat about one-twentieth of their body weight per day during the summer. There seems to be a limit to their capacity, which can generally be measured as the total amount of food they will consume on an empty stomach. When a fish has been fed until it will eat no more, it takes very little food during the following twenty-four hours. The time varies with different species. Even if this quantity of food is divided into a series of feedings, a fish will eat very little after it has reached its capacity. This may explain why fish sometimes do not bite, especially in seasons of abundant natural food production in the lakes and streams.

Seasonal changes in temperature and the length of daylight bring about changes in the feeding habits of various fishes. All species consume less food in winter than in summer. Some fishes, such as northern pike and walleyes, feed more or less continuously throughout the winter, while others, such as black bass and sunfish, seem to become semidormant in winter. In the aquariums at the University of Minnesota largemouth bass, sunfish, and bowfins almost cease feeding during the winter months, although the water never freezes. One winter the water in the aquariums was kept at summer temperatures, and these fishes continued feeding; in a month's time they had exhausted their normal winter supply of minnows.

Crappies alone of the sunfish family are heavy winter feeders in northern waters. Although they bite readily throughout most of the winter, often during the late winter months or the early spring there comes a time when they almost stop feeding. We find that crappies frequently change their diet entirely during the late winter months and feed almost exclusively on planktonic crustaceans which at other times do not form an important part of their diet. Bluegills do not bite readily in Minnesota lakes in winter, and it has been assumed that they do not feed extensively during the colder months. The Minnesota bluegills kept in aquariums also feed very little in winter. It has been discovered, however, that Michigan bluegills bite on certain live aquatic insect larvae in winter; the larvae are now used extensively as bait for winter angling.

Northern fishermen have long complained that fishing is poor in late July and in August, and creel censuses of northern lakes bear this out. Several factors may be responsible for this. Summer is the period of greatest food production in northern waters and consequently the fish tend to be well fed and not hungry. Also, the water reaches its highest temperature during the last part of July and the first part of August, and many species of fish seek the cooler and deeper waters. There is the further possibility that some species do not feed much when the water temperature is above their optimum, just as many species feed little or not at all when temperatures are extremely low.

How fish detect their food — whether by sight, taste, or smell — is a controversial question. In some species the sense of taste must be poor, for otherwise they would not eat such unpalatable objects as pieces of wood and bits of corncob. Undoubtedly many game fishes are attracted to their food by sight, but since they are rather nearsighted they apparently detect their food by the movement of the object rather than by recognizing its detailed appearance. Bass and northern pike, even those kept in captivity, do not exhibit much interest in nonliving food unless it is moved over the surface of the water. One smallmouth bass kept in captivity for some years was first fed on live mice from the janitor's traps. Dead mice held no attraction until someone discovered that if he pulled a dead mouse by the tail over the surface of the water the bass would take it readily. The bass also learned to strike at a finger moved through the water.

The manner in which fish attack their food varies from one species to another. Bass, walleyes, and bowfins spot their prey, turn and eye it momentarily, and then seize it. Sometimes they mouth it for a second before swallowing it. Northern pike and muskellunge typically poise themselves while aiming at a minnow. As long as the minnow is stationary they do not strike, but when the minnow moves they strike it almost faster than the eye can follow. Gars slide smoothly alongside their prey, dead or alive, and with an easy and graceful sideswipe seize it in their long jaws, often completely severing a large fish into halves. Most game fishes, however, swallow their food headfirst; the prey may be seized by the tail, but it is usually shifted into the proper position before being swallowed. Because of the propensity of many game fishes to strike moving objects, the fisherman can fool them with artificial minnows, plugs, and spinners. Frequently fish follow an artificial bait of this nature but seem unable to make a decision to strike. An angleworm or a minnow on the hook or spinner will often induce a fish to strike when otherwise he might not.

Some fishes, particularly those that feed at night, find their food by their sense of smell or taste rather than by sight. The sense of taste in fishes may be contained in the lips, the skin, or the barbels. Bullheads become very excited when food is thrown to them, swimming and gyrating about it as they try to locate it, but they must come close to it or touch it before they will seize it, and there is no evidence that they see it even then. Other species rely on other sensory combinations to locate their food. For instance, the carp kept in aquariums at the University of Minnesota are fed corn. They mouth over the bottom until they locate the corn and suck it up with some sand and mud; then they forcibly eject the entire mouthful and, swimming ahead, suck the corn back in before it settles to the bottom. In the process of separating the corn from the sand and mud they make the water turbid.

Paddlefish feed almost automatically, apparently without need of sight, taste, or smell, although it has been claimed that they locate water rich in microscopic food by means of taste or smell. When a paddlefish feeds, it swims slowly with a spiral motion and with its mouth wide open so that water passes in through the mouth and out through the gill clefts. Microscopic organisms are continuously strained out of the water and swallowed as they accumulate. The paddlefish's diet seems somewhat monotonous, but as a group fish probably have a greater range of food than most animals.

In the matter of palatability, most fish have some individual flavor in addition to the "fishy" taste which is not limited to these animals but is a property of aquatic life in general (for example, some water plants taste fishy). The individual flavor of each species is partly influenced by the food it eats. Any fish, no matter how high it ranks as a game species, may become highly unpalatable if it feeds on certain substances. Bullheads, carp, suckers, crappies, sunfish, and buffalo feeding on muddy bottoms, particularly where decayed vegetation is abundant, have a decidedly muddy or weedy flavor. However, when the same species are transferred to waters with clean bottoms, the taste of the flesh becomes much more palatable in a few weeks. The same is true of the flavor of game species but to a lesser degree because such species usually restrict their diet to living prey. Fish from waters polluted by sewage usually have a flavor reminiscent of sewage gas. The fisherman should always remember that the cleaner the water from which he catches his fish, the better the flavor will be.

To become a successful angler one must have some knowledge of the habits and the requirements of the various species of panfish and game fish. It is part of the purpose of this book to supply some of that knowledge, not by giving explicit directions for catching certain species of fish but by providing information about the various species which will enable the fisherman to direct his efforts wisely.

Fishing Techniques

The art of fishing has become a highly complicated one with a variety of techniques. It is outside the scope of this book to give detailed information about fishing techniques; there are excellent field manuals of that sort available. If fish could read and learn the rules, fishing would be a much simpler and more certain art. Then it would be possible to lay down a definite technique for catching each species. Nevertheless, a general discussion of fishing methods may be helpful to the amateur angler.

Each of the accepted methods of fishing has its own group of devotees who worship their particular art to the utter disregard of all others. The scorn and disdain of the fly fisherman for the cane-pole fisherman is scarcely equaled. In the lake states a great many anglers belong to the cane-pole class. The cane-pole fisherman sits on a bank or in a boat hour after hour, holding his long pole; the hook is baited with anything from angleworms to bits of liver or perch. Patiently he watches the bobbing float and waits for some fish to swallow the bait, seldom pulling in the line until he is certain the nibbling fish has securely swallowed the hook. He usually is not particular about the species he catches but is glad to get any one of a wide variety. A modification of this technique is used by the tight-line fisherman, who fishes without a float and often without a pole, using only a handline with which he expertly hooks any fish that nibbles at his bait. The cane-pole fishermen and the tight-line fishermen together constitute the great majority of the anglers who fish in the northern lakes. They are usually more interested in catching enough fish to cover the frying pan than in refined methods of fishing or in the technical aspects of fish habits.

Another group of fishermen are the bait casters, who make up a sort of middle class. They have graduated from the cane pole and place their trust in short casting rods. Using various artificial minnows, plugs, spoons, and spinners, they troll and cast into all possible habitats, hoping to entice certain game fishes to strike at their moving lures. Frequently they embellish their lures with substantial bait such as minnows or frogs.

Young members of the cane-pole set. Photo: John Dobie, Minnesota
Department of Natural Resources.

The aristocrats among anglers are the fly fishermen, who may be divided
into dry-fly and wet-fly devotees. Using the lightest of tackle, they limit
their catches to the game fishes that will rise to artificial flies. Most trout
fishermen belong to this class. Of all fishermen, fly fishermen may truly
be said to fish more for sport than for fish. Although the fly fishermen

are relatively few in number, they are very enthusiastic and constitute one of the most active groups of anglers.

Fishing is usually a warm weather sport, but in many northern states winter fishing through the ice has long been popular. Certain fishes can be taken through the ice by spearing or by angling. Spearing is done from the shelter of a tiny dark house placed over a hole in the ice; a live minnow or other lure is usually suspended through the hole to decoy the fish. The fisherman sits in the dark house watching the dimly lighted water below, his spear ready to impale any fish that approaches his lure. This type of fishing is highly selective because the fisherman can see and choose his fish before spearing it. Consequently, larger northern pike and other species are taken by this method than by ordinary angling. In many states spearing is now restricted or prohibited by law.

Angling through the ice is the most popular form of winter fishing because it requires only simple tackle — a hook, a line, a float or a bobber, a short rod or a stick, and some kind of implement for cutting a hole in the ice. Usually a live minnow is used for bait. The fisherman is exposed to the wind and cold as he patiently waits for a bite. Less rugged fishermen drive their automobiles alongside the holes and turn on the heater and the radio. Great numbers of crappies and perch and an occasional walleye or northern pike are caught by winter angling.

Some of the fish houses found on Minnesota lakes during the winter season are complete with kitchen, bedroom, and carpeted living room (or fishing room) and are provided with electricity and a television antenna. Many resort owners rent fish houses by the week or for the season, and on lakes such as Mille Lacs the winter business rivals that of normal summer vacation months. As many as a hundred houses may be grouped in certain ''hot'' fishing areas which come to resemble small villages with a car parked in front of each house, especially on weekends. The houses can be towed from place to place as the concentrations of fish change during the winter season. In late winter the houses are towed off the ice and stored until the following season. Most of the lake areas have weekend fishing contests that attract fishermen from near and far to compete for prizes ranging from new automobiles to minnow buckets.

The catching of a fish involves many details that confuse amateurs and bother even experienced fishermen. The correct method of baiting a hook is not simply the common practice of spearing the bait with the hook — many minnows and frogs are lost because they are improperly placed on the hook.

Hooking a minnow through the tail, the jaws, the gills, or the belly usually results in a waste of bait. For casting, the minnow should be threaded on the hook by passing the hook in through the mouth and out through the side as far back of the dorsal fin as possible. Some safety-pin hooks are on the market which thread the minnow on a pin alongside the hook. For still-fishing, when it is desirable that the minnow display some motion, the hook should be passed through the back muscles just under the dorsal fin.

Most fishermen hook frogs through one or both jaws, allowing the body and the legs to dangle below the hook. After a few casts the frog becomes loose and soon falls off. Furthermore, the fish generally has to grab and swallow the entire frog before it reaches the hook. There are available several varieties of special frog hooks, some with a harness which places the frog far enough up on the hook so that the fish is likely to be hooked when it first grabs the frog.

Worms can simply be threaded on the hook, leaving any surplus to dangle from the end, but a more attractive arrangement can be made by looping the worm and passing the hook through each loop. Several worms can thus be crowded onto a single hook, providing a tempting bait that may attract a bass even when all else fails. One trouble with such a bait in many northern lakes is that small perch and sunfish delight in nibbling off the loops without touching the hook. Grasshoppers and various other insects should be threaded on the hook.

Fishing rods and a large variety of tackle are used for the more specialized methods of fishing. The equipment necessary for fly fishing, bait casting, and spin casting includes rods, reels, lines, leaders, and lures. These items differ greatly for the various methods of fishing as well as for the types of fish sought, but a certain amount of interchangeability is possible. For example, many species other than trout can be caught with a fly rod. Great sport can be had using a fly rod for both largemouth and smallmouth bass, striped bass, rock bass, crappies, sunfish, walleyes, northern pike, and perch.

Fly rods range in weight from light to heavy and have a whiplike action. Many modern fly rods are made from hollow or solid fiber glass, whereas older models were usually made of split bamboo or steel. Although split bamboo rods are still the favorite with many experienced fly fishermen, the modern fiber glass rods have the same smooth action as the bamboo rods but do not require the continued upkeep that the bamboo rods do. Despite the advantages of the synthetic rods, there is something fine and appealing about classic hand-crafted bamboo fly rods of the pre–World War II era.

An expensive rod usually lasts longer than a cheap one, but its action may be no better than that of the less expensive rod. Rods are often gauged by their weight, but the value of a fly rod is in its casting ability rather than in its weight. Rods of the same weight and length can differ greatly in casting ability.

A number of reels for fly fishing are on the market, most of which are single action reels. They may or may not have an automatic action for reeling in excess line. Most fly fishermen believe that a reel should balance the weight of the rod. Fly reels serve mostly as a storage place for the line, which is stripped off the reel by hand as it is cast out. Some anglers use the reel to pull in the fish when it is caught while others merely strip the line in.

In the past fly lines were usually made of silk or linen and had to be treated with oil or dressing material to make them float. After each fishing trip the line had to be carefully dried to protect it from rot. Modern fly lines are manufactured from synthetics and require little or no attention. The new dry-fly lines have a hollow core to make them buoyant; they are either single or double tapered. In wet-fly, nymph, or streamer fishing, sinking lines are used; these lines have thin soft-lead cores to increase their density and to assure that they sink. The line is fastened to the lure by means of a nylon leader. The leader may be of uniform thickness or tapered, and its length may vary from three to twelve feet. The leader gives a semi-transparent connection (invisible to the fish) between the lure and the line. The old-fashioned gut leader, rarely used these days, must be soaked before using. It is not necessary to soak nylon leaders, but they seem more pliable and appear to sink more readily if soaked before being used.

There are two methods of fishing with a fly rod. One method is with dry flies, which float on the surface; the other is with wet flies, which sink below the surface. In either kind of fishing, a large assortment of flies and other fly-rod lures is necessary since the bait used successfully one day may fail the next. Most artificial flies are made to imitate the various insects that form part of the fishes' diet. A vast number of patterns have been designed for trout, salmon, and other species. A true fly fisherman studies the type of insect that he thinks the fish are feeding on and then tries to offer them his best imitation. Dry flies must float, so they usually have a large body which is "doped" with paraffin oil or a similar synthetic water repellent. The line should also be kept well oiled. The aim in dry-fly fishing is to drop the fly on the water so that it resembles an insect alighting on the surface or a newly metamorphosed aquatic about to start its terrestrial life. Consequently, dry flies should resemble adult insects.

Wet flies are unoiled and are constructed to sink readily. They resemble immature insects (nymphs) and larval insects, which normally live under water, as well as adult insects. Wet flies should be allowed to sink slowly in the water and then should be reeled in slowly. Streamers are special wet flies that are designed to imitate minnows or small fish instead of insect larvae or adults. Other fly-rod lures, some of which can be used either dry or wet, are often very effective. These consist of spinner combinations, tiny wooden or cork plugs, spoons, and feather combinations, which by proper handling of the rod can be made to imitate a darting minnow. There are other popular lures — cork and feather combinations, small rubber frogs, and hellgrammites — which often prove attractive on the surface.

The task in fly fishing is to drop the lure into the desired spot in such a way as to make the fish think it is natural food and unconnected with a line. For dry-fly fishing, always cast upstream so that the fly can float downstream in a natural manner. Try to drop the fly on the water so that it will fall lightly. The art of fly casting is not as complicated as it seems but depends largely on practice. Holding the rod in front of you, strip off ten or twelve feet of line with your left hand, and then, quickly raising the rod, cast the line behind you. As the rod reaches a vertical position, hesitate long enough for the line to straighten out behind you. Then cast forward, stripping out more line with your left hand. If you do not have the desired amount of line out as the lure reaches the water, cast it back again and repeat until you have sufficient line to allow the lure to drop in the water where you want it. The important rule is not to allow the rod to go back any great distance past a vertical position and to allow sufficient time for the line to straighten out behind but not enough for it to drop into a bush or into the water. If the line is not allowed to straighten out, the lure is apt to be whipped off. Many fishermen advocate using the motion of the right forearm and wrist, holding the elbow close to the body, but others cast successfully with the open arm movement.

Bait casting involves the use of a short and relatively heavy rod to cast plugs and other lures which are then reeled in slowly to imitate a live fish or other natural bait. The art of bait casting demands some practice, but almost anyone can soon manage to get the lure out to some distance and to drop it where a fish should be. If the fisherman casts too vigorously, the frustrating snarl of line known as a backlash will appear on the reel,

A trout fisherperson on the Cascade River, Cook County, Minnesota.
Photo: William D. Schmid.

but as he gains experience in using his thumb for a brake he will have
fewer backlashes. The lure should be reeled in slowly, allowing it to hesitate
every few feet in case some doubting fish needs time to make up his mind.
In trolling it is especially important to give the fish plenty of opportunity
to strike at the bait. If the fisherman trolls too fast, the striking fish may
miss the hook or it may be hooked in the tail instead of in the proper place.
When trolling, let out from seventy-five to one hundred feet or more of
line. It is well to keep from twenty-five to fifty feet of line in reserve on
the reel.

In the past two decades the spin-casting rod has nearly replaced the older
bait-casting rod, and the spin-casting reel has largely replaced the older level-
wind casting reel. A generation of anglers has grown up with the new spin-
casting technique and has little or no familiarity with the older casting
methods. Spin-casting is similar to bait casting, but the rod is longer, lighter,
and more flexible. The reel operates on a quite different principle with the

line uncoiling off the reel spool rather than the spool turning to release the line. When the reel handle is turned, a pick-up arm engages the line and recoils or winds it around the spool, which is parallel to the long axis of the rod. There are two major types of spinning reels, open face and closed face, and each has its advocates. The line used is usually monofilament nylon ranging in strength from ultralight 2-pound breaking test to 50 pounds or more in breaking test. Spin casting has several advantages over bait casting: backlashes usually do not occur unless the line is badly twisted; the lures used can be very small, weighing as little as one-quarter ounce, and can be cast farther than bait-casting lures; and it takes only a few moments to learn to spin cast in contrast to weeks or months to become a competent bait caster. The popularity and versatility of spin casting is phenomenal, and it is now a rarity to see a bait caster except at sportsmen's shows or in tournaments. Bait casting is fast becoming a lost art among modern anglers.

The array of lures displayed by the average sporting goods store is bewildering. Most of the many lures displayed are only modifications of several basic types. The main purpose of all lures is to present an imitation of some natural food animal or to make such a dazzling flash that no respectable game fish can resist it. Any lure that has plenty of action when drawn through the water has possibilities because game fish are largely attracted by motion. One type of lure utilizes spinner combinations. Spinners may be combined with various artificial flies, bucktails, or hooks baited with live minnows or with pork strips. The spoon types are very popular for northern pike and many other fishes. Spoons come in a large assortment of colors and in various sizes. Some people are very particular about the color of the lures they use, but we doubt that the fish are so discriminating. We have often used brightly colored spoons until the paint was worn off and yet the spoons continued to be as effective as when they were new.

Wooden baits or plugs are made in a wide variety of forms. Some imitate a minnow and become submerged when in action. Others skim over the surface, and a fish striking at them breaks from the water with a spectacular splash. One kind of wooden lure that has become very popular dives deep into the water and darts swiftly from side to side. Some of these lures are made in small sizes suitable for a fly rod. The hooks on various lures tend to become dull after long usage so that a hard-striking fish may escape being hooked. The hooks should be inspected frequently and sharpened when necessary; a small whetstone or file should be part of every fisherman's equipment.

All artificial bait-casting or spin-casting lures should be fastened to the line by a swivel or a strong wire leader combined with a swivel. The line may be selected to suit the fisherman's taste. Braided and nylon lines are popular. Better casting can be done with a light line; lines of 12-pound to 18-pound breaking test are most satisfactory, although even lighter lines are used. Heavier lines are better suited for trolling. After fishing, dry the line by stringing it between two trees or posts. Wet lines deteriorate very rapidly.

Some fish grab the lure hard, but on finding it unpalatable they quickly spit it out unless the fisherman sets the hook. There is no positive rule for setting the hook, but the usual method is to pull back strongly on the rod after feeling the first sharp tug as the fish strikes and then to start to reel in the line. If the fish is hooked, it will give several tugs as it tries to throw the hook from its mouth. It may even start to pull away and may break water. Whether one is bait casting or fly fishing, it is necessary to keep a tight line on the fish at all times. It is easy for a poorly hooked fish to throw off the hook if the line is slack. Start reeling in the fish, but always be prepared to let it have line if it begins to move away. Usually it will make several short rushes away and then continue to move toward the fisherman as the line is reeled in.

When the fish nears the boat or the fisherman, it usually starts fighting in earnest. Give it line and then reel it in the moment it weakens. Keep this up until the fish is tired and can be brought up for landing. Many a fish escapes because it is not sufficiently subdued; when it is close enough for landing, it is likely to make a wild dash and break the line unless the fisherman is alert and releases the reel to give it line for this final rush. The surest way of landing a fish is with a dip net, although some expert fishermen can successfully divert the final rush of a large fish so that it will flip over into the boat. Many fish, both large and small, are lost when they are lifted out of the water by the line because the fish's weight, which was largely displaced in the water, tears the hook from its mouth.

Fish caught in warm weather spoil quickly. Sometimes a fish placed on a stringer early in the morning dies in a short time and shows signs of decomposition by afternoon. If possible, fish should be kept alive until they can be dressed and placed on ice, but often they are fatally injured by the hook, especially if the hook penetrates the gills or the nearby circulatory structures, and die soon after being caught. Fatal injuries can also occur through careless handling; it is wise to avoid touching the gills because slight injuries to these delicate structures can kill the fish.

If a fish is not seriously injured, it can be kept alive all day on a safety-pin stringer with the pin passed through the lower jaw. The upper and lower jaws should not be pinned together because this prevents the fish from opening its mouth for respiration. Never pass the stringer through the gills. If live-boxes or tanks with cold running water are available, fish can be kept alive for several days. Fungus growths are likely to occur if the water is warm. Fish placed in a creel spoil quickly unless they are killed by a blow on the head, eviscerated, and packed in moss or grass.

State laws should be consulted when it is necessary to transport fish for some distance. In certain states the law requires the head to be retained on fish in transit. (Gills and entrails should be removed, however, because they spoil very quickly and may taint the rest of the fish.) Portable iceboxes are very useful for transporting fish by automobile, and sphagnum moss, plentiful in the bogs in the far north, makes an excellent insulator. Fish packed with a few pieces of ice in a box lined with sphagnum moss will stay fresh for several days. If ice is not immediately available, the body cavity should be filled with sphagnum moss or grass. The catch should be protected from flies at all times.

Further preparation depends on the size and the kind of fish and on the fisherman's preferences. Most people merely scrape off the scales, cut out the fins, and remove the head and the viscera. The fish is then either sliced or split into pieces convenient for cooking or it may be left whole for baking. If excessively slimy fish are skinned rather than scaled, much of the strong fishy taste is eliminated. For skinning, start by making an incision with a sharp knife around the body behind the gills and lengthwise along the middle of the back and the belly, taking care to cut around both sides of all fins unless they have already been removed. The skin can then be removed from each side by chipping it away with a sharp knife. A more tidy result can be obtained by loosening the skin with the fingers aided by the knife along the incisions and then pulling the skin off backward.

Fish such as walleyes can be easily skinned by splitting them and laying the halves skin downward on a board. A sharp knife is then passed between the flesh and the skin behind the shoulder. The half is held firmly on the board, and the knife with the edge turned slightly downward is passed toward the tail, severing the skin and the scales from the meat. Walleyes, tullibees, whitefish, and some other species can be easily filleted by splitting and lifting out the backbone and the ribs with a knife. Many fish can be filleted by merely cutting the flesh away from the backbone and the ribs on both sides.

Fishing is an art, and to be truly successful in it one must study and know fish. It is also necessary to know how to conserve and maintain the supply of fish. The chapters immediately following are devoted to the dynamics of lakes, the maintenance of conditions that enable fish to live, and the management of waters for greater production of fish.

Lake Dynamics

Lakes are usually more or less closed bodies of water, each forming in a broad sense a small world of its own. The characteristics of each lake reflect in large part the surrounding landscape, the climate, the vegetation, land use, and other factors. In each lake many complex activities which we are just beginning to fully understand and appreciate proceed automatically, making it possible for life to continue almost indefinitely. From a geological point of view, most lakes are ephemeral; sediments slowly fill them in or, in the case of those lakes with outlets, erosion or downcutting may eventually drain them. The lake regions of the world with but a few exceptions are in the most recently glaciated regions of the Northern Hemisphere. Lakes that were formed in earlier glacial periods have been filled in or have been destroyed by erosion. The various types of Minnesota lakes and their origins were studied in detail by Zumberge (1952), who also presented a very useful classification of glacial lakes. The study of fresh waters, both lakes and streams, is called *limnology (limne, marsh)*.

Fish represent the end of the long cycle in which various chemical elements and compounds producing food pass from raw substances in the water and on the lake bottom into food for higher forms of life. Studies of northern lakes show that these lakes vary considerably in the production of both food organisms and fish because of differences in chemical and physical conditions from lake to lake. The most beautiful clear blue lakes are not necessarily the most productive of fish life. In fact, the rockbound lakes with the clearest water are among the least productive in pounds of fish per acre. Although the fish in these lakes may run larger on the average than those in other lakes, there are not as many of them.

The sizes and kinds of fish present in a lake are not a useful measure of the lake's fish production. The actual productivity of a lake can be estimated in a number of ways (Ruttner, 1963; Goldman, 1966), but since we are concerned primarily with fish, we make our measurements in terms of the total number of pounds of fish that can be produced per unit of time.

19

Unlike the fisherman, we are not concerned with the size of the individual fish but only with the total poundage of fish protein.

In matters of production a lake may be considered in the same way as a piece of land which furnishes the food or the general environment (grain, pasture, or forest) from which a crop of livestock or upland game is produced. As illustrated especially well by fish farming in the southern United States or in those Minnesota lakes managed as sport fisheries, fish can indeed be considered a water crop that takes from two to three years or perhaps longer to mature. Consequently, a lake must raise abundant food in the summer and also provide suitable winter conditions for several years in succession in order for a fish crop to mature. In this way fish production differs from the production of upland game, wherein a crop reaches maturity at the end of each summer.

Fish production is based primarily on the richness of a body of water, just as the production or yield of a farmer's field is based on the fertility of the soil. The factors that determine fertility in a lake are the same as those that make the soil productive, but just as a farmer's crops depend not only on fertility but also on proper drainage and cultivation, fish production in a lake depends on a number of conditions including water temperature and predator relations as well as the availability of spawning areas, food for the young, and shelter. The most important factors, however, that determine the productivity of a lake are the chemical elements of fertility, which include various forms of nitrogen, phosphorus, calcium, and many other elements. The availability of these is influenced by additional factors such as depth, temperature, bottom types, and the kind and amount of dissolved gases.

Food production is usually considered first in the dynamics of a lake. Plant life is the basis for most fish foods, and so plants are the first stage in the cycle from the chemical elements of fertility to fish production. These plants include not only the large water weeds along the lake margins but also the myriads of tiny and often invisible algae that swarm throughout the water. Although only a few species of fish eat large quantities of plants directly, plants form the food of many of the lower animals eaten by the forage fishes, which are in turn eaten by the game fishes.

Rooted plants obtain their essential nutrients from the bottom sediments, and the algae obtain theirs from chemical substances dissolved in the water. Since the water contains many substances dissolved from the bottom, it is possible to estimate the chemical fertility or the potential fertility of a lake by an analysis of the water. Many of the compounds making up the fertility of a lake are eventually lost by being incorporated into the sediments that gradually accumulate on the bottom. During the spring and fall overturn of the lake, when there may be complete circulation of the water from top to bottom, many of the substances are returned from the sediments to the water, but some are incorporated into the sediments and no longer are available to the aquatic organisms. Therefore, if a lake is to maintain its nutrient level or chemical fertility, those substances lost to the sediments must be replenished by springs, by streams entering the lake, by runoff from the surrounding land, or by artificial fertilizer.

As mentioned earlier, the elements of fertility necessary for maximum production of food and fish are various forms of nitrogen, phosphorus, calcium, and some other substances — in general the same substances which constitute the elements of fertility in the soil. Pure water, that is, water with few chemicals dissolved in it, is usually almost sterile in terms of food and fish production. On the other hand, it is also possible to have too much of these substances in the water. In some lakes in western Minnesota the calcium and sodium concentrations are so high that we have what are called mineral lakes. In these lakes the concentrations of various dissolved substances are so high that they inhibit the growth of both rooted plants and algae; many mineral lakes lack fish of any kind.

Lakes have been classified in many ways (Welch, 1952; Hutchinson, 1957; Reid, 1961; Ruttner, 1963), but the system most universally used is based on the amounts of various nutrients present in the body of water. Lakes low in nutrients are referred to as *oligotrophic (oligos*, scant; *trophos*, nourishing); those rich in nutrients are *eutrophic* or well nourished. The majority of the lakes in the northeastern part of the state are oligotrophic, and most of the lakes found in the remainder of the state are eutrophic. Hutchinson (1969) has suggested that we should not think of lakes as being oligotrophic or eutrophic but rather that we should think of lakes and their drainage basins as forming oligotrophic or eutrophic systems.

The process by which nutrients are added naturally or artificially to bodies of water is termed eutrophication. It is this process that has been of such great concern to biologists, the state and federal governments, and the public at large for at least a decade. The process of eutrophication or the increase in the supply of nutrients should be distinguished from the *effect* of the addition of nutrients. In some instances the effect may be beneficial and increase the pounds of fish produced, or it may be undesirable and kill the fish or change the composition of the fish population to one less desirable for the angler. Eutrophication is a natural process, and except for those instances where man has added biologically poisonous wastes to the water, man in his activities has only changed the rate of the process. The examination of sediment cores from the bottoms of many lakes indicates that many of our drainage systems were eutrophic long before man's influence became a factor. Similarly the lakes of northeastern Minnesota have been part of an oligotrophic drainage system since the last glacial ice wasted away. With our present knowledge of the process of eutrophication, it is possible to reduce the rate of nutrient input to a level such that the lakes can return to a condition approaching that about which our ancestors wrote such glowing accounts.

Carbonates, usually found in some form of calcium carbonate or lime, are among the important chemical substances present in lake water. When a considerable amount of lime is present, the water is usually called hard; if the amount is small, it is called soft. Lake Superior, the border lakes, and the lakes in the northeastern portion of Minnesota where limestone is scarce or absent usually contain soft water. The waters of lakes of this type, esthetically so pleasing, produce only a small amount of vegetation, algae, and fish food.

Lime and other carbonates in the water are necessary for proper plant growth because certain forms of lime (bicarbonates) are the source of the carbon dioxide necessary for the manufacture of plant food and the liberation of the oxygen so vital to aquatic animals. The carbonates are less soluble than the bicarbonates, but in the presence of carbon dioxide or carbonic acid they change into bicarbonates. When plants utilize some of the carbon dioxide from bicarbonates, they change the bicarbonates back to carbonates which sometimes precipitate to form extensive marl deposits such as those common in some northern lakes. The precipitated carbonates form a gray covering over the leaves of the rooted aquatic plants and give the plants a rough, crustlike coating; in a few lakes in central Minnesota small concretions of calcium carbonate are formed by algae. Carbonates are so important that they can be used as an index to the potential fertility of a body of water.

The important food elements all pass from one stage to another, eventually ending in the body of some aquatic plant or animal which dies and decomposes, liberating the elements into the water to be used again; if the body is preserved in the sediment, however, the constituent elements are lost from the chemical cycle within the lake. The cycle is similar in many respects to the one that takes place in the farmer's field when crops are plowed under in order to maintain the fertility of the soil.

It is interesting to find that the production of food in a lake in actual pounds per acre is far greater in areas where the surrounding soil consists of fertile farmlands. Some of the lakes in central Minnesota carry as much as 80 pounds (dry weight) of animal food per acre in the shallow waters. The lowest number of pounds of food per acre is found in the lakes that are in areas of rocky and thin infertile soils. Some of the rocky lakes along the Gunflint Trail carry only two-tenths of a pound (dry weight) of food per acre. In general this correlation comes about because the lakes obtained their original supply of fertile elements from the drainage waters of the surrounding areas, and they rely on the same source to replenish the elements lost through ground seepage or outlets. A lake can produce only as many pounds of fish per acre as there are available agents of fertility, and in general a lake is no more fertile than the surrounding soils.

Equal in importance to the dissolved contents of the water are the types of bottoms present in a lake. Plants and food organisms have distinct preferences for certain bottom types. It is impossible for most species of plants to grow in any abundance on solid rock bottoms, and as a result few forms of animal life can find subsistence there. Shifting sands are too unstable for the existence of plants or food organisms. On the other hand, although soft muds foster luxuriant plant growth, they smother many animals. The best type of bottom for food production is a relatively firm, fertile bottom, such as one of mud and sand.

The contour or shape of the bottom of a lake has an important effect on the total amount of food produced. The conditions of warm fertile lakes usually make only the bottoms above the 30-foot level suitable for food production. In these lakes the maximum production of food is found above the 15-foot level, which is the usual limit of sufficient light penetration for plant growth. Deep fertile lakes with steep bottoms are relatively low in production, while shallow, or only moderately deep, fertile lakes with gently sloping bottoms are relatively high in production. The shape of the shoreline also influences the total production of a lake. Since most food is produced in the shallow waters near the shores, a lake with an irregular shoreline and many bays has much more productive area than a lake with a smooth shoreline and few bays.

The fertility of a lake is not inexhaustible. It is conceivable that a lake may become reduced in fertility just as soil can be depleted from overfarming. Although we have no evidence that such reduction in fertility has taken place to any serious extent in Minnesota lakes, it is only good conservation practice to watch for and to correct factors which may reduce the fertility of the lakes in the future.

No matter how fertile a lake may be, the oxygen conditions sometimes prove to be a limiting factor on the production of fish. Fish, like all living things, must have a constant supply of oxygen in order to live. Oxygen depletion during a severe winter or as the result of excessive vegetation may make it impossible for fish to survive in an otherwise suitable lake. The oxygen is dissolved in the water, just as salt or sugar may be dissolved. Although water can hold only a small amount of oxygen, the dissolved oxygen is the only source available for the respiration of fish and most other water animals. The oxygen in water comes from two main sources — aquatic plants and the atmosphere.

All green plants release oxygen as a by-product of photosynthesis, the process in which carbon dioxide or carbonic acid gas is taken in and used to manufacture starch for plant food. This process is the natural way of disposing of the carbonic acid gas produced by decomposition and the respiration of animals and plants. Photosynthesis takes place only in the presence of sunlight. Water plants, from the big weeds to the microscopic algae that constitute the green scum, liberate oxygen on days when the sun shines. On a bright day one can observe many streams of tiny bubbles ascending through the water from the leaves of a healthy water plant. These bubbles are pure oxygen. They become smaller as they ascend, and many disappear before reaching the surface because they dissolve completely in the water. The water over a weed bed on a bright day is usually supersaturated with oxygen, while on a cloudy day or at night the same water may be seriously deficient in oxygen because the plants cannot liberate this important gas in the absence of sunshine. Even in summer a lake may occasionally suffer oxygen depletion when there are long periods of cloudy weather without any wind action.

The only other source of oxygen in a lake is the air above the water. When dissolved, oxygen diffuses or spreads very slowly in the water. The surface of the water in contact with the air absorbs large amounts of oxygen, but owing to the slow diffusion rate the oxygen seldom travels beyond a thin film next to the surface unless the water is agitated by strong waves or currents. In rivers the current alone, through its changing contact with the air, keeps the water well aerated, but in lakes currents are usually weak or entirely absent. Thus the main source of oxygen in lake water is from aquatic plants.

The oxygen in a lake is consumed in three principal ways: by fish and other aquatic animals; by plants that produce oxygen as well as use it; and last, and perhaps most important, by bacteria and decomposing organic matter. The organic matter consists of dead animals and plants and the partially rotted ooze that covers the deeper bottoms of lakes; as these decay slowly through bacterial activity, they create a heavy drain on the oxygen supply. Consequently, lakes that have abundant vegetation and bottoms covered with rich muds draw heavily on their oxygen supply, particularly during the winter. The production of oxygen ceases when the ice is covered with snow, and the supply of oxygen in the water at that point must last throughout the winter. In deep lakes, which have a considerable volume of water, the supply is usually sufficient, but in shallow lakes (6 to 10 feet deep) the volume of oxygen that can be stored is seldom sufficient to meet the demands. The situation is further aggravated by the fact that shallow lakes produce the greatest amount of vegetation and consequently have a large amount of dead plant life to decay during the winter. In shallow waters the ice may be so thick that the remaining volume of water is reduced to a point where it cannot hold sufficient oxygen to last all winter. This critical condition results in a fish-kill. In northern Minnesota many rocky infertile lakes, as little as 8 feet deep do not lose their oxygen, while in southern and central Minnesota mud-bottom fertile lakes of twice that depth lose their oxygen.

During the winter many species of fish are semidormant and require much less oxygen than when fully active, but even so fish-kills as a result of oxygen depletion often occur. The fish are sealed in the lake throughout the winter by the ice, which is thicker in Minnesota than in most other states. The survival of the fish depends on the presence of sufficient oxygen under the ice at the time of the freeze-up or on the penetration of sufficient sunlight to enable the plants in the lake to release enough oxygen to meet the demands of the fish until spring. This was demonstrated some years ago in a Minnesota lake containing thousands of bullheads; the lake was approximately 6 to 15 feet deep with a rich mud bottom. Late in November it froze over solidly, and the water was sealed off completely from the air by at least 12 inches of ice. Tests made frequently through holes cut in the ice indicated that the oxygen supply was normal. Although the ice increased in thickness to 20 inches by mid-December, the oxygen levels remained high into the second week in January. The plants were receiving enough sunlight through the ice to enable them to maintain the oxygen content of the water at a level equal to that found during the summer months. In the second week in January the ice was covered with 6 inches of snow, and the sunlight could no longer penetrate. Two days later the oxygen was exhausted throughout the waters of the lake. In the spring thousands of dead bullheads lined the shore as the ice melted. Not one living fish could be found in the lake. In a similar fashion smaller lakes may support fish populations for years, and then a series of events such as low fall water levels, early freezing of the lake, and heavy snowfall may produce a total winterkill. Quite probably some of the smaller lakes that currently lack fish populations and yet seem suitable for panfish or other fish are lakes that were subject to these winterkill conditions at some point in the past.

In addition to oxygen depletion as the cause of winterkills, other conditions may arise and become important factors in killing fish. Fish-kills have been noted under conditions of relatively low oxygen content in one lake, whereas in another lake of equally low oxygen content the fish survived, indicating that other factors probably associated with the decomposition of organic material (such as changes in the concentrations of hydrogen sulphide or carbon dioxide) must play an important part. Furthermore, there is no doubt that the physiological condition of the fish determines their tolerance to various stresses. Of all these factors, however, oxygen depletion is undoubtedly the chief cause of most fish-kills.

Temperature plays an important part in determining which areas of a lake will be productive. Most animals and plants grow better and more abundantly at high temperatures, although there are a few fishes (such as members of the whitefish family and various species of trout) that must have low temperatures. The temperature of the water depends primarily on the depth. The heat a lake receives in the summer comes through the surface area exposed to the sunlight. Two lakes of equal surface area, one deep and the other shallow, receive the same amount of heat, and so the deep lake never warms up as much as the shallow one. Consequently, there are cold-water lakes and warm-water lakes, depending largely on their depth and surface area. The deepest lake in the region covered by this book is Lake Superior, which because of its great depth of more than 1,000 feet does not receive enough heat during the summer to raise the water temperature more than a few degrees.

The major effect of temperature on most lakes is the establishment of stratification which makes only certain parts of the lake bottoms available to animals. During the summer, the warm water, being lighter than the cold, rises to the surface. By the time summer is well established, a layer of warm water, the epilimnion, usually from 20 to 45 feet thick, lies over the deeper and heavier cold water, the hypolimnion. The intervening area is called the thermocline. In very deep lakes the cold water may have a summer temperature as low as 39° F (4° C). The cold water is so heavy that it remains at the bottom, and the heat from the sun is absorbed by the warm upper layer before any of it can reach the cold layers beneath. The stratification becomes so pronounced that after a while the two layers do not mix at all. Even at times when the wind blows heavily in one direction, piling the warm layer on one side and tilting the bottom layer, the currents in the upper layer slide over the lower layer without mixing. During the spring and fall, when the lake is either warming or cooling, there comes a time when the temperature of the upper layer is the same as that of the lower layer and the thermocline disappears. At this period there is complete circulation or mixing from top to bottom in the deepest parts of the lake.

The temperature stratification just described is found only in lakes of 25 feet or more in depth and not more than several miles in diameter. In large lakes like Mille Lacs and Red Lake, the action of wind and waves creates powerful undertows and keeps the water well mixed at all times, preventing stratification. The size of the body of water with the consequent action of wind and waves probably also accounts for the fact that no definite stratification occurs in Lake Superior (Eddy, 1943).

The effect of stratification in fertile lakes is stagnation in the lower layers. The oxygen is soon depleted by any life present and by the decomposition of the bottom muds and organic materials continually settling down from above. Experiments have been made by lowering different species of fish in wire baskets to different depths in various lakes. In the summer the fish died in a few minutes when lowered to depths below 30 feet, while those closer to the surface always lived. In the fall and the spring when there was no stratification, the fish in the baskets lived at all depths, thus indicating that it was the lack of oxygen and not the pressure that killed the fish in the summer experiments.

Deep bottoms may be richly fertile, but because of the lack of oxygen sometimes only a few worms and other lower life forms can exist there. How these forms live without oxygen is an interesting biological question.

Because of the lack of sunlight at this depth, plants cannot grow and form oxygen. Lower LaSalle Lake in Hubbard County, for instance, is 208 feet deep, one of the deepest lakes in Minnesota, and rich in nutritive elements, but the bottom oxygen is nearly exhausted during the summer months. In some very deep lakes such as Clearwater, Tuscarora, and Saganaga lakes in Cook County, Minnesota, which are low in natural fertility, the volume of water in the lower layer is enormous. When the lake stratifies, the lower layer contains more oxygen than will be used up during the summer by the decomposition of organic wastes. In addition, since these lakes produce relatively few plants and animals in the upper layer and in the shore waters, there is only a small amount of organic material to decay and use up the oxygen. Furthermore, the water is very clear, so that sunlight penetrates farther than in the more turbid fertile lakes, thus enabling oxygen-producing plants to grow at much greater depths. Consequently, the deep cold bottoms in these lakes have sufficient oxygen to support trout and other cold-water fishes.

Population Dynamics

The fertility of a lake, determined by the amount of dissolved phosphates and nitrates in the water and by the other conditions described previously, is a controlling factor in the poundage of fish produced, and to a lesser extent it controls the species of fish which thrive in a lake. The size and the rate of growth of the fish, however, are governed by other factors.

One of the more vexing problems associated with the management of fish populations in many lakes is the unsatisfactory size of the dominant species. In such lakes the enormous number of stunted fish is a result of the density of the population in proportion to the carrying capacity of the lake. If a given lake has the capacity to support an average of 100 pounds of fish per acre, in theory it can support one 100-pound fish, or two 50-pound fish, or one hundred 1-pound fish, or four hundred 4-ounce fish, or a combination of various sizes totaling 100 pounds. The last example is probably the most realistic, but in pond fisheries or in hatcheries the other examples may apply. The farmer knows that grazing land can support only so many cattle or sheep, but in the feedlot (equivalent to the pond fishery or the hatchery) larger numbers can be supported per unit of area. In both the feedlot and the pond fishery, a larger area is required to supply the feeds than is represented by the production area itself. Finally, fish ponds usually are monocultures involving a single species or at most two or three species, a condition that is rarely the case in natural lakes.

We have long known that we can calculate the number of pounds of fish that a given pond can support or produce. Furthermore, it is known that if the population density is low and the food supply is constant, the growth rate of individual fish is rapid, but if the population density increases, the average growth rate decreases. There are obvious species limits to the growth rate, and at high densities behavioral problems associated with crowding may affect the growth rate. While it is simplistic to say that the total available food is the only factor governing production, it remains one of the most important factors.

29

Under natural conditions the effect of population density upon the growth rate is difficult to determine. One problem is to obtain a representative sample of the population of a single species or of the various species constituting the fauna of a lake or a stream. Seines, gill nets, electrofishing, anesthetics, and other means have been used singly and in combination to make estimates of the population's size and age structure. A number of attempts have been made to determine population densities in several Minnesota lakes, but they have met with varying success. In general, the effect of population density upon the growth rate must be determined largely from scattered examples. Each lake is unique in a sense and must be sampled, despite the fact that we are able to make estimates of its potential productivity based on the water chemistry, the morphometry of the basin, the extent of rooted plant growth, and other characteristics. With 15,000 lakes present in Minnesota it would be an impossible chore to sample them all thoroughly, but an attempt has been made to study a number of lakes which are typical of many others in the state. In early studies of the fish populations in a series of lakes in Ramsey County, the population densities were determined by seining large areas and calculating the number of fish per acre; for example, data were secured on the bluegill populations in six lakes. These lakes were all of the same type — comparatively fertile hard-water lakes in glacial drift basins wherein the amount of dissolved solids ranged from 140 to 270 parts per million. Three lakes had populations of fish ranging from 25.3 to 48.6 fish per acre; in these lakes the fish displayed rapid growth, taking 2.3 to 3.5 years to reach a length of 7 inches. The other three lakes had high population densities ranging from 80 to 450 fish per acre, and in these lakes the fish took 4.3 to 4.8 years to attain a length of 7 inches. The separation into two groups was definite, clearly indicating the correlation between population density and growth.

These studies may explain in part why fishermen catch large numbers of small fish in one lake and small numbers of large fish in nearby lakes. In Long Lost Lake in Clearwater County a number of years ago, the bass population was so dense that a fisherman might get his limit of largemouth bass within an hour, but the fish were small, ranging from 7 to 9 inches in length. In this lake growth was so slow that the bass required about 5.5 years to reach a length of 12 inches. In nearby Lake Itasca, only a few bass were caught each year, but they were 12 inches long when only 3.5 years old. A similar situation was found among the bluegills in the two lakes. The bluegills in Lake Itasca were found to grow 1.5 times as fast as those in Long Lost Lake. In Morrison Lake in Itasca Park the bass population at present is dense, but the bass are small, usually less than 10 inches in length, and their growth rate is slow, while in Lake Itasca bass 20 inches long and weighing up to 5 pounds are not uncommon, but rarely, except in late fall, do fishermen catch limits. To take another example, the crappies are so abundant in some lakes in Chisago County that an angler can easily catch his limit in a short time, but these crappies are usually not over 6 inches long and their average weight is 27 percent less than that of crappies of the same length in other lakes. The growth rate of crappies in these lakes is slower than that exhibited by crappies from most other lakes in the state. The bluegills are also small, weighing only two-thirds as much as bluegills of the same age in other lakes. Apparently population density in these lakes has become so great that the growth rate has been markedly reduced. Density studies of crappies, sunfish, perch, bass, northern pike, and other species in these lakes often show large populations of stunted fish, and examination of individual specimens reveals very slow growth rates.

There is another piece of evidence that population density is an important element in controlling the rate of growth. It has often been noted that when a species is successfully introduced into a new habitat its growth rate is usually good, largely because of the small number of individuals present and the lack of competition within the species (Eddy and Carlander, 1939). Walleyes grew more rapidly in the northeastern part of Minnesota when they were first introduced than the native walleyes did elsewhere in the state, undoubtedly because of the lack of competition within the species during the early stages of population growth. In many of these lakes the walleyes now tend to be small, displaying much lower growth rates than previously.

Creel censuses on many Minnesota lakes have thrown further light on this subject. With the aid of the Civilian Conservation Corps, creel censuses were conducted throughout the summer of 1940 on six lakes in northern Minnesota. Every fish caught was measured, and scales were taken to determine the growth rate. The species studied were primarily walleyes, northern pike, largemouth bass, and crappies. In many of the lakes the catch was small, numbering 500 to 3,000 fish for the season and averaging from 1 to 5 pounds per acre. However, in one lake the catch was very heavy, numbering 12,000 fish for the summer and averaging nearly 20 pounds per acre. The rate of catch per man-hour was approximately the same for all the lakes. The growth rate of the fish was equal to or slightly above the average for that region in all the lakes except in the one where the catch was unusually heavy. In that lake the growth rate was decidedly lower than the average for the region. From these studies it appears that population density is a factor of great importance in modifying the growth rate of fish. The productivity of a lake seems to determine the total number of pounds of fish, but the population density seems to control the growth rate.

Studies show that the fish in easily accessible lakes usually have a lower growth rate than the fish in lakes that are not reached so easily. Accessible lakes are usually in fertile agricultural districts and are usually quite productive, whereas inaccessible lakes are usually in infertile nonagricultural districts and are relatively low in productivity. Accessible lakes are often subject to interference by man and may also be subject to very selective fishing, and these factors become more important than the fertility in determining the growth rate or the size of the fish. Today it is difficult to find fish populations that have not been disturbed in some fashion by man's activities, and in most lakes (with the exception of certain lakes in Canada) it is impossible to determine what the natural mortality might be. In many lakes these factors may take on great importance and in part mask the relationship between population growth and size and the potential fertility of the lakes.

Although the evidence is far from conclusive, it seems that large populations of undersized fish are associated in certain instances with heavy fishing. The fisherman is by nature selective and tends to remove the larger fish out of proportion to their abundance in the population. Under normal conditions most species produce many more fry than the lake can support. The large individuals which are more desirable as game fish are the natural checks upon the small fish, even those of their own kind. When the large fish are removed, the small fish have no check and so survive in great numbers and in some instances become crowded and stunted. The selectivity of the angler is also responsible for fish population troubles such as the important perch problem. Perch are not as popular with Minnesota anglers as they are with fishermen in some other states. In many large lakes such as Otter Tail and Mille Lacs the fisherman's catch consists predominantly of walleyes and contains very few other species. In these lakes the fish population comprises almost equal numbers of walleyes and perch along with a very small proportion of other fish. These proportions, which do not constitute a highly desirable balance, can be attributed in large part to heavy fishing for a single favorite, the walleye. Such methods are bound to create undesirable population balances and should be corrected. The methods available to correct such imbalances are limited. If the lake is small, it can be poisoned and restocked at a later date and the introduction of undesirable species can be restricted as in the trout lakes of northeastern Minnesota. The limits on desirable species can be reduced and the restrictions on harvesting less desirable species can be removed in the hope that, for example, the perch will be removed in larger numbers. Fishing methods can be restricted so that in some streams only fly fishing for trout would be allowed. In many lakes it is impossible to do more than to improve the species balance because the cost of other methods far outweighs the gains to be made.

Experimental work carried on in other states shows that the poundage of rough fish as opposed to the poundage of game fish supported by a given body of water is also affected by its fertility and that more pounds of rough fish than game fish can be supported per acre. Under a given set of conditions, however, the total poundage remains the same, regardless of the total number of fish or the proportion of rough fish to game fish. Accordingly, if the fish are numerous, they are stunted or undersized; if there are few individuals and the total poundage remains the same, then the fish are large.

Fish have enormous reproductive capacity. Ordinarily they produce more eggs and fry than a lake could possibly support if all the fry survived to become adults. Usually the worst enemies any game fish has are larger individuals of its own kind; cannibalism is common among them. The abundant lower age groups must be thinned out to allow normal growth, and the natural agents of such control are the large predacious fishes.

Each year game fish produce countless millions of eggs in Minnesota lakes, and thousands of the eggs hatch into fry. The question is, what happens to these fry? Studies of sunfish and crappies have shown that only a small number of fry, ranging up to 3 percent, survive to become fingerlings or one-year-old fish. From 10 to 75 percent of the fingerlings survive to become two-year-olds, and from 10 to 40 percent of the two-year-olds survive at the end of the third year, at which time most of these fish reach what might be called adult size. The results of the studies clearly indicate that a large number of fry must be produced annually, since only a very small fraction will survive to become adults. In an analysis of perch populations one sample of 15,000 perch taken from Otter Tail Lake in 1939 contained only a few fish over one year of age. If we assume that the present ratio of age classes represents the survival of past years, only 2.8 percent survived to the second summer, 2 percent survived to the third summer, and 1 percent reached the fourth summer.

In Lake Winnibigoshish thousands of walleyes were tagged before 1940.

Although not of the same age, these tagged walleye samples may be assumed to be a cross section of the adult population. The percentage of survival can be determined by the returns from fishermen's catches in subsequent years. In 1937, 3,000 walleyes were tagged. In that season approximately 13 percent were caught by fishermen; 5 percent were caught in 1938; 3.5 percent were caught in 1939; and 1 percent were caught in 1940. The diminishing returns are indicative of the rate at which the 1937 adult population decreased. The catches account for a total of only 23 percent of the original population. What happened to the other 77 percent? No serious epidemic was noted, so it is reasonable to assume that natural mortality accounted for the losses. Population samples tagged in subsequent years showed a similar decline.

In experimental work where all factors were favorable for growth, walleyes and both largemouth and smallmouth bass have been reared to a weight of 1 pound in one year (whereas it takes about three years for them to reach the same weight in an average lake). It is not possible for fish to grow at this rate in most Minnesota lakes because the population is highly mixed in both sizes and kinds of fish, creating an extremely complex system of competition. The elastic growth rate of fish would have great possibilities if it could be utilized under natural conditions. As noted earlier, it is responsible for the rapid growth frequently noted in fish newly introduced into suitable lakes in which there is little competition, particularly from their own kind. Well-balanced and abundant fish populations are what we are seeking in order to provide the best fishing, but until methods can be developed to utilize the growth-rate potential in Minnesota lakes we shall no doubt continue to find unsatisfactory growth and size ratios.

Upper Red Lake and Lower Red Lake have been studied intensively for over two decades by Professor Lloyd L. Smith, Jr., and his associates (Smith and Butler, 1952; Pycha and Smith, 1955; Grosslein and Smith, 1959; Smith and Pycha, 1960; Magnuson and Smith, 1963; Smith and Kramer, 1964; Peterka and Smith, 1970). These studies provide data on the commercial catch from the lower lake from 1917 to the present and the best statistics on the fish populations of any lakes in Minnesota. Thirty-eight species are present in the lakes, and eight are harvested by the fishery. Marked fluctuations were found in the year-class strength of perch from the lakes (Heyerdahl and Smith, 1971), and a group of factors, acting independently or together, were found to be responsible for differences in the survival of year classes. The researchers had no food data but felt that the availability of food for the fry determined the survival or the strength of a year class. In addition they found that in years with good hatching and survival of perch fry there was also good hatching and survival of walleye fry. Walleyes and perch spawn at different times in the spring, yet the survival of both species was affected in the same way. Heyerdahl and Smith suggest that meteorological factors may influence survival directly by controlling the availability of food organisms to the fry of both walleyes and perch. In other words lack of food may be the proximate cause of success or failure of a given year class, but the ultimate factor or factors determining the availability of food organisms is a matter for speculation. Since many species of fish are the last link in the food chain, it is not too surprising to discover that the success or failure of a given year class — or the fast or slow growth rate exhibited by a species from year to year in the same lake or in different lakes — cannot be explained in a simple fashion. Great progress has been made, but there is still much to be learned before we fully understand the dynamics of fish populations.

It is clear, however, that for maximum production fish crops must be watched carefully. A good farmer would not think of having his grain too thick or of allowing weeds to take the place of grain; the same considerations are important for fish crops. The quality of a fish crop is determined by a number of environmental conditions while the total amount of fish is limited specifically by the productivity of the body of water. It is possible to increase this productivity by improving the environment — that is, by lake and stream management.

Management of Waters
for Fish Production

The lakes of Minnesota have long been famous for their game fishing. With the growing population of the state and the greater amount of leisure time available, however, fishing pressure has steadily increased and as a consequence good fishing is disappearing from many lakes. The new highway systems have made a weekend fishing trip possible in almost any area of the state. Each weekend the main highways north and west of the Twin Cities area are filled with bumper-to-bumper outgoing traffic on Friday and incoming traffic on Sunday. Many of these people are on their way to various lakes and streams in the state, and many are going fishing. Where a decade or two ago such a trip was an annual excursion of one or two weeks, it is now a regular weekend affair. No one seems to mind the prospect of driving several hundred miles for a weekend outing. Add to this throng the increasing numbers of nonresident tourists, many of whom are fishermen, and one begins to understand the tremendous task facing the state Department of Natural Resources in order to assure satisfactory fishing for all. What is amazing to us is the fact that the fisheries personnel have met this challenge with so few workers and with budgets that are rather modest when compared with the total value of water recreation to the state. Fishing is only one part, but a very important part, of the water recreation picture. We trust our readers will realize that we are aware of the other uses of water resources and we appreciate the value of these uses, but in this chapter we wish to stress the use of the waters of the state to produce fish and fishing pleasure.

More and more families are acquiring a second residence, usually on a lake, river, or stream, which compounds the problems of water-oriented recreation. Not only are the shores lined with cabins but the lake may be crowded with boats. Some of the boats are used by fishermen, others by people out for a ride, and still others by people water-skiing. In the winter the lake ice is dotted with fish houses, cars, and snowmobiles. There are only two times during the year when the lake surface is likely to be deserted — when the ice is forming in the late fall and when it is melting in the spring. Even lakes miles from the nearest road are within easy reach of terrain vehicles and snowmobiles.

In 1939 one of us took a canoe trip into what is now part of the Boundary Waters Canoe Area and in ten days saw only two other parties, an Indian family and a Canadian forest ranger. Today it would not be too surprising to find two parties at each end of a portage. The impact of large numbers of people on the fragile canoe country ecology and the deterioration of the forests and the waters is a major concern of the Superior National Forest Administration.

Where once the fishery biologist had only a small number of problem lakes to be concerned about, he now has hundreds. Many of the problems are directly related to people — too many people. Obviously new and better regulations are required to assure that future generations will have the recreation activities that we enjoy. Too often problems such as the sea lamprey depredations on the native fishes of the Great Lakes must reach crisis proportions before we respond. It is often said that education is the answer, that an educated public will not allow such things to occur, but we are perhaps the best educated generation to date. When fishery biologists with good educations and years of experience are consulted, very often old husbands' tales hold sway over the facts. It is safe to say that every fisherman considers himself to be an expert because of his years of fishing experience; after all, "experience is the best teacher." We have not given up on education as a solution, but we feel that some profound changes in attitudes will be necessary before the present trend can be altered. Meanwhile, steps are being taken; for example, many of the northern counties of the state have rather stringent building codes covering summer and lake residences, and owners of lake homes are being required to upgrade their sanitary systems. Zoning laws prevent overdevelopment of the lakeshore. Unfortunately these regulations are too late in many situations, and there is little that can be done to improve the lake and its surroundings. A few lake communities have put in sewers and treatment plants, but only after conditions had made the lake a health hazard.

Over the past forty years a great deal of information has been gathered on the lakes and streams of the state. During this period our knowledge of the requirements of fish and of the management of lakes and streams has been increasing. Lake management is the control of a body of water and its contents in such a way as to produce a sustained yield of the fish species best suited to the conditions of the lake. By indicating the amount of fish that can be removed without disturbing the conditions necessary for maximum production, lake management seeks to prevent the damage done by intensive fishing. It undertakes to improve the environment for fish life and to maintain a balanced size ratio in the fish population.

The management of waters should be based on information obtained by surveys of all the conditions affecting fish life. Lake and stream surveys are not cures, but they are the chief means of diagnosing fishing problems. The surveys determine the potential productivity and carrying capacity in terms of the elements of fertility. Such surveys were initiated in the 1930s in many of the northern states including Minnesota. They are still carried on during each field season, and in some lakes surveys have been repeated at about ten-year intervals to document any changes that have occurred in the intervening years. Sampling methods and techniques have changed over the past forty years, but many of the same procedures used in 1935 are

The *Megalops*, vessel of the University of Minnesota Zoological Survey, on the Mississippi River near Brownsville, Minnesota, in 1900. Photo: Department of Zoology, University of Minnesota.

still used today. A complete survey includes basic mapping of the lake with a recording fathometer and a census of bottom fauna, plankton, and fishes. The chemical nature of the water, especially the carbonate content and usually the phosphate, nitrate, and sulphate content, is determined. The summer temperatures at different depths are recorded. The bottom types, the spawning beds, and the weed beds are measured. The results constitute an inventory of all the conditions necessary for fish life. To date approximately 3,000 lakes have been surveyed in the state.

The chief result of the lake surveys is the determination and classification of the types of lakes suitable for various game fishes. Each lake should be managed to produce the species of fish for which it is naturally suited. It is not practical, for example, to attempt to manage a walleye lake for lake trout or a bass lake for walleyes. Minnesota lakes can be divided into soft-water and hard-water lakes and also into cold-water and warm-water lakes. The proper combination of hardness and temperature determines whether a lake can support cold-water fishes. Minnesota lakes can also be categorized into at least six types according to the species of game fish for which they are best suited. Surveys of lakes in neighboring states have revealed similar types.

The first type is the lake trout lake. It is more or less infertile, with much rocky bottom. The shore drops steeply, is almost entirely of bedrock, and is unproductive. These lakes are deep, with a maximum depth of more than 100 feet. The water in such a lake is low in both mineral and organic content. Owing to the depth of the lake and the low organic content, there is plenty of oxygen at the bottom. Although the surface waters may warm up, the bottom waters are always cold enough for lake trout. Northern pike, suckers, tullibees, and sometimes walleyes are also found in these lakes. Such lakes are confined mostly to the border region, from Lake of the Woods through the Superior National Forest, in an area of surface igneous rock and soils of low fertility, and the drainage waters are very soft. In the same area there are some small lakes that have proved to be suitable for stream species of trout. The waters are cold and may be about 40 feet deep. These lakes are usually fed by springs or cold bog drainage. Brook trout, brown trout, and rainbow trout have been introduced in these waters and have done very well.

The second type of lake is one of two kinds in which walleyes thrive. It is difficult to determine the factors necessary for a walleye lake, but walleyes apparently do best in lakes where they have plenty of range. The only small lakes in which they thrive are those that have channels opening into other lakes, forming a chain. The first kind of walleye lake is similar to the lake trout type. It has rather rocky shores and is relatively infertile. In fact, it has all the characteristics of a large lake trout type except that it is too shallow for lake trout. Many of these lakes are only 75 or 80 feet deep. The cold water below the thermocline has insufficient volume to carry enough oxygen through the summer. Lakes of this type are located on rocky soils in Lake and Cook counties. These lakes contain a few lake trout, many northern pike, and usually some suckers and perch, but most of them did not originally contain walleyes. The walleyes have been introduced and are doing better in these lakes than in any other waters in Minnesota.

The other type of walleye lake is entirely different, being warmer and quite fertile. These lakes are large and have sand and mud bottoms which support abundant submerged vegetation in the shoal waters; they range in depth to as much as 200 feet. A number of deep lakes in Minnesota are of this type, but they are not suitable for lake trout because they are fertile and the bottoms are very rich in organic matter. The waters are hard, for they contain relatively large amounts of carbonates in solution. The cold underwaters become stagnant and deficient in oxygen for at least part of the year, and the fish are therefore confined in summer to the warm surface waters.

A number of large lakes in central and northern Minnesota, such as Upper Red Lake, Lower Red Lake, Leech Lake, Mille Lacs, and Cass Lake, are of the same type but relatively shallow. They are from 35 to 40 feet deep and from 8 to 15 miles across and consequently are subject to much wind and wave action. The wave action prevents bottom stagnation and makes the bottom available to fish throughout the year. Walleyes are the dominant species in these large lakes, while perch, northern pike, suckers, and many other species are common. Sunfish, bass, and crappies are not common except in bays. The majority of the larger lakes in central Minnesota are of this type with its several variations. They are located in areas where the soils are fertile and therefore are sometimes surrounded by agricultural land.

The fourth type of lake is the bass, crappie, and sunfish lake. These lakes are small but may have numerous bays and inlets. They are rich in organic matter and support much vegetation. The waters contain relatively large amounts of carbonates. The shores and bottoms are generally mud and sand. This type of lake is usually over 20 feet deep, and a few exceed 100 feet. When the lakes are deep enough, bottom stagnation and the loss of bottom oxygen occurs. Since large areas of bottom are inaccessible, the deep lakes of this type are not as productive as some of the shallow ones. Bass, crappie, and sunfish lakes are found in most areas of Minnesota but rarely in the northeastern corner of the state. Northern pike, suckers, perch, and other species are also present in most of them.

Many Minnesota lakes are a combination of the last two types — the second kind of walleye lake and the bass, crappie, and sunfish lake — and are suitable for all these species. These lakes make up the fifth type of lake. They are large and have many bays and inlets, thus virtually combining the conditions of small and large lakes.

The sixth type of lake comprises the prairie lakes of the southwestern and central parts of Minnesota. These are fertile hard-water lakes with rich mud bottoms and shores supporting abundant aquatic vegetation. Most of them are shallow, ranging from 6 to 20 feet in depth. This type of lake is largely inhabited by bullheads, buffalo, carp, and sometimes walleyes and other game fishes. Local sportsmen often want to have the rough fishes removed and replaced by game fishes, but these lakes are not very suitable for game fishes, and only by continuous effort can such fishes be maintained. Because of the shallow depths and the high oxygen consumption, winterkills occur frequently.

Since it is impossible to survey each of Minnesota's lakes, these types have been established for the purpose of classifying the other lakes. Most Minnesota lakes and to some extent Wisconsin lakes can be classified on the basis of a few factors such as the chemical condition of the water, the depth and the area of the lake, and the type of shore vegetation. A few intergradient types do not fit into the categories just described. In other states local conditions may alter the categories, so these must be worked out for each region.

Lake surveys determine the type of lake and the kind of fish suitable for it and also give some idea of the basic fertility of the lake, but most of the surveys commonly used in Minnesota give only rough estimates of the number of fish in the lake or the number that can be supported. Determination of these figures is one of the great problems in fish management and must be done before an intelligent management plan can be made. Of all aquatic animals fish are the most difficult to study quantitatively. They move about so readily that no collection obtained from any specific area can be considered an absolute quantitative sample. The only absolute measurement of quantity would involve the removal of every fish, for which the only practical method would be poisoning. Obviously such a measure would mean the end of the existing fish population and also of further study. Sampling with seines and nets may give some idea of the population, but the results cannot be regarded as more than crude measurements. Most of the work done on the Minnesota fish populations has of necessity been confined to sampling with electrofishing, seines, and various types of nets, giving at best only rough estimates.

In a state with as many lakes as Minnesota, surveys in which the fish in all the lakes are quantitatively measured are practically impossible. Furthermore, fish populations change from year to year, and so such a census would have to be repeated annually. An ordinary lake survey, however, such as has been developed and used in Minnesota, determines the general fertility of the lake and provides an index to the potential production of the kinds of fish for which the lake is suited. Certain lakes are surveyed at various intervals to provide some insight into the changes that occur. The surveys provide us with an inventory of the fishery resources of the state and must be continued in years to come.

The total weight of fish that can be removed from a lake without disturbing the overall production has never been worked out. Fish managers believe, however, that there is a yield limit, just as there is a limit to the amount of game that can be taken from land areas without depleting the necessary breeding stock. In some Minnesota lakes anglers take as much as 20 pounds per acre annually, while in others, including many of the northern lakes, the annual catch is less than 3 pounds per acre. Obviously it is important that this yield limit be determined, and it will probably be necessary to limit the amount of fish taken from a lake to conform with it.

Several factors within the fish population may prevent a lake from producing a maximum crop of fish. Surveys should include a study of the existing conditions of the fish population not only to determine the species present but also to determine the predominant age groups and the growth rate of the important species. The ratio of forage fishes to predacious fishes must be established, since forage fishes are a basic food supply for predacious fishes. The ratio between the two-year, three-year, and other age groups of the predominant species must also be determined.

As we mentioned earlier, some lakes are overpopulated with small fish and have too few big fish. In many fertile lakes that support a sizable fish population, heavy selective fishing keeps the number of large individuals in the game fish population reduced to a low level. However, population balances are difficult to regulate because such regulation involves restricted fishing. If fishermen could be induced to remove small game fish in proportion to the number of large individuals they catch, the competition within younger age groups would be relieved and a satisfactory growth rate would probably result. The average fisherman, however, can hardly be expected to follow such a radical procedure. Nor does this method take into consideration the populations of non-game species that are little affected by fishermen but that should likewise be controlled.

A very serious problem for lake management is the lowering of lake levels through drainage projects and drought. The lowering of lake levels creates oxygen deficiencies in the winter and reduces game fish lakes to bullhead lakes, or it may even make them unsuitable for any species. The extent of the problem is indicated by lake surveys, which thus provide another basis for the management of lakes for fish production.

Finally, water pollution is a factor that has become of greater significance in the past twenty-five years. Pollution is not something new, but with the tremendous increase in the human population the problem has become more serious. All forms of pollution — from agricultural, domestic, and industrial sources — have increased. The topic is the subject of many books and appears daily in the news media. Recent legislation, stimulated by public outcry, may prevent further increases in pollution and perhaps will help make it possible to restore better quality to polluted waters. It remains to be seen whether the public is willing to make the sacrifices and to pay the increased taxes and costs that go with water treatment. In addition to managing the sport fishery, the aquatic biologist today must also contend with the problems of maintaining water quality in lakes, rivers, and streams under his supervision.

Improvement of Lakes and Streams

Most of the problems in fish conservation are concerned with the factors that result in poor fishing. Because of the ever-increasing pressure by fishermen, maintenance of good fishing conditions becomes imperative, and the improvement of waters for better fishing is one of the fundamental goals of fish management. Lake improvement consists of activities to restore or to enhance any of the environmental or ecological conditions which affect the fish species for which the lake is managed.

As we have seen, food production is one of the most important factors determining the amount of fish a lake will produce. It is possible to increase the natural fertility of many lakes by adding commercial fertilizers or even ordinary barnyard manure. The proper use of these substances increases the productivity of the lake in food and consequently in pounds of fish. Unfortunately the increase is a short-term one because many of the added nutrients are quickly lost to the sediments at the bottom of the lake. In Europe fish ponds have been fertilized for centuries, and continuous research has been carried out in Israel on the relation between the use of fertilizers and the yields of carp and other fish from managed ponds. Wiebe (1931) and others have shown that certain commercial fertilizers increase the yield in rearing ponds, and fertilization is now a standard practice in pond operations. Although a few Minnesota lakes have been fertilized, no check has been made to determine the results; studies in other states have indicated that the benefits are evident for only two or three weeks before the additional nutrients become incorporated into the sediments.

Many northern lakes are too far from any source of commercial fertilizers for the use of them to be feasible. Moreover, in Minnesota the large size of some lakes that might otherwise be profitably fertilized makes the expense prohibitive. In addition, the problem in the present era is frequently one of *reducing* the influx of nutrients from summer homes and untreated sewage. The increase in fish production, while a primary goal of the fishery scientist, must be consistent with other recreational uses of the body of water. Increased

44

fertility promotes the growth of rooted aquatic plants, which the cottage owner may find undesirable near his swimming beach, and an increased algal population may produce obnoxious "blooms." Changes in fertility may also alter other characteristics of the lake and result in a change in the species composition of the fish population. At present it would appear that the addition of fertilizers for the purpose of increasing fish production is best restricted to small, easily managed bodies of water such as ponds.

In some waters the food supply may be increased by introducing forage fishes that do not compete with the species already present and so do not disturb the balance. Such a procedure has been followed in some northern trout lakes where tullibees were absent. Lake Superior ciscoes, which feed on material not utilized by trout, were introduced to provide additional food for the trout. Although the ciscoes were introduced only a few years ago, they have multiplied to such an extent in some lakes that fishermen occasionally complain that the trout will not bite because they are too well fed. This step is only the first one, but it seems to indicate the success of the procedure. In time presumably the lake trout population will grow and eventually the trout fishing will be greatly improved.

A good many remedies have been suggested to prevent the serious problem of winterkills which occur when the water in a lake does not contain enough oxygen to maintain fish all winter. Cutting holes in the ice to allow surface aeration has been tried, but this method does not allow sufficient oxygen to enter the water and, as mentioned earlier, the diffusion or spread of oxygen in the water is so slow that the effects are not found more than a few inches away. (The limited effectiveness of surface aeration is evident in the summer when, although the entire lake is exposed to the air, fish-kills sometimes occur because the plants have become so abundant that under special conditions their respiration reduces the oxygen to very low levels.) In addition, large numbers of fish force their way into the area directly below the holes and smother as a result of overcrowding. Furthermore, in a winter climate like that of Minnesota the holes quickly freeze over again. The remedies for oxygen depletion as well as the factors involved have been discussed in detail by Greenbank (1945).

One remedy that is practical where small bodies of water are involved is to clear the snow from large areas of clean ice. Removing the snow allows sunlight to penetrate to the plants below, enabling them to keep up the liberation of oxygen. In several lakes where this procedure has been tried, it has been successful. But clean ice is not always available. If there is a snowfall very soon after the permanent ice has formed on a lake, the weight of the snow depresses the ice and water comes up through the cracks, producing a slush surface. The slush then freezes, forming an opaque ice layer which reduces the light penetration and therefore the oxygen production of the aquatic plants. Ice cores we have examined indicate that several opaque layers may be formed during any given year.

Oxygen depletion may also be prevented by removing excess vegetation along the margin of the lake before the freeze-up. Although vegetation usually functions to increase the oxygen supply, it becomes one of the heaviest oxygen consumers when it dies and decomposes. There are usually enough microscopic plants in the open water to liberate oxygen so that the lake will not suffer if the large aquatic plants and water weeds are taken out. The method of removing excess vegetation has been followed in a number of states, particularly in Ohio, to prevent summerkills as well as winterkills. It is expensive, however, because it requires considerable labor and special machinery. If Minnesota had only a few lakes in danger of oxygen depletion, vegetation removal would be feasible. However, in a state with hundreds of lakes in this condition — and some of them of enormous extent — this method is far too expensive for general use. Furthermore, very careful studies would be required to ascertain whether the removal of the vegetation would upset the chemical or nutrient cycle and produce other detrimental effects.

Various other approaches to the problem have been developed. For example, there are aerators on the market which operate on the general principle of pumping air through the water and then circulating the water by propellers or other devices. The aeration method is effective over a limited area, but it seldom improves the oxygen conditions more than 50 feet away. As a result, pumps may be beneficial and feasible on a small lake or a pond, but a hundred or more pumps might be necessary to maintain the oxygen in a lake of considerable size. Moreover, some of the pumps are expensive to operate, and many of them require considerable attention lest they freeze.

In some lakes raising the water level a few feet seems to be the best remedy. In many lakes now suffering from low-oxygen conditions this would provide a sufficient volume of water to hold the necessary oxygen supply through the winter. The procedure is particularly effective with lakes (such as Big Kandiyohi Lake in Minnesota) which fell many feet during the drought years of 1932–1935 and which have never regained their former levels. If the water levels of these lakes could be restored and maintained, oxygen might once again be retained in sufficient quantities to hold fish over the winter.

Remedying oxygen depletion is very difficult. There is no definite amount of oxygen that can be said to be absolutely necessary to sustain fish life. Moreover, fish species differ greatly in their requirements. Unfortunately most game fishes require more oxygen than many rough fishes do; hence often the game fishes die while the rough fishes survive. When the oxygen supply is reduced to about one-third of the amount normally present in the summer, the fish population is in danger. At times fish survive on much less, but at other times they die when this point is reached. These differences are probably related to the condition of the fish and to the temperature and other conditions of the water. A careful study of the oxygen supply in various lakes during the late winter can be made to determine when the supply will approach the critical point. Often in cases where the oxygen is disappearing rapidly there is no immediate or practical remedy. If no means are available for the application of some method of aeration, the only procedure left is to rescue or salvage as many fish as possible before it is too late.

Another aspect in which many lakes can be improved involves the spawning conditions. Conditions for natural propagation should be maintained at the highest possible level in order to maintain natural reproduction. Keeping up natural reproduction is much cheaper than undertaking artificial propagation and stocking. For gravel-nesting species, gravel beds should be constructed in lakes with muddy shores. In lakes with very soft mud bottoms, boxes of sand may be placed for bass nests. Bluntnose minnows, one of our most valuable forage fishes, deposit their eggs on the underside of submerged objects; their production can be greatly increased by placing spawning boards in shallow water. The protection of spawning beds from disturbance during the season when the adult fish are on the nests is important. Several bays containing good spawning beds will produce as many fry as the best rearing pond.

The control of rough fishes is another important step in lake improvement. Species such as carp and dogfish may compete with the more desirable species or may destroy the conditions necessary for them. In some states carp are used as forage fish because they multiply rapidly and produce a large amount of food for game species. However, Minnesota and several other states cannot follow this plan because of the destructiveness of carp in northern lakes, long proved by their devastation of vegetation and of the feeding grounds and the spawning beds of other fish. In this way carp have already eliminated most other species from some lakes in southern Minnesota. The only sure way of exterminating the carp in a lake would be to kill every fish in the lake with dynamite or with some poisonous chemical. This procedure is expensive and does not ensure against the reintroduction of carp, which may occur through the use of young carp as bait. The present method in general use is to control them by seining, by trapping them on their favorite spawning beds, and by screening inlets where they may be gaining access from other waters. They are exceedingly prolific, which adds to the difficulty of controlling them.

Proper vegetation in a lake is necessary for successful maintenance of the fish population. Vegetation is not only an important agent in oxygen production but also shelters small fish and is the basis for the food of all fish. The shore waters of many lakes have been cleared of all types of vegetation, particularly in front of cottages and around bathing beaches. These clean sand bottoms may be ideal for bathing, but they are deserts as far as fish food and fry production are concerned. At the other extreme some lakes in the late stages of eutrophication are literally choked with vegetation. The vegetation may become so thick that it fills in the open water and prevents free movement of the fish. It may result also in an accumulation of decaying plant waste during the winter, which uses up the oxygen and causes winterkills. In some lakes conditions may be improved by restoring or increasing the areas of vegetation, in others by removing the vegetation and restricting its growth. Each lake seems to be a special case and must be examined in detail before a solution is proposed because the results of the ''cure'' may be even worse than the problem. There are examples of lakes that have become practically fishless because of the overzealous removal of rooted aquatic plants.

Low and fluctuating water levels are one of the most serious obstacles to fish production in many northern lakes. In some lakes the levels have been lowered by drainage; in others the summer water supply has been reduced by the removal of surrounding forests which had acted as reservoirs. Many lakes are subject to great fluctuations in their levels because of power dams. Today we have the additional problem of thermal changes associated with discharges of warm water into rivers and lakes from industrial sites. The lowering of water levels in moderately shallow lakes may reduce the volume of water to such an extent that the lakes become subject to winter oxygen depletion. Some lakes lose their fertile marginal bottoms, which are replaced by the less productive muds of the deeper bottom deposits. Lakes subject to frequent fluctuations caused by dams are always in danger of having important spawning beds left high and dry at a critical time. They are also subject to frequent destruction of their most important food production areas. Under such conditions no lake can produce its maximum yield of fish. In order to maintain the maximum fish production every effort should be made to keep lake waters at their normal levels.

Streams differ from lakes mainly in the conditions caused by the current, the absence of great depths, and the absence of complications caused by stratification. Lakes depend primarily on vegetation for their oxygen supply, but streams secure much of their oxygen from the atmosphere through the action of the currents. Streams also differ from lakes in that they have a continual supply of nutritive salts and other elements washing in from land sources.

Many streams in Minnesota have deteriorated as a result of manufacturing, agricultural, and lumbering operations, and they are no longer supporting the fish populations they once carried. Because of the numerous lakes available, our warm-water streams were neglected until the increasing popularity of canoeing led to renewed interest in them; nevertheless, it is still possible in many cases to rehabilitate fishable streams. The restoration of good fishing in these streams and rivers would also help to relieve the fishing pressure on the lakes.

Scientific surveys of streams are essential before any major improvement can be attempted. Data on the source, the volume, and the chemical conditions of the water and on temperature, shade, food organisms, depth, bottom types, pools and rapids, and present fish populations should be secured first in order to isolate the conditions requiring correction. In recent years detailed biological surveys have been carried out by the Department of Natural Resources on many of the large streams in the state, for example, the Cloquet, Crow Wing, and Snake rivers.

Streams may be divided into a number of types. Small streams are usually swift; large streams tend to be slower and often have deep, pondlike areas. Streams may contain cold water or warm water, depending on the source and the local conditions of shade, depth, and current. Cold streams are usually suitable for various species of trout. Warm streams are not suitable for trout, but if large enough they can support largemouth and smallmouth bass, sunfish, channel catfish, bullheads, and various species of suckers. In the largest streams many additional species may be found, particularly those that prefer quiet waters and muddy bottoms (large catfish, buffalo, gars, carp, sheepsheads, and paddlefish).

Pollution, loss of cover, erosion, and extreme fluctuations of the water levels caused by extensive drainage and by the cutting of moisture-retaining forests have combined to render some streams unsuitable for the support of large fish populations. In many streams unrestricted seining of minnows has destroyed the food and the spawning and feeding grounds of game fishes. All these conditions must be remedied in order to restore such streams to their former productivity.

Trout streams have been surveyed and some attempts at improvement have been made where feasible. Because of their small size, most trout streams are easier to work with than are the larger rivers. Detailed instructions for surveying and improving trout streams have been given by investigators such as Hubbs, Greeley, and Tarzwell (1932), Davis (1938), and Needham (1938).

Improvement involves remedying the conditions found to be the most unsatisfactory to the extent that the results justify the expense. Most important is the maintenance of a flow of water uncontaminated by warm water, sewage, or refuse from industrial operations. Silt from eroded watersheds must be reduced because it smothers food organisms, destroys spawning beds, fills up pools, and sometimes even smothers the fish themselves. The silt in streams can be controlled by stopping soil erosion in the cultivated fields of the drainage basin. Siltation as a result of intensive cultivation adjacent to the streams is a major source of our present problems. The construction of deflectors and various types of dams may direct and concentrate the stream currents so that they will sweep silt downstream and will also wash out holes, providing deeper waters for the larger fish, but unless these structures are constantly maintained nature destroys them in a few years. In some instances beavers use these man-made structures as the foundation for their dams and hence defeat the human engineer. In the case of small streams which are so shallow that they freeze to the bottom in winter, judicious regulation of current and depth is required to eliminate deep freezing.

In many trout streams the maintenance of low temperatures in the summer is one of the greatest problems. Trout do best in water with summer temperatures ranging from 50° to 65° F. The destruction of shade along the banks may allow the sun to warm the water until the temperature is too high for trout. In such places shade can be restored by planting trees or shrubs, and the stream can be narrowed and the current forced into the shady part. A cover of bushes and brush can be pulled over the stream. The water can be further cooled by cleaning and enlarging the lateral feeder springs. The few streams that are too cold may be warmed by widening them with dams to spread out the water and expose it to the sun.

Spawning conditions can be improved in almost every stream. All trout require coarse gravel for spawning. In streams with bottoms of soft mud or sand, spawning beds of coarse gravel should be constructed at intervals. Spawning conditions can be further enhanced by opening small lateral feeder streams and building spawning beds in them.

Food production is of as much concern in stream management as in lake management. Most of the aquatic insects that form an important part of the diet of trout, for instance, are produced on beds of coarse gravel and small boulders, while sand and solid rock beds are low in food production. Weed beds on silt bottoms produce large quantities of small crustaceans and insects and are important assets for increased productivity. For best results a trout stream should have ample feeding beds with sheltered water easily accessible. Good trout waters usually have alternate pools and rapids. Although long straight stretches of swift water often produce abundant food, they are usually barren of trout because they do not offer pools for shelter. Pools can be made by damming the stream with logs and rocks in locations sheltered with overhanging banks or logs. If the pools are too deep, suckers and other fish may enter and compete with the trout for food and space. Too many pools may result in a shortage of the swift water in which many food organisms develop. Small trout, on the other hand, need weed beds for feeding and cover, and such beds are best developed in the feeder streams. When streams have so much vegetation that they are partly choked by it, some of the cover should be removed.

In some streams rough or undesirable fish are an even greater problem than in lakes. In large streams that are silted and muddy game fish tend to become scarce and rough fish very numerous. It is difficult to control the numbers of rough fish present in a stream because they can enter an area from either downstream or upstream except where impassable dams are present. Continual removal is the only practical solution, although it can be supplemented by encouraging predatory game species.

The procedures for improving warm-water streams are similar to those for improving trout streams and involve many of the same considerations. The existing conditions must first be measured in order to determine what needs improvement. Clean water is always necessary, and undisturbed feeding and spawning areas should be provided. Wherever possible, pools and sheltered areas should be created and protected. When these conditions have been developed as much as possible, the streams should be stocked with the desired species of game fish and panfish. If these fish can become established, they may aid in reducing any surplus of rough or forage fish. In all cases the cost of improvement must be considered in order to determine whether the results will justify the expenditures.

Although fish population imbalances can constitute a problem in streams, the problem is not usually as serious as in lakes. Streams, like lakes, have a limited productivity and can support only a certain amount of fish, but if this amount is exceeded and competition becomes too great, it is usually possible for stream fish to escape to areas of less competition. The tendency of many species to move upstream or downstream, often for great distances, makes continued stocking necessary in some heavily fished areas. There is much less danger of overstocking in streams than in lakes.

Another method by which lakes and streams have been improved is the introduction of fish species that were not originally native to those lakes and streams. There is a type of lake referred to as a "two-storied" lake, one in which walleyes and other spiny-rayed or warm-water fishes live in the warm surface waters and rainbow trout live in the cold deep waters. These lakes are generally very clear and quite deep, usually over 80 feet, with a narrow fringe of beach supporting a meager growth of rooted aquatic plants, and they have a large volume of cold water in the hypolimnion. Long Lake in Clearwater County is a lake of this type. Long Lake and others like it originally supported only walleyes, bass, panfish, and a few northern pike, but surveys by the Department of Natural Resources showed that the deep waters were cool enough and contained sufficient dissolved oxygen throughout the year to support rainbow trout. Rainbow trout were stocked as fingerlings in the early summer and within a few years reached weights of up to 7 pounds. They have not succeeded in spawning in the lake, however, so it has been necessary to restock the lake at regular intervals to maintain the population. Since the initial success of experiments of this type, a number of lakes elsewhere in the state have been stocked with trout and managed for trout as well as the native fishes. While there are no data available on production, it appears that the addition of trout has increased the overall yield to the angler and has provided the angler with a sport fish that is very highly prized.

Similarly the Department of Natural Resources has planted brook trout, brown trout, and rainbow trout in many streams throughout the state where detailed studies have shown conditions for trout growth and survival to be very good. Many of these streams, such as the Straight River in Hubbard County and the Clearwater River in Beltrami and Clearwater counties, are known for excellent fishing and large fish. Other streams, particularly small spring-fed brooks, afford some of the best brook trout fishing in the entire state, in some cases surpassing the trout streams along the north shore of Lake Superior. In a few instances the trout have been able to maintain their populations by natural reproduction, but more often the populations have had to be supplemented by annual stocking. A list of these streams and other trout streams in the state has been prepared by the Department of Natural Resources to provide the public with information on their locations and the actual mileage that is managed in the various streams.

A number of new species have been introduced in Minnesota lakes to augment the native fishes. The grayling has been stocked in a few small lakes in Lake and Cook counties, and a fast-growing variety of the rainbow trout, the Donaldson, has been introduced in several lakes. Most fishermen are aware of the much-touted introduction of coho salmon in Lake Superior. Other species of fish have been introduced, all cold-water species and members of the salmon or trout family. The success of these introductions has yet to be determined in most instances, but they do represent a continuing effort on the part of the fisheries scientists in the Department of Natural Resources to improve and augment fishing for the thousands of fishermen who live in Minnesota and the additional thousands who visit the state each year.

The Natural Diet of Fish

The food of the various fish species ranges from microscopic algae and protozoans to ducklings and small muskrats. Only a few fishes have restricted diets; most utilize a wide range of food sources and usually eat whatever is most readily available within that range. Many fishes are omnivorous, eating both plant and animal matter. Some are mainly insectivorous, while others are predacious or piscivorous. Still others feed almost exclusively on plankton or are strictly herbivorous, eating only plant food. The diets often change with the age of the fish and sometimes with the season of the year. As a group, fish eat several thousand kinds of food, and in this chapter we will describe only the main types of foods or the most common forms. Many of these common forms are not recognized by fishermen and others, to whom they are just bugs or grubs. Although common names have been given to some of them by biologists, these names are of little help if they are not known to the layman. Consequently, we have used anglicized scientific names or generic names for most of the food organisms because many people do not know them by any common name.

The basic type of fish food is plankton. Years ago few people had ever heard this term and even fewer knew what it meant. Today the vast number of popular articles on water purity and pollution published in magazines and newspapers have made it almost a household word. Plankton is a collective term covering a vast conglomeration of microscopic or semimicroscopic plants and animals that live a free-floating or drifting existence in more or less open water. The planktonic animals are only feeble swimmers at best. In an ecological sense the plankton constitutes an independent community with its own producers and consumers. The microscopic plants, mostly algae, utilize dissolved nutrients in the water, and sunlight enables them to convert the nutrients into their body substance. Some algae are minute one-celled forms, others are filaments. The higher algae, which live on rocks and sticks in long strands often several feet long, are not classified as plankton, but they are used as food by some fishes. The algae (phytoplankton) furnish

54

food for minute animals (zooplankton) which in turn are food for still larger animals until the ultimate consumers are fish. Plants and animals of the plankton at all levels of the food chain die and settle to the bottom to become food for those animals restricted to bottom life. The community of organisms associated with the bottom is called the benthos or the benthic community.

The protozoans are the lowest level of consumers among the planktonic animals and feed on the algae and the organic detritus from the decay of various planktonic forms. In the next level of consumers are many species of minute rotifers which teem in the plankton, feeding on algae and protozoans. In this same food level we find large numbers of tiny crustaceans (Entomostraca) and a few insect larvae which feed on all the lower levels. Plankton flourishes in lakes and ponds and in quiet waters of large rivers. Strong currents are unfavorable for plankton.

The growth of plankton depends on the nutritive quality of the water. Water rich in nutrients such as phosphorus and nitrogen may have so much plankton that it becomes turbid. A great increase in some kinds of algae may cause it to float to the surface and to form heavy scums or algal blooms. Sometimes the plankton may become so dense that it causes oxygen depletion, and large quantities of senescent plankton settling to the bottom tend to hasten eutrophication.

Plankton constitutes the basis for most of the food production of lakes and ponds and to a more limited extent that of rivers. In these waters plankton or its equivalent is food for nearly all fish in the first few weeks of life and for the adults of quite a few large species. Adult paddlefish, for instance, feed mainly on plankton strained from the water by means of their fine gill rakers. The senescent plankton settles to the bottom and forms a rich ooze on which many small benthic animals browse until they in turn become food for fish.

The tiny planktonic crustaceans are often referred to as entomostracans. At one time this was a scientific name reserved for certain minute crustaceans, but today it is also in common use as a term referring generally to all small crustaceans. Most entomostracans fall into two groups, the cladocerans and the copepods, although there are several larger crustaceans that also occur in plankton.

The cladocerans include a large number of species, some of which are true plankton forms while others live in the weeds and on the bottom ooze. Practically all are eaten by fish. The most common and best known are the several species of *Daphnia* (Figure 1). These are often abundant in plankton along with a number of other common species of cladocerans that are important food items for fish (Figure 1). The large *Daphnia* are visible to the naked eye, but they very rarely exceed 1/16 inch in size. Many of these tiny cladocerans can be seen in a vial of water held to the light. We have found large predacious fishes such as crappies and lake trout gorging on them. They are cultured in fish hatcheries to feed newly hatched trout fry. The largest of the cladocerans is *Leptodora*, an elongated form nearly an inch in length, which in midsummer becomes quite abundant in the plankton of warm lakes.

Fig. 1. Cladocerans common in Minnesota lakes. *Left, Daphnia; right, Bosmina.*

The copepods are another important group of entomostracans present in plankton. Although some species of copepods live on the bottom, several species are common as planktonic forms. They are jointed animals with many legs and are usually less than 1/8 inch in length. They are eaten by nearly all young fish and are important food even for adults. Stomachs weighing 8 to 10 pounds have been removed from paddlefish and have been found to contain nothing but copepods. The most common copepod species are those of the genera *Cyclops* (Figure 2) and *Diaptomus*.

In the deep waters of Lake Superior and a few inland lakes such as Lake Saganaga, we find *Mysis* (Figure 3), a shrimplike animal belonging to the higher crustaceans. It is only about 1/2 inch in length, and although it may be found near or even on the bottom, we usually find it in open water and consider it as a plankter. It is an important food item for many deep-water fishes such as lake trout and whitefish.

Plankton plays only a small part in the food production of small rivers and streams where there is little quiet water to promote its production. The food material in small streams is primarily from two sources. Because of the proximity to land, terrestrial items including vegetation, leaves, seeds, and insects furnish one source of food. The other source is within the stream itself. On any solid object — a stone, a stick, or a log — microscopic plant life, primarily diatoms and algae, forms an adhesive slimy covering called the periphyton. Some small fish browse on the periphyton, but it is most important as food for worms, snails, and many browsing aquatic insects which in turn are food for fish. Beds of higher plants such as watercress

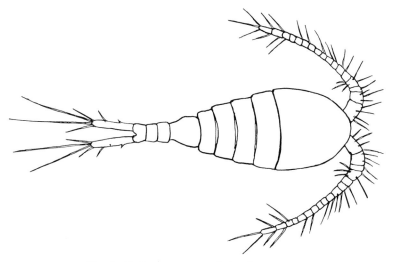

Fig. 2. *Cyclops*, a common planktonic crustacean

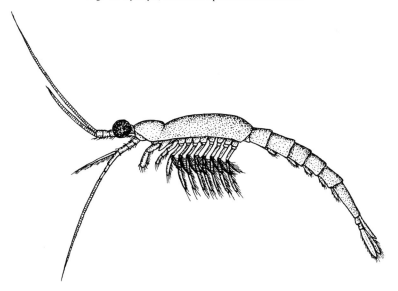

Fig. 3. *Mysis relicta*, a crustacean found in Lake Superior and Lake Saganaga

support a large number of immature insect forms and higher crustaceans (Amphipoda), which are also food for fish. Although streams are capable of producing considerable fish food, the amount varying with depth, bottom type, and current, they offer much food derived from the adjacent land sources. The deeper and quieter pools of streams and rivers have productive bottom oozes that support a variety of aquatic insects, worms, and small mollusks.

In both lakes and streams a vast number of species of animals live on the bottom and practically all are eaten by fish. Because of their size, the minute bottom forms related to those found in plankton are not as important as the worms, snails, and larger crustaceans and the many kinds of adult and immature insects. The shallow bottoms of lakes and streams down to depths of about 10 feet support populations of food animals when the bottoms are rich in ooze, and the ooze-browsers constitute the basis of food production. In creeks and small streams lacking ooze bottoms, the food basis may be the minute plant forms (diatoms and algae) which form a coating of ooze on rocks and other objects. In these streams an additional large food contribution comes from the land animals that fall into the water. The shallow marginal waters of lakes produce the bulk of the food there. Beyond the depth at which water weeds grow, food production becomes less as the depth increases.

The bottom ooze, which is of organic origin, is converted into animal food by various browsing organisms. Aquatic worms are some of the most common browsers. Although related to the common terrestrial earthworms, the aquatic worms are much smaller; some fish eat large numbers of them. The leeches, commonly called bloodsuckers, are another kind of worm. While many are capable of sucking fish blood, they are not very important in this regard. The largest leeches stretch to a length of over 10 inches, and we often see them swimming with undulating movements in northern lakes. Many of the large leeches do not feed on blood but on bottom ooze. Some of the smaller species are predators on snails. When the larger leeches are abundant in midsummer, northern pike, walleyes, and even black bass gorge on them. The leeches are quickly killed by the powerful digestive juices of the fish. Some bait dealers now stock large leeches for bait.

Mollusks are part of the food chain in both lakes and streams. Large clams, mussels, and snails are not very important as fish food, although the larvae of clams are natural fish parasites. Small clams and snails are eaten by many fishes, some of which eject the shells while others do not.

Many small species of snails (about 1/4 inch in size) feed on the ooze and the microscopic plant growth covering sticks, stones, and water weeds in the shallow waters of streams and lakes. Minnows, perch, sunfish, and many other fish feeding in shallow water nibble eagerly on these snails. The only clams eaten to any extent by fish are the tiny fingernail clams, the most important of which are species of *Pisidium* and *Sphaerium* (Figure 4). The *Pisidium* species are tiny clams, usually not over 3/16 inch in size, which are often abundant on the bottoms of very deep lakes; they are one of the few food organisms living on the bottom ooze of Lake Superior below depths of 400 feet. Lake trout and other deep-water fishes eat large numbers of these clams. The *Sphaerium* species are larger forms, up to 1 inch in length; these forms are common in streams and in the shallow waters of lakes.

Fig. 4. Fingernail clams found in Minnesota waters. *Left*, *Pisidium*; *right*, *Sphaerium*.

The more important crustaceans which live on the bottom and serve as food for fish are not minute entomostracans but the larger and more advanced forms which are either ooze-browsers or scavengers. One group consists of the amphipods; they are small, usually less than 1/2 inch in length, and live in the ooze or on the water weeds. The most common amphipod is the small *Hyalella* (Figure 5), which swarms by the millions on the shallow bottoms and the water weeds of all Minnesota lakes. If water weeds are shaken in a pan of water, the abundant *Hyalella* can be seen swimming about on their sides. The amphipods furnish an almost inexhaustible food source for sunfish, perch, young game fish, and others feeding near shore. A similar amphipod, *Gammarus*, sometimes occurs in Minnesota lakes, but it is usually most abundant in the weed beds of small streams, especially in watercress beds of trout brooks where it may be a major item in the diet of stream trout. In Lake Superior and most very deep inland lakes with

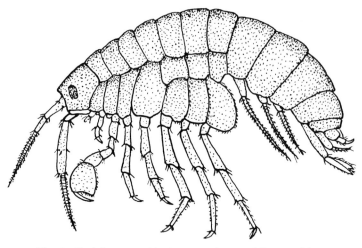

Fig. 5. *Hyalella*, an amphipod common in many Minnesota lakes

oxygen at the bottom, we find the deep-water amphipod *Pontoporeia* at depths over 100 feet. This amphipod is an important food for lake trout and other deep-water fishes.

Other large crustaceans include *Mysis*, already described in the discussion of plankton, and the crayfishes (Figure 6), which are sometimes incorrectly called crabs. Several species of crayfish are common in the shallow waters

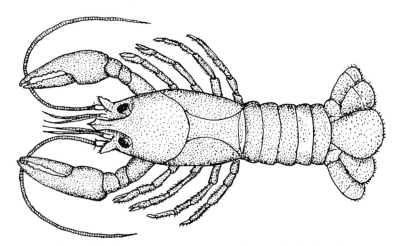

Fig. 6. Crayfish *Orconectes*, an important food item in the diet of bass, walleyes, and perch

of hard-water lakes and streams; they are also abundant at greater depths and are frequently seen by skin and scuba divers. Crayfish up to 6 inches in length as well as small juveniles are eaten by almost all game fishes feeding in marginal waters. The crayfish themselves are scavengers which feed on both plant and animal matter. The tail portion is an excellent fishing bait. Until they produce a hard "skin," they are known as soft crayfish, the type which is considered best for bait. Black bass, northern pike, and walleyes eat both hard-shell and soft-shell crayfish. Sunfish, crappies, rock bass, and perch gorge on any small ones available. Even large brown trout seem to relish crayfish.

Insects form a very important part of the diet of most fishes, large and small. All aquatic insects are eaten by various fishes, and many terrestrial insects also become prey when they fall into the water or fly too close to the surface of it. Four groups or orders of insects are known as aquatic orders; although the adults are terrestrial flying forms, they deposit their eggs in the water, and the resulting immature stages are strictly aquatic. Most of these live in the water for about a year before becoming mature flying forms. Other orders of insects have members that live in the water both as immatures and as adults. Orders such as Diptera (flies) have certain species that deposit their eggs in the water, and the resulting larvae are aquatic until they emerge as adults. The larvae are carnivorous and feed on all sorts of bottom animals. The nymphs of the order Odonata, containing the dragonflies and the damsel flies (Figure 7), reach a length of several inches. They crawl onto the shore or upon the weeds and shed their skins, emerging fully developed for flying. Perch, sunfish, and many other fishes prowling in the shallow water consume large numbers of the nymphs.

The order Ephemeroptera, containing the mayflies (Figure 8), is another aquatic order. The immature nymphs live for about a year on the bottom in relatively shallow water in streams and lakes. In Lake Pepin and other large lakes, they are extremely abundant and usually emerge at the same time. All predacious fishes and various bottom-feeding fishes eat large numbers of them. The nymphs are usually distinguished by three caudal filaments and a row of fuzzy gills on each side of the abdomen. Some live on sticks and stones, others bury themselves in the ooze. The adults live only about a day, just long enough to mate and drop their eggs in the water. They are attracted to lights; during a heavy emergence, dead ones sometimes pile up under the streetlights in river towns and create a traffic hazard. At times they are so numerous that housewives are forced to hang their laundry indoors, and freshly painted houses become a mess. Some of the species living in small streams emerge in a premature state and fly to nearby trees or bushes to complete their final molt. They then mate, drop their eggs in the water, and die. Thousands may be strewn over the water where the

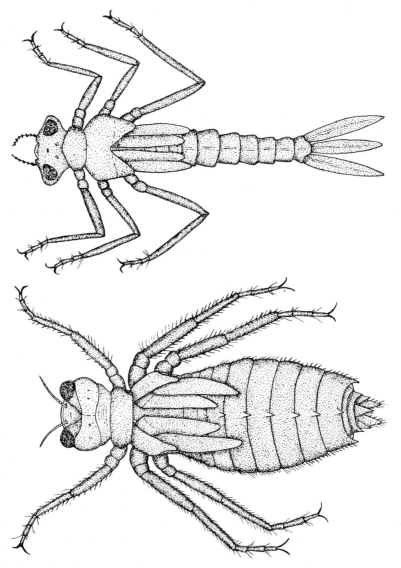

Fig. 7. Larvae of order Odonata. *Top*, damsel fly larva; *bottom*, dragonfly larva.

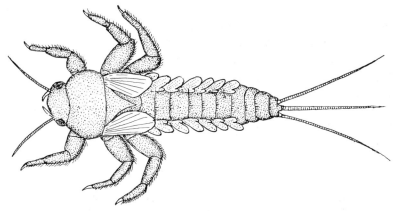

Fig. 8. Mayfly nymph (order Ephemeroptera)

eager fish devour them. Lures for fly fishing are often made to imitate both adult and immature mayflies.

The caddis flies of the order Trichoptera all have aquatic larvae. They prefer the shallow water of lakes and streams, where they live on rocks, sand bottoms, and soft mud bottoms. The adults are mothlike flying insects that hide on tree trunks or bushes near the water during the day and become active at night. They live about a month as adults, depositing their eggs on the water. The resulting larvae are grublike forms with short legs just behind the head. The larvae of various Trichoptera species build many different kinds of cases. Some possess glands that produce a silk material with which each larva constructs a case around itself, leaving only the head end protruding. Sticks, tiny shells, sand grains, small pebbles, and bits of vegetation are used by other species to make cases (Figure 9). Some species prefer to live in swift water where they attach their cases of sand and pebbles to rocks. One species builds a case equipped with webs or nets fashioned to resemble wings which the larva uses to catch prey. Other species make cases that look like bundles of tiny sticks; it is quite startling to see a bunch of sticks slowly moving over a smooth mud bottom. Another species uses tiny sand grains to build a coiled case that looks like a snail's shell. Still another species makes an elongated case of tiny sticks crossed in a symmetrical log-cabin pattern. The larvae are seldom separated from their cases and they even pupate in them. Many fishes feed on them, eating the cases along with the larvae.

The stone flies form the aquatic order Plecoptera. The nymphs are restricted to swift water in streams and are well adapted for clinging to logs and rocks. The adults are dusky insects with elongated transparent wings. They are commonly found hiding under the leaves and the bark of trees and bushes along most trout streams. The nymphs (Figure 10) reach a length of about an inch and have well-developed clawed legs for clinging to the underside of rocks and logs. Most nymphs stay well hidden, and they are eaten by trout and other fishes only when they stray from their shelters. They resemble some mayfly nymphs but can be readily distinguished by

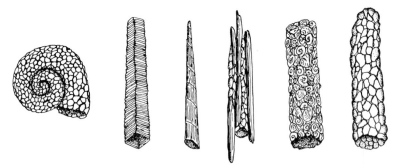

Fig. 9. Typical caddis fly cases found in streams, lakes, and ponds

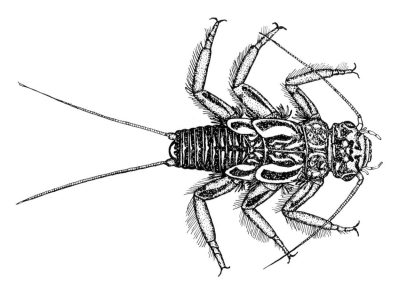

Fig. 10. Stone fly nymph (order Plecoptera)

the presence of two long caudal filaments and by the thoracic gills. Lures for fly fishing are often made to resemble the nymphs.

Most of the other orders of insects are primarily terrestrial, but many of these orders have species that are wholly or partly aquatic, and some are so abundant that they are important as fish food. The order Diptera, which contains a vast number of species, includes many species that have aquatic larvae — mosquitoes, blackflies, crane flies, horseflies, and many others. Some of these live in shallow and sometimes foul water hardly suitable for fish. The eggs of the nonbloodsucking midge *Chaoborus* develop into "phantom" larvae, which are predacious members of the plankton of warm-water lakes. These are transparent wormlike forms about 1/2 inch long with a pair of black air sacs at each end of the body (Figure 11). Phantom larvae are eaten by many fishes.

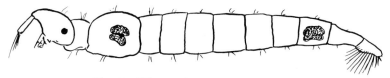

Fig. 11. "Phantom" midge larva (*Chaoborus*)

The most significant aquatic members of the order Diptera are the gnatlike midges or chironomids (Figure 12). These are the tiny midges or gnats that often swarm in clouds near water, especially on summer evenings when their nuptial flights high above the trees make a loud hum. At times they

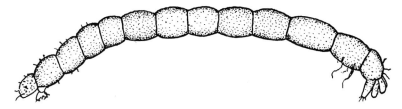

Fig. 12. Chironomid or bloodworm, the larval stage of a midge (order Diptera)

are a nuisance on lakes such as Lake Vermilion at Tower, Minnesota. Great windrows of cast skins and dead and dying adults may form on the beach, attracting hordes of flies and producing a most unpleasant odor. At times midges rival the mayflies in their swarming. There are many types of midges, and they deposit their eggs in almost any water environment. The wormlike maggots live in the bottom ooze even at depths of 900 feet in Lake Superior. They are ooze-browsers, and all fishes that feed on or near the bottom eat large quantities of them. Some of the larvae found on deep bottoms deficient in oxygen are bright red and are sometimes called bloodworms. The color is from the blood pigment hemoglobin, which is slightly different from the pigment in the blood of vertebrates. As a group the larvae of midges or chironomids constitute a very important part of the fish food produced on the bottom of lakes and rivers. No other group of aquatic insects is distributed as widely or as abundantly as these.

The lacewing flies of the family Sialidae include several species that have aquatic larvae. The best known is the Dobson fly, a large clear-winged insect that may be found flying around lights near the water in southern Minnesota on summer nights. The adult is about 3 inches long with very slender jaws (about an inch long in the male but only half that long in the female). The eggs are deposited on overhanging bushes and trees, and the newly hatched larvae drop into the water and live under rocks and in the mud until they pupate. They are commonly known as hellgrammites (Figure 13) and are excellent bait for bass and trout.

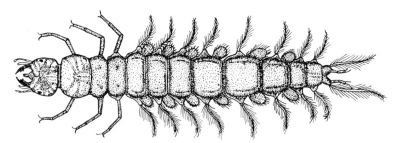

Fig. 13. Dobson fly or hellgrammite (order Neuroptera)

The true bugs form the large order Hemiptera, all possessing leathery wing covers and piercing, needlelike mouth parts. Although many species are strictly terrestrial, others are wholly or partly aquatic. Some of the adults live in water but are capable of leaving it and flying to other bodies of water. The aquatic forms are predacious, and the larger ones can straddle and sink their beaks into small fish and can even pierce a human hand. The giant water bug (which can leave the water and fly about electric lights), the water boatman (which skims over the surface), the back swimmers (which swim upside down), the long and slender water scorpion in the weeds, and the spidery water striders (which skate on the surface) all belong to this order. Although these forms are eaten by fish, we seldom find many in fish stomachs.

The large order containing the beetles (Coleoptera) has a few families with aquatic species (Figure 14). The adult diving beetles carry air bubbles and swim under the surface, and the whirligig beetles gyrate on the surface film. Some beetles are scavengers while others, such as the diving beetles, are predacious and feed on all manner of aquatic animals including small fish. None of these beetles ranks high in the diet of fish.

The foods of various fish species do not always include the aquatic animals just described. Plants may be eaten at times. Plants play an important role in the food chain and provide food for the animals that make up a large proportion of the food eaten by fish. Many insects with no aquatic relatives (for example, grasshoppers) are eagerly eaten if they fall into the water. Frogs are eaten by most predacious fishes. The same is true for ducklings, muskrats, and other small animals. Woe to the meadow mouse that falls in the water if a northern pike, black bass, or trout is present. Minnows and other small or immature fish furnish a large part of the diet of the large game fish. The small fish are part of the food chain in which still smaller animal forms and even plants are converted into food for game fish.

It is always wise to examine the stomach contents of your catch because this will often give you a clue to the preferred natural foods of the species. Armed with such knowledge on days when there is a long time between bites or when you are about to go home empty-handed, you might try as bait one of the items in the natural diet of the fish. The organisms in the fish's stomach may also indicate where the fish are feeding — in the shallows, in the deeper water (on mayfly nymphs or bloodworms), or on the reefs (on crayfish). You may be amazed at the varied contents of a fish's stomach.

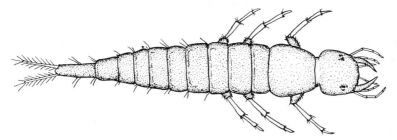

Fig. 14. Larval stage of aquatic beetle *Dytiscus* (order Coleoptera)

Parasites and Infections of Fish

Fishermen are frequently disturbed when they find small yellow or black spots on the fish they catch. These spots are caused by one or more of a large variety of parasites with which almost all freshwater fish are infected. In fact, it is unusual to find fish that do not harbor at least a few parasites. With a single exception (the broad fish tapeworm, *Dibothriocephalus latus*) these parasites are not harmful to human beings, but they can cause extensive damage among fish populations. Some of the parasites are external, living on the skin or the gills; others are internal parasites which live in the intestine or in and among the various organs. Many larval forms are found as cysts in the muscles and the skin.

Many adult parasitic worms live in the digestive tract and are usually not discovered by the fisherman who discards the viscera without exploring the contents of the intestine. The parasites most often detected are the larval forms of worms encysted in the body or the viscera. The most conspicuous are the larval flukes — the yellow grubs that live just under the skin and the black grubs that live in the skin. Some tapeworm larvae appear as yellow cysts in the flesh. Most flukes and tapeworms of fish have complicated life histories, the adults living in one species and the larvae living in one or more other species.

A wide variety of parasites attack the surface of the gills and the skin of fish. The largest of these are the lampreys, which are primitive fishlike vertebrates. The native Minnesota forms measure 6 to 15 inches in length, while the marine lampreys of the Great Lakes grow to a length of several feet. Lampreys attach themselves by their funnellike suckers to the skin of the fish and rasp a hole up to several inches in diameter. They retain their hold until gorged with blood, leaving the fish in a weakened condition with a large gaping wound which often becomes infected by fungi and bacteria. These lampreys should not be mistaken for leeches, which are commonly called bloodsuckers in many regions, although many species of leeches do attack fish. Some of the smaller leeches attach themselves to the gills and to the lining of the mouth and the opercle. Others fasten themselves to the outer skin. If bloodsucking leeches are numerous, they can cause considerable damage to the fish.

Tiny copepods belonging to the Crustacea may be found crawling over the gills and the skin of fish, and some species burrow into the fins and the gills. These parasites, which are sometimes called fish lice, also can do much damage, if they are sufficiently abundant, because they leave the fish emaciated and subject to fungus infection.

The larvae or glochidia of freshwater mussels are common skin parasites of fish. Before the larval forms can develop into adult mussels, they must pass through a stage as a fish parasite. The glochidia of some species of mussels have toothed valves which enable them to bury themselves in the skin, particularly that of the fins. The glochidia of other species have only small toothless valves; these forms attach themselves to the gills and become buried in the soft tissues. The glochidia remain on the host for several weeks or longer, depending on the temperature. There is some question whether they do much actual damage to the fish.

There are several species of microscopic protozoans that sometimes infect the skin and the gills of fish, eventually causing death. Some of these are large enough to be seen under a magnifying glass. When a fish is infected, small spots and pustules appear on the skin. The infection can spread from fish to fish as an epidemic. Minute flukes belonging to the flatworms also infect the gills and the skin. Some of these cause serious losses in fish hatcheries.

A common white fungus (Saprolegnia) may attack the skin of fish wherever the protective mucous coat is broken by careless handling or by wounds. This fungus is present in most warm waters and lives on dead animal matter. It grows rapidly in warm water but does not thrive in cold water; hence it is most prevalent in the summer. For some reason fish in natural open waters are usually not infected with this fungus unless they are in a weakened condition. However, fish in confinement are highly susceptible to it. The fungus first appears as a white fuzzy patch, which spreads rapidly and unless checked usually proves fatal. The most common remedy is a bath for about two minutes or even longer in a 3 percent salt solution. Fish that are already in bad shape may die under the treatment, but they would probably die anyway.

Bacteria are another source of infection, causing fin rot, gill disease, furunculosis or boils, and various other diseases. They are usually more prevalent on fish confined in hatcheries or aquariums than on those in natural waters. Davis (1937) describes many of these parasites in detail and cites the known treatments.

Threadworms or roundworms (Nematoda) are very common internal parasites of fish. They are slender worms, ranging from microscopic size to several inches or more. Frequently they infect fish to such an extent that the fish die or become emaciated and susceptible to other infections. These worms can be distinguished from other fish parasites by their shape and their lack of attachment spines. They usually occur in the digestive tract but may be found in the body cavity and in cysts embedded in the flesh and the viscera. As far as we know, the species found in fish are harmless to man. Since they usually occur in the viscera, most of them are discarded in dressing the fish. Spiny-headed worms (Acanthocephala) also occur frequently in the intestines of fish. They resemble roundworms in size but differ in other ways. They possess an anterior proboscis covered with minute hooks by means of which they attach themselves to the wall of the intestine. Often large numbers infect fish and cause considerable damage.

The larval stages of a number of parasitic worms live in the flesh and the skin of fish. One common species is the yellow grub (*Clinostomum marginatum*), which is a larval form of one of the flukes or flatworms (Trematoda). This worm appears as a yellowish swelling in or just under the skin of fish such as rock bass and perch. The adult worm lives in the mouth of the great blue heron and various other fish-eating birds. The eggs pass into the water and hatch into free-swimming larvae (miracidia) which enter snails. Inside the snails these larvae reproduce and eventually leave as tiny free-swimming forms (cercaria); the cercaria burrow into the skin of a fish and become encysted there, remaining until the fish is eaten by a bird. In the bird the parasites complete their development and become adult worms. They are harmless to man and do little damage to fish. They are practically impossible to eradicate because it would be necessary to destroy all fish-eating birds or all snail hosts.

Another very common parasite in northern fishes is the black grub (Neascus), which causes black spots in the skin of perch, northern pike, and many other fishes. This worm is another larval flatworm or fluke. The adults live in the mouths of kingfishers, from which the eggs pass into the water. As in the case of yellow grubs, the larvae find their way into snails and eventually into fish, where they form black cysts in the skin and remain until the fish is eaten by a kingfisher in which they can complete their development. Frequently a fish is so heavily parasitized that it is fairly covered with these black cysts. The parasite does not infect man, and the cysts can be removed by skinning the fish. Fish that spend most of their lives in open water and do not come near the shores where snails live are least frequently infected with this parasite. In Lake Superior, where snails are relatively rare, the parasite is not common.

Some tapeworms also have larval stages that form cysts in the muscles of fish. The most common of these are several species of *Triaenophorus*, which form elongate yellow worms in the back muscles of tullibees and whitefish in inland lakes. The adult tapeworms live in the intestine of the northern pike. The eggs are released into the water and develop into free-swimming larvae (coracidia), which are eaten by copepods (*Cyclops*) in which the larval procercoid stage develops. When the minute crustaceans are eaten by a tullibee or a whitefish, the parasite is liberated and it burrows into the back muscles, forming a large cyst enclosing the plerocercoid stage. When an infected tullibee or whitefish is eaten by a northern pike, the parasite develops into its adult form and attaches itself to the wall of the intestine. This parasite is abundant in the lakes of northern Minnesota and Canada and is responsible for the condemnation of large quantities of tullibees by state and federal authorities as unfit for human food. There are other larvae of related species that infect trout-perch and the livers of perch (with the adult forms occurring later in walleyes). These parasites are harmless to man. The waters of Lake Superior are not highly suited for northern pike, and consequently ciscoes and whitefish from these waters are not heavily infected.

Another common tapeworm is the bass tapeworm (*Proteocephalus ambloplites*), which is commonly found in both largemouth and smallmouth bass. This worm lives as an adult in the intestine of the bass, and its eggs pass into the water. The eggs contain a larval stage called the oncosphere. The eggs are eaten by a small copepod, such as a species of *Cyclops*, and within the copepod the procercoid stage of its life cycle develops. When the copepod is eaten by a small bass or other fish, the parasite is liberated in the intestine and undergoes further development, burrowing into the body cavity where it forms a large plerocercoid. At this stage the parasite causes great damage because it tends to destroy the reproductive organs, rendering the fish sterile. When the infected fish is eaten by a large bass, the parasite completes its development into an adult tapeworm in the intestine. In addition to rendering the bass sterile, the parasite causes it to become thin and vulnerable to other infections.

The only known fish parasite capable of infecting man is the broad fish tapeworm (*Dibothriocephalus latus*) originally found in northern Europe and probably brought to this country by infected immigrants. It is a serious menace to man but fortunately is prevalent only in limited localities in the northern states. It has been found in walleyes, perch, and northern pike. Human infection occurs only from eating raw or improperly cooked fish; the parasite is killed and rendered harmless when the fish is thoroughly cooked. The adult form of this worm lives in the intestine of man and some carnivores. The eggs pass out with the feces and hatch into motile coracidia. When a coracidium is eaten by a species of *Cyclops*, it develops into a procercoid larva within the body cavity of the copepod. The copepod is eaten by a walleye, a northern pike, or a perch, and the larva escapes and burrows through the intestine into the flesh of the fish, where it encysts and elongates into a plerocercoid. When the flesh is eaten by man or a suitable carnivore such as a fox or a bear, the larva is released in the intestine and develops into an adult tapeworm. In a few weeks, the worm is mature and eggs appear in the feces of the host.

Anatomy and Physiology of Fish

All of our present-day fishes have a long evolutionary history of millions of years. The ancestors of the lamprey go back to the Ordovician period, over 500 million years ago, and the remains of bony fishes are found in rocks of Devonian age, which are 350 million years old. The anatomy of modern fishes is highly specialized for an efficient aquatic life. All of the fishes constituting our present-day fauna are modern forms, but some (the paddlefish, the bowfins, and the gars) retain primitive ancestral characters. In their long period of evolution and specialization some fishes lost or modified many fundamental structures such as fins, scales, and teeth.

Body shape varies greatly among the many species of fish, but the most characteristic and least specialized shape is a streamlined or fusiform modification of an elliptical or ovoid form. Some species (for example, the sunfish) are thin and deep-bodied or *compressed*. Others (for example, the catfish) are broad and shallow-bodied or *depressed*. The most extreme body shape found among Minnesota freshwater fishes is the long slender *anguilliform* shape of the eel. Body shape is correlated with the life activities of the various species: fish with the shape of the trout or the salmon are fast swimmers and travel great distances; those with the long slender shape of the gar or the northern pike are swift predators and lie in wait to seize their prey. Those depressed like the sturgeon and the catfish are bottom-feeders, while those with flattened, upturned mouths skim their food from the surface of the water.

In describing fish certain general anatomical terms are used. *Anterior* refers to the front or forward part of the body, and *posterior* refers to the rear or hind part. *Dorsal* refers to the upper side or back, and *ventral* refers to the underside of the animal (Figure 15).

The body of a fish consists of three parts: the *head*, the *trunk*, and the *tail*. Fish do not have a neck, but the posterior margin of the gill cover marks the end of the head and the beginning of the trunk. It is usually difficult to determine where the trunk leaves off, which is at the vent or

73

anus, and the tail or caudal region begins. The tail or caudal region is usually defined as the region posterior to the vent which bears the tail fin or caudal fin posteriorly. The tail fin, the tail, and the trunk musculature are important organs of locomotion for most fishes, and the other fins are used for stabilization, turning, or stopping.

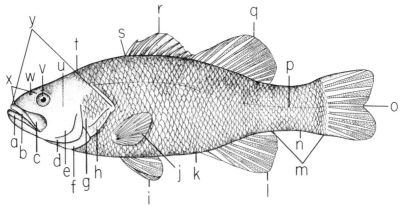

Fig. 15. Hypothetical drawing of a spiny-rayed fish. *a*, lower jaw or mandible; *b*, premaxillary; *c*, maxillary; *d*, *e*, preopercle; *f*, interopercle; *g*, opercle; *h*, subopercle; *i*, ventral or pelvic fin; *j*, pectoral fin; *k*, anus (vent); *l*, anal fin; *m*, caudal peduncle; *n*, depth of soft caudal peduncle; *o*, caudal fin; *p*, lateral line; *q*, soft-rayed portion of dorsal fin; *r*, spinous portion of dorsal fin; *s*, insertion of dorsal fin; *t*, nape (occiput); *u*, cheek; *v*, eye; *w*, nostril (nares); *x*, snout; *y*, length of head.

Various body dimensions (Figure 16) are used in the keys for identification of the families and species of Minnesota fish later in this book. The *standard length* of the fish is used chiefly by the fish specialist or the ichthyologist and is the length measured as a straight line from the tip of the snout to the end of the vertebral column at the base of the caudal fin. The last vertebra cannot be seen without dissection, but the posterior margin of the last vertebra can be determined rather simply by flexing the caudal fin and noting the small crease which appears at the base of the tail fin and marks the end of the last vertebra. A pair of calipers or dividers and a long millimeter rule are useful in making accurate length measurements of the body dimensions. Fishery biologists use *total length*, the distance measured as a straight line from the tip of the snout to the tip of the tail fin, instead of standard length. The total length is the measurement used by fishermen when telling about the big one that was caught or that got

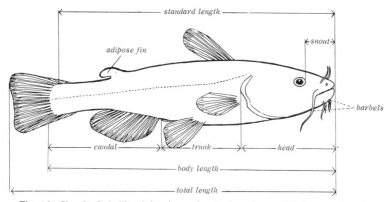

Fig. 16. Sketch of a bullhead showing various body regions and their measurements

away. It is often unreliable; the tail or caudal fin may be broken or injured, and the total length may be altered by environmental factors not related to the growth of the fish.

Fish continue to grow or at least have the potential for growth until they die, although there are changes in the rate of growth and the younger fish grow more rapidly than the older individuals. Proportional measurements or ratios are of greater value than most measurements, but even the ratios may vary for individuals of different sizes. The variability in the ratios is caused in part by the different rates of growth of one part of the fish's body when compared with the growth of another part; for example, the head may increase in size at a rate greater or less than the increase in size of the trunk, or the orbit may increase at a rate less than the head. In addition to the problems of relative growth rates there are differences in the growth of parts of the body between the two sexes. The average measurements and the range of these are usually given and, where measurements differ between the sexes, the ratios for both males and females are given.

The head of a fish is considered to be that portion extending from the tip of the snout to the posterior margin of the opercular membrane. The *opercle* is the large bony flap, flat and thin, that covers the branchial chamber or gills. The front of the opercle bordering the cheek is the *preopercular region*, the area along the lower margin of the opercle is the *subopercular region*, and the bone beneath the preopercle and in front of the subopercle is the *interopercle*. The *snout* is the region from the anterior end of the upper jaw to the front rim of the orbit of the eye. The *cheek* is the area lying between the eye and the preopercle. The mouth is said to be *terminal* when it forms the extreme anterior tip of the head and *subterminal* when the snout extends beyond it. The lower jaw is formed largely by the *dentary* bone, but the *splenial*, *articular*, and *angulare* bones form minor portions of it. The upper jaw is mainly formed by the *premaxillary* bone and the *maxillary* bone. Sometimes a supplementary *supramaxillary* bone is present as a splint above the maxillary. The bones of the upper jaw are covered with a thin skin and can be observed externally. The head is said to be *depressed* when flattened from above or dorsoventrally, as in the catfish. Located on the inner margins of the upper and lower jaws are the *oral valves*; these membranous valves can be seen easily in live fish.

The membrane on the underside of the opercle is the *gill* or *branchiostegal membrane*. The membrane contains a series of supporting bony rays, the *branchiostegal rays* or *branchiostegals*. The fleshy space under the throat and between the gills is the *isthmus*. In some species (for instance, in the perch) the gill membranes join the isthmus far forward (Figure 17), in which case they are described as being free of the isthmus. In the suckers and in some darters, the gill membranes are joined or united to the isthmus directly (Figure 17).

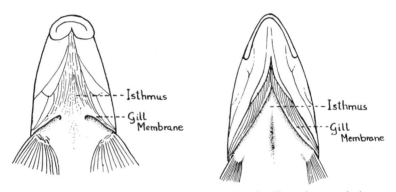

Fig. 17. Structure of gill membranes and isthmus. *Left*, gill membranes united to isthmus; *right*, gill membranes free from isthmus.

Teeth may be present on almost any bony structure in the mouth. In a few fishes teeth are absent or vestigial. The teeth of most freshwater fishes are conical in shape and vary in size from numerous tiny spines in the bullhead to large fanglike teeth in the muskellunge. Many species have teeth called *vomerine teeth* on the vomer bone in the roof of the mouth, and some have teeth on the rudiments of a tongue, although most fishes have no true tongue development. Teeth may also be located on the *palatine bones* just behind the vomer and on the *pterygoid bones* located behind the palatines. Frequently toothlike structures known as *pharyngeal teeth* are found in the throat region on the margins of the gill bars. The pharyngeal bones are paired structures formed by the fusion of two dorsal bones with a single ventral bone and they represent the fifth gill arch. Pharyngeal teeth are useful in the identification of many suckers and minnows. The teeth of suckers may be numerous in a single comblike row or fewer in number and molariform (Figure 18). Minnows have one, two, or three rows of teeth: all native North American minnows have one or two rows, and the introduced carp has three rows (Figure 18).

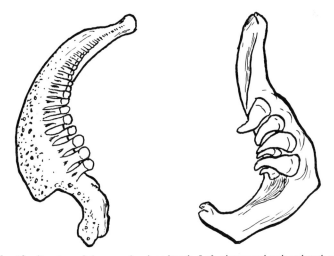

Fig. 18. Structure of pharyngeal arch and teeth. *Left*, pharyngeal arch and teeth of a sucker; *right*, pharyngeal arch and teeth of a New World minnow.

Pharyngeal tooth counts are very useful in identifying various species of Minnesota minnows. For example, the common shiner has a tooth formula that is written 2,4–4,2, which means that the pharyngeal teeth are in two rows with two teeth in the outer row and four teeth in the inner row on the left arch and the same on the right arch. The golden shiner has the formula 0,5–5,0, indicating a single inner row of five teeth. For the carp the formula is written 1,1,3–3,1,1, showing that there are three rows of teeth on each arch with one tooth in each of the two outer rows and three teeth in the inner row.

The pharyngeal arches are movable and have large muscles attached to them; hence, the teeth are used in chewing, tearing, and grinding. On the ventral surface of the *basioccipital bone* of the skull there is a *chewing pad* which is used in mastication. (The effectiveness of the chewing pad becomes evident when you put your finger into the throat of a big minnow.) Large molariform teeth are found in the freshwater drum or sheepshead; the drum sometimes feeds on snails and clams and the heavy pharyngeal teeth are used to crush the shells of its prey. Other fish have finer pharyngeal teeth similar to those on the pharyngeal bones of the perch and the northern pike.

Barbels are present on the heads of some fishes. These are soft threadlike structures above and below the mouth, the so-called whiskers of the bullhead. The barbels are important sensory structures containing many nerve endings, some of which are similar in many respects to the taste buds of higher organisms. They are used to locate food in murky and turbid waters, and many minnows living in such habitats have very prominent barbels.

The fins of fish are of two types, the paired ventral fins and the unpaired median fins. The paired fins consist of the *pectoral fins* and the *pelvic fins*, which are respectively homologous to the front and hind limbs of land animals. The pectoral or shoulder fins are located just behind the gill arches. The pelvic fins may be located just anterior to the anus or vent, in which case they are termed *abdominal*, but frequently they are located anteriorly in close proximity to, but slightly behind, the pectoral fins, in which case they are referred to as *thoracic*. When they are anterior to the pectoral fins, they are said to be *jugular*. The number of rays in a fin at times is useful in identification. In counting the rays in the paired fins the first complete ray is counted as one, the thin and splintlike rudimentary ray at the base of the first true ray is not counted, but each additional complete ray is counted from the origin to the posterior base of the fin. The fin rays of small fish are counted most easily with the aid of a dissecting microscope and with the fin spread as much as possible. Usually the fin rays are counted on the left pectoral or pelvic fin. The length of these fins is the distance from the anterior base of the first fin ray to the farthest tip of the fin.

The unpaired fins are always median in position and consist of the *dorsal fin* on the back, the *caudal fin* or *tail fin*, and the *anal fin* located under the tail and just behind the vent. The anterior base of an unpaired fin is referred to as its origin. Frequently the dorsal fin is divided into a front or anterior part and a hind or posterior part. The length of the dorsal fin or the anal fin is the distance from the origin to the tip of the fin when it is depressed or flattened.

The caudal fin may be of either the *heterocercal* or *homocercal* type (Figure 19). The heterocercal type is found only in primitive fishes such as sharks, sturgeons, and paddlefish. In the heterocercal caudal fin the backbone extends into the elongated upper lobe. A modified heterocercal type is present in gars and bowfins. In these species the ventral lobe is only developed in the adults and the caudal fin is rounded; in the young fish

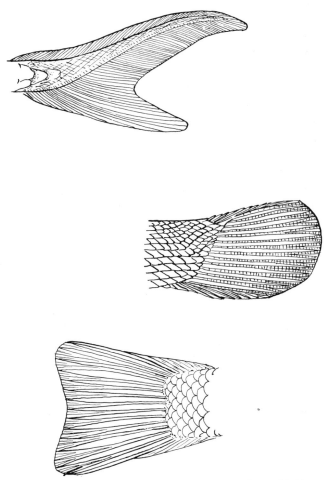

Fig. 19. Types of caudal fin. *Top*, heterocercal caudal fin; *middle*, modified heterocercal caudal fin; *bottom*, homocercal caudal fin.

the dorsal lobe is very prominent (Figure 28). The homocercal type is found in most freshwater fishes. In this type of caudal fin the lobes usually are of equal length, although in some species the fin may be forked and one lobe may be slightly longer than the other. The backbone does not extend into either lobe. The *adipose fin*, located posterior to the dorsal fin, is a small dorsal median fin that lacks fin rays or spines. Several unrelated families of fish — salmonids, smelt, catfish, and trout-perch — have adipose fins; the function of the adipose fin is conjectural.

The fins are supported by bony structures known as *soft rays* and *spines*. The soft rays are usually segmented and branched and are always divided longitudinally into two symmetrical halves. The spines are of two types, *hard spines* and *soft spines*. Both types have stiff pointed tips and are unsegmented, but the hard spine is a single structure and the soft spine is divided longitudinally into symmetrical halves. Freshwater catfish have a stout spinous ray in each pectoral fin and in the dorsal fin, and carp and goldfish have a similar spinous ray in the dorsal fin. The spines are formed by the fusion of soft ray elements during embryonic development.

Many fishes have fins containing both spines and rays. Usually the number of spines is expressed in roman numerals and the number of rays in arabic numerals. For example, in the white bass there are 3 spines and 11 to 13 rays in the anal fin; a description of the anal fin would be written III,11–13; for the slimy muddler, which has 1 spine and 3 rays in the pelvic fin, the formula would be I,3. The first rays of the unpaired fins are usually short and not branched and are termed *rudimentary rays*. The first long ray, often unbranched, is regarded as the first ray in a count of the fin rays.

The spines and rays of the median fins and the paired fins are counted in different ways. The number of rays in the pectoral and pelvic fins is the total number of rays regardless of whether the ray is divided or branched. In the dorsal fin and the anal fin, only those rays that are separated clearly at the base of the fin are counted, as noted previously; to determine whether there is a separation, the fin should be spread out and examined with magnification.

All fish have a thin skin covering the scales and the plates, and the skin contains numerous glands that render the fish more or less slimy. The slime or mucus serves to protect the fish from bacteria and fungi or molds, especially Saprolegnia. Infections frequently result when fish are handled carelessly and the slime is rubbed off. When large numbers of fish are kept in aquariums or holding ponds, such infections occur often and can be very serious. There is also evidence that the mucus reduces the friction or drag of the water on the fish when it swims.

Fish have many sensory structures in the skin. The most conspicuous of these is the *lateral line*, which appears as a line running from the operculum to the base of the caudal fin about midway on the side of the body. The line consists of a canal with many nerve endings running beneath the skin. Most Minnesota fishes have well-developed lateral lines, but some species have only a partially developed lateral line, and a few have none. The lateral line continues on to the head region where it divides up into a complicated interconnecting network. The lateral line is described as *complete* if there are pores present in the scales from the margin of the head to the base of the caudal fin, *incomplete* if the pored scales do not extend to the base of the caudal fin or if some of the lateral line scales lack pores, or *absent* if no pored scales are present. Various functions have been associated with this structure, but the best evidence at present indicates that it is concerned with detecting vibrations and water currents, enabling the fish to swim in darkness or in turbid waters. The lateral line nerve is associated with the auditory portion of the brain.

Scales are of at least four general types. The most primitive type is the *placoid scale*, found only in sharks and their near relatives. Placoid scales do not overlap but have their flat bases embedded in the skin with a conical point or spinelike tip protruding through the epidermis. The points give the rough, sandpaperlike texture to sharkskin. Placoid scales are similar in structure to a tooth, being composed largely of dentine and covered with enamellike material called *vitrodentine*. In the course of evolution, scales of this type located on the rim of the jaw became enlarged and developed into teeth. The true teeth of all vertebrates are derived from these early toothscales.

A second kind of scale, the *ganoid scale*, is found in a few primitive fishes such as the gars. Ganoid scales consist of rhomboid bony plates covered with a hard, enamellike substance known as ganoin, which differs from vitrodentine. Ganoid scales are derived from the inner layer of the skin, the *dermis*, rather than the upper layer, the *epidermis*, and growth takes place along the margins of the scale, from beneath it, and on its surface.

A third type of scale is the *cycloid scale*, which is thought to be the simpler of the two kinds of scales found on most bony fishes. It is the scale found on trout, salmon, whitefish, smelt, and some other fishes. Cycloid scales are more or less circular in outline, although indentations may occur on the inner margin. The cycloid scale is a bony structure that lacks the dentine and enamellike layers characteristic of placoid and ganoid scales. Growth of the cycloid scale is on the outer surface and from beneath. These scales are covered by a thin epidermis.

A fourth type, the *ctenoid scale*, is found on the majority of modern bony fishes. It differs from the cycloid type by the development of tiny spines or *ctenii*. This type is bony with a scalloped margin and a series of tiny prickles or spines on the exposed posterior margin of the scale. The *ctenii* give the rough or sandpaper texture to the skin of perch, walleyes, and sunfish.

A few fishes such as the catfishes have lost all of their scales in the course of evolution. The brook trout and the burbot have minute or almost microscopic scales.

All the cycloid and ctenoid scales are fully formed during the first few weeks of the fish's life. No new scales are added as the fish grows, but as overall growth proceeds the scales also grow by the deposition of successive layers of fibrous connective tissue plus some calcification. The outer surface of the scale is gradually covered with concentric growth rings (*circuli*). Since fish grow more rapidly in the summer when the waters are warm than during the winter and since the rate of growth of the scales is related to the growth of the fish, corresponding changes occur in the deposition of scale substance. The crowded circuli produced by these changes constitute an annual mark, the *annulus*, and in many species it is possible to determine a fish's age by counting the number of annuli on the scales. Actually the procedure for establishing the age of a fish is somewhat more complicated than this, especially if the fish spawns after the new year's growth has begun. Growth may slow or stop during the spawning period and a false annulus may be laid down on the scales; it is necessary to recognize these "spawning checks" and to distinguish them from true annuli. Another difficulty is that from time to time fish lose scales accidentally, and the lost scales are replaced by new scales which obviously will not exhibit the circuli and annuli of the original scales. If we know the age of the fish and its length at the time of capture, it is also possible to calculate the size of the fish at earlier ages, although a correction must be made for the size of the fish at the time the scales first appear. Knowledge of the age of fish and their rate of growth is of great importance in fish management and is one of the fundamental tools of the fisheries biologist.

Bony plates embedded in the skin and covered by a thin epidermis form an outer skull in primitive fishes such as sturgeons, gars, and bowfins. In the higher bony fishes many of the bony plates of the head unite with the bone beneath the plates and become part of the skull, no longer forming part of the skin covering. In some bony fishes the head is naked — that is, it is covered with smooth skin only — while in others the head is partly covered by scales. Many fishes, especially the males, develop tubercles on the head, the trunk, and the fins, particularly during the breeding season.

The size and the number of scales on various regions of the body are useful in identifying various species of fish. Characters such as the number of scales, spines, or fin rays are referred to as *meristic* characters. The most important of these counts is the number of scales in the lateral line. The lateral line count is the total number of pored scales counted from the first scale at the posterior margin of the head to the caudal fin base at the margin of the last vertebra. If the fish lacks a lateral line or has an incomplete lateral line, the number of scale rows along the middle of the left side of the fish from the head to the caudal base is counted.

Two other counts which are often used are the number of scales above the lateral line and the number of scales below the lateral line. The first is based on the number of scales in an oblique line from the origin of the dorsal fin to but not including the lateral line. The second is based on the number of scales in an oblique line from the origin of the anal fin to but not including the lateral line. In the description of a perch, for example, the scale formula would be written 5–55–17, indicating that there are an average of 5 scales above the lateral line, an average of 55 scales in the lateral line, and an average of 17 scales below the lateral line. There is some variation in the number of scales in individuals of the same species from the same population, so in addition to the average count the ranges of the counts are also included.

There are still other methods of making scale counts. A count of *circumference scales* begins with the scale immediately in front of the origin of the dorsal fin, and all the scale rows around the body are counted. A count of the *caudal peduncle scales* is based on the number of scales around the narrowest portion of the caudal peduncle; this count is best made by starting with a lateral line scale and then counting ventrally or dorsally to the starting point. Occasionally the circumference count is separated into circumference scales above and below the lateral line. Therefore it is best to count the scale rows above and below the lateral line separately and to add the individual counts later. The circumference count of the mimic shiner would be written

10–2–10, indicating there are 10 scale rows above the lateral line, 2 lateral line scales (one on each side), and 10 scale rows below the lateral line, making a total of 22 circumference scales.

Other important characters in identification are measurements of various divisions of the body. *Head length* is the distance from the tip of the snout to the most posterior margin of the opercle or gill cover (including the membranous portion of the opercle). *Head in length* is the number of times the length of the head is contained in the standard length of the fish; for example, if it is stated that head length is 4.0 to 4.5 in standard length, this means simply that the length of the head is contained 4.0 to 4.5 times in the standard length. This kind of measurement can show the amount of variability in the ratio of head length to standard length in a large sample of individuals. The *body depth* is the greatest distance from the back or dorsal side to the belly measured as a straight line at right angles to the long axis of the body. *Body depth in length* is the number of times the depth of the body is contained in the standard length of the fish. *Eye in head* refers to the number of times that the diameter of the eye goes into the length of the head. Another measure often used is *eye in snout* or the diameter of the eye divided into the length of the snout. The *caudal peduncle length* is the least distance from the posterior margin of the base of the anal fin to the end of the last vertebra or the caudal fin base, and the *caudal peduncle depth* is the least depth of the caudal peduncle. (The caudal peduncle is the part of the fish from the posterior base of the anal fin to the base of the caudal fin.) *Head depth* is the maximum distance measured as a straight line from the top of the head to its ventral margin at right angles to the long axis of the head. The *predorsal length*, often used in identification, is the distance measured as a straight line from the tip of the snout to the anterior base of the first ray or spine in the dorsal fin. Various other body proportions are also used but less frequently than those we have discussed.

The gills of a fish are complex structures anatomically, and casual observation of the gills of a dead fish gives only a very elementary knowledge of the anatomy and the morphology of the gills. The blood in the gills flows in a direction opposite to the flow of water over the gill surface in a countercurrent system, assuring maximum efficiency in the absorption of oxygen from the water and in the discharge of carbon dioxide from the blood. Most species of fish are dependent on gills to extract dissolved oxygen from the water. A few species (gars and bowfins) are able to use the gas bladder as a primitive lung for breathing air at the surface of the water to supplement their gill respiration, but most modern fishes are completely dependent on oxygen dissolved in the water for their respiration.

Four pairs of gills are present. Each gill is composed of a *gill bar* or *gill arch*, on the outer edge of which are two rows of delicate *gill filaments*, the respiratory structures of the fish. Each gill filament is further subdivided into many small *lamellae* or folds which serve to increase the surface area of the filament. The extremely thin lamellae are the sites of oxygen exchange. Since the small vessels or *capillaries* carrying the blood through the lamellae have a bore somewhat smaller than the diameter of a red blood cell or erythrocyte, the red cells are deformed slightly as they pass through the lamellae. The fish erythrocyte has a nucleus and contains a red pigment, *hemoglobin*, which transports oxygen to the various cells of the fish. The lamellae and the deformation of erythrocytes assure the maximum exchange or diffusion of oxygen. In addition, fish blood contains white blood cells or *leucocytes*, proteins, and plasma — in other words, it has the same major constituents as the blood of higher animals.

Rudimentary gills are frequently present. These are relicts from a time when fish had more gills than they now possess. Such gills, known as opercular gills, are found on the lower inner surface of the opercle of gars and sturgeons. This type of gill has the same circulation as a normal gill, receiving venous blood or nonoxygenated blood. *Pseudobranchia* are gill-like structures (not true gills) found on the upper inner surface of the opercle of some other fishes. Pseudobranchia do not have normal circulation; they receive only arterial or oxygenated blood. They appear as small patches of red filaments.

The water used by fish in respiration enters through the mouth and passes out through the openings between the gills, the *gill slits* or *gill clefts*. The gill cleft behind the fourth gill is closed in some species. The gill clefts are guarded by numerous projections known as *gill rakers*, which are attached to the inner surface of the gill bar. In many fishes the gill rakers are a series of coarse projections along the inside surface of the gill arch, but in some species — tullibees, whitefish, and paddlefish, for example — the rakers consist of long fine filaments. The function of the gill rakers is to strain the water and to prevent particles of food from passing out through the gill clefts.

Anyone who has had an opportunity to observe a fish in an aquarium has noticed the rhythmic opening and closing of the mouth and the equally rhythmic movements of the opercle or gill covering. The mouth and the buccal region act as a pump; the opercular movement functions as a second pump, forcing water over the respiratory surface of the gills. This arrangement assures a continuous flow of water from the mouth posteriorly into the pharyngeal region and out over the surface of the gills. A single pump would produce spurts of water over the gills, comparable to our inhaling and exhaling. A brief description of the two pumps in operation may help to illustrate the process. The buccal cavity is expanded by muscular action, drawing water into the mouth. At the same time the opercular opening is closed, preventing backflow over the gills. The buccal cavity then contracts, forcing the water from the mouth into the pharyngeal region. The path of least resistance is the mouth opening but inside the margins of the upper and lower jaws are flaps of skin forming *oral valves* which prevent the escape of water from the mouth. The water flow is thus directed posteriorly into the pharyngeal region and over the gills. The second pump works reflexly and in synchrony with the buccal pump. Muscles associated with the pharyngeal region and the opercular apparatus contract to increase the volume of the pharyngeal cavity. A close examination of the margin of the opercle reveals a flap of skin that extends considerably beyond the bony portion of the opercle. The flap is evident only in living or freshly caught fish. When the opercle swings out from the body, the opercular flap remains in contact with the side of the fish. It is finally pulled free from the body as the opercle swings wide open, drawing water out over the gill's surface. Next the opercle is drawn back against the body, the pharyngeal region is reduced in size, and the water is forced out of the opercular region in a posterior direction. All these movements can be seen in resting fish in an aquarium. The oral valves are most easily observed in the northern pike, which has rather long jaws.

Gill respiration is similar in principle to respiration in lung-breathing vertebrates. Oxygen diffuses from a region of high concentration (water or air) into the blood, which is low in oxygen and high in carbon dioxide as it returns from the body through the capillaries of the gills or the lungs. The diffusion occurs through the moist surface of the gill or lung epithelium. At the same time the dissolved carbon dioxide is released to the water or the air. On the whole respiration is not very different in aquatic and terrestrial vertebrates. The most important difference is in the medium, water or air, which carries the oxygen and the carbon dioxide.

Our knowledge of gills and gill function was based mostly on preserved material until several British physiologists devised a transparent covering which was substituted for the bony opercle in an experimental fish; with the transparent covering in place they were able to observe for the first time the actions of the gills in a living fish. Their observations brought about a complete change in our understanding of gill function and morphology. The gills form a very close mesh, like interlocking pickets, with very little space for the water to flow between the individual filaments. The delicate filaments have lamellae that extend out from the surface and interdigitate with the lamellae of the adjacent filaments. The arrangement of the filaments and the lamellae assures very efficient extraction of oxygen from the water.

These recent findings indicate that the resistance to water flow over the gills is much higher than it was formerly thought to be, and far greater energy is required to run the respiratory pump. Alexander (1967) and others have calculated the energy requirements of a fish's respiratory activities under different oxygen concentrations in the water. A resting fish in air-saturated fresh water (8 milliliters of oxygen per liter) will use only 5 percent of the oxygen absorbed from the water to supply the muscles of respiration. If the same fish is placed in water with a low concentration of oxygen (1 milliliter of oxygen per liter), the fish must pump 20 times as much water to get an equivalent amount of oxygen. Alexander calculated that to accomplish this feat the work of respiratory activity must increase 2,000 times and respiration alone would require all the oxygen absorbed from the water. When the water temperature rises and the oxygen-carrying capacity or solubility drops, the metabolic rate and the oxygen requirement of the fish rises. Theoretically it is possible to reach a point where the available dissolved oxygen in the water is just sufficient for respiratory energy, leaving none for other vital activities such as swimming and digestion. These conditions can occur in either the summer or the winter, resulting in massive fish-kills. Most of the deeper waters of northern lakes become anaerobic in late summer, and although these waters are cold, they will not support fish life. Both temperature tolerance and critical oxygen tensions vary with the species. There are marked physiological differences among the various families and among species in the same family which are as pronounced as the morphological differences that we depend on for distinguishing the species. Temperature and oxygen solubility are closely related in the aquatic environment, and the interaction between these two factors results in conditions not encountered by land animals.

The *gas bladder* or *air bladder* is an important structure found in most modern bony fishes. It is associated with buoyancy in many fishes but is used for respiration and other purposes in some species. The gas bladder is a tough membranous sac lying in the body cavity dorsal to the digestive system. It is usually elongated but is sometimes divided by one or more constrictions. It is common to all bony fishes except flounders and a few other species that usually live on the bottom, sharks and their relatives, and cyclostomes or lampreys. The gas bladder originates in the embryo as a dorsal pouch in the wall of the pharynx and later pushes back into the body cavity. In a few species (the physostomic fishes) the connection with the pharynx is retained as an open duct, but in most modern species (the physoclistic fishes) the connection becomes almost or wholly closed, often forming a ligament.

The first appearance of the gas bladder in the history of fishes is uncertain, but apparently it arose early in some primitive groups. All bony fishes that retain primitive characteristics possess a gas bladder with an open duct. All evidence indicates that the gas bladder had a function in respiration and that the lungs of land animals developed from it. In gars and bowfins, which have retained many primitive characteristics, the opening of the duct is very large. In these fishes the bladder has vascularized walls and a well-developed circulatory system. The bladder in gars and bowfins functions as a respiratory aid to gill respiration, and it is so effective that they can live in water that is practically devoid of oxygen. Gars are so dependent on air respiration that they may drown when entangled in a net and unable to reach the surface. Both gars and bowfins can live for many hours out of the water. When large gars are removed from the water, the gulping and expelling of air becomes very rapid and quite audible. Other species of fish such as climbing perch and eels can live out of water, but they respire with their gills, which are kept moist in a chamber with a small opercular aperture.

In most of Minnesota's bony fishes the duct of the gas bladder is practically or wholly closed, and the gas bladder functions primarily as a hydrostatic organ regulating the buoyancy of the fish. The density of the body of a fish is slightly greater than that of water, 1.08 compared with approximately 1.00 for water. Consequently, fish have a tendency to sink, and if they did not possess a gas bladder they would have to swim constantly to maintain a position in the water above the bottom. They are able to adjust their density, however, by means of the gas bladder along with slight movements of the pectoral fins for orientation. The adjustment is accomplished by increasing or decreasing the volume of gas in the bladder. In physostomic fishes the bladder is filled with air, but in physoclistic fishes the bladder is filled with a variety of gases including oxygen, nitrogen, and carbon dioxide, mostly secreted from the blood by a vascular structure, the *rete mirabilis*. The rete mirabilis, usually located on the anterior ventral surface of the bladder, is a network of capillaries in the wall of the gas bladder that secretes gases from the blood into the bladder. Another vascular region, the *ovale*, located on the dorsal surface of the bladder, is able to absorb gases from the bladder and hence to reduce the volume and the pressure of the gases contained within it. The resorbed gases are taken up by the blood and eliminated through the gills. Almost any gas dissolved in the water can enter the gills during respiration and eventually find its way into the gas bladder.

It is much easier for a fish to travel downward to great depths than to come up from them, but if the fish is to remain at a greater depth without actively swimming, it must increase the pressure of gas in the bladder. When a fish rises to the surface, on the other hand, it must adjust the pressure of the gases in its bladder to the pressure exerted by the water column at the different depths. This requires time enough to eliminate some of the gases. When fish from depths of 500 feet or more are brought too rapidly to the surface in a net, they may literally explode from the sudden decrease of external pressure on the gas bladder. Even lake trout caught by anglers at depths of 100 feet are helpless from the disequilibrium between the pressure in the gas bladder and the sudden decrease in the water pressure around them as they are brought to the surface. When freed, they float belly up and soon die. (Carp, catfish, and other physostomic fishes with a tiny duct may be able to discharge some gases through the mouth to reduce the pressure in the gas bladder.) When commercial fishermen raise nets from great depths in Lake Superior, they puncture each fish with a sharp spike in the end of a club in order to release the pressure in the gas bladder. If the pressure is not reduced, it may cause the stomach to protrude from the mouth and the intestine from the anus.

Physoclistic fishes appear to be able to use the gas bladder as a reservoir to store oxygen for emergencies. Perch have been reported to use oxygen from the gas bladder for short trips into the oxygen-depleted hypolimnion of lakes. In experimental fishes that have just died of suffocation in water depleted of oxygen, the gas bladder has been reported to contain much carbon dioxide but no oxygen.

A few fishes have found other uses for the gas bladder. The freshwater

drum or sheepshead produces a very audible sound by muscular vibrations
of the gas bladder. Minnows, catfish, and bullheads have a bony connection
between the gas bladder and the inner ear region of the skull; whether this
carries sound or pressure is controversial, but the freshwater fishes with
this adaptation are the dominant group in lakes and streams.

Everyone accepts the fact that a fish swims, but few understand how
it swims. The technique used by a fish as it rushes, jumps, and turns is
exactly what makes fishing a sport. When a fish swims, it moves by means
of alternate contractions and relaxations of the muscle segments on opposite
sides of the body, producing bends in the body along the flexible vertebral
column or backbone. The wave of contraction passes from the muscle segments adjacent to the head posteriorly through the tail; in the dense medium
of water, this results in forward motion. The same contractions cause the
apparently aimless flopping exhibited by a fish in the bottom of a boat.
In the far less dense medium of air these rhythmic contractions result only
in alternate bending of the body to right and left along the long axis. If
a fish is placed on a board with many pegs arranged in rows, the fish's
swimming movements will enable it to move off the board. The expression
"like a fish out of water" reflects the loss of mobility of a fish when it
is out of its normal medium. There are notable exceptions: the eel can wriggle
on land like a snake, and a few exotic fishes (such as the walking catfish
recently introduced into Florida) can scramble about on their paired fins.
Most modern fishes are not well adapted for locomotion on land.

In swimming, a fish must overcome the drag of water on its body, a
problem that is of little importance for a land animal. The caudal fin con-
tributes to the forward propulsion; although it describes a sinuous path
through the water, it makes possible the straight-line path of the fish. In
order to move forward a fish must exert sufficient force through muscular
contraction to overcome the drag on the body and the tail. Slow-motion
films of a swimming fish show that the waves traveling down the length
of the body move at about 1.5 to 2.0 times the swimming speed. These
movements are so rapid that to the eye the fish is moving like an arrow
through the water. Only by slow-motion photography can we see the rhythmic
contractions or undulations of the body. If you know the film speed, the
size of the fish, and the distance traveled in a unit of time, it is not difficult
to calculate the swimming speed. Most observations have been made in
circular tanks where the water is moving and the fish swims to remain in
one place. Mathematicians have been able to demonstrate that fish swim

in a manner that holds their power requirements to a minimum. Most fish, despite allegations of fishermen to the contrary, are unable to swim very rapidly for extended periods of time or even for several minutes. Sustained swimming at speeds greater than 3 to 5 times the length of the fish per second seems highly improbable. A bony fish may dart at a speed of about 10 times its length per second, but such speeds are maintained for only a few seconds (Alexander, 1967). Such are the quick rushes of the rainbow trout or the black bass when it feels the barb of cold steel or the northern pike as it first views its would-be captor. If these measurements are translated into more conventional units or terms, a trout 12 inches long can swim conservatively at a sustained rate of 3 feet per second and for a short period at 8 miles per hour. Any fisherman would argue with these rather low rates because a startled fish certainly disappears in an instant and at speeds apparently in excess of those mentioned, but the quick disappearance of the startled fish is an optical illusion. When a fish crosses one's line of vision at right angles, the eye cannot keep up and the fish is gone. If the fish moves directly away from the observer, the eye can follow it with greater ease, but despite this it is almost impossible to judge accurately the distance and the time involved and the tendency is to overestimate the velocity. In addition there are complications involving refraction and water clarity that make field observations difficult and unreliable.

The force a rainbow trout, a largemouth bass, or a northern pike exerts when checked by the fisherman's line is little understood by most fishermen. Once the fisherman brings the fish to a halt by thumbing the reel or applying the brake — or in extreme conditions when the supply of line on the reel is exhausted — the kinetic energy of the fish is converted into mechanical energy. If a 5-pound trout moving at a rate of 6 feet per second is stopped in a distance of 2 feet, it will exert a force of 90 foot-pounds. It is obvious that a 5X tippet on the leader or a 3-pound-test monofilament line will part when exposed to this force. If a large northern pike comes to the boat initially in its normal mild way and then takes off with a burst of speed equal to 2 or 3 times its body length per second, the power required to bring it to a stop will be approximately 2 or 3 times that for the 5-pound trout. If the angler is not careful and the drag is set too tight, the line parts under a force of over 200 pounds. The traditional cries of "Don't horse him!" or "Give him line!" are based on practical experience with the equation

$$\text{work} = \frac{\text{weight} \times \text{velocity}^2}{\text{distance}}$$

The answer is to slow the fish down gradually: the value of distance in the denominator will be larger and the force exerted by the change of kinetic energy to mechanical energy will be spread over a longer period of time. Meanwhile, the fish will expend more energy, tire more quickly, and come to the net more readily. The fact that a fish breaks a new 6-pound-test monofilament or a 30-pound-test line usually does not mean that you have lost a monster; in most instances it means that you have experienced the application of a physical law.

If you hook a 10-pound rainbow trout traveling at 2 feet per second and you try to stop it in the last 6 inches at the end of the pool before it reaches the rapids, you will require a leader or a line whose breaking strength is not less than 40 pounds. It is better to flounder and get wet following the fish through the rapids to the next pool than to lose the prize. Unfortunately, nice fish can be lost both ways, for once a fish is in the current, it utilizes the additional force of the flowing water to frustrate the fisherman's efforts. Try to keep the fish headed upstream so that it not only has to contend with the drag of the line but also must swim against the current. In desperation you can try to stop the fish from reaching the security of a brush pile, a fallen log, or some other snag, but otherwise all you can do is to exert enough pressure to slow the fish and perhaps turn it from its path. As a last resort most fishermen clamp down on the brake or the line and the fish is gone. When the relatively unintelligent fish turns the laws of physics to practical advantage, it is not only the big ones that get away.

The fins and the trunk musculature of a fish enable it to swim and to control its movements in the water. The fins are flexible structures made up of movable spines or rays and connecting membranes, and each spine and ray can be controlled by means of antagonistic paired muscles. The caudal fin is mainly concerned with locomotion, while the other fins function more as stabilizers.

A fish in motion experiences the same tendencies as a moving ship or boat to roll, pitch, and yaw. The fish may roll or have a tendency to rotate about the long axis of the body; it may pitch or have an up-and-down movement along the long axis, pivoting on the center axis; or it may yaw, showing sideways movements in the plane of the long axis. The fins, either singly or in combination, serve to inhibit these tendencies, enabling the fish to maintain a straight course, to turn sharply, or to come to a stop exactly where it wishes.

In some species the fins have other functions, or they are used in different ways. Bowfins can move through the water by generating rhythmic waves that pass down the dorsal fin. Perch and sunfish use the pectoral fins to some extent for locomotion. In many species the paired fins (the pectoral and pelvic fins) are used as brakes or even as rudders to control the direction of swimming. During rapid swimming the pectoral and pelvic fins are usually pressed close to the body. A sunfish approaching the aquarium wall will display slow pectoral finning. If it is startled, it darts quickly away, stops, by braking with its pectoral and pelvc fins, and turns to see what disturbed it. The same thing occurs when a fishing fly lands with an unintentional splash and the bluegills flee, turn back, and slowly rise to suck in the fly.

A fish's movements are the result of complete coordination of its nervous system, muscles, fins, and gas bladder. Unfortunately, we must treat each unit separately in order to present a picture of how each functions, yet only rarely, if in fact ever, does any unit work independently. The adipose and pelvic fins seem least essential to the well-being of the fish, but this may be simply because we have not yet learned their real functions. The adipose fin present in several very different and distantly related families — Salmonidae, Ictaluridae, and Percopsidae — does not seem to have any specific purpose.

Fish possess virtually the same internal systems of organs as land vertebrates. The *pharyngeal cavity* or *throat cavity* opens through the very short *esophagus* just behind the gills into the stomach. The stomach is so close to the mouth that it is possible to remove food from the stomach of many species by inserting an ordinary pliers down the fish's throat. The stomach is often modified in accordance with the fish's diet; as mentioned earlier, some fishes are herbivorous, some are carnivorous, and many are omnivorous. Many fishes have a simple saclike stomach, but a few, such as the gizzard shad, have complex stomachs. The stomach is absent in the fishes belonging to the minnow family (Cyprinidae), and the esophagus leads directly into the intestine which is modified to hold food but which lacks the digestive secretions produced by the stomach. The digestive action of the stomach of many fishes is very powerful and food is digested rapidly, enabling the fish to consume huge quantities of food daily.

The stomach empties into the intestine. Near the union of the intestine and the stomach, fingerlike pockets known as *pyloric ceca* are sometimes present. In some species the pyloric ceca are filamentous and very numerous. In sharks and a few primitive bony fishes (paddlefish and sturgeons) the intestine is short and consists of a complicated spiral tube called the *spiral valve.* Most modern fishes have a more or less coiled tubular intestine similar to that found in land vertebrates. Generally the intestine is short in carnivorous fishes and very long in herbivorous fishes. The intestine discharges waste through the anus, commonly called the *vent*, which is near the opening for the *excretory* and *genital ducts.*

The *liver*, the *pancreas*, and the *spleen* function about the same as those organs of land vertebrates. The *kidneys* are straplike organs on the dorsal wall of the body cavity; they appear as dark red streaks on each side of the backbone. The ureters or ducts of the kidneys usually empty near the anus. The *gonads* (ovaries and testes) are located in the dorsal portion of the body cavity in the same area as the kidneys. They are difficult to find and to distinguish in immature fish, but during or just preceding the spawning season they become very large. When the ovaries contain ripe eggs, they often fill much of the body cavity. They are enclosed in a reddish vascular membrane through which the numerous eggs can be seen. The testes are smooth, white or yellowish white, and straplike. All Minnesota fishes are egg-laying (*oviparous*) forms with the exception of the introduced mosquitofish (*Gambusia affinis*). The eggs are laid before they are fertilized. The male liberates *sperm* or *milt* over or near the eggs, and fertilization is accomplished when the sperms actually swim or float to the eggs and unite with them. Reproductive behavior differs among the various species — some species scatter their eggs while others build elaborate nests and guard their eggs and young for various lengths of time.

The *heart* is located far forward under the gills. It is composed of four chambers — the *sinus venosus*, the *atrium* (auricle), the *ventricle*, and the *bulbus arteriosus* — arranged in a linear pattern. The blood is pumped directly from the bulbus of the heart to the arteries leading to the gills and through the capillaries of the gills where the blood is oxygenated. The oxygenated blood passes to the dorsal aorta and is distributed to all parts of the body. The bulbus arteriosus functions to maintain steady blood pressure and flow through the gills. The hepatic portal system carries the blood from the intestine to the liver, and the hepatic vein takes it from the liver to the sinus venosus. Numerous other veins return the blood from various tissues elsewhere in the body to the sinus venosus.

The *brain* of a fish is small in proportion to the size of its body. A catfish weighing almost as much as a man has a brain not much larger than a man's thumb. Although the fish brain has most of the parts found in the brain of a land vertebrate, many parts are not as well developed.

Fewer cranial nerves are present. The *forebrain* or *cerebrum*, the "thinking" region of the human brain, is undeveloped in fish.

The major sensory organs such as eyes and ears are present in fish, although they are modified to meet the conditions of the aquatic environment. The *eye* is well developed and contains essentially the same structures as the human eye. The eyes of most fish are more or less fixed and can be moved only slightly. Fish cannot readily adjust their vision for distance; the sight of most species is fixed for near vision. Since water is so opaque that under any circumstances it is impossible to see a great distance, this myopic condition is probably not a serious handicap. Most freshwater fishes that have been examined have color vision not greatly different from that of man, although their ability to discriminate shades of violet and gray may exceed that of humans. The *ears* are entirely internal, buried in the sides of the skull. Structurally, the inner ear of a fish contains the receptors of balance and hearing. In some bony fishes, such as the freshwater drum, large *otoliths* or "ear stones" are present in the inner ear. These function in maintaining the equilibrium of the fish. There is evidence, both observational and experimental, that fish can hear, although the perception of sound in water is quite different from the perception of sound in air. Fish are more sensitive to sound vibrations originating in water than to those originating in air. Many species of fish can produce sounds and may be able to communicate to a limited extent. The auditory system is intimately connected with the lateral line system, and there is speculation that the inner ear is a specialized portion of the lateral line system. In amphibians the lateral line disappears, and the inner ear becomes the sole auditory structure. The inner ear of fish may be more important for maintaining a sense of balance than for hearing.

The *nostrils* in modern fishes have no respiratory function. Usually two on each side, they open into a pair of blind pits over the snout. In native northern species the nostrils do not open into the throat as they do in land animals, whereas in a few exotic fishes (lungfish, for example) the nostrils lead into the throat. The nostrils in Minnesota species serve only as organs of smell and have the same olfactory connections to the brain as those of higher animals. The nostril is a simple pouch with a single or double flap; the water passes in through one opening over the sensory lining of the pouch and out through the posterior opening. The innervated olfactory organs are located in the nostrils, and the sense of smell is well developed. Fish have good odor discrimination and can be trained to recognize various substances at very low concentrations of one part per million. A tremendous body of evidence exists indicating that salmon find their way to their home stream by odor. When a salmon reaches the coast after its migration through the open sea, it identifies by smell the stream where it hatched, recognizing the odor of the stream in which it completed its embryonic development two or three years before the spawning migration. The coho salmon introduced recently into Lake Superior and Lake Michigan also exhibits this ability. Some very interesting experiments have shown that freshwater fishes, especially minnows, can distinguish the odors of various kinds of aquatic plants. "Stink baits" are widely used for many fish by anglers, and there is reason to believe that they often are effective.

The many small sensory structures scattered over the skin have been assigned various functions, and part of the sense of taste may also be located in the skin. In an aquatic medium it is difficult operationally to separate taste from smell, but there are sense organs on the barbels of catfish and certain minnows that in their microscopic structure resemble very closely the taste buds found in higher vertebrates including man. The various species of minnows that inhabit muddy and turbid streams possess well-developed barbels with numerous taste buds; presumably these sensory organs make up for the lack of visibility and in a sense enable some fish to find food by taste rather than by sight. Some night-feeding fishes such as catfish depend almost entirely on external taste structures aided by smell to locate their food.

The skeleton of a fish is relatively complex. The skull, when fully developed, contains an enormous number of bones. Except for the bones associated with the unpaired fins, many of the bones found in fish correspond to those in land vertebrates, but in land vertebrates the number is greatly reduced by the fusion of some of these bones to form single bones. Fish have extra ribs, being provided with an inner and outer pair for each trunk vertebra. Together with the accessory bones between the muscles, the ribs make some species exceedingly bony.

Factors in the Aquatic Environment

Of all our animals with vertebrae or backbones, fish are the most numerous in kinds and individuals. Like amphibians (frogs, toads, and salamanders) and reptiles (turtles, lizards, and snakes), fish are referred to as cold-blooded animals because they have body temperatures that are the same as or close to the temperature of their habitat. The velocity of activities such as locomotion and digestion in cold-blooded animals is generally correlated with the temperature of their habitat, increasing at higher temperatures and decreasing at lower temperatures.

Fish have been a very important source of food for man from very early in his history. Fish bones are found in many ancient kitchen middens and prehistoric garbage piles. We suspect that the most important reason for man's failure to understand fish better than he does is his inability to appreciate the problems of another animal when the organism comes from an environment completely different from his own. From man's historic association with fish we know much about their habits, but we live under such entirely different conditions that it is difficult for us to understand how or why they act as they do. We have little idea of how a fish feels or thinks or if it feels or thinks at all. The world of the fish is a three-dimensional one, as is that of the bird, but most of us live in a two-dimensional world. Furthermore, our field of vision under the water, in all but the most pristine mountain lakes and streams, is so limited that we can rarely observe the activities of fish in their natural environment. Recently scuba and skin divers have been able to carry on some helpful observations, but only in very clear waters.

One characteristic of water that is extremely important to the activities of fish is its density. Pure water has a density of 1 gram per cubic centimeter — 700 times that of air. A man walking in water up to his shoulders finds it much more difficult than walking on land because of the greater density of water. A swimmer tends to tire quickly and comes to a stop abruptly when he stops swimming, and friction drag brings a fish to a halt

97

just as quickly. Because of the density of water fish are not able to move quickly from the depths to the surface with the ease that pigeons fly to the top of a tall building. We ourselves experience only slight changes in the weight of the column of air sitting above us when we go to the top of a 20-story building. The changes we experience are so minute that we require an instrument, a barometer or an altimeter, to detect the changes. A fish, on the other hand, is very much subject to the weight of the water above it. A column of water the height of a 20-story building exerts a pressure of approximately 60 kilograms (132 pounds) per square centimeter. Finally, although the density of fresh water is 1.0, the density of most fish is about 1.08; hence, a fish slowly sinks to the bottom if it does not expend energy by swimming to maintain its position.

As mentioned earlier, freshwater fish have a gas bladder that allows them to control their buoyancy by changing their density, enabling them to maintain their position at various depths without tremendous expenditures of energy in swimming. A fish adjusts its density by changing the volume of gas in the bladder until it is nearly equal to the density of the water around it. The fish with a gas bladder is not free to move rapidly upward or downward in the water, however, because it must make changes in the volume of gas in the gas bladder. Downward movements can be made with greater freedom than upward movements, but they require an expenditure of energy and eventually necessitate changes in the volume of gas in the bladder in order for the fish to achieve neutral buoyancy at the greater depth.

Temperature ranges and variations in aquatic habitats are less than those encountered by terrestrial animals. With the exception of the ice fish of the Antarctic, fish do not live at temperatures below freezing. In Minnesota the annual temperature range of the air may be from $-30°$ F in late January or early February to a high of 100° F in July or August, a range of some 130° in a year. In aquatic habitats the variation is from slightly over 32° F immediately adjacent to the ice in the winter to 90° F in early August, a range of about 58°, less than half the range experienced by man in the course of a year. In streams the range may be far less; the water temperature of springs varies only a few degrees during the year, and spring-fed streams vary only about 30° to 40°. The daily temperature variations in terrestrial habitats may vary as much as 40°, but the great heat capacity of water prevents any marked daily fluctuations in most aquatic habitats. At Lake Itasca the lake temperatures vary only a few tenths of a degree from day to day. The lake may be covered with a morning mist or fog, but the most sensitive thermometers are unable to detect a change in the lake's temperature. Stream temperatures may vary several degrees during the day-night cycle as the moving and constantly mixing water gives up heat and regains it more rapidly than the relatively stable lake water. Nevertheless, the fish are not subjected to daily variations in temperature or to annual ranges in temperature equivalent to those affecting terrestrial animals.

Another important difference between the terrestrial environment and the aquatic environment is in the availability of two very important gases, oxygen and carbon dioxide. Oxygen and carbon dioxide concentrations in the air may vary slightly, but the earth's atmosphere is roughly 21 percent oxygen and 0.033 percent carbon dioxide by volume. These percentages do not fluctuate noticeably daily or annually under ordinary conditions. The oxygen available to fish is limited and variable. The solubility of oxygen in water varies with the temperature and is greater in cold water than in warm water. As the temperature of lake water rises through the late spring and early summer, the amount of oxygen the water can hold in solution decreases. Since the fish is an ectotherm, its body temperature rises as the water temperature increases, and its metabolic rate approximately doubles with each increase in temperature of $10°$ C ($18°$ F), thus increasing the need for oxygen. The overall result of the warming trend is a greater demand for oxygen by fish at a time when less oxygen is available to them in the water.

The solubility of carbon dioxide in water is about two hundred times greater than the solubility of oxygen. Since fish live in an environment where carbon dioxide concentrations are so high, we might expect that they would be subject to great respiratory stimulation. For instance, we know that carbon dioxide is always present in the blood of mammals as an end product of metabolism but that a slight increase in the concentration of it causes a mammal's breathing rate to double in an effort to restore the normal balance of gases in the blood. Contrary to our expectations, fish do not respond to high concentrations of carbon dioxide in the water but only to low oxygen concentrations, and the effects of carbon dioxide are observed in fish only under very unnatural experimental conditions. We are still uncertain about the influence of very high carbon dioxide concentrations on respiratory movements in fish, but the levels required to produce changes in the breathing rate are markedly different from those in land vertebrates.

Among the vertebrates the fishes have almost completely dominated the ecology of both marine and fresh waters. The impact of man's activities on fishes was not great until the past century. The collapse of important fisheries for Atlantic salmon, lake trout in the Great Lakes, and sturgeon in Lake of the Woods is indicative of man's disregard for fishes and their environment. Water is, to all too many people, an unlimited and renewable substance used for drinking and bathing. Water, however, is also the home of the fishes, the largest group of vertebrates in term of numbers of species.

Classification and Origin of the Fishes

The animal kingdom is classified in major divisions known as *phyla*. The fishes belong to the phylum Chordata, which includes all the vertebrates as well as several minor groups of organisms. Each phylum is divided into subunits (taxa) called *classes*, each of which is divided into *orders*. The orders are subdivided into categories known as *families*, and these in turn are subdivided into *genera* containing one or more *species*. If a genus contains only one species, it is referred to as a *monotypic* genus. Most genera contain two or more species and are referred to as *polytypic*.

Each species is designated by a binomial *scientific name* consisting of a generic name and a specific name. For example, the brook trout has the scientific name *Salvelinus fontinalis*; the generic name is *Salvelinus*, and the specific name is *fontinalis*. We want to stress that the scientific name of the species we recognize as the brook trout is *S. fontinalis* and that the specific name *fontinalis* has no scientific meaning except in combination with the generic name. The scientific name is latinized and is always printed in italic type or underlined in handwritten material. The first time a scientific name is used in a descriptive text, both the generic and specific names are spelled out, but in subsequent occurrences of the scientific name in the same text passage the generic name may be abbreviated.

The scientific name is usually followed by the name of the author of the specific name (the person who described the species for the first time). As an example, the common carp has the scientific name *Cyprinus carpio* Linnaeus. Linnaeus, the early Swedish biologist who originated the system of binomial nomenclature, gave the species name to the fish we recognize as the carp. The brook trout mentioned previously was originally described by Mitchill as belonging to the genus *Salmo* and was named *Salmo fontinalis* Mitchill. A later study of the brook trout and other species of the genus *Salmo* by Jordan and Gill indicated that the brook trout was more closely related to the chars, so the scientific name was amended to *Salvelinus fontinalis* (Mitchill). Mitchill's name is put in parentheses to indicate that he

101

first described the species but that the species subsequently has been placed in another genus. In this book a man's name following the scientific name of a species may be in parentheses for one species but not in parentheses for another species. This just means that as more species were described and as revisions of groups were undertaken, the presumed relationships among various species also changed. Such changes are still taking place as new information comes to light and new techniques are applied in the field of systematics. Nevertheless, our own inclination is to be somewhat conservative in accepting recent revisions.

The fundamental unit in classification and the most objective unit biologically is the species. In some species various parts of the population, usually occupying different but contiguous geographical areas, differ slightly from one another; in that case we refer to the species as being polytypic because it has two or more forms which constitute an actual or potential interbreeding group. Such units of the species are referred to as *subspecies* or geographic *races* and are designated scientifically by a third name. For example, Louis Agassiz, an eminent Harvard zoologist, described the subspecies *Rhinichthys atratulus meleagris* Agassiz (the western blacknose dace) from a collection of fish made during his trip to Lake Superior in the middle of the nineteenth century. He also proposed the generic name *Rhinichthys*. Throughout this book we have used the binomial in our treatment but will note the subspecies that various ichthyologists feel are represented in our waters. Our personal opinion is that in many instances the recognition of subspecies is difficult and that their validity is often controversial.

For many years all fishes were included in one class of vertebrates under the name *Pisces*, but in the late 1800s zoologists began to realize that there are fundamental differences among the fishes and that some groups are as different from each other as frogs and reptiles or birds and mammals. The fishes actually can be divided into several classes. One group, the lampreys, lacks jaws and paired fins; these belong to the class Cyclostomata. The sharks, skates, and rays with jaws and cartilaginous skeletons but lacking gas bladders and some other characters belong to the class Chondrichthyes. Another group with jaws, bony skeletons, and gas bladders are in the class Osteichthyes. Of these three classes, only two, Cyclostomata and Osteichthyes, occur in Minnesota waters. The jawless fishes (Agnatha) first emerged during the Ordovician period. The first jawed vertebrates (Placodermi) appeared in the Silurian period. The Osteichthyes appeared early in the Devonian period, and the Chondrichthyes evolved later in the same period. The Devonian is often referred to as "the age of fishes."

The agnathans of the class Cyclostomata are represented by modern lampreys and hagfishes. The extinct agnathans bear little resemblance to modern agnathans, and the latter must be viewed as highly specialized modern relicts. There is evidence, however, in fossil deposits from the Pennsylvanian period of lampreys which do not differ greatly from modern lampreys. The lampreys (Petromyzoniformes) are represented in both marine and freshwater habitats, but the hagfishes (Myxiniformes) are all marine. Their ancestors, the ostracoderms, are the oldest well-known fossil remains of the vertebrates. Many theories have been proposed on the ancestry of the ostracoderms, and it is fairly certain that they arose very early from some invertebrate ancestor. These early vertebrates left little evidence of well-developed internal skeletons, but it is known that some were covered with plates. They lacked upper and lower jaws and paired fins. From what little evidence we can glean from the fossil remains, it would appear that the early vertebrates were filter feeders, sifting organic matter from the water for their nutrition. Perhaps the ammocoetes (larvae) of the lamprey will provide us with further clues to the earliest vertebrates.

The class Placodermi, known only from fossils, is important because representatives of this class were the first vertebrates to have jaws. Despite the fact that they were destined to become extinct (presumably eliminated by their more adaptable progeny, the bony fishes and the sharks), they achieved considerable adaptive radiation, and a number of quite distinct orders are represented in the fossil record. The placoderms were presumably derived from some agnathan ancestor, but the evidence has been hidden by time, erosion, and the vagaries of the fossilization process.

The Osteichthyes or bony fishes are the largest group of modern fishes in terms of numbers of species and numbers of individuals. They have dominated the marine and freshwater aquatic habitats since they first evolved. Subsequently the Chondrichthyes arose; while successful, they were never able to achieve the dominance of their bony relatives. It is as if the bony fishes had the ideal plan and the necessary plasticity virtually to explode into both the marine and freshwater habitats. The freshwater fishes are almost entirely members of the class Osteichthyes.

The first Osteichthyes had primitive characteristics, some of which are retained in sturgeons, paddlefish, and bowfins. Their skeletons are partly or entirely cartilaginous. One group of primitive bony fishes (the Cros-sopterygii), now virtually extinct, used the gas bladder to breathe air. By means of lobed fins they were able to crawl out of the water onto the banks of lakes and streams. They found a terrestrial world free of competitors, but until the higher plants evolved and insects appeared to feed on the plants, their food supply may have been limited to their neighbors. Many biologists think that their ability to breathe air and thus survive when lakes and ponds dried up was an important fact in their initial success. They were able to move from one body of water to another while other fishes, unable to survive out of water, died. These lung-breathing fishes were apparently the ancestors of terrestrial vertebrates. The paired fins used in swimming and maneuvering in water developed into the fore and hind limbs of the ancestors of land vertebrates. Another vast group of primitive bony fishes underwent changes to become the modern bony fishes. In these species the bony plates that formerly covered the head were incorporated into the skull. They also lost one gill slit, replaced most of the soft cartilage in their skeletons with bone, and developed bony spines and rays to support the fins. Most of the recent fishes have departed as widely as the land vertebrates have from the form and structure of their common ancestors, and the bony fishes differ from one another as much as whales, bats, and man among the mammals.

Over 20,000 species of fish are known today, a figure that is almost equal to the total number of known species of mammals, birds, reptiles, and amphibians combined. New species of fish are being described each year, even in the fresh waters of the United States, but the vast majority of new species described are marine forms and members of the class Osteichthyes.

To aid in the identification of the fishes known to occur in Minnesota waters, taxonomic keys to the families and the species are included in this book. Use of the keys assumes that the reader is familiar with the anatomy and the morphology of fish as outlined in the preceding chapter. If the family to which the fish belongs is not known, it can be found by referring to the key on pages 106–107. To use the key, select the couplet that accurately describes the structure of the fish and continue to the couplet indicated by the number at the righthand side of the key until the family name is found. Then locate the chapter covering that family and follow through the key given there to identify the genus and the species. In those families represented by only one species in Minnesota waters, no key to the genus or the species is necessary.

With but a few exceptions we have used the common names recommended by a special committee of the American Fisheries Society, although there are no binding scientific rules on the subject of common names. We have also attempted to arrange the various families, genera, and species in phyletic sequence.

Artificial Key to Families
of Northern Fishes

15. Jaws elongated, shaped like a duck's bill; large irregular teeth; tail deeply forked ...
.... ESOCIDAE (p. 198)
Jaws not elongated; weak teeth; tail more or less rounded 16

16. Upper jaw not protractile, formed by maxillary bone .... UMBRIDAE (p. 196)
Upper jaw protractile, formed by premaxillary bone 17

17. Anal fin of male similar to that of female; third anal ray branched ....
.... CYPRINODONTIDAE (p. 322)
Anal fin of male modified and unlike that of female; third anal ray unbranched .....
.... POECILIIDAE (p. 324)

18. Gill membranes united to isthmus (Figure 17) 19
Gill membranes free from isthmus (Figure 17) 20

19. Dorsal fin with 10 or more rays; pharyngeal teeth numerous, in only one row ......
.... CATOSTOMIDAE (p. 273)
Dorsal fin with fewer than 10 rays (except in the introduced carp and goldfish); pharyngeal teeth fewer than 10 on each side, in one or more rows .... CYPRINIDAE (p. 209)

20. Lateral line present; tongue with sharp teeth .... HIODONTIDAE (p. 139)
Lateral line absent .... CLUPEIDAE (p. 142)

21. Body scaleless but covered with tiny spines or prickles; head large; eyes in top of head; pectoral fins large .... COTTIDAE (p. 390)
Body with scales 22

22. Vent anterior to pectoral fins .... APHREDODERIDAE (p. 317)
Vent posterior to pectoral fins 23

23. Single median barbel on chin .... GADIDAE (p. 319)
No barbel on chin 24

24. Anal spines, 2 or fewer 25
Anal spines, 3 or more, first spine sometimes rudimentary 26

25. Spinous and soft-rayed portions of dorsal fin distinctly divided ... PERCIDAE (p. 363)
Spinous and soft-rayed portions of dorsal fin confluent .... SCIAENIDAE (p. 332)

26. Without longitudinal dark stripes on side of body or with only one stripe; spinous and soft-rayed portions of dorsal fin confluent (but deeply notched in largemouth bass) ....
.... CENTRARCHIDAE (p. 338)
With 5 or more narrow dark longitudinal stripes, usually distinct, on side of body; spinous and soft-rayed portions of dorsal fin either separate or deeply notched ....
.... PERCICHTHYIDAE (p. 335)

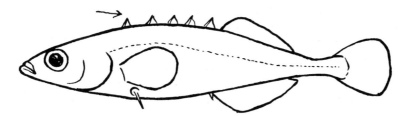

Fig. 20. Structure of dorsal fin in family Gasterosteidae. Free dorsal spines anterior to dorsal fin.

Class CYCLOSTOMATA
The Hagfishes and the Lampreys

The only true parasitic vertebrates are found among the cyclostomes. Some zoologists classify the cyclostomes as fishes while others recognize them as a distinct and different group, more primitive than the fishes and somewhat degenerate. While they are quite distinct, it seems reasonable to treat the cyclostomes along with the fishes. These eellike forms are contained in two important divisions, the hagfishes and the lampreys. The hagfishes are entirely marine, but the lampreys are found in both marine and fresh waters.

The cyclostomes are characterized by the absence of several structures common to most fishes: paired fins or appendages, true teeth, scales, and upper and lower jaws. They are often considered to be primitive vertebrates in which these structures never developed, but they are highly specialized for their mode of life. The brain and skull are rudimentary when compared with those of the higher vertebrates. There are no bones in the skeleton, the vertebral column is poorly formed, and the supporting structure consists mostly of a stiff, rodlike notochord. The latter is not supportive in the sense that the human vertebral column is; its function is to prevent the shortening of the animal's body when the muscles contract. Water serves to support the organism, and the notochord maintains the anterior-posterior axis of the cylindrical organism. The gills open externally through separate slits and are supported by basketlike cartilaginous structures. The gills are not really primitive but are respiratory structures which have been modified for a parasitic life.

Most members of this group are carnivorous or semiparasitic, and they are often referred to as parasites or predators. The marine hagfishes are very destructive, for they burrow into the bodies of living fish and devour their flesh until nothing remains but skin and bones. Many of the lampreys also are injurious to fish. The adult lamprey attaches its mouth like a suction cup to the side of its host or prey. It then rasps a hole in the side of the fish by means of its filelike tongue and sucks the fluids from the fish's body. Glands in the buccal region secrete hemolytic and histolytic substances which prevent coagulation of the blood and which digest externally the tissues of the host fish. Once the lamprey has completed its meal, it releases the fish and settles to the bottom, where it remains inactive until it is time to feed again. We have observed lampreys feeding on fish in our aquariums at the University of Minnesota and have noted that the attack rarely kills the fish; more often the fish succumbs later to secondary bacterial or fungal infection. Fish disfigured by fresh lamprey sores lose their market value and are usually in very poor condition. Species which lack scales (catfish and sturgeons) or which have very small and fine scales (trout) are particularly vulnerable to lamprey attack. Carp, which have large and heavy scales, are less vulnerable and in our laboratory tanks have survived a number of lamprey attacks without marked adverse effects.

The lampreys and the hagfishes, while considered primitive, are actually highly specialized modern forms retaining many characters of the earliest fishlike vertebrates. Their specialized structures and mode of life have enabled them to survive for over 250 million years.

Family PETROMYZONIDAE
The Lamprey Family

The lampreys are characterized by a circular funnellike mouth or buccal cavity armed with toothlike horny spines. Members of this family lack scales and paired fins and possess a single median nostril. The skeleton is wholly of cartilage or a cartilagelike substance and consists of an imperfect skull and a poorly developed vertebral column made up of a series of cartilaginous disks on a notochord. The notochord persists throughout the life of the lamprey and consists of a mass of vacuolated cells which are enclosed in a fibrous sheath. Seven pairs of external gill openings are present. The gills are supported by an arrangement of cartilage known as the branchial basket. The toothlike spines immediately surrounding the mouth opening are called the circumoral teeth. Bordering the opening of the mouth anteriorly are horny plates bearing spines known as the supraoral laminae, and bordering it posteriorly are the infraoral laminae. The transverse lingual laminae and the longitudinal lingual laminae form the teeth on the tongue.

The lampreys all pass through a nonparasitic stage in their life history as ammocoetes. These larvae are blind, eellike forms which live a sedentary life buried in the mud and silt. During their larval life they are filter feeders, straining algal and bacterial cells and other organic matter from the surrounding water. The water and food are carried in through the mouth, which is surrounded by a U-shaped hood; the food particles are collected on a mucous strand secreted in the pharynx, and the water then passes out through the gills. One of the functions of the rhythmic movement of the branchial apparatus is to move water through the mouth for the purpose of feeding as well as for respiration. The larvae remain in the mud in small burrows for a number of years, the time spent in the larval stage varying with the species, and eventually they metamorphose to adults. The adult may be parasitic or nonparasitic, depending on the species.

There are three genera and four species of lamprey now present in Minnesota. Three of the species are native to Minnesota and the neighboring states; all three species are small, usually less than 16 inches in total length. The sea lamprey, *Petromyzon marinus*, found originally along the Atlantic coast and in the Lake Ontario drainage system, may reach a length of over 2 feet. In the past thirty years the sea lamprey has invaded and all but destroyed the native fish fauna of the Great Lakes.

110

KEY TO MINNESOTA SPECIES OF FAMILY PETROMYZONIDAE

1. Dorsal fin separated into two distinct parts 2
   Dorsal fin continuous, never separated into two distinct parts 3
2. Buccal funnel with three radiating rows of teeth, 4 or more teeth in each
   row on each side of buccal opening ....
   ....Sea lamprey, *Petromyzon marinus* Linnaeus
   Scattered groups of teeth not in radiating rows, usually in three groups of
   1 or 2 large teeth on each side of buccal opening ....
   ....American brook lamprey, *Lampetra lamottei* (LeSueur)
3. Circumoral teeth, with rare exceptions, all unicuspid (single-pointed);
   myomeres (body segments) between last gill slit and anus usually 49 to
   52; transverse lingual lamina moderately to strongly bilobed ....
   ......Silver lamprey, *Ichthyomyzon unicuspis* Hubbs and Trautman
   Circumoral teeth in part (usually 6 or 8 teeth) bicuspid (double-pointed);
   myomeres between last gill slit and anus usually 51 to 58; transverse
   lingual lamina usually linear or weakly bilobed ....
   ....Chestnut lamprey, *Ichthyomyzon castaneus* Girard

Genus *Petromyzon* Linnaeus

Only one species, *Petromyzon marinus*, is found in Minnesota waters;
the characters of the species describe the genus.

SEA LAMPREY

Petromyzon marinus Linnaeus

The sea lamprey (Figure 21) is a relative newcomer to Minnesota and
is restricted to the Lake Superior drainage of the state. The freshwater sea
lampreys, 12 to 25 inches in total length, are larger than the native lampreys
but tend to be smaller than those in the sea. The dorsal fin has a very
wide notch that separates the fin into two parts. Usually the teeth of the
circumoral series are bicuspid, and they are large, long, and sharp. The
myomeres usually number 65 to 80. The body is mottled or spotted gray
or chocolate (bluish black in spawning adults).

Fig. 21. Sea lamprey, *Petromyzon marinus*

The sea lamprey spends four to seven years as a larval ammocoetes,
metamorphoses to an adult, and spends twelve to twenty months as a parasitic
adult. Spawning generally occurs in the period from March to June over
gravel and rubble riffles in tributary streams. The male lampreys migrate

a few days before the females and begin to construct nests; they are later helped by the females. Sea lampreys are monogamous and rarely does more than one male attend a female. Breeding behavior is quite elaborate, and only a few eggs are laid at a time; repeated egg-laying occurs until the female is spent. It may take two days for the pair to complete spawning, and a female 20 inches in total length may lay as many as 95,000 eggs. Once spawning has been completed, the adults die.

The eggs hatch and the larval ammocoetes leave the nest after about twenty days, depending on the water temperature. If the temperature is low, hatching takes a longer period of time than at higher temperatures. The newly hatched ammocoetes drift downstream and settle into backwaters and eddies and burrow into the silt or mud bottom. In such areas they can burrow easily and also can find an abundance of microorganisms on which to feed. As a rule the burrows are crescent-shaped or broadly U-shaped. The ammocoetes squirms to the mouth of its burrow and extends its oral hood to the surface of the substrate. The branchial chamber is expanded and contracted, drawing water into the mouth over a sieve apparatus and then passing it out through the gills. The sieve apparatus serves to strain out food material brought in with the water current. The food passes into the intestine where it is digested.

Metamorphosis involves a number of radical changes in the larvae: the U-shaped hood fuses ventrally to form a sucking disk; the sieve apparatus disappears and is replaced by a rasplike tongue; rudimentary eyes appear on the dorsal lateral surface of the head; the body color changes from various shades of brown to bluish gray; the dorsal fin becomes larger. The gill chambers change and enable the adult to pump water in and out through each aperture as it feeds. When metamorphosis is complete, the adult lamprey moves downstream into the lake and begins its parasitic or predacious existence.

The sea lamprey has been present in the St. Lawrence River drainage and in Lake Ontario since postglacial times, and a dwarf population occurs in the Finger Lakes of New York (Hubbs and Pope, 1937). For years Niagara Falls prevented the sea lamprey from invading the other Great Lakes, but in 1829, when the Welland Canal was constructed connecting Lake Ontario and Lake Erie, the sea lamprey gained access to the upper lakes. Despite the fact that the barrier to migration was removed, however, it was almost a century before the first sea lamprey was collected from Lake Erie on November 8, 1921 (Trautman, 1957). The sea lamprey did not become common in Lake Erie, but in Lake Huron and Lake Michigan the lamprey population virtually exploded after its initial appearance in 1936. Ten years later the first specimen was reported from Lake Superior. No doubt lampreys were present before these dates, but their populations were probably scanty and the likelihood of collecting a specimen was poor.

By the mid-1950s sea lampreys were very abundant in Lake Michigan

(Applegate and Moffett, 1955), and they quickly reduced the number of native salmonids and larger coregonids found there. The lake trout, probably because of its small scales, was the first species to feel the brunt of this new predator, but soon the whitefish was attacked. The average annual yield of lake trout in good years had been about 5 or 6 million pounds and was worth nearly $8 million, but the catch in Lake Michigan fell from 5.5 million pounds in 1946 to 402 pounds in 1953 (Applegate and Moffett, 1955). Once the trout were scarce, the lampreys began to prey on whitefish, suckers, and other species, and these species soon showed similar declines in numbers. S. H. Smith (1968) provides a detailed chronology of the changes in the Great Lakes fish populations from the late 1800s to the late 1960s.

The dramatic disappearance of lake trout and whitefish elicited a public clamor for control or eradication of this destructive predator. The federal government responded with funds for research on the biology and the control of lampreys, and one of the results of this research is our present detailed knowledge of the life history of the sea lamprey. The development of a larvicide or a selective poison which kills the ammocoetes but does not harm other fish has brought about some control of the lamprey. Electric weirs have been used in an attempt to prevent spawning runs up tributary streams, but they have not proved to be practical. It now appears that total elimination of the sea lamprey will not be possible and that we can only hope for control. Apparently the sea lamprey has no natural enemies in the Great Lakes, so biological control does not appear to be a long-range solution to the problem. If we wish to maintain the trout sport fishery in Lake Superior, we must control the lamprey by other than biological means. The alternative is to substitute for the lake trout a species of game fish which is able to survive in the presence of the lamprey.

Environmental changes, mostly man-made, taking place in the Great Lakes may complicate the lamprey problem. Present control of the lamprey must not lure us into a false sense of security. Organisms change or evolve, and the lamprey may undergo changes as a result of the heavy selective pressures imposed by larvicides. If sea lampreys are able to spawn in lakes even though they prefer streams, for instance, by treatment of the streams we could be inadvertently selecting for lake-spawning forms which would be equally difficult to control, but there is some evidence to indicate that this is not taking place (Hansen and Hayne, 1962). At present we must assume that the sea lamprey is a permanent part of the ecological system of the Great Lakes.

Few lampreys appear in the streams on the north shore of Lake Superior; the population of sea lampreys in Minnesota waters is maintained by lampreys that spawn in the streams entering the south shore of Lake Superior in Michigan and Wisconsin. The bedrock and poor nesting bottoms characteristic of most streams on the north shore plus the barrier falls near the mouths probably account for the small number of lampreys spawning in these streams. In the Mississippi River several native freshwater lampreys have always coexisted with the native fishes. A similar ecological balance seems to have been established long ago in Lake Ontario and in the Finger Lakes of New York.

Lampreys have always been present in European rivers and have been utilized to some extent for food. (The ancient Romans considered them a delicacy.) As far as we know, they have never been used for food in North America.

Genus *Ichthyomyzon* Girard

The species belonging to this genus are medium-sized, usually less than 16 inches in length. The adults can be distinguished from members of the genus *Lampetra* by the presence of a single emarginated dorsal fin which is continuous with the caudal fin. Only two species, *Ichthyomyzon unicuspis* and *I. castaneus*, are known from Minnesota waters.

SILVER LAMPREY

Ichthyomyzon unicuspis Hubbs and Trautman

The silver lamprey (Figure 22) is slender and eellike and reaches a total length of 8 to 12 inches. The large funnel-shaped buccal cavity has a diameter

Fig. 22. Silver lamprey, *Ichthyomyzon unicuspis*

greater than that of the body. The circumoral teeth (Figure 23) are usually unicuspid, but approximately 15 percent of Minnesota specimens have one or more bicuspid circumoral teeth. The number of circumoral teeth ranges from 13 to 23, with an average of about 18. There are about 51 myomeres or muscle bands between the posterior margin of the gill opening and the cloacal slit or vent; the range in our specimens is from 47 to 57 myomeres. The transverse lingual lamina is usually strongly bilobed. The supraoral cusps are usually 2 (occasionally 3) in number. There are two or three rows of teeth anterior to the mouth, with 5 to 8 teeth in the lateral rows. In counting the teeth, a jet of air should be used to expose the smaller marginal teeth for inclusion in the total count.

The silver lamprey ranges from the St. Lawrence drainage throughout the Great Lakes, the Ohio River, the Mississippi River south to Missouri (Hubbs and Trautman, 1937), and the Missouri River (Bailey, 1959; Cross and Metcalf, 1963). Specimens have been taken in the St. Louis River and in the Duluth-Superior harbor in the Lake Superior drainage. We also have specimens from the Minnesota River, the Mississippi River below St.

Anthony Falls, and the St. Croix and Rainy river drainage basins in Minnesota. Most of our specimens have come from Lake of the Woods, Lake Pepin, and Lake St. Croix, where they are quite common on fish taken by commercial fishermen. We have not collected specimens from above Taylors Falls in the St. Croix River.

Fig. 23. Silver lamprey, *Ichthyomyzon unicuspis*. Buccal funnel showing unicuspid circumoral teeth.

The silver lamprey is parasitic on fish and has been quite destructive in the Lake of the Woods area. It is the species commonly seen by fishermen in Lake St. Croix on northern pike, catfish, and walleyes. The silver lamprey should not be confused with the marine lamprey which is restricted in its distribution to Lake Superior in Minnesota. From time to time we see fish, particularly suckers, with large circular holes in their sides; these holes are the result of a lamprey attack.

When sexually mature, the adult lampreys ascend small streams to spawn and die soon afterward. The eggs develop into ammocoetes which are carried passively downstream to quiet pools where they burrow into the mud and spend several years as filter feeders. Eventually they metamorphose into parasitic adults, preying on fish in large streams and lakes until they become sexually mature.

The silver lamprey apparently has always lived in association with other native fishes and an ecological balance seems to have been established in their interrelations. Lamprey sores and scars are frequently found on the native species, but we know of no ill effects such as those produced by sea lampreys on lake trout and whitefish. We know little about the population dynamics of the silver lamprey, and we have only bits and pieces of information on the life history of the species. The silver lamprey is more characteristic of large stream and lake habitats and preys on larger fish than does its close relative, the chestnut lamprey.

CHESTNUT LAMPREY

Ichthyomyzon castaneus Girard

The chestnut lamprey is similar in many respects to the silver lamprey. It is slender and eellike in appearance, usually 8 to 12 inches in total length. It has a large funnel-shaped buccal cavity which when expanded is greater in diameter than the body. There are 21 to 24 circumoral teeth and 45 to 54 myomeres. Usually 4 to 10 of the circumoral teeth are bicuspid. The transverse lingual lamina is weakly bilobed. There are four or five rows of teeth in the anterior part of the mouth with 6 to 8 teeth in the lateral rows.

The chestnut lamprey is not common in Minnesota, and most of our specimens have come from the St. Croix River and its tributaries above Taylors Falls. We have one specimen from Lake St. Croix and another from the Mississippi River near Hastings. Woolman reported a single specimen from the Red Lake River in 1892; this specimen, in the University of Michigan collection (UMMZ 77424) is the only specimen extant from the Red River drainage in Minnesota. The chestnut lamprey is found in the Mississippi River from Louisiana and Mississippi northward through Oklahoma, Arkansas, Missouri, and Illinois into Iowa, Wisconsin, Minnesota, and Michigan (Hubbs and Trautman, 1937). It is also found in the Missouri River drainage of Missouri and Kansas (Cross and Metcalf, 1963).

The chestnut lamprey is similar in habits and life history to the silver lamprey but occupies smaller rivers and streams. Hubbs and Trautman (1937) indicate that the chestnut lamprey preys on smaller fish than does the silver lamprey, but our information on the ecology and the life history of both species is rather fragmentary.

Genus *Lampetra* Gray

In members of this genus the dorsal fin is divided into two parts by a deep notch and is almost separate from the caudal fin. Only one species occurs in the Upper Mississippi Valley in Minnesota. Several other species are found in the Pacific drainage of North America.

AMERICAN BROOK LAMPREY

Lampetra lamottei (LeSueur)

The American brook lamprey (Figure 24) is small and slender, seldom over 8 inches in length. The funnellike buccal cavity is small; when extended, the diameter is only slightly greater than that of the body. Most of the teeth are blunt and small; 3 medium-sized bicuspid teeth are located on each side of the mouth. The adult is not parasitic and has a degenerate digestive tract which is nonfunctional and is reduced to a small strand. The dorsal fin of the adult consists of an anterior and a posterior portion separated by a deep notch. The number of myomeres ranges from 63 to 73 (Trautman, 1957).

Fig. 24. American brook lamprey, *Lampetra lamottei*

The brook lamprey ranges northward from Tennessee and Missouri to western Pennsylvania and through the Great Lakes drainage to Minnesota. It also occurs in the Atlantic drainage from the Connecticut River south to Maryland. In Minnesota it is restricted to the Minnesota River, the St. Croix River below Taylors Falls, and the Mississippi River below St. Anthony Falls. There are no records of the brook lamprey from the Red River or the Rainy River and Lake of the Woods basin. Hubbs and Lagler (1964) state that the same species, *Lampetra lamottei*, or a virtually indistinguishable form is in the Yukon River system in Alaska and northeastern Asia. The Arctic lamprey, *L. japonica* (Martens), has a large seagoing form which is parasitic (McPhail and Lindsey, 1970). McPhail and Lindsey have presented meristic and other data indicating a close similarity between *L. lamottei* and *L. japonica* and have further suggested that an imaginative search for new characters might be useful in resolving taxonomic and nomenclatural difficulties in the lamprey group.

The brook lamprey is confined to small clear streams, where the species is often very numerous, but the adults are seldom seen except when they congregate for spawning. In the Credit River, a small tributary of the Minnesota River near Savage, Minnesota, the brook lampreys used to spawn by the hundreds each year from May 5 to May 20. They congregated in gravel riffles and attached themselves to stones by their suckerlike buccal funnels. Shallow nests were hollowed out in the river bottom, and the eggs were deposited in them. Frequently several males attended a single female. These tremendous spawning migrations were last observed in the late 1940s; annual visits have failed to reveal populations in the Credit River since that time. Their disappearance was probably caused by disturbances associated with the post-World War II development of the Credit River drainage basin.

Once the eggs hatch, the ammocoetes drift downstream into pools or backwaters where they settle to the bottom and burrow into the mud. They live as larvae for about five years, feeding on algae and bacteria. (Some ammocoetes found in the Credit River were larger than the adults that had just recently metamorphosed.) The larval individuals have lighter pigmentation than the adults, which are brown or fawn to bluish black in color. The dorsal fin of the ammocoetes is continuous with the caudal fin, and the buccal hood is smaller in the larvae than in the adults. The adults do not feed (hence they are nonparasitic), and they die after they spawn. The life cycle has been described in detail by Gage (1893, 1928).

Class OSTEICHTHYES
The Bony Fishes

Most modern freshwater fishes are characterized by the presence of bone, which distinguishes them from the cartilaginous fishes (Chondrichthyes) such as the sharks and their relatives. (The cartilaginous fishes are characterized by a skeleton entirely of cartilage and uncovered gill clefts. They are mostly marine, and none are found in the fresh waters of North America.) Most of the bony fishes are highly developed forms. A few primitive forms (sturgeons, gars, paddlefish, and bowfins) have very little bone and retain many characters common to the ancestors of the highly developed bony fishes.

The bony fishes are differentiated from the cyclostomes by the development of upper and lower jaws and two pairs of appendages or fins. Scales of some type are usually present, although in some species they have been lost. Teeth are also usually present, but a few species have lost their teeth or have only vestigial ones. The skeleton is fully formed and is of bone except in some of the more primitive forms in which the bones are not completely ossified and remain partly or wholly of cartilage. The gill clefts are always covered by an opercular flap (Figure 15).

Family POLYODONTIDAE
The Paddlefish Family

This is an ancient family which has only two representatives living today. One is the American paddlefish and the other is *Psephurus gladius*, a huge fish said to reach a length of 20 feet in the Yangtse River of China. These are smooth-skinned primitive fishes with an internal skeleton composed mostly of cartilage. They possess a heterocercal caudal fin and (at least in the American species) a long paddlelike snout. The vertebrae are cartilaginous and are strung on a notochord — an embryonic forerunner of the vertebral column — which usually disappears in adults.

Genus *Polyodon* Lacépède

There is only one living species in this genus, the characters of which distinguish the genus.

PADDLEFISH

Polyodon spathula (Walbaum)

The paddlefish (Figure 25) is dull lead gray in color with a smooth skin. The only scales are a small patch of rhomboid scales on the caudal fin. The intestine is a peculiar structure known as a spiral valve — a type that

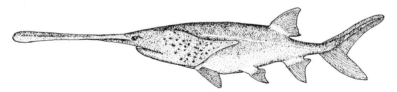

Fig. 25. Paddlefish, *Polyodon spathula*

is found in all sharks. The head of the paddlefish terminates in an enormous paddlelike snout which is one-third the length of the entire fish. The mouth is subterminal and contains tiny teeth only in the young individuals. The gill rakers are long and fine, forming an efficient organ for straining minute organisms from the water. The opercle ends in an unusual pointed flap that extends back almost to the pelvic fins. The eyes are small and located

120

anteriorly over the front of the mouth. Spiracles are present; these are small apertures anterior to the upper end of the opercular cleft which represent vestigial first gill clefts. Spiracles are common in sharks but are found in only a few bony fishes including paddlefish and certain sturgeons. The gas bladder retains its connection with the esophagus, but to our knowledge it does not function in respiration.

The strange form and the primitive characters of the paddlefish make it one of the most unusual fishes of the Mississippi Valley. It resembles a marine shark in many ways. In fact, when it was first studied in the early 1800s, it was incorrectly classified as a shark. Although its skeleton is mostly cartilage as in the sharks, after more thorough study the paddlefish was found to represent a primitive type of bony fish. The species reaches a large size. Several individuals we have taken from Minnesota waters in recent years weighed over 40 pounds. Harlan and Speaker (1969) report one weighing over 200 pounds taken from the Okoboji lakes in Iowa many years ago.

The distribution of the paddlefish once extended to the large streams and the connected lakes of much of the Mississippi drainage. The species ranged in the quiet waters of the Mississippi River and its larger tributaries from St. Anthony Falls to the Gulf of Mexico, and it occurred in the Minnesota River as far west as Mankato and in the St. Croix River up to Taylors Falls. It is no longer common in much of this range and has practically disappeared from many areas. In recent years, however, paddlefish have reappeared in parts of their original habitat in Minnesota, and they are caught occasionally in commercial seining operations in Lake St. Croix and in the Mississippi River below Lake Pepin. At the turn of the century they were very abundant in Lake Pepin, and seine hauls often yielded as much as a ton of paddlefish; their almost complete disappearance from the Lake Pepin area since then can be blamed on the gross pollution of the Mississippi River below the Twin Cities. Dams and overfishing may be other factors accounting for their scarcity. Meyer and Stevenson (1962) report that female paddlefish in Arkansas do not mature until they are over 25 pounds in weight and that paddlefish may not spawn every year, indicating a slow reproductive replacement. Harlan and Speaker observe that paddlefish are not abundant in the Iowa part of the Mississippi River.

The function of the paddlelike snout has long been the subject of much conjecture, but the matter has not yet been resolved satisfactorily. The snout is covered with numerous nerve endings and seems to be a sensory structure. Years ago it was thought that the fish used the snout to knock food animals from the weeds. Some claimed that the paddlefish used the snout to stir up the mud so it could strain out food organisms from the debris. Others thought that the snout served as a directional aid in swimming through muddy water. We have observed the activities of many paddlefish and have seen little evidence that the snout serves as an aid in feeding except that it may help to detect the presence or the density of the plankton upon which the paddlefish relies heavily for food. It seems possible that the snout acts as a directional aid in the same way that the lateral line system does.

Eddy and Simer (1929) examined the stomachs of numerous paddlefish, some of which held as much as a quart of food. In most cases cladocerans and copepods, which were the largest entomostracans present in the plankton at the time of capture, made up more than 98 percent of the stomach contents, and a few aquatic insects constituted about 2 percent. Direct observations showed that the paddlefish habitually swims through the water waving the paddlelike snout back and forth. It feeds on the large plankton organisms by keeping its mouth open and allowing the incoming water to pass through the gill clefts where crustaceans and other edible items are strained out by the filamentous gill rakers. Needless to say, this fish does not feed in the ordinary sense but is fed continuously by merely swimming with its mouth

Over a thousand pounds of paddlefish taken from Lake Pepin in 1900 by the University of Minnesota Zoological Survey. Photo: Department of Zoology, University of Minnesota.

A large paddlefish taken by the University of Minnesota Zoological Survey from Lake Pepin in 1900. Photo: Department of Zoology, University of Minnesota.

open. This is perhaps why we find paddlefish most abundant in waters which support a high production of plankton.

The spawning habits of the paddlefish have recently been recorded (Purkett, 1961), but before this our information was limited to a very few reports. The field notes of the late Henry Nachtrieb, the first professor of zoology at the University of Minnesota, indicate that in 1901 he caught paddlefish containing eggs which were almost ripe from early March until May in Lake Pepin but that in May he began to find spent females. Later in the year he caught young fish from 3 to 4 inches long, although he did not know if they were from that year's crop. David Thompson of the Illinois Natural History Survey (1933) secured a very young paddlefish which showed that the snout is undeveloped in newly hatched individuals. It was almost thirty years before Purkett (1961) found paddlefish actually spawning in Missouri; they spawned on gravel bars in swift water in the late spring after the high-water stage. He also observed that the newly hatched fish did not have the paddlelike snout.

Paddlefish are rarely caught on baited hooks unless they are snagged accidentally, but they are commonly taken in seines and traps. The flesh is excellent in flavor and is almost without bones. In some southern states it is highly esteemed and is sold as "boneless catfish." In South Dakota there is an important sport fishery below the Fort Randall Dam at Lake Andes, and the paddlefish there are referred to as "spoonbill catfish."

Family ACIPENSERIDAE
The Sturgeon Family

The sturgeons are remnants of an ancient and primitive group of fishes in which the cartilaginous skeleton is retained and the bony skeleton is confined largely to prominent bony plates in the skin. Sturgeons are found throughout northern Europe, Asia, and North America. Some species live in the sea and are anadromous, ascending rivers to spawn. Other species live in fresh water almost entirely. In North America two anadromous species are found on the Pacific coast; one of them, *Acipenser transmontanus* Richardson, has been reported as weighing well over 1,000 pounds. Two other anadromous species occur on the Atlantic coast, but they have become rare in recent years. Three freshwater species are found in the Mississippi drainage and nearby waters; two of these, the lake sturgeon and the shovelnose sturgeon, occur in Minnesota. The third species, the pallid sturgeon, has been found in the Mississippi River south of Minnesota and in the Missouri River but has not been reported yet in Minnesota.

Sturgeons have been one of the important commercial fishes of the world. Both the flesh and the eggs (for caviar) have been valuable products. Russia has been famous for caviar and other sturgeon products, but according to recent reports some of the Russian sturgeon fisheries have been lost because of dams, pollution, and exploitation. The same factors have affected sturgeon fisheries in the United States.

The sturgeon is characterized by a shovellike snout, on the underside of which is a protractile subterminal mouth with thick papillose lips which are extensible and efficient for sucking up food. No teeth are present except in the very young. A transverse row of four barbels is present on the underside of the snout, just anterior to the mouth. The caudal fin is a primitive heterocercal type. The dorsal fin and the anal fin are inserted far back. The four pairs of gills are covered by a bony opercle, but there are no bony branchiostegal rays in the opercular membranes which are joined to the isthmus. The internal skeleton is composed of cartilage, and the cartilaginous vertebrae are strung on a retained embryonic notochord. The head is completely covered by bony plates, and rows of prominent bony plates cover the sides of the body.

KEY TO MINNESOTA SPECIES OF FAMILY ACIPENSERIDAE

Small aperture or spiracle between eye and upper corner of opercle; caudal peduncle heavy and not entirely covered by bony plates; lower lip with two

slightly papillose lobes . . . .Lake sturgeon, *Acipenser fulvescens* Rafinesque
No aperture or spiracle between eye and upper corner of opercle; caudal
peduncle very slender and completely enclosed by bony plates; lower lip with
four papillose lobes . . . .
. . . . .Shovelnose sturgeon, *Scaphirhynchus platorynchus* (Rafinesque)

Genus *Acipenser* Linnaeus

The genus *Acipenser* is characterized by the description of the following
species, which is the only member of this genus found in Minnesota. The
anadromous sturgeons on the Pacific and Atlantic coasts belong to this genus.

LAKE STURGEON
Acipenser fulvescens Rafinesque

The lake sturgeon (Figure 26) is known by several common names in
Minnesota, but most frequently it is known as the rock sturgeon. It reaches the
largest size of any Minnesota fish. Individuals weighing over 200 pounds
have been taken in past years, but it is doubtful if any over 100 pounds exist
today. It is easily distinguished from the shovelnose sturgeon by the blunt and
heavy snout which becomes heavier with age. The thick tail, which is only
partly covered by plates, and the presence of a spiracle between the eye and
the upper corner of the opercle also characterize the lake sturgeon. The
appearance of the lake sturgeon changes with age. The snout is sharper in
young individuals but becomes more blunt and shorter in older individuals.
The juveniles have rough plates with strongly hooked spines on their sides,
but as they grow older the side plates become smooth and smaller until they
practically disappear in the very old individuals. The juveniles are usually
reddish brown above and have dark blotches but become greenish olive or
gray and lose the blotches as adults. Lake sturgeons reach a length of 6 feet in
some lakes. The record size is probably that of a sturgeon caught in 1911 off
Long Point in Lake of the Woods. It was 8 feet long and weighed 236 pounds.

Lake sturgeons ranged originally in parts of the Hudson Bay drainage, the
Great Lakes drainage, and the Mississippi drainage south to Alabama and
Missouri. They prefer the relatively quiet water of large rivers and lakes.
They are not nearly as abundant in Minnesota waters today as they were at the
turn of the century. They have never been abundant along the deep-water
shores of Lake Superior but have been reported in the shallow water of St.

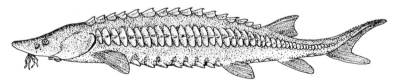

Fig. 26. Lake sturgeon, *Acipenser fulvescens*

Louis Bay, in the relatively shallow waters of Keweenaw Bay and the Apostle Islands, and in some of the shallow bays along the Canadian shore of Lake Superior. At one time lake sturgeons were quite abundant in the Mississippi River below St. Anthony Falls. Cox (1897) reported them from Lake Pepin, the St. Croix, Snake, Cross, and Kettle rivers, and Lake Pokegama in Pine County. They have been taken from the Red River, Red Lake, Lake of the Woods, and the Rainy River and its tributaries. They disappeared or became rare in most of these waters soon after 1900, probably because of pollution and overfishing. Since the passage of protective laws, the lake sturgeons are slowly increasing in the Snake, Cross, and Kettle rivers and in Lake Pokegama and Lake St. Croix.

Lake sturgeons frequent the shoal waters in those lakes where they still occur and ascend streams in the spring to spawn, but there are some exceptions. In Lake of the Woods in 1911 and 1912, for instance, Surber found sturgeons spawning off some rocky islands not far south of Kenora, but their favorite spawning beds were formerly at the Soo Rapids on the Rainy River, where at one time they arrived in great numbers at about the time the ice broke up in the spring (Eddy and Surber, 1947). Surber noted that their spawning migrations began as early as April 5 and often lasted until the middle of June. In recent years we have observed sturgeons congregating in shallow water at spawning time. In May and early June large numbers pass from the St. Croix up the Snake River and gather below the dam at Cross Lake. A large female may deposit as many as 3 million eggs. The eggs are large and sticky and adhere to sticks and stones; they are deposited at random, and they receive no care. They hatch in about two weeks, depending on the temperature. The young sturgeons require five years to reach a weight of 2 pounds and about twenty years to reach sexual maturity. It is claimed that they spawn only every second or third year, which may be part of the reason it takes so long to restore their depleted numbers. Several recent studies have indicated that fish 5 or 6 feet long are seventy or more years of age.

The young sturgeons seek shallow water and feed on minute planktonic crustaceans and other tiny aquatic organisms until they reach a length of 7 or 8 inches. Sturgeons are bottom feeders, and their protractile mouths efficiently suck up small clams, snails, crayfish, amphipods, and aquatic insects. They eat some algae and other plant material as well as a few small fishes; the latter may be carrion because sturgeons are not equipped to pursue and catch healthy and active fish. Surber reported that 10 out of a total of 27 adult stomachs examined in 1911 contained little but pebbles and sand. One early fisherman of Lake of the Woods repeatedly kept sturgeons in confinement for long periods; he found that they thrived on such grains as wheat and barley.

Sturgeons were so abundant in Lake of the Woods in the late 1800s that one writer referred to the lake as the greatest sturgeon pond in the world. They were considered such a nuisance by the pound-net fishermen (who were interested in walleyes) that special barges were built to haul the sturgeons away. Thus one of our valuable natural resources was seriously depleted through stupidity and wanton destruction. The present pollution from the Rainy River and the slow growth of the species have prevented restoration of the population in Lake of the Woods to anything like its former abundance.

Some idea of the rapidity with which the sturgeons disappeared from Lake of the Woods can be seen from the statistics given by Evermann and Latimer (1910): "In 1893 the catch of sturgeon in American waters amounted to 1,300,000 pounds. . . . By 1903 the catch had dwindled to 45,239 pounds." Surber noted that during the first nineteen days of September 1911 the catch of sturgeons at the Curry fishery at the mouth of the Rainy River was only 20 adult fish (that is, individuals exceeding 15 pounds in net weight). The number of undersized fish taken during the same period was 808. During the second half of May 1912 the same fishery obtained 15 adults and 65 undersized fish. One 6-foot female caught by Curry in 1911 yielded 30 pounds of eggs for caviar, and the value of the fish and the eggs netted the fisherman $54.80. In the late 1930s it took Eddy two years to secure a mature sturgeon from Lake of the Woods for the university's collection. In recent years the sturgeons have increased slightly in abundance, but they are caught only occasionally. Until World War II sturgeons from the Canadian waters near Kenora were served regularly in several restaurants in Warroad, Minnesota. They were considered a delicacy well worth driving out of the way to obtain.

In the late 1800s the value of sturgeon began to increase as the supply decreased, and the eggs used for caviar commanded a premium. Although the flesh was excellent, it was not in such great demand as the eggs. During the period 1888–1891 sturgeon eggs sold at 10 cents per pound for caviar; in 1897, at 60 cents; in 1900, at 80 cents; and in 1909 at a peak of $1.50. The air bladder ("sounds") also had considerable value for use in making isinglass (a transparent substance composed mostly of gelatine). Air bladders maintained a price of $1.00 per pound from 1888 to 1902, then dropped to 75 cents; by the end of 1904 they were worth only 50 cents per pound. Apparently the increasing use of celluloid and other substitutes was responsible for the drop in price.

In an early experiment in artificial propagation in the 1890s the Michigan Conservation Department succeeded in securing some sturgeon eggs and managed to hatch several thousand fry. Later the United States Bureau of Fisheries also secured some eggs and hatched them at their Vermont station. At the time the difficulty in securing eggs, the slow growth of the fish, and the heavy mortality seemed to make this method impractical for any extensive propagation of the lake sturgeon. The United States Bureau of Fisheries undertook another study of artificial propagation in 1911. Surber, then the senior scientific assistant at the fishery station at Fairport, Iowa, was assigned to the problem. He obtained a number of adults which were 5 to 6 feet long and wintered them at Le Claire Point in an enclosure at the Curry fishery, continuing his observations on them during the spring of 1912. Observations were also made on additional sturgeons procured at the mouth of the Rainy River. Surber found that under natural conditions the lake sturgeons spawned over a period of several months, depositing a few eggs at a time wherever they might be at the moment. In Surber's study of the captive sturgeons the ovaries of over forty females were examined carefully. Eggs in all stages of development — from those scarcely 1/15 inch in diameter to those 1/5 inch in diameter and nearly ready for extrusion — were found in the same female. Thus it seemed impractical to try to strip the eggs from the females for artificial propagation.

Most sturgeons are taken with pound and gill nets, although they may be accidentally caught or snagged by anglers if the baited hooks are on or near the bottom. The occasional reports of giant fish hooked by anglers but escaping by breaking the tackle could be encounters with large lake sturgeons. There are still a few around.

Genus *Scaphirhynchus* Heckel

This genus includes two American species of which only one is known definitely to occur in Minnesota. Both are strictly freshwater species. The characters for the genus are the same as for the following species.

SHOVELNOSE STURGEON

Scaphirhynchus platorynchus (Rafinesque)

The shovelnose sturgeon (Figure 27), sometimes known locally as the hackleback, is a small sturgeon; it rarely exceeds a length of 3 feet and a weight of 5 to 6 pounds, although at least one weighing 20 pounds was

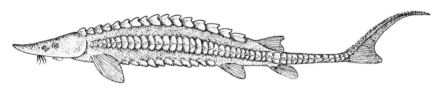

Fig. 27. Shovelnose sturgeon, *Scaphirhynchus platorynchus*

reported from the Missouri River. The shovelnose sturgeon can be distinguished from the lake sturgeon (which may occur in the same waters) by its longer and thinner snout and by the absence of a spiracle. The body is more slender than that of the lake sturgeon; the peduncle or tail is long and slender and is entirely enclosed with bony plates. The heterocercal caudal fin ends in an elongated filament nearly equal in length to the rest of the fin. This filament is often broken off. The body is yellowish olive in color and has no blotches. There are several rows of bony plates on the sides, and small bony scalelike plates cover the belly.

The shovelnose sturgeon ranges from the Hudson Bay drainage of the Canadian plains southward to New Mexico, Arkansas, and Kentucky. It is present in much of the Mississippi River and its larger tributaries and in several coastal streams of the Gulf of Mexico. In Minnesota the species seems to be restricted to the Mississippi, Minnesota, and St. Croix rivers. We have never found shovelnose sturgeons above St. Anthony Falls on the Mississippi River. Apparently Granite Falls on the Minnesota River has prevented them from reaching the Red River drainage, although they have been reported from Lake Winnipeg. We have never found them above Taylors Falls on the St. Croix River. Although shovelnose sturgeons were common years ago, they are no longer very abundant. They are still taken occasionally from Lake St. Croix in commercial seining operations, but it has been many years since any have been recorded from the Minnesota River. Like lake sturgeons, they do not bite readily on a baited hook but are sometimes snagged when the hook lies on the bottom.

The shovelnose sturgeons in Illinois spawn in April, May, and June (Forbes and Richardson, 1908). We have found them spawning in Minnesota in May and June. At Taylors Falls large numbers come up from Lake St. Croix and gather under the dam at the falls in an apparently unsuccessful attempt to pass upstream to spawn. As far as we know, they are forced to spawn on the rocks in the swift water below the dam. They have adhesive eggs like those of the lake sturgeon, and they seem to prefer swift water for spawning. Years ago we thought that perhaps the swift discharge of the dams into the 9-foot channel in the Mississippi River would aid spawning conditions, but we have no evidence that the dams have helped. We know little else about the spawning habits, growth, or feeding habits of shovelnose sturgeons, but we have reason to believe their food is about the same as that of lake sturgeons. Eddy and Surber (1947) examined a number of stomachs and found that the contents were composed of bottom organisms including many kinds of aquatic insects, snails, fingernail clams, and amphipods. The few stomachs we have examined had similar contents.

Shovelnose sturgeons used to find a ready market in the river towns years ago. The eggs were suitable for caviar, and it is reported that they were sometimes mixed with paddlefish eggs and sucker eggs and even then produced edible caviar. The flesh is firm and flaky and has an excellent flavor when fried or broiled.

PALLID STURGEON

Scaphirhynchus albus (Forbes and Richardson)

The pallid sturgeon belongs to the same genus as the shovelnose sturgeon, but so far it is not known in Minnesota. This sturgeon was originally described from Illinois and for a long time was not regarded as a valid species. It is now recognized as a species quite different from the shovelnose sturgeon, having a lighter color and no scalelike plates on the belly. The inner barbels under the snout are shorter than the outer barbels, and the snout is longer and sharper than that of the shovelnose sturgeon. It is quite common in the Missouri River in South Dakota, but it is reported as rare in the Mississippi River in Iowa (Harlan and Speaker, 1969). Although we have not identified this sturgeon in the Minnesota portions of the Mississippi River, it is possible that it may work its way upstream.

Family LEPISOSTEIDAE
The Gar Family

The gars are primitive fishes which have persisted into modern times as remnants of an ancient fossil group. A number of species are found in Central America, Mexico, the West Indies, and the southern states. The largest is the alligator gar, which is found in the Lower Mississippi Valley as far north as St. Louis. It is huge, reaching a length of well over 10 feet. (At one point it was Eddy's ambition to hook one with suitable tackle. When he finally caught one in a seine in Louisiana and found that it took three men to land it and a day to mend the seine, he decided it would be a waste of tackle to hook one.) Some of the Minnesota species reach nearly 6 feet in length.

Gars have long cylindrical bodies and long jaws armed with numerous sharp teeth. The internal skeleton is only partly of bone. The skull is largely cartilage protected by bony plates. The body is covered with diamond-shaped ganoid scales; these scales are extremely hard because their surfaces are covered with ganoin, an enamellike substance which takes a high polish. The ganoid scales form a tough and hard armor or shell which protects the fish from all manner of enemies. It is difficult to pierce this armor with a fish spear. The pre-Columbian Indians used the larger scales for arrowheads and the shells for breastplates, and the early settlers in America occasionally covered their wooden plowshares with scales.

Gars possess a highly vascular gas bladder with an open passage to the throat, and they can use the gas bladder as a lung to supplement their gill respiration. They rise to the surface periodically to discharge waste air and to gulp in a fresh supply, trailing bubbles behind them as they descend. Their ability to breathe air enables them to live in polluted water unfit for any other fishes except the bowfins. We have seen cases of total oxygen depletion where all the other species were killed, but the gars and the bowfins still swam about unconcernedly. We have known gars to drown when entangled in a net and unable to reach the surface for fresh air. Their air-breathing ability may be one of the characteristics which enabled these primitive fishes to survive. The gas bladder was probably not uncommon among certain of the ancient fishes.

The gars in Minnesota are warm-water fishes which spawn in weedy waters in the spring. Their eggs are greenish in color and quite toxic to warm-blooded vertebrates. People who have eaten them have become violently ill and have taken weeks to recover. For some reason the eggs do not seem to bother egg-eating fishes. The young gars have a black stripe along their sides, short jaws, and a long heterocercal caudal fin (Figure 28). As they grow older, the jaws lengthen and part of the caudal fin disappears, leaving a rounded fin with the vertebral column extending into the upper portion.

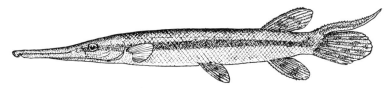

Fig. 28. Gar (juvenile, about 6 inches in total length). Short jaws and heterocercal caudal fin.

KEY TO MINNESOTA SPECIES OF FAMILY LEPISOSTEIDAE

Beaklike snout long and slender; length of snout about 20 times the least width . . . . .Longnose gar, *Lepisosteus osseus* (Linnaeus)
Beaklike snout short and broad; length of snout about 5.5 times least width or less . . . . .Shortnose gar, *Lepisosteus platostomus* Rafinesque

Genus *Lepisosteus* Lacépède

Six species of this genus are found in the United States, but only two species are known from Minnesota. Since gars are warm-water fishes, they are restricted to the southern half of the state. Some of the characters for the genus are the same as those for the following species.

LONGNOSE GAR
Lepisosteus osseus (Linnaeus)

The longnose gar (Figure 29) has a very long cylindrical body covered with regular rows of small platelike ganoid scales. The jaws are slender and very elongated, and both the upper and lower jaws are armed with long sharp teeth. Color, length of snout, and body proportions of the longnose gar are quite variable. The general body color is greenish olive above, silvery on the sides, and white below; both body and fins are marked with numerous black spots. The lateral line has 60 to 63 scales. The elongated snout is more than twice the length of the rest of the head. Some of Minnesota's longnose gars attain a length of over 5 feet, but the average length is much less. The young are very

Fig. 29. Longnose gar, *Lepisosteus osseus*

pretty little creatures, each marked with a broad black lateral band. Especially noticeable is the lance-shaped upper lobe of the caudal fin which becomes modified as the individuals grow older.

The longnose gar ranges from Montana eastward through the Mississippi, Great Lakes, and St. Lawrence drainages to Vermont and southward to northern Alabama and Mexico. It occurs in the Mississippi River and its tributaries as far north as Minneapolis, and we have taken it in most of the lakes in the Mississippi drainage. We have not found it in the Lake Superior drainage, although it appears in other parts of the Great Lakes. We have not taken it in the Red River or in the Rainy River system, but Woolman (1895) reported it from the Otter Tail River of the Red River drainage. Longnose gars frequent quiet waters and are most common in the large sloughs along the Mississippi River below St. Paul and along the Minnesota River. They are abundant in some of the large shallow lakes of the southern half of Minnesota.

The spawning habits of the longnose gar are the same as those described for the shortnose gar. Longnose gars feed mostly on fish of all kinds, both dead and alive. They glide alongside their prey and seize it with a sudden sideswipe of their long jaws. They often lie quietly near the surface and attack any unsuspecting fish which swims near them.

This fish is very destructive of game and forage fishes and is seldom used for food. It has no commercial value and fortunately is not abundant in good fishing lakes.

SHORTNOSE GAR

Lepisosteus platostomus Rafinesque

The shortnose gar (Figure 30) is somewhat similar to the longnose gar, but it differs greatly in several respects. The jaws are shorter, the back is shorter and broader, and the snout is broader and only 1.3 times longer than the rest of

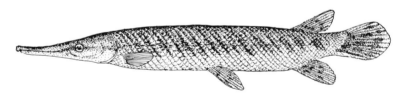

Fig. 30. Shortnose gar, *Lepisosteus platostomus*

the head. The newly hatched fish have short jaws and a wide black lateral band. The young have a lance-shaped upper lobe on the caudal fin (Figure 28) which later is replaced by a modified heterocercal fin with a rounded lobe. The scales in the lateral line number 60 to 64. The shortnose gar seldom exceeds a length of 2 or 3 feet.

The shortnose gar ranges from South Dakota through the Ohio Valley and south to Alabama and Texas. For some reason not many records from Minnesota were reported in the early days. Cox (1897) reported only two specimens, both from the Mississippi River near Minneapolis. Several gars were obtained from a slough near Savage in 1920 and from sloughs in Goodhue County between 1921 and 1923. However, numerous shortnose gars were obtained by Nachtrieb in the 1890s from sloughs near Winona. The northernmost record we have is for a gar collected by Friedrich (1933) from the Mississippi River near St. Cloud. No specimens have been taken in recent years by survey crews from the Mississippi River above St. Anthony Falls. The species is common in Lake St. Croix and in many shallow lakes in southern Minnesota.

The shortnose gar does not differ much from the longnose gar in spawning habits, although the shortnose gar prefers grassy sloughs for spawning, whereas the longnose gar prefers open sloughs and backwaters. They spawn in the spring, usually in June, in shallow water, depositing the eggs amid the aquatic weeds and grass. The large greenish eggs are poisonous to humans.

Fishermen detest shortnose gars because of their predatory habits and because they have little sport or food value. War is waged on them whenever possible, but the cylindrical shape of their bodies coupled with their activity makes them hard to hold in any ordinary seine and most of them escape before the seine can be hauled in. Although these fish may have some value as scavengers, they also consume food that could be used by northern pike, walleyes, and bass. Fortunately, they seem to thrive in waters not highly suited for game fishes.

The flesh of the gar is rarely used for food and has little or no value in Minnesota. In some southern states it is occasionally smoked or cooked on the half shell. The flesh is firm and there is no reason why it cannot be used. In the south sport fishing for gars has been attempted. A large gar of any species can put up a tremendous fight, but they are hard to hook because their mouths are tough; a copper noose on the lure is recommended. We know of no cases where this has been tried in Minnesota.

Family AMIIDAE
The Bowfin Family

Bowfins have stout bodies covered with cycloid scales. The head is covered with smooth bony plates. The mouth is horizontal and rather wide. The jaws are well armed with teeth, and the vomer, palatine, and pterygoid bones in the roof of the mouth bear small teeth. Bowfins are the only survivors of an ancient family which is known mostly through fossils.

Genus *Amia* Linnaeus

The characters for this genus are given in the following description of the only living species, which is restricted to eastern North America.

BOWFIN

Amia calva Linnaeus

The bowfin (Figure 31) has a rather primitive skeleton, partly of bone and partly of cartilage. The skull, also composed partly of cartilage, is covered with an outer sheath of bony plates. A bony plate known as the *gular plate*

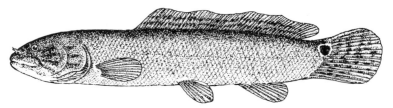

Fig. 31. Bowfin, *Amia calva*

(Figure 32) covers the space between the lower jaws. The body is rather stout and is covered by large smooth cycloid scales. The back and sides are olive or brownish green and more or less mottled, but the belly is white. There is a pair of short barbels on the nostrils. The dorsal fin is very long and low and reaches almost to the tail fin. The caudal fin is rounded and is of a modified heterocercal type. The dorsal and caudal fins are marked with dark wavy bars. The male bowfin has an ocellus (eyespot) on the base of the caudal fin. The gas bladder is bifid in front and quite vascular and retains a large connection

136

with the pharynx; it functions as a lung to aid gill respiration. The bowfin reaches a length of over 2 feet and a weight of more than 10 pounds.

Bowfins are known locally in many places as dogfish, but this name is deceptive because it is often applied to other fishes. They range over most of the Mississippi River drainage and eastward through the Great Lakes drainage (excluding Lake Superior) to Vermont and southward to the Gulf of Mexico. They are very common in the warmer waters of southern Minnesota. We find them in some lakes and tributaries of the Mississippi River above St. Anthony Falls and in the Red River drainage, but we have no records of their presence in Lake of the Woods or in the Rainy River drainage. Bowfins are not known from Lake Superior or its tributaries.

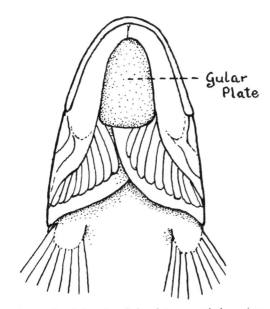

Fig. 32. Bowfin, *Amia calva*. Gular plate present in lower jaw.

Bowfins rise to the surface of the water every few minutes to expel waste air from the air bladder and to take in a fresh supply. Like the gars, they can live in water too low in oxygen for other species. They are very tenacious of life; specimens kept out of water at cold temperatures for twenty-four hours survive without apparent harm. One bowfin was inadvertently left in an aquarium without food and was discovered a year later, still alive although quite gaunt.

Bowfins are voracious, feeding on all kinds of animal life, although fish (including other bowfins) form a large part of their diet. They are very destructive of game and forage fishes alike, often feeding at night. One bowfin in our aquarium attacked a bowfin about half its size and carried it in its mouth for twenty-four hours before completely swallowing it. Bowfins in aquariums do not feed much during the winter, but in some lakes they bite occasionally on a baited hook when anglers are fishing through the ice. The lake bowfins seem to be quite active during the winter, and many are caught by commercial fishermen while seining under the ice.

Bowfins spawn in May and early June when the water becomes warm. They move in large numbers up small streams or into weedy bays. The males at this time assume brighter colors, and the fins become a vivid bluish green. A 5-pound female, 19 inches long, had 23,000 eggs in her ovaries. A larger female, 21 inches long, contained 64,000 eggs. Bowfins prepare a nest in shallow water by fanning out a depression in the mud and sand bottom, usually in a weedy area. They tear out the weeds and fan the mud away until the tiny rootlets are exposed. Spawning takes place at night, with the male guarding the nest. When the young hatch, they cling to the rootlets at the bottom of the nest by means of an adhesive organ on the snout. The male guards the young until they are able to care for themselves. The young are black and have at first a lance-shaped caudal fin, beneath which develops an inferior lobe which becomes the permanent caudal fin. After leaving the nest, the young travel about in a dense school attended for some time by the male.

Bowfins are often hooked by fishermen casting into the weeds for bass. They are hard fighters and fool many a fisherman into thinking he has hooked the largest bass in the lake. They would make a first-class game fish if they had much food value, but the flesh is very soft and mushy and is of poor flavor. During rough fish removal in winter some are used by local people who soak them in brine and smoke them. Smoked bowfin is reputed to be very good, but we have never tried it. In past years small bowfins were recommended for bait because they can live for hours on a hook, but in our opinion to use them for bait is to risk introducing this destructive fish into waters where it is not now present.

Family HIODONTIDAE
The Mooneye Family

The mooneyes are silvery fish with compressed bodies, small heads, feeble mouths, and large eyes with adipose eyelids. They reach a length of more than 12 inches. No spines are present in any of the fins. The body is covered with large cycloid scales; the head is naked and has a blunt snout. The mouth is of medium size and is obliquely set with jaws of equal length. The teeth are well developed on the jaws and on the vomer, palatine, and pterygoid bones lining the mouth as well as the hyoids on the tongue. The gill membranes are free from the isthmus. There are from 8 to 10 branchiostegal rays, and the gill rakers are short and straight. The mooneyes have a large gas bladder and a horseshoe-shaped stomach with only a single pyloric cecum. No oviducts are present in the female; the eggs are discharged through the body cavity.

Genus *Hiodon* LeSueur

This genus contains two species which are found in Minnesota.

GOLDEYE
Hiodon alosoides (Rafinesque)

The goldeye (Figure 33) may reach a length of over 12 inches. The body is bluish above; the sides and belly are silvery with a more or less golden luster anteriorly. The eye has a golden tinge. In shape and general appearance the goldeye resembles the mooneye but can be distinguished by the sharp scaleless ridge on the belly extending anterior to the pelvic fins and by the smaller number of dorsal rays (usually 9 and not more than 10). The anterior margin of the dorsal fin is inserted just above or slightly behind the anterior margin of the anal fin. The anal fin has 30 rays. The maxillary reaches past the middle of the orbit. The lateral line has 56 to 58 scales and may be incomplete.

139

Goldeyes range through northwestern Canada into the Hudson Bay drainage and southward to the Ohio River drainage in Tennessee. They are not uncommon in the Mississippi River below St. Paul and in the larger tributaries such as the Minnesota River and the St. Croix River as far north as Taylors Falls, but they are most abundant in the large northern waters such as Red Lake and Lake of the Woods. They seem to prefer the quiet areas of large streams and their backwaters or connected lakes. They feed on all kinds of aquatic and terrestrial insects, snails, small crustaceans such as crayfish, and small fish.

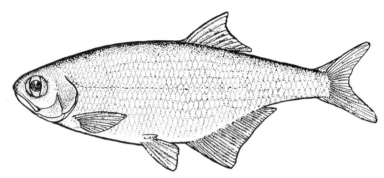

Fig. 33. Goldeye, *Hiodon alosoides*

We know relatively little about their spawning habits. They spawn in the spring (into June), moving up tributary streams and depositing their eggs at random on gravel in shallow quiet water. The resulting young move downstream in late summer to lakes and rivers.

Large numbers of goldeyes are caught in the commercial fisheries of Lake of the Woods and Red Lake. Smoked goldeye is popular in the northern part of Minnesota and in Canada. Some are eaten fresh, but they are not as good as the smoked ones. Goldeyes bite at times on flies and other lures, including baited hooks. Like the mooneyes, they are quite game fighters when hooked.

MOONEYE

Hiodon tergisus LeSueur

The mooneye (Figure 34) usually reaches a length of 10 to 12 inches. The body is silvery with a pale olive-buff back. The mooneye differs from the goldeye in that the dorsal fin has 11 or 12 dorsal rays and has its anterior margin inserted well in front of the anal fin. The naked ridge or keel on the belly is developed only between the pelvic and anal fins. The anal fin has 28 rays. The eye is large and is contained about 3 times in the length of the head. The maxillary extends to the center of the orbit. The lateral line has about 55 scales and is usually complete.

Mooneyes are found from Hudson Bay to the St. Lawrence drainage and

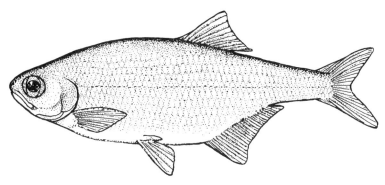

Fig. 34. Mooneye, *Hiodon tergisus*

southward into Arkansas and Alabama. In Minnesota they often occur in the same waters as goldeyes. Cox (1897) reported that they were widely distributed in Minnesota in the 1890s. We find them to be very common in the Mississippi River and its large tributaries and backwaters from St. Paul southward, in the Minnesota River drainage, in the St. Croix River as far north as Taylors Falls, in Lake of the Woods, and in the Red River drainage including Red Lake. They seem to prefer the quiet waters of rivers and lakes.

It is known that mooneyes enter streams in the spring and pass upstream to spawn at random in shallow water. They feed mostly on aquatic and terrestrial insects, snails, small crustaceans, minnows, and other small fish. At times they will strike at a fly or even a baited hook and will put up a game fight. However, they are not highly esteemed for food, and most anglers catch them only by accident. In the removal of rough fish and in commercial seining mooneyes are often caught in large numbers, but they have little commercial value. Young mooneyes are probably of considerable importance as food for game fishes.

Family CLUPEIDAE
The Herring Family

The herring family contains many important marine species including the true herring, which is one of the most important commercial fishes of the world. Several species are anadromous and enter fresh water to spawn. A few species live in fresh water but may be able to live also in brackish water along the coasts. Three species are known to occur in Minnesota.

Herring are characterized by a row of modified scales (sometimes called scutes) along the entire edge of the belly; these scales form a distinct saw-toothed margin. The body is more or less slender; it is silvery in color with a bluish back. All species have a transparent eye covering with a vertical slit known as an adipose eyelid (Figure 35). They are spring spawners, and the anadromous species crowd into the streams in spectacular runs. The eggs are deposited at random, and no care is given to them or to the newly hatched young.

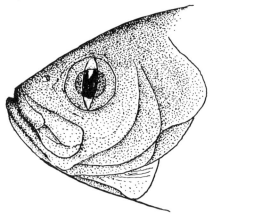

Fig. 35. Alewife, *Alosa pseudoharengus*. *Left*, head showing adipose eyelid; *right*, lower jaw extending slightly beyond upper jaw.

KEY TO MINNESOTA SPECIES OF FAMILY CLUPEIDAE

1. Last dorsal ray greatly elongated; snout blunt; lower jaw not projecting .
. . . . .Gizzard shad, *Dorosoma cepedianum* (LeSueur)
Last dorsal ray not elongated; snout sharp; lower jaw projecting 2

2. Spot on side behind opercle; upper jaw without teeth on rim; gill rakers long . . . . .Alewife, *Alosa pseudoharengus* (Wilson)
No spot on side behind opercle; upper jaw with teeth on rim; gill rakers short . . . . .Skipjack, *Alosa chrysochloris* (Rafinesque)

Genus *Alosa* Cuvier

Two species belonging to this genus are known from Minnesota waters. One species is native to the Atlantic drainage and has recently invaded the Great Lakes; the other, formerly common in the upper Mississippi River, is probably extinct. In members of this genus the vomer is without teeth, the belly is compressed, the ventral scutes are strongly developed, and the pelvic fins are below or slightly behind the front of the dorsal fin.

ALEWIFE
Alosa pseudoharengus (Wilson)

The alewife (Figure 36) is ordinarily from 4 to 8 inches in length but may reach a length of 15 inches. The body is thin and deep with a sharp serrated ridge of scales on the margin of the belly. The body is silvery with a dusky

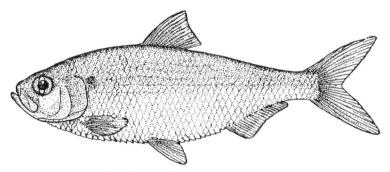

Fig. 36. Alewife, *Alosa pseudoharengus*

back; there is a spot behind the opercle and above the pectoral fin. The upper jaw extends back to the center of the eye in adults. The eye is large with a distinct adipose eyelid. The lower jaw (Figure 35) is narrow and extends slightly beyond the upper jaw but does not fit into a notch in the upper jaw as in the gizzard shad. The anal fin is not as long as that of the gizzard shad and has from 15 to 20 rays. The lateral line has from 45 to 54 scales. The gill rakers are long and slender, numbering 20 to 40 on the lower limb of the first branchial arch.

The alewife is native to the Atlantic coastal area and is a newcomer to Minnesota waters. In its native range the species is anadromous, and populations have become landlocked in lakes in the eastern states. The species apparently was introduced into Lake Ontario where it has been present for over one hundred years. It entered Lake Erie (by way of the Welland Canal), where the earliest specimens were recorded in 1931 (R. R. Miller, 1957); from there it passed through Lake Huron into Lake Michigan. The species began to multiply with great rapidity, and in a few years it was so abundant in Lake Michigan that the fishermen complained that alewives were clogging and fouling their herring nets. Alewives were first caught in the east end of Lake Superior in 1954. Undoubtedly they had entered earlier because some time was required for them to multiply before specimens were likely to appear in fishermen's nets. The first authentic Minnesota record for the species was based on a fish taken near Two Harbors in 1956. The species has increased in abundance since then, particularly in the eastern part of Lake Superior, but it has never become as abundant as in Lake Michigan. The waterfalls in Minnesota streams form barriers which prevent spawning runs, and the lack of shoals for spawning along the north shore of Lake Superior may be a limiting factor. Most of the alewives taken in Minnesota waters are caught in herring nets, and they rarely constitute a large percentage of the catch.

The migration of this fish into the upper Great Lakes has given rise to a controversial problem. Wherever the species appeared in Lake Michigan, in several years it increased to an enormous population. At first this was blamed on the simultaneous decline of the lake trout, which was the most prominent of the predacious fishes in the Great Lakes and which may have kept the alewife under control earlier. But when the species increased in Lake Ontario, it was *after* a decline in the trout population, just as in Lake Michigan, and its appearance and increase in Lake Superior also occurred *after* the depletion of the lake trout. The lake herring has shown a similar decrease in the eastern lakes with the increase in the alewife population, and this is thought to be the result of competition between species with similar feeding habits. The alewives may eventually adapt to their new environment and reach an ecological balance with the other fish species present in the Great Lakes. Meanwhile, the controversy centers around the wisdom of introducing other exotic predacious species in the hope of controlling the alewives.

The alewife is subject to summerkills which can occur anywhere from late spring until midsummer and which have been noted annually for many years in the eastern lakes. In Lake Michigan literally tons of alewives die in some summers and wash up on the beaches where they become an intolerable nuisance. Apparently these kills are a periodic event, the cause of which is uncertain; no evidence of any epidemic disease has been noted. They may be related to the inability of the alewife to adjust to sudden changes in temperature. Alewives are subject to low temperatures (down to 3° C) in winter; when they move into warmer water in the spring and summer, the sudden change in temperature may be fatal. Graham (1956) found that ordinarily a temperature of over 20° C is fatal, but if the fish are slowly acclimated to it they can endure a temperature of 23° C. Alewives in Lake Superior have not been subject to the summerkills so common in Lake Michigan.

Alewives become mature at four or five years of age and gather in enormous numbers for the spawning runs in April and May. Usually they run up tributary streams, but apparently they are able to spawn on shoals in lakes. The eggs are deposited when the temperature is between 55° and 60° F, preferably in quiet water. The eggs adhere to stones or sticks and hatch in about six days. The young remain in the spawning area from four to six weeks and then move out into the lake. Alewives are very prolific, producing from 60,000 to 100,000 eggs. They feed principally on plankton entomostracans but are known to take a few insects. During their spawning runs they apparently do not feed, but they will strike at a small fly or similar lure.

In the eastern states alewives have some importance as a food fish. However, they are thin and bony and do not have much popularity elsewhere. They are caught commercially in nets and seines, and some have been marketed for fertilizer and for fish meal. In the past they were an important forage fish for many game fishes in eastern waters. The abundant lake trout populations that used to exist in Lake Ontario fed heavily on alewives. The presence of such an abundant supply of fish food in Lake Michigan led to the introduction of the coho salmon as a predator to control the alewife. Reestablishment of the lake trout would probably serve the same purpose. The rapid spread and success of the coho salmon may complicate the problem. If the salmon deplete the alewife population, it may be necessary to restore the alewives; at the same time the presence of the salmon may prevent the restoration of the lake trout. The future of the competitive lake herring in this ecological mess is uncertain because it feeds on much the same food as the alewife.

SKIPJACK

Alosa chrysochloris (Rafinesque)

The skipjack is usually 8 to 10 inches in length but may be more than 15 inches. The body is streamlined, slender but elliptical, and the margin of the belly is sharply serrated or keeled. The head is slender with a strongly projecting lower jaw. Small but definite teeth are present on the premaxillaries of the upper jaw. The caudal fin is deeply forked. The back is bright steel gray, the sides are silvery with a golden tinge, and the belly is silvery. Even in very clear water the skipjack's movements are so swift that the eye can seldom follow them, and its coloration also helps to obscure its movements.

Originally the skipjack ranged from Minneapolis southward into the brackish waters of the Gulf of Mexico. At present it is practically extinct in Minnesota. Before construction of the Keokuk Dam on the Mississippi River in 1913, this species was more or less abundant as far north as Minneapolis and in the St. Croix River to Taylors Falls. It occurred in the Minnesota River and was at one time fairly common in Big Stone Lake, where Surber examined specimens in 1920. Between 1911 and 1913 many specimens from Lake Pepin were forwarded to the United States Bureau of Fisheries laboratory at Fairport, Iowa. These included both adults and young, which indicated that they must have spawned somewhere in that vicinity. Specimens taken before 1910 from Lake Pepin and from the Minnesota River at Mankato are in the collections at the University of Minnesota. Surber obtained specimens from the Mississippi River at Homer, Minnesota, in 1913 and 1914, but since then few records have been reported. In about 1950 a few specimens were reported from the Mississippi River on the Wisconsin side below Prairie du Chien, but no Minnesota specimens have been reported since those of Surber at Big Stone Lake in 1920. The skipjack was probably a strictly migratory fish in the upper Mississippi River. For several weeks after the waste gates of the Keokuk Dam were first closed during the spring of 1913, the skipjacks literally swarmed in the swift current below the powerhouse in a fruitless effort to reach the waters above. The Keokuk Dam and the many dams which came later probably contributed to the extinction of this fish in Minnesota.

The skipjack feeds on small organisms and algae of the plankton, on small insect larvae, and even on small fishes. It is a very active fish, jumping clear of the water in play or in pursuit of its prey. It frequents the swiftest waters and is often found around the ends of old wing dams. The angler finds it a savage fighter on light tackle. It readily takes a small spoon or live minnows and occasionally will take flies. Eddy caught many in recent years in the Mississippi below St. Louis. Unfortunately, the fish has little value as food, for it is excessively bony.

At one time the skipjack performed at least one valuable function in the general scheme of nature. In Surber's studies on freshwater clams or mussels in 1912, he discovered that the skipjack is the only specific host of the glochidia or larva of the species of clam which is used extensively in the mother-of-pearl industry. With the passing of the skipjack from the upper Mississippi River and particularly from Lake Pepin (which sixty years ago was the best area in Minnesota for clam production), that species of clam became extinct; along with it disappeared part of the livelihood of many people who worked as clammers or who were otherwise associated with the mother-of-pearl industry. In 1929, Eddy could not find a living specimen of that species of clam in Lake Pepin, only old shells.

Genus *Dorosoma* Rafinesque

This genus contains several species found in the southern United States, Mexico, and Central America. One species is common in parts of Minnesota.

GIZZARD SHAD

Dorosoma cepedianum (LeSueur)

The gizzard shad (Figure 37) is usually 5 to 6 inches long, but old individuals may be much larger. The body is silvery with a bluish tinge on the back. Young individuals are distinctly marked with a spot behind the opercle and above the pectoral fin which fades as the fish grow older. The body is thin and quite deep, with a sharply serrated or sawtoothed margin on the belly. The species is readily distinguished by an elongated filamentous last ray on the dorsal fin. This ray is about as long as the head; it is shorter in the young, and it may be broken off accidentally. The young gizzard shad have teeth, but these are poorly developed or absent in adults. The mouth is small and weak. The upper jaw is short and has a notch into which the tip of the lower jaw fits. The lower jaw is equal to the upper jaw in the young but is shorter than the upper jaw in adults. The gizzard shad possesses a muscular, gizzardlike stomach and a long coiled intestine. The gill rakers are long and extremely fine, with 90 to 275 rakers on the lower limb of the first arch.

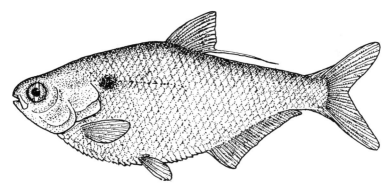

Fig. 37. Gizzard shad, *Dorosoma cepedianum*

Gizzard shad frequent large rivers and muddy lakes, especially those connected with large rivers. They range from central Minnesota eastward to the St. Lawrence drainage and southward to New Jersey and the brackish waters along the Gulf of Mexico and into Mexico. They are common and often abundant in the backwaters of the Mississippi River, the Minnesota River, and the St. Croix River below Taylors Falls, which seems to be their northern boundary. They are quite abundant in Lake St. Croix, where we have taken adults ranging up to 18 inches in length. The young often travel in schools in the open waters of muddy lakes in southern Minnesota and skip along the surface in front of a rowboat. This habit has earned them the local name of skipjack, which is misleading because it is sometimes applied to several other fishes.

Gizzard shad spawn in the spring in shallow water. The young fish feed at first on entomostracans. They soon move out into the open water to congregate in schools and to feed on plankton which they obtain by means of their fine gill rakers. It is reported that the young fish eat more copepods and cladocerans than the adults do. This may be because they find more of the large entomostracans in the shallow waters where they spend the first few weeks of their life. The older fish utilize even the minute microscopic algae of the plankton; this appears in their stomachs as a gray substance occasionally mixed with mud. Gizzard shad seem to retain all the plankton their fine gill rakers strain from the water and thus are not as selective as many plankton-feeding fishes.

Gizzard shad are not very palatable, and they are seldom used for food. Although they do rarely bite on a baited hook, occasionally a large shad is caught on a minnow or on a lure. They can put up quite a fight when hooked. Vast numbers are caught by commercial seining, and commercial fishermen consider them a nuisance. Nevertheless, they serve an important function by converting plankton into food for more desirable game fishes and panfishes. If they were not preyed upon, these highly prolific fish would rapidly fill up some of our lakes. Those not eaten by other fishes soon become too large for food and can create a management problem. Gizzard shad have been used as a source of food for hatchery trout, swine, and cattle in some states. They have also been steamed and pressed for oil.

Family SALMONIDAE
The Salmon Family

Despite the fact that this family does not contain many species, it includes many important game fishes and some of the most valuable commercial fishes in the world. The family contains the whitefishes and the related ciscoes, the Pacific salmon, the Atlantic salmon, the trout, the chars, and the grayling.

The fishes in the salmon family are all cold-water species native only to the Northern Hemisphere. All are characterized by the presence of a soft rayless adipose fin between the dorsal fin and the caudal fin and the presence of soft fin rays in all but the adipose fin. All of these species spawn in fresh water, but some mature in the ocean or have seagoing species; most of them spawn in the fall. The eggs are large; if they are refrigerated, they can be transported long distances, and consequently they have been widely distributed to suitable waters in all parts of the world. In many species the juveniles have vertical bars known as parr marks.

The family Salmonidae contains three subfamilies which have been considered by other workers as separate families. These are the subfamily Coregoninae, consisting of the whitefishes and related forms; the subfamily Salmoninae, containing the Pacific and Atlantic salmon, the chars, and the trout; and the subfamily Thymallinae, including two species of grayling. Native or introduced species representing each of these subfamilies are present in Minnesota waters.

KEY TO MINNESOTA SPECIES OF FAMILY SALMONIDAE

1. Dorsal fin shorter than head and with fewer than 15 rays 2
   Dorsal fin longer than head and with more than 15 rays . . . .
   . . . . .Arctic grayling, *Thymallus arcticus* (Pallas)
2. More than 100 scales in lateral line; maxillary extends behind center of eye (Salmoninae) 3
   Fewer than 100 scales in lateral line; maxillary does not extend behind center of eye (Coregoninae) 13
3. Anal fin with 13 to 19 rays; 19 to 40 gill rakers on first arch; 13 to 19 branchiostegals; vomer narrow and long with weak teeth; dorsal fin seldom with spots (*Oncorhynchus*) 4
   Anal fin with 9 to 12 rays; fewer than 20 gill rakers on first arch; usually 10 to 12 branchiostegals; dorsal fin with spots 7
4. Lateral line scales more than 200 . . . .

149

................Pink salmon, *Oncorhynchus gorbuscha* (Walbaum)
Lateral line scales fewer than 200 5
5. Gill rakers long, 30 to 50 on first arch.............................
..........Kokanee salmon, *Oncorhynchus nerka kennerlyi* (Suckley)
Gill rakers short, 19 to 28 on first arch 6
6. Anal fin with 13 to 15 rays ....
.................Coho salmon, *Oncorhynchus kisutch* (Walbaum)
Anal fin with 15 to 17 rays ....
...........Chinook salmon, *Oncorhynchus tshawytscha* (Walbaum)
7. Body with dark spots on light background; fewer than 190 lateral line scales; teeth on shaft of vomer in alternating series or zigzag row (*Salmo*) 8
Body with light spots on dark background; more than 190 lateral line scales; no teeth on shaft of vomer (*Salvelinus*) 11
8. Hyoid teeth (small teeth behind those on tip of tongue) always present; lateral line scales more than 150; 9 to 11 dorsal rays, usually 10; red or pink streak on underside of each mandible ....
......................Cutthroat trout, *Salmo clarki lewisi* (Girard)
Hyoid teeth absent; lateral line scales usually fewer than 150; 10 to 13 dorsal rays, usually 11 or 12; no red or pink streak on underside of mandible 9
9. Anal fin with 9 rays; adults with X-shaped spots on side ....
.........................Atlantic salmon, *Salmo salar* Linnaeus
Anal fin with 10 to 13 rays; sides usually with round spots (except in very old specimens) 10
10. Caudal fin profusely covered with spots ....
......................Rainbow trout, *Salmo gairdneri* Richardson
Caudal fin without spots or with only a few spots restricted to dorsal portion of fin ....Brown trout, *Salmo trutta* Linnaeus
11. Caudal fin deeply forked; body covered with light spots on dark background, belly sometimes spotted; fins not emarginated 12
Caudal fin not distinctly forked; body with light spots and some red spots on sides; fins strongly emarginated with whitish or cream margins ....
......................Brook trout, *Salvelinus fontinalis* (Mitchill)
12. Lateral line scales 163 to 183; body depth 3.1 to 3.8 in standard length .
....................Siscowet trout, *Salvelinus siscowet* (Agassiz)
Lateral line scales 195 to 218; body depth 4.1 to 4.8 in standard length
....................Lake trout, *Salvelinus namaycush* (Walbaum)
13. Two flaps on septum dividing nostril; gill rakers of first arch more than 23 (*Coregonus*)..14
Single flap on septum dividing nostril; gill rakers on first arch fewer than 20 (*Prosopium*) 20
14. Premaxillary wider than long, extending downward and backward to form a rounded or blunt snout; gill rakers fewer than 23 ....
...............Lake whitefish, *Coregonus clupeaformis* (Mitchill)

Premaxillary longer than wide, extending downward and forward to form an acute or pointed snout; gill rakers more than 32 15
15. Lower jaw more or less hooked 19
    Lower jaw not hooked 16
16. Gill rakers on the first branchial arch 43 to 52 . . . .
    . . . . .Cisco, *Coregonus artedi* LeSueur
    Gill rakers on first branchial arch usually fewer than 43 17
17. Body ovate (deeper anterior to center) . . . .
    . . . . .Blackfin cisco, *Coregonus nigripinnis* (Gill)
    Body elliptical (deepest at center) 18
18. Gill rakers on first branchial arch usually fewer than 39; lower jaw with considerable black pigment . . . .
    . . . . Shortnose cisco, *Coregonus reighardi* (Koelz)
    Gill rakers on first branchial arch usually more than 39; lower jaw without much pigment . . . .
    . . . . .Shortjaw cisco, *Coregonus zenithicus* (Jordan and Evermann)
19. Body ovate; gill rakers on first branchial arch usually fewer than 41; lateral line scales usually more than 75 . . Kiyi, *Coregonus kiyi* (Koelz)
    Body elliptical; gill rakers on first branchial arch usually more than 40; lateral line scales usually fewer than 76 . . . .
    . . . . .Bloater, *Coregonus hoyi* (Gill)
20. Lateral line scales fewer than 75, usually 55 to 60; length usually less than 8 inches . . . .
    . . .Pygmy whitefish, *Prosopium coulteri* (Eigenmann and Eigenmann)
    Lateral line scales more than 75; length usually more than 8 inches . . .
    . . . . .Round whitefish, *Prosopium cylindraceum* (Pallas)

SUBFAMILY THYMALLINAE

This subfamily contains one genus with two species. The European grayling, *Thymallus thymallus* (Linnaeus), is found in the cold waters of northern Europe and Asia; the second species, *T. arcticus* (Pallas), occurs in North America from Hudson Bay westward. Two relict populations of the latter were originally found in the United States.

Genus *Thymallus* Cuvier

Since only a single species occurs in North America, the description of the species will serve to characterize the subfamily and the genus.

ARCTIC GRAYLING

Thymallus arcticus (Pallas)

The Arctic grayling (Figure 38) reaches a length of 18 inches or more. The body is an iridescent purplish gray and silver sprinkled with small spots. The saillike dorsal fin is the most outstanding character of the species. The dorsal fin has 21 to 24 rays and is very long and high; the base of the dorsal fin is longer than the head and greater than the depth of the body. The fin is dark gray with rows of violet or blue spots set off by light borders, and the upper margin of the fin is bright red. The first branchial arch has 12 short and slender gill rakers.

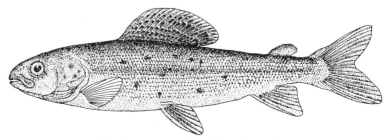

Fig. 38. Arctic grayling, *Thymallus arcticus*

The grayling is a recent introduction to the Minnesota fish fauna. It is native to the Arctic drainage of North America from Hudson Bay into Alaska. A closely related species is found throughout northern Europe and Asia. Two isolated relict populations of grayling once existed in the United States. One was in the Otter River of Upper Michigan and in several rivers of Lower Michigan. Another population was present in the headwater streams of the Missouri River, principally in Montana. Although these have been treated as separate subspecies, they were probably Arctic grayling that survived as postglacial relict populations. Shortly after the turn of the century the Michigan population was reduced to the point where it was thought to be extinct. The reduction was probably caused by overfishing and habitat modification resulting from lumbering operations. During this period grayling from Montana were planted to replace the depleted Michigan stock; it is doubtful that any of the original Michigan strain exists today. The Montana grayling has for years been the main source of stock for various northern waters. The Montana and Michigan grayling live only in clear cold streams and lakes. Although they are sometimes found in rapids over gravel bottoms, they appear to prefer pools.

Introduction of the grayling into new waters seems to be difficult, even within its natural range in the Rocky Mountains. Many attempts to introduce it in the northern states have resulted in only occasional and sometimes only temporary success. Eggs from Montana were secured and hatched by the Minnesota Department of Conservation, and the resulting fry were planted in Twin Lake (near Isabella) and in Musquash Lake (near Grand Marais). The introduction was a success, but reproduction has not been satisfactory to date. However, it may be possible to maintain a sport fishery in the lakes by means of hatchery propagation.

Grayling spawn in shallow water on sand and gravel bottoms in small streams from May to July. They feed extensively on aquatic and terrestrial insects which light on or fall into the water. They feed to a lesser degree on bottom organisms and on small fish.

Fishermen have always considered the grayling to be one of the finest of game fishes, and it is not so wary as some of the trout species. It is easily taken with both wet and dry flies, particularly in the late summer, and feeds primarily in the late afternoon and early evening. Grayling also take small spinners, and they are reported to be great sport on ultralight spinning gear.

SUBFAMILY SALMONINAE

The subfamily Salmoninae contains the Pacific salmon (*Oncorhynchus*), the Atlantic salmon (*Salmo*), various trout species (*Salmo*), and the chars (*Salvelinus*, including the lake trout, the brook trout, and the fat trout). All of these have fine scales, well-developed teeth, and coarse stubby gill rakers. Many of the species in the subfamily show great variation in their morphology and coloration. They are all predacious, feeding on various small animals; the larger individuals tend to become piscivorous. All lay large eggs containing large amounts of yolk. The eggs are usually deposited and covered in prepared nests called redds, which are deserted following the spawning period. There is no parental care of the nest or the young. The Pacific salmon dies after spawning, but the trout and the Atlantic salmon live to spawn again.

No species of salmon is native to Minnesota, although many species have been introduced at various times with mixed success. The same is true of the trout species, except that the introduced populations have been much more successful and have become a very important addition to the sport fishery. The chars are native to Minnesota waters.

The popularity of trout with the angler is so great that in many cases it is impossible to maintain satisfactory populations in streams and lakes. Their natural reproduction does not produce enough progeny to keep up with the removal by fishermen and must be supplemented heavily by stocking with hatchery-reared fish. Propagation has progressed to the stage where the trout approaches being domesticated, and we are now producing by artificial selection strains with faster rates of growth, higher temperature tolerances, and other desirable traits. Many streams are stocked at regular intervals throughout the fishing season to maintain a satisfactory sport fishery. It is probably safe to say that a large proportion of stream trout taken by the angler were reared in one of the Minnesota hatcheries. Trout rearing and breeding is quite scientific and has been carried on for about ninety years in Minnesota. At present there are five trout hatcheries in the state and more are on the drawing boards.

Brood stock is maintained in ponds fed by cold water. The eggs and the milt are stripped from the brood fish, and the fertilized eggs are hatched on trays in running water at temperatures of 47° to 49° F. The trays are watched carefully, and any damaged eggs are removed. In from eight to eleven weeks when the eggs are about to hatch, they are transferred to hatching tanks. The fry live for a number of days on the yolk contained in the yolk sac. Subsequently, the fry are placed in pools where they are fed on scientific diets to assure that they obtain all the vital amino acids and vitamins. Once the fish reach fingerling size, they can be placed in aerated tanks on trucks and transported to suitable streams. Others are allowed to remain in the rearing ponds until they are a year or more of age before they are planted in streams. This method provides the angler with sizable fish and avoids losses from natural mortality that occur when fingerlings are planted. In 1969 Minnesota produced 11,000 pounds of fingerlings, 71,000 pounds of yearling trout, and 2,500 pounds of adult trout to be released in state trout waters.

The trout species, particularly the stream trout, have been so manipulated that we wonder where it will all end. In the past someone suggested facetiously that recently stocked trout taste like liver — and it is true that years ago liver was a common food supplied to trout in rearing ponds. Today fishermen often follow the hatchery truck and fish in the pools where the trout have been released. The economist, even if a fisherman, would probably recommend selling the fish by the pound or allowing the fishermen to fish in the rearing pond and billing them for their catch. At least this would reduce the loss of fish to causes other than angling. The throngs of fishermen at Eagle Creek (west of Savage, Minnesota) and along similar streams on opening day give a measure of the popularity of catching hatchery-reared fish. The fact is that the streams are incapable of maintaining natural trout populations at levels that will satisfy the fishing public. Fishery biologists are doing their best to increase the trout populations artificially to meet the demand and to augment the natural populations in less popular streams. The Donaldson trout, a rainbow strain recently developed in Washington after years of breeding, may prove ideal for some of the small lakes which are too warm for other trout strains. Unlike the wild rainbow, this strain does not seem to be much of a traveler so it can be stocked safely in warm streams. The splake, a tough, fast-growing hybrid between the brook trout and the lake trout, has been introduced into Pierz Lake in Cook County.

Recently a few commercial trout farms have been developed in Minnesota. These farms usually buy trout or rear their own and stock streams and ponds for angling. In 1970 twenty-two trout hatchery licenses were issued in Minnesota, and of these eighteen were for angling sales. The fisherman is charged a flat fishing fee, or he pays for the fish he catches. Some of these farms rear trout for the restaurant and grocery trade. In the eastern states trout waters are often owned or leased by fishing clubs, which is also the case in Scotland and in northern Europe. In Scotland annual leases for the use of a few hundred yards of a trout stream may cost thousands of dollars. Fortunately, Minnesota has not reached this stage, but it may do so in the future. Eastern trout fishermen are required to buy a separate license to fish for trout, and the funds obtained from license sales go into the trout management fund of each state's department of natural resources; in these areas the trout fishermen pay their way and are not subsidized by the anglers who seek warm-water fishes.

Genus *Oncorhynchus* (Suckley)

The Pacific salmon species include some of the most valuable commercial fishes of the world. They are also popular game fishes and perhaps could become an important asset to sport fishing in fresh water. For many years attempts have been made to introduce various species of salmon into Minnesota waters with little success, but the recent introductions of several species into Lake Superior seem to have been effective and to have added several new species to the game fish fauna.

The anal fin of the salmon has 13 to 19 rays; an adipose fin is present. The vomer is long and narrow and has weak teeth which become obsolete in old individuals. The first branchial arch has 19 to 40 gill rakers, and there are 13 to 19 branchiostegal rays. The scales are small. In their first year of life young salmon have rows of spots or short vertical bars on their sides known as parr marks. Similar parr marks appear on the sides of young trout and a few species of whitefish.

Salmon differ in several ways from trout. All salmon are naturally anadromous, spending their adult life in the ocean and returning to fresh water to spawn, whereas only a few trout have developed anadromous races. However, many species of salmon have evolved landlocked races which pass their entire lives in fresh water. When the mature salmon start their spawning runs back to the lakes and streams where they were hatched, the males develop prominent sexual characteristics such as the strongly elongated hooked snout known as a kype. Male trout develop a similar dimorphism but to a lesser degree.

Salmon spawn in headwater lakes and streams that may be thousands of miles from the sea. They spawn in relatively shallow water over beds of gravel from late summer into late fall; thousands of pairs use the same section of stream for spawning. After spawning has been completed, the emaciated and battered adults die. The eggs develop during the winter, and the young remain in the gravel beds until late winter or early spring. Then the pink salmon and certain other species begin their migration downstream to the sea; the sockeye salmon spends up to three years in fresh water before entering the sea. The number of years spent in the ocean before the adults mature is species specific; the sockeye salmon spends three or four years at sea, the coho returns in its third year, and the pink salmon returns in its second year. All salmon exhibit a homing instinct and return to spawn in the stream where they were hatched. It is thought that they migrate by means of a "sun compass" from the ocean to the mouth of the river system and then trace specific environmental odors to the stream in which they hatched.

PINK SALMON

Oncorhynchus gorbuscha (Walbaum)

The pink salmon (Figure 39) usually weighs from 3 to 5 pounds, although some have been reported to weigh up to 10 pounds. The body is silvery with a bluish back. The dorsal and caudal fins and the posterior part of the back are profusely covered with black spots; the spots on the caudal fin are large and oblong. The anal fin has a light tip, and the base is longer than the longest anal ray. The juveniles do not develop the parr marks found in most young salmon. The scales are small with more than 200 in the lateral line.

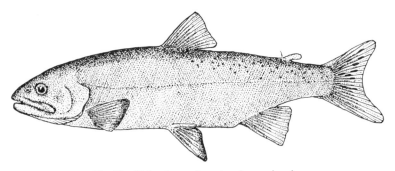

Fig. 39. Pink salmon, *Oncorhynchus gorbuscha*

We believe the pink salmon was introduced into Lake Superior by accident. The species has successfully reproduced since it was first seen in 1959. The first records were based on two salmon caught by fishermen in the Cross River (Cook County) and in the Sucker River (St. Louis County). Both specimens were males and had started to develop hooked jaws, indicating that they were approaching sexual maturity. A search for information about the original introductions revealed no records of plantings, but it was learned that some eggs had been hatched at the former Port Arthur hatchery for planting in the Hudson Bay drainage in 1956; in the process of transferring the fingerlings to a seaplane, about a hundred of them escaped into Thunder Bay. It seems certain that this accident was responsible for the introduction of the species into Lake Superior. Since the pink salmon matures in two years and since the specimens recorded in 1959 were just approaching maturity, it was evident that the original fingerlings had spawned and that the specimens were from the second generation. This was of particular interest because earlier the pink salmon had always been considered to be incapable of maintaining a population in fresh water.

In British Columbia where pink salmon are native, they usually enter the streams in September and move upstream to spawn in October. After the eggs are deposited in the gravel bed, the adult fish die. The eggs hatch in about 125 days, and the newly hatched fry emerge from the gravel bed in April and May and almost immediately start downstream to the ocean, where they live until maturity. Lake Superior takes the place of the ocean for the pink salmon in Minnesota.

Pink salmon fry feed on small crustaceans and later on small fish. Although these salmon do not feed when spawning, they strike at intruding objects such as spoons, spinners, and other lures, frequently the same artificial lures that are used for lake trout. Many times they simply make a pass at the lure and become snagged by the gang hooks.

In the fall of 1969 Underhill observed several dozen pink salmon crowding into the mouth of the Cascade River and spawning on gravel and sandbars were the water flowed in shallow riffles. Some of the fish weighed up to 4 pounds. Fishermen reported the same activities in the mouths of some streams on the north shore of Lake Superior. Most of the fish were covered with sores and fungus and a few had already died and washed up on the shore. In the fall of 1971 pink salmon were observed spawning in the mouth of the Cascade River. After about nine generations, the species is now firmly established and is breeding successfully in the Lake Superior drainage.

COHO SALMON

Oncorhynchus kisutch (Walbaum)

The coho salmon (Figure 40) is one of the latest additions to the Minnesota fish fauna. This salmon usually weighs from 4 to 5 pounds, although some may weigh over 8 pounds. The back is metallic blue, and the sides and the

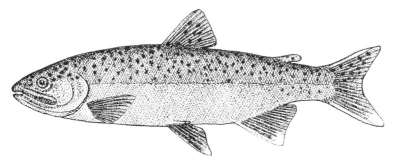

Fig. 40. Coho salmon, *Oncorhynchus kisutch*

belly are silvery. Black spots may be present on the back and on the upper lobe of the caudal fin. When the fish matures and begins its spawning run, the sides become reddish and the belly darkens. In the mature males the jaws become strongly hooked. Young individuals have pronounced parr marks.

The mature salmon migrate upstream and select a gravel riffle in which to spawn. Spawning usually takes place in October and November, and the eggs hatch in about 110 days. The young fish usually remain in the stream for a year before migrating to the lakes or the ocean. In the fall of their third year they reenter the spawning streams.

Coho salmon were first introduced into Lake Superior and Lake Michigan

by the Michigan Department of Conservation in an attempt to find a predacious fish to control the rapidly increasing alewife population and to take the
place of the depleted lake trout population. The Michigan hatcheries secured
Columbia River coho eggs from Oregon in the fall of 1964 and hatched them
at Oden, Michigan, in 1965. They later released approximately 800,000
one-year-old fingerlings into suitable streams emptying into Lake Superior
and Lake Michigan; the majority of the fingerlings were released into the
Huron River. In the fall of 1966, only a year after the first release of salmon
into the two lakes, a few cohos showed up in fishermen's catches, and about
2,000 were caught in 1967. Some of the fish in the 1967 catch weighed up to 8
pounds, indicating phenomenal growth in comparison with their Pacific ancestors. In the spring of 1967 Michigan released an additional 2,300,000
salmon fingerlings into Lake Superior and Lake Michigan; the fingerlings
included approximately 850,000 chinook salmon.

More recently Minnesota and Wisconsin biologists have begun to propa-
gate and plant coho salmon. Minnesota has not been as successful as
Michigan with the initial introductions. Minnesota fisheries biologists obtained eggs from Oregon and released over 100,000 fingerlings in the French
River in 1968. In November and December of 1970 cohos appeared at the
mouth of the same river, and in 1971 young jack salmon were taken from it.
The females did not enter the river but were taken in test nets set at the mouth.
Apparently the fish could not adjust to the cold waters of Lake Superior and
the north shore streams. The few fish that did enter the river found the water
temperature too cold (39° F), and as a result did not spawn. Some of the fish
taken in the test nets were stripped at the French River hatchery, and the eggs
were hatched at the French River, St. Paul, and Lanesboro hatcheries in
preparation for another attempt to establish coho runs in the north shore
streams. Many of these streams are not well suited for salmon because they
have impassable falls close to the lake which prevent the fish from proceeding
upstream to suitable spawning habitats. Also the steep and rocky character of
the shores does not offer shoal areas which could be used for spawning. The
Devil Track, Baptism, Brule, and Split Rock rivers and several smaller
streams provide marginal spawning habitats. In several instances the Department of Natural Resources is creating bypasses around barriers in streams to
open more of them to both salmon and rainbow trout spawning runs.

Fishermen have caught Minnesota cohos, but the fish were reported to be in
less than prime condition because they were too far developed sexually. A
coho weighing 8 pounds, 7 ounces, caught near Beaver Bay, holds the present
record for Lake Superior. A 33-pound coho was taken from the Manistee
River in Michigan in 1970.

It is reported that cohos strike readily at spoons, spinners, flatfish, flies, and
a variety of other artificial lures. They also strike at objects when they are on
the spawning beds, despite the fact that they have ceased to feed by this time.

CHINOOK SALMON
Oncorhynchus tshawytscha (Walbaum)

The chinook salmon (Figure 41), sometimes known as the king salmon, is the most desirable of all the Pacific salmon. It is also the largest salmon species, usually weighing about 20 pounds, but weights up to 125 pounds have been recorded. It furnishes the most valuable grade of commercial red salmon and is highly esteemed as a game fish on the Pacific coast. The body has silvery sides and a dusky back. There are numerous black spots on the back and the tail; the dorsal and caudal fins are also spotted. The anal fin has from 15 to 19 rays. The chinook salmon usually matures at sea in the third or fourth year, but some take as few as three years and others as many as seven years to reach maturity.

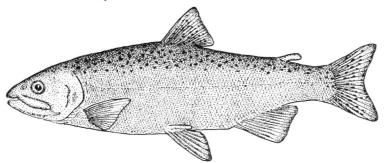

Fig. 41. Chinook salmon, *Oncorhynchus tshawytscha*

Numerous attempts, dating back many years, have been made to introduce this salmon into Minnesota. Unfortunately the early plantings were a shotgun attempt in which a wide variety of waters were liberally stocked; we know today that many of these waters do not provide suitable environments for any kind of salmon. In 1876 and for several succeeding years many stockings of chinook fry and fingerlings were made in the lakes of Rice, Blue Earth, Washington, Ramsey, Hennepin, Meeker, Wright, Faribault, and several other counties and in the Cannon, Blue Earth, St. Croix, and Red rivers. There are records in the annual report of the Minnesota Fish Commission for 1878 of an occasional catch in Rice County of fish planted two years previously. They had reached a length of 10 to 13 inches. A chinook salmon that died in Sunfish Lake in Dakota County had reached a length of 16 1/2 inches and a weight of 2 pounds, 2 ounces. Again in 1881 many yearlings and several hundred thousand fry were planted widely throughout the state as far south as Nobles County, and a generous stocking was made in the upper Mississippi River at Brainerd. Many years later the United States Fish Commission made plantings in Lake Superior but with little success.

There is only one record of a chinook salmon which reached mature size in a small lake. The specimen, 20 inches long, was taken in Lake Minnie Bell in Meeker County in 1919. Fingerlings had been planted in the lake in 1916. A few specimens have been reported from Lake Superior, but many of these reports are based on large steelhead trout. We have at least one authentic record from Lake Superior: a specimen weighing 12 pounds was caught off Susie Island in 1921 and was sent to the office of Minnesota's Governor Preus, where it was examined by Surber. Several chinook salmon were caught in nets set for lake trout in 1934 and 1935. The most recent record of a chinook salmon was a specimen weighing 8 pounds, 8 ounces, which was caught in 1970 in Lake Superior near Beaver Bay. The specimen was verified by personnel of the Minnesota Department of Conservation. In the spring of 1967, the Michigan Department of Conservation hatched over 800,000 chinook salmon and released the fingerlings in the Huron River, a tributary of Lake Superior. We think the recent Minnesota record from Beaver Bay is probably from the Michigan planting.

KOKANEE SALMON

Oncorhynchus nerka kennerlyi (Suckley)

The kokanee salmon, sometimes called the redfish, is a landlocked dwarf subspecies of the sockeye salmon (*Oncorhynchus nerka*) and is native in lakes from Oregon north into Alaska. The kokanee is usually about 12 inches long and weighs about 1 pound, but occasionally an individual may reach a length of 15 inches and may weigh as much as 4 pounds. The kokanee ordinarily has a bluish back and silvery sides, but in mature fish in spawning condition the sides become bright red. A few spots are present on the back and on the caudal fin; the sides are finely speckled with black pigment. The juveniles have parr marks on their sides. There are 122 to 139 scales in the lateral line.

The spawning habits of this relative of the sockeye are similar to those of the other salmon species. Kokanees are landlocked, however, and spend their entire lives in fresh water and mature in the fourth or fifth year. When mature they enter tributaries to the lake, usually in the early fall, and migrate to their spawning grounds upstream. They generally select gravel beds for spawning but are known to spawn on gravel beaches and bars when tributary streams are not available. Shortly after spawning is completed, the adults die. The newly hatched fry descend into the lakes where they spend most of their lives.

In a recent attempt to introduce a sport fish in a number of deep oligotrophic lakes, the Department of Natural Resources secured kokanee eggs from the West Coast; the resulting fingerlings were planted in Larson Lake in Itasca County and in several lakes in Cook County after potentially competitive fishes had been eliminated from the lakes to assure optimum conditions for survival and growth of the fingerlings. The results have not been encouraging, but perhaps it is too early to judge the success of the program.

The kokanee bites readily on both wet and dry flies and is reported to be a good game species. Most kokanees are caught at the start of the spawning run. In the West Coast lakes they are taken by trolling a small fly or a worm behind a spinner in deep water. Cowbell spinner combinations have also been found to be productive lures at times.

Genus *Salvelinus* Richardson

The representatives of this genus in Europe are known as chars. They are closely related to the other trout. The American species have usually borne the common name trout; our native brook trout is properly a char, and so are the lake trout and the siscowet. The Dolly Varden trout of the Rocky Mountains and the northern Pacific drainage and the Arctic char of the far northern Arctic drainage are also members of this genus. The chars have smaller scales than the trout of the genus *Salmo* and differ in a few other respects. The only species which are native to Minnesota are the brook trout, the lake trout, and the siscowet.

BROOK TROUT

Salvelinus fontinalis (Mitchill)

The brook trout (Figure 42) has a dark olive back with light marbled streaks. The sides are also dark olive, sprinkled with light spots and numerous red spots with light brown margins. The scales are very small, numbering

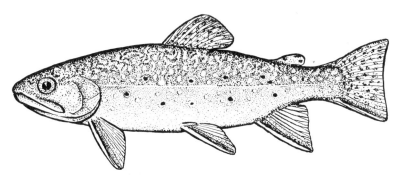

Fig. 42. Brook trout, *Salvelinus fontinalis*

about 230 in the lateral line. The caudal fin is slightly notched in the young but is square in the older trout. The dorsal fin has 10 rays, and the anal fin has 9 rays. All the fins except the dorsal fin are strongly marked on the ventral margin by a white or cream streak which is emphasized by a dark streak. The males are characterized by slightly longer pectoral and pelvic fins and by a hook at the tip of the lower jaw during the spawning season.

Although brook trout may reach a length of nearly 25 inches, the trout caught in small Minnesota streams seldom exceed 8 or 10 inches. This may be a result of the crowded environment offered by trout streams which are only 3 or 4 feet wide. Furthermore, heavy fishing pressure prevents most trout from reaching old age and the increased size that goes with it. Investigations show that brook trout in small streams are seldom more than three years of age. In small lakes they are often larger, and in the shore waters of Lake Superior they reach lengths up to 24 inches. One of the largest individuals on record was from the Nipigon River in Ontario; it was 31 1/2 inches long and weighed 14 pounds, 8 ounces.

The brook trout is a prime favorite with anglers and is a choice food fish. It is the only species of trout or char native to the cold brooks and streams of Minnesota. The species prefers clear brooks and rivers in which the mean temperature rarely exceeds 50° F. The optimum temperature is reported as ranging from 55° to 66° F. Brook trout also thrive in the small cold-water lakes of northern Minnesota, provided that suitable spawning conditions exist. In early times brook trout were commonly called speckled trout, which seems to us a far more appropriate and descriptive common name than brook trout. Large adults are referred to as squaretails.

Brook trout ranged originally through the Great Lakes region northward into Labrador and southward through the Appalachians into Georgia. They are native to certain cold-water streams in eastern Minnesota, and they have been widely introduced in similar streams elsewhere in the state. They also have been introduced successfully in small cold lakes in St. Louis, Cook, and Lake counties after competitive fishes such as perch, northern pike, and suckers were eliminated. Cox (1897) reported that brook trout were native in Minnesota streams flowing into Lake Superior. Early settlers in the area claimed that brook trout were native in several small lakes above Beaver Bay and north of Grand Marais and in some small lakes between the Baptism and Manitou rivers but that none were present in the streams above the lower falls except in the Reservation River. Brook trout were always abundant about the mouths of the rivers entering Lake Superior and along the shore. (We know that Lake Superior is now constantly restocked by trout passing downstream from above the lower falls; the upstream areas are heavily stocked, and the trout cannot pass back over the falls once they are swept below.) It is thought that brook trout were present in the many cold-water brooks entering the St. Croix River long before the streams were stocked with trout from hatcheries. Brook trout are also native to many spring-fed streams in southeastern Minnesota. In 1857 the abundance of "speckled trout" in the vicinity of Winona was advertised as an inducement for people to settle there.

Brook trout spawn from late October to December when the water temperature is 40° to 49° F, although they may start spawning in September in streams flowing into Lake Superior. The females often spawn when they are a year old and are still quite small, but some do not mature until the second year. As the spawning season approaches, they move upstream into small headwater brooks where they select gravel bottoms in shallow riffles for the spawning beds. There the female prepares a nest (a redd) by sweeping out a depression

Barrier Falls on the Baptism River, Lake County. Such falls are found on most streams tributary to the north shore of Lake Superior. Photo: William D. Schmid.

in the gravel and sand. While the female prepares the redd, the male starts a courtship, darting and quivering around the busy female and driving all intruders away. The female then takes a position close to the bottom of the redd. The male darts to her side and arches his body over her, discharging milt as the female deposits her eggs. Sometimes a second male may join them. The male deserts the female a few minutes after spawning. The eggs are adhesive and stick to pebbles in the bottom of the redd. The female pushes the loose pebbles to the center and covers the entire redd with sand. She may spawn several times, and the number of eggs varies from 90 to 4,800, depending on the size of the female. Spawning usually occurs during the day. The eggs remain in the redd without hatching until the water becomes warm the following spring. Natural hazards sometimes account for great losses of eggs. For instance, many eggs may be swept away by the current as they are laid. Other fishes and even male trout may rush in and seize some of them. After the redd is covered, however, the majority of the eggs are safe.

The redds are constructed in swift water which is seldom over a foot deep, and they are more or less exposed to the direct rays of the sun for several hours daily. Any eggs in the upper portions of the redd are killed by the exposure to

163

the sun and become covered with fungus. These eggs are usually eaten by suckers, sculpins, and other fish. It is probable that the removal of these eggs is beneficial; if they settled deeper into the gravel, the fungus might spread to the good eggs. The sculpins which are common in the spawning streams have been blamed for extensive depredation of trout spawn, but studies of the feeding habits of brook trout and sculpins (Dineen, 1951) indicate that sculpins eat only a few trout eggs (although trout eat many sculpin eggs). Dineen concluded that trout eggs are not an important part of the sculpin's diet, but he found that trout consume quite a few of their own eggs. In the stomachs of mottled sculpins and brook trout caught in several spawning areas, the trout stomachs contained many of their own eggs, while the sculpin stomachs contained only a few trout eggs, usually no more than three.

Under natural conditions newly hatched trout establish small feeding territories in the streams and feed on tiny aquatic insects and their larvae. Fingerlings and adults subsist largely on aquatic insects in the winter and any terrestrial insects that fall into or light on the water in the summer. Small fish are occasionally eaten. In some streams the amphipod *Gammarus* forms an important part of the trout's diet. In many brooks, beds of watercress support large quantities of *Gammarus* and aquatic insects. Trout often wait below these beds and feed on any organisms which are swept downstream; they also forage within the cress beds. The peak feeding times for brook trout occur in the early evening and in the morning.

In recent years hybrids between the brook trout and the lake trout have been produced in hatcheries. The hybrids, known as splake, are suitable for stocking cold waters. Like many hybrids, the splake grows faster than either parent and shows typical hybrid vigor. In an experiment with the hybrid in Minnesota, Lake Pierz in Cook County was poisoned and cleared of native fish and then stocked with splake. At present the technique of securing fertilized eggs to produce the hybrids must be improved. So far we have been forced to secure eggs from neighboring states. Although Minnesota hatcheries maintain brood stocks of both brook trout and lake trout, their eggs are not highly viable. It is possible that the hatchery water supplies are too hard chemically and that it will be necessary to build hatcheries where soft water is available. Further research on splake production is presently being carried out by personnel of the Department of Natural Resources.

Brook trout are not easy to catch, and they usually hide under logs and overhanging banks. They are extremely wary, and the angler must exercise caution, keeping out of sight as much as possible. They are most active during the early morning and in the evening and strike on both dry and wet flies. Although worms are disdained by many fishermen, brook trout are known to bite on them. Often worms are the only bait one can use in narrow brooks where the heavy overgrowth of brush, grass, and weeds makes casting impossible. The worm should be dropped into the water and allowed to float naturally downstream past the hideouts and the weed beds.

The bright orange flesh of the brook trout is a delicacy when broiled or fried. The scales are so tiny that many people are not even aware of them, and the fish are usually cooked without having been scaled. They can be eaten scales and all, or the skin can be left uneaten. There are many recipes for sauces to serve with trout, but brook trout are excellent even without them.

LAKE TROUT
Salvelinus namaycush (Walbaum)

The body color of the lake trout (Figure 43) varies greatly in intensity and ranges from slate gray to almost black, shading to gray or almost white on the belly. No colored spots are present on the body, but it is profusely covered with light spots which extend over the median fins. The body is rather slender. The head is large, and the ratio of the head length to the body length (to the base of the caudal fin) is 4 to 4.5. The mouth is large and extends past the posterior margin of the eye. There are well-developed teeth on the jaws, on the tongue (hyoid), and on the roof of the mouth (vomer). The lateral line contains from 185 to 210 scales. The caudal fin is deeply forked. All the fins are without spines. A small adipose fin is located behind the dorsal fin and has several spots. The dorsal fin and the anal fin have 11 rays. Lake trout are the largest of all Minnesota trout. In inland lakes they achieve weights of 18 to 20 pounds, and some probably exist which are even larger. However, the Minnesota record for Lake Superior is 43 pounds, 8 ounces. (A 63-pounder was caught elsewhere in Lake Superior in 1952.) The average trout caught in small inland lakes usually weighs about 3 pounds.

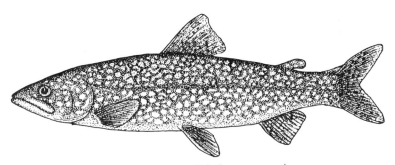

Fig. 43. Lake trout, *Salvelinus namaycush*

The lake trout has always been a popular although elusive game fish in Minnesota, and it has had various local names. Years ago many resorts in northern Minnesota advertised "landlocked salmon" fishing, referring to the abundant lake trout in their area, although the term applies only to the landlocked form of the Atlantic salmon. In the western states the lake trout is often called the Mackinaw trout.

Lake trout are distributed throughout northern North America from Alaska across Canada and south to the northern New England states. They range through the Great Lakes to the headwaters of the Fraser and Columbia rivers and have been reported from the headwater lakes of the Hudson River. The species has been widely introduced in the lakes of the Rocky Mountain region. In Minnesota lake trout are native in the deeper lakes of the northern parts of St. Louis, Lake, and Cook counties and in several lakes in Itasca and Koochiching counties. The lake trout's area of greatest abundance is Lake Superior. It is doubtful that the fish is native in any lakes in the Mississippi drainage in Minnesota, but it is known to be native in certain Minnesota lakes in the Arctic and Great Lakes drainages. Before the turn of the century the species was introduced in lakes of central and southern Minnesota, but the lakes were not suitable for lake trout and the introductions were not successful except perhaps in Lake Pokegama at Grand Rapids. It is not certain whether the lake trout in Lake Pokegama are natives or are survivors from early introductions. Cox (1897) found lake trout in Lake Pokegama, which is closely connected with the Mississippi River, and a small population replenished with hatchery stock survives there today. Some years ago Grindstone Lake in Pine County was found to contain some survivors of an early introduction, and this population also has been successfully maintained by stocking.

Lake trout are cold-water fish and do not thrive in water with temperatures over 65° F. They require rock or boulder shoals for spawning and adjacent cold water for the fry. These are probably the most important factors determining their distribution. For this reason trout lakes should be over 100 feet deep with rock or boulder shores. In such lakes oxygen is always abundant in the deeper waters because little is consumed by the scanty vegetation and the resulting organic detritus. Although the surface waters may become too warm for the trout, they can always find cold water with sufficient oxygen near the bottom. Rocky lakes of less depth, unless fed by springs or cold bog waters, often do not have a sufficient volume of cold water to carry the trout through the summer. Lake trout rarely are found in streams; along the shores of Lake Superior they may enter the mouths of streams, but they seldom travel upstream very far.

The adult trout spend much of the year in the deepest waters of the lake, but in the fall and the spring they may be found in shallower water. In Lake Superior, where the surface water never becomes very warm, they can be found at all depths down to about 600 feet in the summer, although as the summer progresses they are most abundant in the deeper water. In the fall as spawning season approaches they move in toward the shore and congregate on the rocky reefs. Tagged trout have been found to range over an area of about 30 miles, although some travel up to 200 miles. Fin-clipped trout recently stocked in Lake Superior in an effort to reestablish the sport fishery there have been taken throughout the lake.

Spawning occurs in the fall, usually from late September or early October until late November or early December, depending on the weather. The optimum water temperature for spawning is near 40° F. In small inland lakes the lake trout usually spawn just before the ice forms. Most spawning occurs on rocky reefs or boulder rubble at depths varying from 3 to 260 feet. Reports indicate that in some of the Great Lakes the trout spawn on hard clay bottoms as deep as 300 feet. On the Canadian shore at the east end of Lake Superior they spawn in the lower reaches of several streams. Lake trout produce about 750 eggs per pound of fish, and the average is estimated at about 6,000 eggs per fish. The eggs are large and hatch in about 16 to 20 weeks, depending on the temperature; no care is given to them by the parents.

The newly hatched fry feed largely on plankton and grow slowly. They soon change to a diet of larger crustaceans including *Mysis*, *Pontoporeia*, and similar forms. The adult trout are usually piscivorous, feeding extensively on other fishes. In Lake Superior they rely on ciscoes, fourhorn sculpins, burbot, and smelt. In inland lakes their diet consists of a large variety of aquatic insects and small fishes such as ciscoes which range into the deeper water. Some lake trout populations are reported to depend heavily on plankton for food. The flesh of the trout varies from light red or deep pink to almost white in various lakes. The cause of this variation in flesh color has been attributed to several factors. Some researchers claim it is hereditary; others feel it is related to diet and that trout which eat large quantities of crustaceans have orange-colored flesh. The carotenoids derived from algal-feeding entomostracans are thought to cause the red or pink color of the salmon's flesh.

The most common method of fishing for lake trout in Minnesota is by trolling a spoon lure with a heavy sinker to keep the lure at the desired depth. In the inland lakes the fisherman should troll at depths of 30 feet in June to 70 feet in July. In Lake Superior, trout will sometimes strike at depths of only a few feet and sometimes, especially in July, at depths down to 200 feet. Lake trout strike hard and put up considerable resistance when brought to the surface, but they seldom leap and clear the surface. Still-fishing with live minnows at depths of about 70 feet is sometimes successful in inland lakes during the summer. Some fishermen are successful in casting flies or other lures in shallow water in the spring, and Underhill can attest to the great fight the lake trout puts up on light fly-fishing tackle. With the development of surf-casting spinning gear it is possible to cast off the mouths of most streams on the north shore of Lake Superior and to catch a limit of lake trout with little difficulty. Lake Superior may lack a surf, but surf casting is a very successful fishing technique for all the salmonids present in the lake and especially for the lake trout cruising near the river mouths.

Lake trout were caught and sold commercially in large numbers from Lake Superior until their populations were decimated by the sea lamprey and perhaps pollution. In 1942 the commercial catch in the United States waters of Lake Superior was reported to be about 3,000,000 pounds. The yield dropped in the following years until it was no longer profitable to operate the fishing boats and the expensive equipment. The commercial fishermen used motorized fishing boats to work fishing areas that were as much as twenty miles offshore, well beyond the range of sport fishing. The fish were usually caught in large-mesh gill nets set at depths down to 100 fathoms. Usually thousands of feet of net were set; the nets were run only once or twice a week because the cold water preserved any fish that died after entering the nets. Trout were also caught on long gangs of setlines (with small ciscoes for bait) extending for miles offshore.

SISCOWET

Salvelinus siscowet (Agassiz)

The siscowet (Figure 44), locally called the fat trout along the Minnesota shore of Lake Superior, is a close relative of the lake trout. It lives at depths of 300 fathoms and seldom occurs in water less than 100 fathoms deep. Although the siscowet is quite common in Lake Superior, it may also occur in

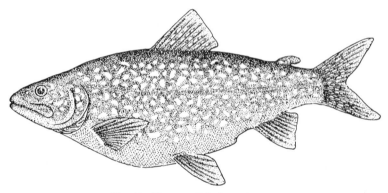

Fig. 44. Siscowet, *Salvelinus siscowet*

some of the other Great Lakes. The siscowet tends to be lighter in color and to have smaller spots than the lake trout. It has a deep layer of fat lining the body wall and covering most of the viscera, which accounts in part for the great depth of the body anterior to the dorsal fin. The depth and body length ratio of the adult siscowet ranges from 3.1 to 3.8, whereas the ratio is from 4.1 to 4.8 in the adult lake trout. The depressed and extended belly causes the vent aperture of the siscowet to be directed posteriorly instead of ventrally as in the lake trout. The scales of the siscowet are larger than those of the lake trout; the siscowet has from 163 to 183 scales in the lateral line, whereas the lake trout usually has from 195 to 218. There seems to be little difference between the two species in the number of scales above and below the lateral line, although the body of the siscowet is appreciably deeper. We have no information on the effect of the lamprey on the siscowet.

The siscowet was first described by Agassiz in 1850 as a distinct species, but it has since been regarded as a peculiar form of the lake trout, which it resembles in many ways. Some workers treat it as a separate subspecies. Since it differs in several characters from the typical lake trout, it is quite evident that the siscowet can be regarded as a distinct species. Most of the siscowets in the University of Minnesota collection were taken along with typical lake trout in gill nets at depths of 80 to 100 fathoms in Lake Superior about twenty miles off Grand Marais. Although the species live together, they have retained their distinctive characters. It is true, however, that small individuals of these species are sometimes difficult to distinguish from each other, and in early studies it was thought that they might be intergrades. Commercial fishermen have long regarded these small trout as half-breeds and have often marketed them as typical lake trout. It is possible that hybrids can occur; in 1923 R. G. Gale of the Minnesota Department of Conservation successfully fertilized siscowet eggs with milt from a lake trout and reared the resulting hybrids to an age of one year. Unfortunately all the hybrids were released and none were available for further study.

Slastenenko (1958) gives the siscowet specific rank and presents comparative measurements and other data for the siscowet and the lake trout. In some respects, such as in the number of branchiostegals, gill rakers, pyloric appendages, and vertebrae, the data overlap or fall within the same range so that only the means are significantly different — and means are of little help in distinguishing individual fish. Slastenenko considers the head of the siscowet to be shorter and smaller and the snout shorter and more blunt than those of the lake trout, but we find much individual variation in both species. He reports that there are 14 or 15 pectoral rays in the siscowet and 12 or 13 pectoral rays in the lake trout. He also indicates that the fins of the lake trout are larger than those of the siscowet, but here again we have noted considerable variation in fin size in both species. Thurston (1962) mentions significant differences in the oil and fat contents of the lean (lake trout) and fat (siscowet) types; the means for his samples were 9.4 percent and 48.5 percent, respectively. Of further significance is the fact that there is no overlap in the oil, moisture, or protein concentrations in the two types. According to Thurston, another unusual feature of siscowets is that they do not "blow up" when taken from depths of 100 fathoms, while lake trout taken from depths of 40 fathoms commonly are ready to burst when they reach the surface. Finally, the stomach of the siscowet appears to be much smaller than that of the lake trout (Thurston, 1962). There seems little doubt that the siscowet is a distinct species and that it is not a variation or a subspecies of the lake trout maintained by environment, diet, or some unknown factor as has long been believed. The siscowet may represent a Pleistocene relict from the periglacial lakes which has survived to modern times only in Lake Superior.

Little is known about the habits of the siscowet, although they are probably similar to those of the lake trout. The two species are separated spatially in Lake Superior (Khan and Qadri, 1970). Siscowets are reported to spawn earlier than lake trout, sometimes even in June, and to continue into November. They have not been found to spawn on the relatively shallow spawning beds of the lake trout, which suggests that they spawn in deeper water. The growth rate is apparently about the same for both species. Siscowets reach a large size; individuals weighing up to 40 pounds are not uncommon in Lake Superior, and there are reports of specimens weighing as much as 100 pounds.

Siscowets feed mostly on deep-water fishes such as coregonids, sculpins, and occasionally burbot and longnose suckers. The stomachs of forty-two of forty-four specimens taken at 100 fathoms off Grand Marais in 1946 contained food: eighteen contained small coregonids (*Coregonus hoyi* and *C. kiyi*); two contained larger coregonids (probably *C. zenithicus*, which is common at that depth); twenty-five contained one or more fourhorn sculpins (*Myoxocephalus quadricornis*); and fourteen contained eggs of this sculpin. Some of the eggs may have been released from the ingested sculpins, but one stomach contained nothing but eggs. A number of stomachs contained small pebbles. Siscowets feed also on insects floating on the surface (Thurston, 1962).

Siscowets do not rank highly as game fish, partly because they live at such great depths that it is difficult for anglers to reach them. They are commonly taken by commercial fishermen in gill nets set for lake trout at 80 to 100 fathoms. Their flesh is so soft and oily that they are not utilized locally for food. When commercial fishing for lake trout was profitable, the fishermen sold the siscowets in their catch of lake trout to be brined, smoked, and marketed in the East.

Genus *Salmo* (Linnaeus)

The species of the genus *Salmo* include the Atlantic salmon and several of Minnesota's introduced stream trout. (The brook trout and the lake trout, however, are chars and belong to the genus *Salvelinus*, as discussed earlier in this chapter.) The species of this genus are regarded as the true trout. They are characterized by a flat vomer in the roof of the mouth bearing two rows of teeth on the shaft and by relatively large scales with fewer than 200 scales in the lateral line.

RAINBOW TROUT

Salmo gairdneri Richardson

The rainbow trout (Figure 45) is bluish or olive green above and silvery on the sides, with a broad pink lateral stripe. The back, the sides, and the dorsal and caudal fins are profusely dotted with small dark spots. The scales are large, numbering 120 to 150 in the lateral line. The caudal fin is very slightly forked. The dorsal fin has 11 rays, and the anal fin has from 10 to 12 rays. Some western varieties weigh up to 50 pounds, but the Minnesota rainbows are much smaller. Those in the streams are rarely over 3 pounds; in Lake Superior and in a few inland lakes they are often larger and may reach 15 pounds.

The rainbow trout is native to the streams of the Pacific coast where many varieties or subspecies have developed. The seagoing form is known as the steelhead trout and is thought to be identical to the strictly freshwater rainbow trout. Many other strains and subspecies are found in other West Coast watersheds. Because of the ease with which the eggs of the rainbow trout can be transported, different strains have been distributed all over the world.

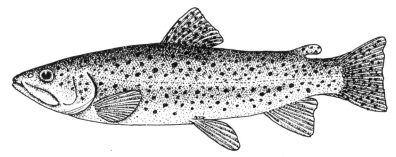

Fig. 45. Rainbow trout, *Salmo gairdneri*

Rainbow trout were among the first fishes to be introduced and stocked in Minnesota nearly ninety years ago. Early introductions of the Shasta rainbow trout (*S. gairdneri stonei*) were made in Minnesota and Wisconsin. Somewhat later steelhead trout (migratory rainbows) were successfully introduced, and they very shortly replaced the earlier Shasta plantings. The steelheads have thrived in Lake Superior as a result of the stocking of tributary streams; once the trout in the streams have passed over the low barrier falls to reach the lake, they are unable to make their way back up the streams. They are very important in the Lake Superior fishery, and they are also important in the fall and spring sport fishery in the mouths of the streams. The steelheads are a spring-spawning strain but may enter the streams in either late fall or early spring. There is evidence that the steelheads range along the shore of Lake Superior and may enter several stream mouths before they select one in which to spawn. Trout of the steelhead strain have been introduced into some small deep lakes in northern St. Louis County and have been very successful, but efforts to maintain resident populations in streams have often ended in failure.

Great success in the development of a stream rainbow trout was achieved later by the introduction of a Missouri strain less prone to migration than the steelhead. Instead of spawning in the spring as is characteristic of other rainbow strains, the Missouri strain spawns from late October until early February. Another bonus associated with the Missouri fish is their ability to adapt to warm-water streams. Until the great drought of the early 1930s, this strain was doing splendidly in several streams in which the summer water temperatures rise to 85° F, which is well beyond the lethal temperature for the brown trout and the brook trout. However, during the protracted drought

many of the streams almost stopped flowing and were deserted by fish of all ,
kinds. The most successful attempt to acclimatize the Missouri strain was in
the Cannon River, where it lived in apparent harmony with smallmouth bass
and even carp until low water levels and pollution ended their existence.

The greatest difficulty with the stocking of rainbows for local angling is
their propensity to migrate from the stream where they were stocked. For
example, during the period of high water in the spring the rainbows in the
Root River system often travel many miles downstream into the Mississippi
River, and commercial fishermen in northern Iowa sometimes take them in
their nets. Consequently in recent years the stocking of rainbows has been
mostly confined to the cold-water lakes of northeastern and north central
Minnesota. Rainbow trout have been stocked in several of the tributaries of
the Red River, such as the Clearwater River in Beltrami and Clearwater
counties, where they appear to be doing fairly well.

Recently the famous Kamloops strain from Washington has been introduced into Minnesota. This form is reputed to reach the enormous weight of
50 pounds. It thrives at higher temperatures than most rainbows, and it is
supposed to be less migratory in its behavior. In 1969 the Minnesota Department of Conservation obtained 70,000 eggs which were hatched at the St.
Paul hatchery. Some of the fry were reared in a cooperatively managed pond
at Fergus Falls. Approximately 300 of these were retained at the hatchery and
150 of the best were sent to the hatchery in Spiro Valley to be kept as brood
stock. Although only 1 1/2 years old, they averaged over 4 pounds. If the
Kamloops strain lives up to its reputation, the future production of this fish
should be a tremendous asset to Minnesota's sport fishery.

The natural spawning activities of the rainbow trout are quite similar to
those of the brook trout. As the spawning season approaches, the males
develop a kype on the lower jaw. Both males and females move upstream to
shallow sand and gravel areas in the headwaters; if confined to lakes, they
move into shallow shoals or reefs of sand and gravel. The female sweeps out a
depression for a redd. Accompanied by one or two males, she deposits her
eggs, which are then fertilized by the males. After spawning, the female
covers the eggs with gravel and sand. She may spawn more than once, and the
number of eggs produced ranges from 400 to 3,000, depending on the size of
the female. The duration of spawning varies with the number of eggs carried
by the gravid female. If spawning occurs in the late fall or in the winter, the
eggs do not hatch until early spring; if spawned in the spring, they hatch by
early July. Our observations indicate that most spawning occurs in the spring.

The cold-water Minnesota hatcheries maintain brood stock from which
eggs and milt are stripped; the fertilized eggs are hatched in trays in running
water. The eggs are kept at a temperature of 50° F or slightly lower. When
they are nearly ready to hatch, they are placed in hatching troughs. The young
hatch in about fifty days and then are placed in rearing troughs or ponds where
they are fed a special diet containing essential vitamins and minerals. Under
such optimum conditions the young fish grow rapidly and reach lengths of 6 to

12 inches in sixteen months. Some of the young are planted as fingerlings, but others are raised to 6 or 8 inches and are planted just before the opening of the trout season and at intervals thereafter. As with other stream trout, the heavy trout fishing pressure on rainbow trout necessitates constant restocking. Many streams close to large metropolitan areas are managed on what is referred to as a "put and take" basis. This is an excellent management procedure which provides maximum recreation and which at the same time minimizes natural mortality.

Wild trout or trout resulting from natural reproduction grow less rapidly than their hatchery relatives. Some estimates indicate that wild trout in Minnesota reach an average length of 4.9 inches the first year, 9.1 inches the second year, and 20.5 inches at the end of the fifth year of life. First-year rainbow trout hatched in the Devil Track or Baptism rivers may be only 2 or 3 inches long. When hatched under wild or natural conditions, the newly hatched trout feed on any tiny animal life available. As they grow older, they feed extensively on small aquatic insects and small crustaceans. The adult trout feed on a wider variety of foods, including fishes such as minnows, sticklebacks, small whitefish, cottids, small perch, and even other trout.

Many anglers regard the rainbow trout as Minnesota's most popular trout species. The best fishing for large rainbows or steelheads is along the north shore of Lake Superior from the Lester River to the Canadian border. The techniques used to catch rainbows are quite varied, and each fisherman has his own favorite method. Some prefer to cast off the mouths of the tributary streams, while others swear by trolling with spinners or spoons just off the shore adjacent to the river mouths. Some of the largest brook trout, brown trout, and rainbow trout have been taken in this manner. In 1970 a steelhead weighing 15 pounds, 7 ounces, was caught in Lake Superior near Beaver Bay. Recent catches from Lake Superior provide encouraging signs of the return of the productive and popular "deep sea" sport fishery in the Minnesota waters of the lake.

Along the shores of lakes and in streams rainbows strike on both dry and wet flies. In small lakes they bite on spinners and spoons. (In Montana on an impoundment of the upper Missouri River Eddy caught rainbows by trolling with daredevil spoons in water warm enough for the carp which were "playing" all along the shore.) A spinner combination baited with minnows, cut bait, floss, or worms is often very good for trolling in small lakes. Within the past couple of decades salmon eggs tied in cheesecloth bags and weighted down with lead sinkers have become an important bait. Sometimes fresh roe from a recently caught female steelhead are used instead of preserved salmon eggs. The roe can be frozen and stored for successive fishing trips. In fishing for steelheads, particularly in the spring, the usual technique is to cast upstream to the foot of some rapids and to allow the bait or the lure to bump along the bottom, keeping a fairly tight line until the bait has passed through the pool. Then the whole procedure is repeated, casting in such a way that the bait will follow a slightly different course through the pool. Patience is the key to successful steelhead or spring-run rainbow fishing, and veteran fishermen may spend half a day or more fishing a single pool. The fisherman must be prepared to lose his baits to snags and to be cautious when this happens because sometimes the presumed snag is his rainbow!

Once hooked, the rainbow or steelhead is the most terrific of all fighters. It may sulk in the pool and be stimulated to run only by the fisherman's tapping on the butt of his rod, and then without a moment's notice it may make a tremendous dash upstream and explode from the water, shaking its head and body vigorously. The fish may jump six or seven times in rapid succession; unless the angler is experienced and able to maintain his composure after viewing his prize (the weight of which is usually magnified in the mind of the angler), the fight may end with the fish breaking the line or throwing off the hook. If this strategy fails to free the fish, it may return to sulk in the current in the shelter of a submerged boulder, or it may make a dash toward the foot of the pool and attempt to escape into the rapids below. If the fish chooses the latter stratagem, the angler must decide quickly either to turn the fish before it reaches the lip of the pool or to race with the fish downstream through the rapids to the next pool. The latter is no mean feat in the high waters of such streams as the Baptism, Split Rock, Devil Track, and Brule rivers. A rule of thumb is to keep the fish upstream so that it must fight the current plus the pressure of the line. The spring trout fisherman might find it useful to visit his favorite streams in the late summer or in the fall and to make note of where the boulders and pockets are located in the various pools so that he will have a better idea of where the fish will be in the high waters the following spring.

Once the water levels drop in late May and early June, a different fishing technique may be used. Large streamers, wet flies, and occasionally dry flies may attract large rainbows at this time. Most of the rainbows migrate back to Lake Superior after they have spawned, but in some years they are stranded by low waters and are forced to remain in the stream until a storm brings water levels back to the stage where the large fish can negotiate the rapids. Under just such conditions Underhill and several of his companions caught eleven rainbows ranging from 4 to 9 pounds in the Baptism River.

Fall-run rainbows provide equal excitement, and similar fishing techniques are used. The fish usually begin to run into the mouths of the Lake Superior streams after the first fall rains when the gravel bars at the mouths have been breached by higher water levels. If you wish to test your skill as an angler, try fishing with ultralight spinning gear; large rainbows will take a 0 Mepps spinner. Be prepared to lose many fish. To many anglers fall fishing in the north shore streams is the ultimate sport because rainbows, brook trout, and brown trout are all available and soon the coho may be added to the list. Fall fishing is more relaxed than spring fishing; there are fewer competitors and they are confirmed trout fishermen. Your hands may freeze, ice may plug the guides, and you may have to carry two reels, but the unique aspects of fall fishing are well worth the effort. Under the recently revised regulations the mouths of many north shore streams are open for fishing all year.

As we mentioned earlier, stream rainbow trout can be taken with flies, spinners, or live bait. Fishing in the smaller streams is best with a fly rod or ultralight spinning gear. In fly fishing the usual technique is to cast upstream and to allow the fly to drift naturally with the current, stripping in the slack line. Either wet or dry flies may be used. Many veteran fly fishermen use nymphs to match the natural larvae and dry flies to imitate the newly metamorphosed adults. To many trout fishermen dry-fly fishing is the ultimate in angling. Stream rainbows are also attracted by streamers, which presumably resemble small minnows, and by small spinners. These lures should also be fished upstream and retrieved in such a way that they give the impression of a darting fish or a wounded minnow. If you take a few moments to observe small fish in a stream, you will notice that the initial reaction of a startled fish is to make a short dash downstream. The angler should attempt to imitate this when he presents the lure or the bait.

CUTTHROAT TROUT

Salmo clarki lewisi (Girard)

The cutthroat trout, like the rainbow trout, is silver gray in color with black spots profusely scattered over the body and the sides. The dorsal and caudal fins are also heavily spotted. The body may have a rosy tinge, but the cutthroat lacks the prominent reddish streak on the side that is characteristic of the rainbow (*S. gairdneri*). The species gets its common name from the very pronounced red streaks present along the underside of each side of the jaw.

Cutthroats are native to streams of the Pacific coast and the Rocky Mountain region. Various attempts have been made to introduce the species into Minnesota waters but with no success.

ATLANTIC SALMON

Salmo salar Linnaeus

The Atlantic salmon is steel blue or brownish in color above and has silvery sides. Numerous small black spots are present on the body and the head and often on the dorsal and anal fins. The spots frequently are in the form of a small X. The caudal fin is moderately forked. The dorsal fin has 10 to 12 rays, and the anal fin has 8 to 10 rays. The lateral line contains from 106 to 125 scales. The juveniles have 7 to 12 vertical parr marks on their sides.

The young Atlantic salmon remain in the headwaters of the stream where they hatch for a year or two or until they are 5 or 6 inches long. At this stage they are called smolts. Then they migrate to the sea where they mature in three to five years. After their first year at sea they are called grilse. The mature salmon move up the rivers in late summer or early fall to spawn when the water temperature reaches about 43° F. The eggs are deposited in prepared beds of gravel and hatch the following spring. Atlantic salmon, unlike Pacific salmon, do not die after spawning but return to the sea. They may spawn again each season for several years. Juvenile Atlantic salmon usually feed on a diet of entomostracans, amphipods, and small fish, while the adults feed primarily on various species of smelts and small herring.

The Atlantic salmon sometimes reach a weight of 60 pounds, and there is a record of a 100-pound monster taken in the British Isles many years ago. Most of those now caught are much smaller. The species has become landlocked in several lakes in Maine, where it is known as the sebago salmon, and also in eastern Canada, where it is known as the ouananiche. These landlocked forms reach a weight of 3 to 10 pounds and have been considered by some workers to be a distinct subspecies (*Salmo salar sebago* Girard).

The Atlantic salmon is native to the Atlantic ocean. It was originally found from the Delaware River northward into Labrador. Dams, pollution, lumbering, and commercial exploitation have brought about its extinction except in areas from Maine northward. At present the species also ranges into the waters of Greenland, the Scandinavian countries, Ireland, and Scotland. In Scotland it has been a popular game fish for centuries, and in earlier times it was reserved for the nobility and the landed gentry. Even in Scotland, where there has been great concern for the preservation of the salmon populations, the salmon runs have declined and in certain rivers they have disappeared. As mentioned earlier, in many of the Scottish salmon streams leases for fishing rights cost thousands of dollars, and salmon fishing tends to be a sport for the wealthy.

Recently commercial fishermen have found concentrations of Atlantic salmon off Greenland, and they are taking large numbers of adults. Before this, commercial fishing for the species was restricted to harvesting fish on their entry into the spawning streams. Such fishing was regulated by federal laws. Regulation in international waters is extremely difficult, however, and there is a fear that overfishing may seriously deplete the already reduced Atlantic salmon stock. In addition to undertaking a very detailed study of the Atlantic salmon, the Canadian government is doing a most remarkable job in cleaning up the salmon rivers and in creating artificial spawning grounds in streams where hydroelectric plants have been constructed. In the United States the Atlantic salmon may benefit greatly as a result of water quality laws. For instance, Atlantic salmon have been reported from streams in New England where they have not been seen for a century or more. Nevertheless, this work may be for naught if we fail to regulate the fishing in international waters.

Many attempts have been made in the past to introduce the Atlantic salmon into Minnesota. Beginning in 1881 it was introduced into many streams and various deep lakes in Ramsey, Rice, Hennepin, Dakota, and other counties. Although several hundred thousand salmon were planted over a period of ten years, there are no records of any adults ever being taken. At the same time attempts were made to introduce one form of the landlocked Atlantic salmon, the ouananiche, into central and southern Minnesota. In 1912 and 1913 they were introduced into Burnside Lake in St. Louis County with no success. In more recent years some have been introduced into Lake Superior, and we have had reports of occasional individual salmon taken by fishermen in the

Wisconsin waters of the lake. Large and very old brown trout resemble the Atlantic salmon so closely that many of them are mistaken for Atlantic salmon. Many years ago Underhill saw a fish taken from the Brule River in Wisconsin which very closely resembled a salmon, but that fish ended up in the frying pan instead of in the laboratory. To the best of our knowledge no form of Atlantic salmon exists at this time in Minnesota waters.

BROWN TROUT

Salmo trutta Linnaeus

The brown trout (Figure 46) is olive brown or greenish, shading to a yellowish white on the belly. The sides are covered with rather large dark spots often interspersed with large red or orange spots with pale margins. Many dark spots are present on the dorsal fin, while the caudal fin has only a few dark spots confined to the upper portion. The latter character readily distinguishes the brown trout from the rainbow trout, in which the caudal fin is profusely covered with spots. The pelvic and anal fins of the brown trout have a yellowish edge on the lower or front margins. The brown trout is also distinguished from the brook trout by the absence of wormlike streaks or vermiculations on its back and the presence of dark spots instead of light spots on the sides. The scales are also larger, numbering about 115 to 150 in the lateral line.

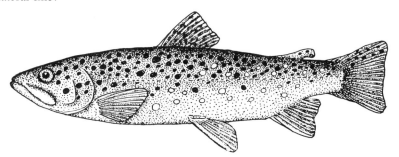

Fig. 46. Brown trout, *Salmo trutta* (adult)

In old individuals the body color becomes silvery, and the large dark spots on the sides may become reduced to small blotches or crosses. (The brown trout in Lake Superior may be so silvery that the spots and dark blotches are not evident until the specimens have faded in the creel.) Spawning males, particularly among stream trout, are brightly colored with reddish sides, and they develop a hook or kype at the tip of the lower jaw.

Brown trout in Minnesota waters seldom weigh more than 12 pounds, but weights up to 30 pounds and lengths of 3 feet have been reported elsewhere. In common with other stream trout, the largest brown trout are found in the shore waters of Lake Superior, where their numbers are constantly replenished from natural reproduction in the stream mouths and from trout planted by the Department of Natural Resources in the tributary streams. A brown trout weighing 29 pounds, 9 ounces, caught near Bayfield, Wisconsin, in 1970, represents the United States record. The world record brown trout was taken more than a century ago in Loch Awe, Scotland; it weighed 39 pounds, 8 ounces. The largest brown trout recorded in Minnesota was from Grindstone Lake in Pine County and weighed 14 pounds, 8 ounces.

The brown trout is one of three species of stream trout which are commonly stocked and maintained in the cold-water streams and lakes of Minnesota. This trout was introduced into the United States from Europe in 1883 and immediately became popular because of its rapid growth, gamey habits, and ability to survive under conditions that are marginal for other trout species. The Continental brown trout is known as the German brown trout, while the brown trout from the British Isles is known as the Loch Leven or Scotch brown trout. For all practical purposes these are the same species although the population from the British Isles has been isolated for several thousand years from its mainland relatives and at least six different subspecies have been recognized by European ichthyologists. In a very informative book on trout Frost and Brown (1967) have discussed the biology of the brown trout in the British Isles and in Europe. It is quite possible that the fish that have been stocked in Minnesota streams and lakes are actually a mixture of German brown trout and Loch Leven trout and are best referred to simply as brown trout. We are not certain when the brown trout was first introduced into Minnesota because eggs were secured at various times from federal hatcheries. Eggs of the Loch Leven strain were first secured in 1923 from federal hatcheries in Montana, and the fry reared from these eggs were planted with the fry of the already established German strain.

The spawning habits of the brown trout are similar to those of the brook trout. The adults mature at about three or four years of age. They spawn in the fall from October into December, ascending streams to the shallow headwater brooks. Every fall they congregate in the lower stretches of the streams tributary to Lake Superior along the north shore, but they are prevented from migrating farther upstream by the barrier falls. In Lake Superior and perhaps other lakes they are purported to spawn on sand and gravel bars at the mouths of the tributaries where there are barriers to migration or where the tributaries are too small. The female prepares the redd by making a depression in the sand and gravel bottom. The male and female then position themselves over the redd, the male brings his vent in close proximity to that of the female, and the pair vibrates vigorously. As the eggs are released, the male simultaneously releases milt. The eggs are fertilized externally and settle into the gravel in the floor of the nest. The female stirs up the bottom of the redd to cover the eggs, and then the pair repeats the egg-laying until the female is spent. The fertilized eggs generally settle to the bottom, while those that are not fertilized are swept away by the current. The nest is then deserted, and the eggs are left to develop and to hatch the following spring. Under the constant temperatures in the hatchery brown trout eggs hatch in 48 to 55 days, but it takes longer when they are subjected to the colder temperatures of streams. The young fish (Figure 47) grow rapidly and reach a length of 7 to 10 inches during their first year of life if food conditions and water temperatures are optimum.

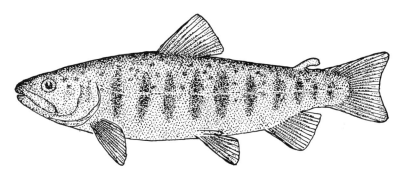

Fig. 47. Brown trout, *Salmo trutta* (juvenile). Typical parr marks on side of body.

The young brown trout feed on small crustaceans and aquatic insects, but as they grow they begin to eat larger forms such as terrestrial insects from the surface of the water. Brown trout reared in hatcheries are fed prepared diets that maximize growth or at least allow them to approach their genetic potential for growth. The large stream trout feed on all sorts of insects, worms, small clams, snails, crayfish, and small fish. On one occasion Underhill caught a 14-inch brown trout that contained seven medium-sized crayfish. The telson or tail of the last victim was still protruding from the esophagus, yet the glutton tried to take an imitation minnow. Frost and Brown (1967) concluded that it is impossible to present a complete picture of how and why trout food varies in quantity and quality from place to place and from time to time. Mayflies, stone flies, alderflies, caddis flies, and midges make up a great portion of the trout's diet, and artificial nymphs and flies resembling the natural insects are usually the most successful lures. Sometimes examining the stomachs of fresh-caught brown trout will give the angler a clue to what fly or nymph to use to match items in the natural diet.

Brown trout are not considered to be as delicately flavored as brook trout, but they have the advantage of growing faster and usually to a larger size. Brown trout are more wary and less vulnerable to angling than brook trout. They rise readily to both wet and dry flies and put up spectacular battles once hooked. Spinners in combination with live baits such as worms or minnows are sometimes successful with large individuals. They are most active in the early morning and in the evening. Sultry oppressive days with threatening storms or soft warm drizzles are ideal times to visit a pool that is home for a big brown trout; on such days the wariest browns seem to strike with abandon.

Why there is such a dramatic behavior change is not clear, but it perhaps has to do with the abundant food supply, including terrestrial insects, associated with the runoff from the stream banks. In states where fishing after 11:00 P.M. is legal, fishing after dark and into the early morning produces good results, particularly with large brown trout. In Minnesota the fishing hours for trout (except lake trout) on all waters are from one hour before sunrise to 11:00 P.M. Patience is the key to success and generally a large trout will remain in the same pool throughout the summer and from year to year until he is finally caught or he dies of old age.

SUBFAMILY COREGONINAE

The whitefish species grouped in this subfamily include some of Minnesota's more valuable fishes. The importance of the whitefish group was recognized over two hundred and fifty years ago when the Jesuit missionary Claude Dablon described the wonderful qualities of the Lake Superior whitefish which the Indians caught at Sault Sainte Marie; the good father subsequently established a mission there. Many early explorers described what seemed to be an inexhaustible supply of whitefish and related species in the Great Lakes. This abundance of fine food available for the catching was one of the inducements used in advertising the area for future settlement.

Some of the earliest attempts at fish planting in Minnesota took place ninety years ago when efforts were made to plant whitefish species in various southern Minnesota lakes. In recent years much attention has been devoted to the propagation of game fishes, but the whitefishes have not been entirely neglected; state and federal hatcheries have continued until recently to propagate and distribute fry annually.

The members of the whitefish group include the whitefish, the lake herring or cisco, and a number of related species. They have often been considered as a separate family (Coregonidae), but they are currently included as a subfamily in the salmon family (Salmonidae). Whitefish possess a small soft dorsal fin and a rayless adipose fin which is located near the base of the caudal fin. In general they are fall spawners. They differ from trout and salmon in having feeble teeth and much larger scales. Their gill rakers are usually longer and finer than those of trout and are better adapted for straining microscopic plankton crustaceans from the water for their food. Because of their ability to feed on small pelagic crustaceans, many species in this group native to Lake Superior are independent of the bottom and the shore and lead a pelagic or open-water existence. Consequently fishes such as the lake trout which prey on whitefish also live far out in the open waters.

All members of the whitefish group are cold-water fishes. They are found in the open waters of the large lakes of North America, Europe, the British Isles, and Asia. In the Arctic and the western part of the United States several species are found in streams, but in Minnesota they are entirely confined to lakes except for a few spawning runs into large tributary streams.

Genus *Prosopium* Milner

Members of the genus *Prosopium* have a single round flap between the nostrils instead of two as in the genus *Coregonus*. The juveniles have parr marks on the sides of the body. The genus is represented in the Minnesota waters of Lake Superior by two species.

ROUND WHITEFISH
Prosopium cylindraceum (Pallas)

The round whitefish (Figure 48) is a rather slender ovate fish with silvery sides and a bronze back which is darker than that of other members of this group. The snout is sharper than that of the lake whitefish (*Coregonus clupeaformis*); the mouth is subterminal. Only a single flap is present between the openings of the nostrils. The premaxillary is greater in width than in length as in the whitefish. The maxillary does not extend all the way to the eye. The premaxillary is usually contained more than 3.8 times in the head length. The mandible is contained more than 3.8 times in the head length. No vestigial teeth are present. The gill rakers number 15 to 20. During the spawning season small tubercles or pearl organs are developed on the sides of both sexes. The young all have parr marks on their sides.

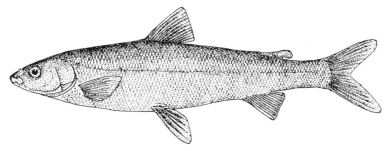

Fig. 48. Round whitefish, *Prosopium cylindraceum*

The round whitefish is distributed from northern New England through the Great Lakes and Canada into Alaska and intergrades with a similar form in Siberia. The species is found in Lake Superior, but it is not as abundant as the lake whitefish and the cisco. Apparently round whitefish do not range far out into the lake or go very deep; they usually travel in schools not very far offshore. A few are caught occasionally in the nets set for herring.

Round whitefish spawn in late November or early December on shoals or on bars at the mouths of the tributary streams. They prefer to spawn on gravel and rock bottoms at depths of 12 to 35 feet. Koelz reported them spawning at the mouths of the Devil Track and Cascade rivers. Surber found them spawning in considerable numbers in shallow waters off the mouth of the French River in 1933. The eggs are large for a member of this group and average 21,300 per quart with a diameter of about 0.15 inch.

Although an excellent food fish, the round whitefish is not sufficiently abundant to be of great commercial value. Those caught by local fishermen are usually reserved for their own consumption.

PYGMY WHITEFISH

Prosopium coulteri (Eigenmann and Eigenmann)

The pygmy whitefish (Figure 49), the smallest member of the whitefish subfamily, usually is about 3 or 4 inches long, although a few reach a length of 6 inches. It is dull silver in color with a dark back. Young individuals bear a row of parr marks on their sides. The head is similar to that of the round whitefish with the premaxillary extending downward and backward. The snout is rather short and blunt. The mouth is subterminal, and the maxillary reaches back to the eye. The nostrils have a single flap as in the round whitefish. Teeth are present only on the tongue. The scales are large, numbering 54 to 74 in the lateral line.

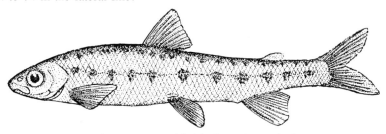

Fig. 49. Pygmy whitefish, *Prosopium coulteri*

The pygmy whitefish is well known on the Pacific coast, where it is found from the headwaters of the Columbia River into Alaska. Its presence in Minnesota waters was not known until the species was taken by trawling expeditions of the United States Fish and Wildlife Service in Lake Superior in 1953 (Eschmeyer and Bailey, 1955). The specimens from Lake Superior were found at depths of 60 to 300 feet, but young fish have been taken in shallower water. The presence of the pygmy whitefish was probably overlooked because its small size allowed it to escape from the large-mesh gill nets which have always been the chief fishing gear used in the lake at such depths. The fact that the pygmy whitefish is found so far from its previously known range suggests that it may be a glacial relict that has managed to survive in Lake Superior.

The pygmy whitefish matures in as little as two years and spawns in shallow water usually late in the fall. Its growth has been reported to be very slow; it may take five years for a fish to reach a length of 5 inches. The young usually feed on very small crustaceans and insect larvae, and the adults feed on a similar diet of larger forms. An examination of the stomach contents of a number of specimens showed mostly bottom crustaceans, primarily *Pontoporeia*, a few entomostracans, and midge larvae (about 9 percent by volume).

Genus *Coregonus* Linnaeus

Members of this genus are characterized by two flaps between the nostrils and by the lack of parr marks in juveniles. Two subgenera are present in Minnesota: *Leucichthys* includes the cisco and the tullibee, and *Coregonus* is represented by the whitefish. The biology, systematics, and anatomy of the subgenera found in Minnesota and of the other species in this very diverse and plastic group of fishes was the subject of a recent symposium (Lindsey and Woods, 1970). The publication resulting from the symposium is highly recommended to anyone with a serious interest in the whitefishes and their relatives. Some of the species covered in the subsequent discussions may no longer be extant, probably as a result of the lamprey depredations and habitat changes of the past decade. We have included those species for which there are authentic museum records, but we have not included the various subspecies which have been described and discussed in previous works (Eddy and Surber, 1947; Hubbs and Lagler, 1964).

LAKE WHITEFISH

Coregonus clupeaformis (Mitchill)

The lake whitefish (Figure 50) is a large, more or less ovate fish with silvery sides that shade to a dark olive-brown back. There are two small flaps between the openings of each nostril. The snout distinctly overhangs the lower jaw. Local sports fishermen sometimes confuse lake whitefish with ciscoes, but the whitefish can be readily distinguished from the deep-bodied cisco of the inland lakes by the pronounced overhanging snout, which causes

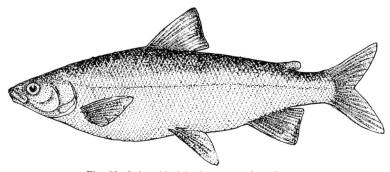

Fig. 50. Lake whitefish, *Coregonus clupeaformis*

the mouth to be inferior. The upper jaw is characterized by a premaxillary which is greater in width than in length. Vestigial teeth may be present on the premaxillaries, the palatines, the mandible, and the tongue. The gill rakers usually number from 23 to 32. During the spawning season pearl organs are developed by both sexes on the sides of the body and on the head. The lake whitefish becomes sexually mature at three to six years of age.

The whitefish is the largest of Minnesota's coregonine fishes. The largest individuals, usually from Lake Superior, may weigh more than 20 pounds, but the average weight rarely exceeds 4 pounds. Individuals weighing over 4 pounds are termed "jumbos" by commercial fishermen. Koelz reports that hybrids between the cisco and the whitefish reach weights up to 11 pounds.

The whitefish was formerly one of the important commercial fishes of Lake Superior. The species also lives in the open waters of some of the northern inland lakes where it has developed various forms or subspecies. The inland lake forms tend to have darker fins than do their relatives in the large lakes such as Lake Superior. In Lake Superior the whitefish range down to depths of 200 feet, and in the inland lakes, if oxygen conditions permit, they go to depths of over 100 feet. They are cold-water fishes, and in some of the shallow lakes large numbers may die during August.

Inland forms of the whitefish are found in large Minnesota lakes of the Arctic drainage (Red Lake, Lake of the Woods, and Rainy Lake), in some boundary lakes as far eastward as Basswood, and in lakes of the Lake Superior drainage (including the lakes at the headwaters of the Pigeon River and Pine and McFarland lakes in Cook County). Inland whitefish are also present in Silver Island Lake in Lake County; in late October they may run up the Island River toward Harriet Lake to spawn. Whitefish are common in a number of large lakes of the Mississippi River drainage in north central Minnesota, such as Whitefish Lake in Crow Wing County. They are numerous in Leech Lake, Mille Lacs, and Cass Lake, where fish weighing up to 8 pounds have been taken. The species is not found in many lakes south of Mille Lacs. Howard Krosch of the Department of Natural Resources took a single specimen in Lake St. Croix while carrying on an intensive study of the fish fauna following the construction of the Northern States Power Company's Allen S. King generating plant. Whitefish from inland lakes vary greatly in size; in some lakes the fish may not survive long after reaching maturity and hence are of small size. Years ago several of the hatcheries in the state hatched large numbers of whitefish eggs and planted the fry in Lake Superior and in several inland lakes, but unfortunately the records of these early plantings are quite vague.

Whitefish are abundant in Lower Red Lake and are next in importance to perch and walleyes in the commercial fishery operated by the Chippewa Indians. Red Lake was also a source of whitefish eggs for the hatchery operations which were conducted by the state in cooperation with the Indian Service. Many thousands of fry from Red Lake eggs were planted in Lake Superior in an attempt to restore the fishery. Although there appears to be little difference between the whitefish of Red Lake and those of Lake Superior, the commercial fishermen on Lake Superior seem to be able to distinguish them. Certainly there is a difference in the size of their eggs. Eggs from Lake Superior whitefish average 34,000 per quart (0.125 inch in diameter) while those from Red Lake average about 50,000 per quart (0.110 inch in diameter).

The whitefish in Red Lake spawn on gravel beds near the shore in water 6 to 8 feet deep. Spawning begins when the water temperatures range from 33° to 35° F. In the inland lakes the whitefish may enter rivers to spawn. After spawning, the adults soon return to deeper water. The eggs hatch in late winter or early spring. The newly hatched fry sometimes move to deeper water, but often they stay for some weeks around the shallow bays feeding on zooplankton. In contrast the Lake Superior whitefish move inshore in early fall and congregate off the river mouths. They spawn in November and early December at depths of 6 to 75 feet on smooth sand or boulder bottoms. No care is given to the eggs. In Lake Superior the young fry swarm around docks along the shores.

Although whitefish will bite occasionally on a baited hook, they are not noted as game fish. In some northern lakes they may be caught throughout the summer by still-fishing in deep water (75 to 100 feet) with minnows or small perch for bait. They are usually caught commercially in either gill nets or pound nets in Lake of the Woods.

The whitefish has a greater commercial value per pound than the cisco, but today, more often than not, when the consumer buys "whitefish" he gets cisco. Whitefish roe is used for caviar and ranks as a delicacy. In many inland lakes the whitefish is infested with the larval stage of the *Triaenophorus* tapeworm, which also commonly infests the inland cisco. While the infestation is not significant in Minnesota waters, it is a serious problem in the Canadian freshwater commercial fishery because the infested fish cannot meet inspection standards.

CISCO (LAKE HERRING)

Coregonus artedi LeSueur

The cisco or lake herring (Figure 51) common to Lake Superior is a rather slender fish that reaches a length of 12 inches or more. The lower jaw is either equal in length to the upper jaw or slightly shorter. The gill rakers usually number more than 43 on the first gill arch. Fewer than 80 scales are present in the lateral line. The cisco can be distinguished from the lake whitefish by the absence of an overhanging snout and upper jaw.

Ciscoes usually stay near the surface of the water, but they may swim down to a depth of several hundred feet. They often run in schools offshore. In late July and early August the Lake Superior ciscoes move close to shore in preparation for spawning. Spawning usually takes place during the last two weeks of November on almost any type of hard bottom from shoal water to a depth of 120 feet. Ciscoes differ from other salmonids in that they undertake no preparation or care of the spawning bed. The eggs are small; in a sample taken from ciscoes off the mouth of the French River near Duluth, the eggs averaged 118,346 per quart.

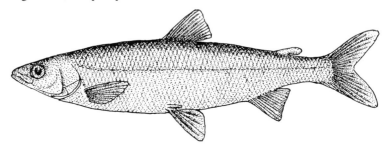

Fig. 51. Cisco, *Coregonus artedi*

The cisco is the best known and the most abundant species of the whitefish group in Lake Superior. It is native in Lake of the Woods and the border lakes and in inland lakes southward to Mille Lacs. The species shows considerable variability in form and shape in some parts of the Great Lakes, but the variations are most pronounced in the inland lakes. The variant forms occur in many northern Minnesota lakes where they may have been native, but there is also the possibility that they were introduced. There has been a tendency among ichthyologists to describe populations that display such variations as separate subspecies, and the result is a very confusing nomenclature for the group. Some of these populations contain small fish weighing only a fraction of a pound; others consist of large, deep-bodied forms weighing several pounds. Individuals described as "jumbos" are known from Lake of the Woods and may weigh as much as 8 pounds. Koelz (1931) described twenty-four subspecies of *Coregonus artedi* from inland lakes in the northern parts of Michigan, Wisconsin, and Minnesota. With few exceptions the ciscoes found in Minnesota's northern lakes are closely related to the ciscoes of Lake Superior. They are relics of the glacial period when the species had a much wider distribution. Sport fishermen usually refer to the inland form as the tullibee (Figure 52). The tullibee tends to have a deeper and heavier body than the Lake Superior form. Because of the numerous specific variations, it seems unwise to attempt to use subspecific names for any of them.

We are certain that many ciscoes were introduced years ago when eggs secured from federal agencies and from other northern states were hatched and planted. The records of these introductions are not clear about the origins or the kinds of ciscoes, but they do show that in about 1878 Lake Superior herring, whitefishes, and herring from other lakes were planted in many central Minnesota lakes such as Cedar Lake in Wright County and Green Lake in Kandiyohi County, where they still exist. The ciscoes in Mille Lacs also may have been introduced. The plantings in Lake Elmo in Washington County survived until the drought years of the 1930s. The isolation of the cisco populations in these small lakes is thought to be the factor which originally brought about the development of variant body forms. In recent years slender-bodied ciscoes from Lake Superior have been introduced into certain lakes of the Superior National Forest in an effort to increase the food for lake trout. Studies of these populations in the future will show whether the change in environment has any effect on their body form.

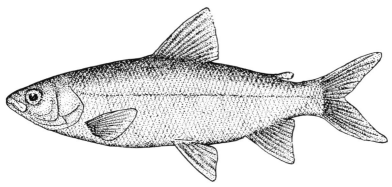

Fig. 52. Tullibee, inland form of cisco, *Coregonus artedi*

In inland lakes, the ciscoes move inshore in the fall. The males enter shallow water (3 to 9 feet deep) when the water temperatures drop to about 41° F, and the females follow a short time later. The females deposit their eggs while swimming slowly about 6 inches above the bottom. One or more males follow each female, emitting clouds of milt to fertilize the eggs. The young fry seek deeper water before the ice melts in the spring.

All ciscoes are cold-water fishes, which is probably the reason many of the early introductions in central Minnesota lakes ended in failure. In certain warm-water lakes the ciscoes have survived, but during the late summer, particularly in August, thousands die and are cast up on the shore. In inland eutrophic lakes, the ciscoes prefer to stay close to the thermocline during the summer; in the winter following the fall overturn, when oxygen is again available in the deeper waters, the ciscoes may go down to depths of 100 feet or more. With few exceptions, the central Minnesota lakes where the ciscoes have survived are those with depths greater than 75 feet and where there is sufficient oxygen in the cool waters near the thermocline. Young ciscoes seem to be able to tolerate higher temperatures than adults; the large adults succumb first in summerkills. In Lake Itasca at the headwaters of the Mississippi River, there are summerkills of ciscoes almost every year, but in nearby Elk Lake such kills have never been observed. Elk Lake is a deep lake while Lake

Itasca is very shallow; both lakes are eutrophic, but in Elk Lake the oxygen supply in the hypolimnion is never depleted while in Lake Itasca it is rare to find more than a trace of oxygen in the waters below the thermocline. The temperatures and the oxygen concentrations related to summerkills in the waters of Lake Itasca have been documented by Nelson (1970). Nelson also observed that the larger and older fish were the first to die during a summer-kill. Furthermore, when the oxygen level remained above 2 parts per million in the waters below the thermocline, the summerkills in Lake Itasca were very light.

Inland lake ciscoes or tullibees feed heavily on plankton which they strain from the water with their fine gill rakers. Ninety-two percent of several hundred stomachs examined contained large quantities of plankton, 12 percent contained insects, 2 percent contained small crayfish, and 2 percent contained small minnows. In the winter, 40 percent of the stomachs contained small sculpins, and one stomach contained a small whitefish. Cahn (1927) found that the ciscoes in Oconomowoc Lake feed on planktonic crustaceans, especially during the winter. A small percentage of the fish he examined had the remains of small fish and mollusks in their stomachs. Lake Itasca ciscoes eat large numbers of midge larvae and may be important predators on chironomids at various times of the year (Underhill and Cole, 1967).

Under certain conditions ciscoes will bite readily on a hook, but usually they are taken in gill nets during the fall. In the spring they enter the cold shore waters of many lakes in large numbers, probably to feed. At this time of the year they afford great sport to the fisherman who casts various wet or dry flies or very small streamers; they are tremendous fighters. Underhill has caught them on small spinners with ultralight spinning gear. The best method is to go out in a boat or a canoe and to watch the surface for schools of feeding ciscoes. Move into the school and cast in front of it, retrieving the lure rapidly. If one is careful, the school can be followed for five or ten minutes with a strike on almost every cast and probably one fish for every four casts. When the school disappears, simply relax and wait for another to appear. On a quiet day the water may be covered with dimples caused by fish feeding near the surface. Ciscoes are taken in the winter by anglers who fish through the ice, using a few handfuls of oatmeal to attract the fish. Goldenrod gall grubs and small minnows are successful baits.

The species has great commercial value and huge quantities are sold annually from Lake Superior and the other Great Lakes. The flesh is excellent; it is easily filleted, and it can be smoked. In the past ciscoes were sold in salt brine. Some fishermen object to using ciscoes for food because in many inland lakes they are heavily infested with the larvae of the *Triaenophorus* tapeworm. The larvae form large yellow cysts on the back muscles and are considered obnoxious, but they are harmless to man and they die when cooked. If the cysts are not too numerous, they can be cut out. The presence of the worms can be detected if the fish is split lengthwise and held to the light. In some northern Minnesota lakes and nearby Canadian lakes where commercial fishing is practiced, large numbers of tullibees are condemned annually as unfit for consumption because of this infection. The ciscoes of Lake Superior are seldom infected because of the scarcity of the northern pike, which is the final host of the tapeworm.

SHORTJAW CISCO

Coregonus zenithicus (Jordan and Evermann)

The shortjaw cisco is a slender fish with a large head. It has a bluish green back, silvery sides, and a white belly. The scales are slightly pigmented on the margins. The mandible is the same length as the upper jaw or slightly shorter. There are 39 to 43 gill rakers present on the first branchial arch. The lateral line contains 70 to 85 scales.

The shortjaw cisco is present in Lake Huron, Lake Michigan, and Lake Superior. It is reported from many large lakes in Canada from Lake Winnipeg to the Northwest Territories. At one time it was abundant in the deep waters of Lake Superior along the entire north shore. It ranges at depths from 60 feet to over 600 feet, but it is most abundant at about 200 feet and relatively close to shore.

The shortjaw cisco spawns from September to late November at depths of 120 to 200 feet and not far from shore. Only the males develop pearl organs. We know very little about their spawning habits. They feed primarily on plankton, especially the larger crustaceans such as *Mysis*, but they also pick up some bottom fauna such as midge larvae and the crustacean *Pontoporeia*.

Several decades ago these fish were quite important commercially, and considerable numbers were netted in deep-set herring nets. They have been marketed as ciscoes and as chubs. When fresh, they are excellent food fish.

SHORTNOSE CISCO

Coregonus reighardi (Koelz)

The shortnose cisco is elliptical in shape and reaches a length of slightly more than 12 inches. Several subspecies are reported to occur in Lake Superior, Lake Michigan, and Lake Ontario. The form found in Lake Superior is lighter in color than the forms in the other Great Lakes. It is light green above with silvery sides, and it closely resembles the shortjaw cisco. The first branchial arch has fewer than 39 gill rakers. The lower jaw is the same length as the upper jaw or shorter. The Lake Superior form does not have as much pigment on the lower jaw as the forms found in the other Great Lakes. The lateral line has from 66 to 77 scales.

Along the north shore of Lake Superior the shortnose cisco is found at various depths down to 400 feet, but it is most abundant at depths of 90 to 100 feet. It feeds on plankton. Its spawning habits are not well known. In some of the Great Lakes it has been reported as spawning from May to June, but in Lake Superior (from the evidence of spent females) it probably spawns in November on sandy or mud bottoms at depths of 250 feet or less.

Shortnose ciscoes are excellent food fish; those taken in deep-set herring nets are sold, but the species is so rare that it has little commercial value. It is one of the fishes sometimes sold at roadside stands as either fresh or smoked chub.

BLACKFIN CISCO

Coregonus nigripinnis (Gill)

The blackfin cisco (sometimes called the bluefin cisco) is one of the large ciscoes found along the north shore of Lake Superior. It may reach a length of 10 to 18 inches. The ovate body has its greatest depth anterior to the dorsal fin. This cisco has a dark bluish back and silvery sides, and the fins are dusky or bluish with dark tips. There are 40 to 52 long and slender gill rakers. The scales in the lateral line number 72 to 89.

The blackfin cisco is quite common in Lake Superior from Duluth to Two Harbors and occasionally as far up the shore as Beaver Bay. It is reported that the species was once abundant from Beaver Bay to the Canadian border. Several subspecies of the blackfin cisco are found in the other Great Lakes with the exception of Lake Erie. The Lake Superior blackfin cisco is less strongly colored than the subspecies that have been described for the other Great Lakes. Inland forms are reported from many large lakes of central and northwestern Canada and from several large northern lakes in Minnesota, but so far we have no specimens of them. These ciscoes are deep-water fishes, usually found at depths of 200 to 600 feet. Not much is known about their spawning habits beyond the fact that they spawn in deep water during September.

Blackfin ciscoes are primarily plankton feeders, as might be suspected from the long and slender gill rakers. We find them often in the stomachs of lake trout and siscowets caught in very deep water. When commercial fishing for lake trout was at its peak, the gill nets set at 400 to 600 feet often caught a few blackfin ciscoes. They are excellent food fishes, but they are caught in such small numbers that they are not commercially important. In the past they were sometimes sold fresh or smoked in the roadside markets that used to be so common along the North Shore Drive.

BLOATER

Coregonus hoyi (Gill)

The bloater, a small deep-water cisco, is a slender fish that seldom exceeds 8 inches in length. The body is silvery with an iridescent bluish streak. The tip of the lower jaw is slightly hooked and is pigmented. The bloater is about the same size as the kiyi, which it resembles rather closely, but the bloater has its greatest depth in the center of the body instead of anterior to the center. The lateral line usually has 68 to 76 scales. The first branchial arch has from 40 to 47 gill rakers.

The bloater is found in all the Great Lakes except Lake Erie. It is reported to occur in Lake Winnipeg and in some of the large Canadian lakes to the northwest. In Lake Superior the species ranges from areas near the shore to as much as twenty miles offshore and at depths of 150 to 600 feet. Not much is known of its spawning habits in Lake Superior. Bloaters have been reported to spawn not far offshore during November and into the winter months. Apparently they feed on plankton, including *Mysis*, and use much bottom fauna for food. Their stomachs often contain considerable amounts of deep-water fauna such as *Pontoporeia*, midge larvae, and the tiny fingernail clam *Pisidium*.

Bloaters are too small to appear in most gill-net catches, but some become tangled in the deep-water sets for lake trout. The large bloaters sometimes taken in herring nets are often smoked and sold in roadside markets. Since bloaters are eaten by the lake trout in deep water and sometimes form an important part of their diet, some of the small individuals caught accidentally are used as bait for setlines in the lake trout fishery. Otherwise these fish have little commercial value and are of no value as sport fish.

KIYI

Coregonus kiyi (Koelz)

The kiyi is a small cisco, 6 to 8 inches in length, with a slender body. The body is bluish below the lateral line, and the dorsal and caudal fins have wide black margins. The mandible is thin and distinctly hooked at the tip. The lower jaw is longer than the upper one. The snout is longer than the diameter of the eye. There are 36 to 41 gill rakers on the first gill arch and more than 75 scales in the lateral line. This species can be distinguished from the bloater, which sometimes occurs at the same depths, by observing that the greatest body depth of the kiyi is anterior to the center of the body and the lower jaw is unpigmented.

Like bloaters, kiyis are found in the deep waters of the Great Lakes with the exception of Lake Erie. In Lake Superior they spawn in deep water in late October, November, and early December, but we know little about their spawning habits. They feed primarily on the small crustacean *Mysis*, on the deep-water organisms *Pisidium* and *Pontoporeia*, and on plankton.

Because of their small size they are not taken often in the large-mesh nets set in deep water for lake trout and siscowets, and they are probably more abundant than we realize. Their primary value is as a food item for lake trout and siscowets.

Family OSMERIDAE
The Smelt Family

The smelt family contains many species of small marine fish, some of which are anadromous and ascend rivers to spawn. They are closely related to the family Salmonidae but differ in having larger scales, stronger teeth, and no axillary process. All have soft rays and an adipose fin. They are all predacious.

Genus *Osmerus* Lacépède

This genus contains one species found in Minnesota but which is widely distributed in the cold waters of the Northern Hemisphere. The characters for the genus are the same as for the following species.

RAINBOW SMELT

Osmerus esperlanus (Linnaeus)

The rainbow smelt (Figure 53) is a small slender fish with a greenish back and translucent violet-blue sides fading to white on the belly. Although similar to trout, smelt have larger scales (only about 68 scales in the lateral line), large sharp teeth, and no axillary process at the base of the pelvic fins. The caudal fin is deeply forked. An adipose fin is present. The mouth is large, and the maxillary extends to below the back margin of the eye.

Smelt are usually 6 to 9 inches long when they become mature. In their third year they may reach a length of 9 to 12 inches, and those few that happen to live to their fourth year may be up to 15 inches long. Those caught in Lake Superior spawning runs are usually in their second year and range from 6 to 9 inches in length.

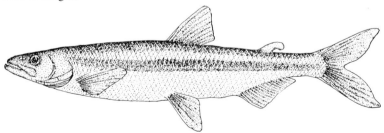

Fig. 53. Rainbow smelt, *Osmerus esperlanus*

192

The rainbow smelt is the common smelt found along the Atlantic coast and on the Pacific coast from British Columbia northward into Alaska. It is also found in northern Europe and Asia. It is anadromous, and vast numbers crowd into the rivers to spawn. Some have become landlocked in certain eastern lakes. The form present on the Atlantic coast is the subspecies *Osmerus esperlanus mordax.*

Trout fishermen at the mouth of the French River, the site where the coho salmon was introduced into the Minnesota portion of Lake Superior. Photo: John Dobie, Minnesota Department of Natural Resources.

Landlocked rainbow smelt prefer cold-water lakes where they can find water below 60° F, and this probably limits their distribution. They are not native to Minnesota waters but were accidentally introduced when smelt planted in several Michigan lakes as food for the landlocked salmon escaped into the Great Lakes. Landlocked salmon in the eastern lakes depend largely on smelt for food, and when attempts were made to introduce the salmon into the Michigan lakes, it was necessary to introduce the smelt at the same time. Smelt were introduced as early as 1906 in the St. Mary's River but with no success. In an attempt in 1912 to establish the landlocked salmon in Michigan, smelt were introduced into Torch Lake (Antrim County), Crystal Lake (Benzie County), and Mountain, Howe, and Trout lakes (Marquette

County). The introductions were successful in Howe, Crystal, and Trout lakes. It is believed that some of the Crystal Lake population escaped and became the source of the Great Lakes population. They spread fast and were found along the east shore of Lake Michigan in 1923. In 1924 they appeared in the Green Bay area, and in 1925 they appeared in Lake Huron. In the next ten years they spread into Lake Erie. They were first noted in the eastern end of Lake Superior in 1930 and apparently entered from Lake Michigan by way of the St. Mary's River. They spread slowly in Lake Superior; although reported earlier by commercial fishermen, their presence in Minnesota waters was not verified until 1946, when specimens were caught in the mouth of the French River. In a few years they became abundant along much of the north shore. In recent years they have become established in Grindstone Lake in Pine County, and in Musquash, West Bearskin, Hungry Jack, and several other lakes in Cook County, where they provide food for the lake trout.

At first the rapid spread of smelt in the Great Lakes caused much concern among the fishery biologists, who feared the small carnivorous fish would work havoc among the young lake trout and other species. However, no harm has been noted, perhaps because the smelt live at depths where important species such as the lake trout are not common. In contrast to introduced fishes such as the carp, smelt have apparently become a valuable asset to the Great Lakes fish fauna because they furnish an additional food basis for lake trout and other fishes. Their spectacular spawning runs have yielded a new resource for sport fishermen as well as for commercial use.

The smelt in Lake Superior usually inhabit water from 50 to 200 feet in depth. The young smelt stay in shallow water until midsummer, when they seek deeper water. As the spawning season approaches, the mature smelt move inshore and assemble in large schools. The spawning run starts when the ice melts, but the peak comes in May when the water temperature rises. The smelt crowd into the mouths of the tributary streams of Lake Superior in incredible numbers, running upstream mostly at night, and in the morning most of them drift back to the lake. They repeat the run on successive nights until they are through spawning. It is possible that some of them spawn in the lake on beaches and shoals where waves simulate a current.

From one to five males accompany a female. They assume positions slightly before and above the female and drive her close to the bottom where she deposits her eggs, usually over 100 of them; then the adults retreat to the lake until the next night. A female may have from 12,000 to 50,000 eggs in her ovaries, depending on her size. The eggs are much smaller than those of trout and whitefish, and they adhere in clusters. They hatch in about ten to thirty days, and the resulting fry are swept downstream to the lake. Although a very large proportion of the eggs are fertilized and large numbers hatch, the mortality of the fry is very high.

The young smelt feed at first on minute plankton organisms, but they soon change to a diet of *Hyalella* and small insect larvae. As they grow and move into deeper water, they start feeding on larger forms such as *Mysis* and

Pontoporeia. At the end of their first year they begin to feed on smaller smelt and other small fishes. As adults they feed on *Mysis, Pontoporeia,* small coregonids, and other fishes including their own kind.

Dipping for smelt at the mouths of the tributaries of Lake Superior has become a popular sport, and people come from hundreds of miles to take part. Thousands of fishermen crowd the banks at night using dip nets, minnow seines, and all manner of dippers. Vast numbers of smelt are taken, but this seems to have little effect on the number which return the next night. Since smelt are highly prolific, this may be one of the ways in which they are held in check. In some eastern lakes smelt are often taken in winter by anglers fishing through the ice. Many are caught by commercial fishermen, particularly in Lake Michigan, and are frozen and shipped to markets.

Smelt are a delicacy when properly prepared. Smelt fries have become very popular in Minnesota. Many people just eviscerate the fish, leaving the heads and scales on. Usually they are rolled in flour or batter, fried crisp, and eaten — bones and all. There are many other ways to prepare them.

Family UMBRIDAE
The Mudminnow Family

The mudminnow family includes three genera and four species in North America, but only one species occurs in Minnesota waters. Mudminnows are soft-rayed fishes with heavy bodies compressed posteriorly. The dorsal surface of the head is flattened. The mouth is of medium size, and teeth are present on the jaws, the vomer, and the palatine bones. The upper jaw is nonprotractile; the maxillary bones form the posterior margin of the upper jaw. The gill rakers are not prominent and the pseudobranchiae are poorly developed. There are from 6 to 9 branchiostegal rays. The head and body are covered with cycloid scales. No lateral line is present.

Genus *Umbra* Müller

The genus Umbra contains two North American species and one European species. The eastern mudminnow, *Umbra pygmaea* (DeKay), occurs in swamps and sluggish streams from New York south into Florida. The central mudminnow, *Umbra limi* (Kirtland), is found in the Upper Mississippi Valley.

CENTRAL MUDMINNOW
Umbra limi (Kirtland)

The central mudminnow (Figure 54) is usually less than 4 inches in length, but specimens up to 7 inches have been taken. The body is usually dark brown and somewhat mottled. A prominent dark bar extends across the base of the caudal fin, and there are about 14 narrow and less prominent light crossbars on the body. The head length is contained 3.75 times in the body length, and the body depth is contained 4.25 times in the body length. The dorsal fin has 14 rays and is far posterior, behind the origin of the pelvic fins. The anal fin has 8 rays, and the pectoral and pelvic fins have 6 rays.

The central mudminnow ranges throughout the upper Mississippi and Great Lakes drainages south to Kansas and Tennessee. It is widely distributed in all parts of Minnesota including the Red River and Lake Superior drainage basins. Mudminnows are very common in the bog country of the north central portion of the state, especially in old drainage ditches, and they are very abundant in the roadside spring-fed ditches just west of the headwaters of the

196

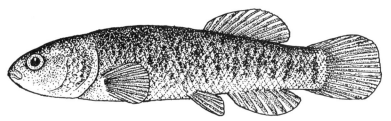

Fig. 54. Central mudminnow, *Umbra limi*

Mississippi River near Lake Itasca. They are also common in beaver impoundments.

The mudminnow is rarely seen by the average fisherman because it lives in waters rarely frequented by panfish and game fish, and it is difficult to seine. It appears to prefer bog habitats, ditches, and streams with muddy bottoms which are often choked with aquatic vegetation. Students at the Lake Itasca Forestry and Biological Station carried out mark-and-recapture studies on the mudminnows in some roadside ditches which provided optimum conditions for seining and which did not give the fish an opportunity to migrate. They observed mudminnows diving into the mud and detritus near the margins of the ditches but could not capture them with either seines or dip nets. However, once the water had become stirred up and turbid, the fish could be taken in the seines. After five weeks of daily sampling the students were still capturing unmarked mudminnows. During the same period the students also marked brook sticklebacks (*Culaea inconstans*), but in contrast to the mudminnows no unmarked sticklebacks were taken after three weeks.

The mudminnow is one of the hardiest of Minnesota fishes and has been found in ponds where the oxygen concentration is less than one part per million. Eddy and Surber (1947) note that mudminnows burrow down into the mud when the water in the pond evaporates. They feed on insects, small crustaceans, and worms, and under some conditions their diet may include small fishes. Stasiak (1972) found the pharyngeal teeth of minnows in the digestive tracts of several large mudminnows. Some of these characteristics help to explain why the mudminnow is often the only species of fish inhabiting swamps, shallow ponds, and bog pools. Mudminnows spawn in late spring and early summer.

Family ESOCIDAE
The Pike Family

The family Esocidae includes the true pikes or pickerels, all of which are members of the genus *Esox*. All members of this family have elongated bodies and heads with long depressed jaws. The jaws are armed with large canine teeth. A single soft-rayed fin is inserted far back on the body.

Four species of pike are found in the United States. The best known species is probably the northern pike, *Esox lucius* Linnaeus. It is distributed over much of North America east of the Rocky Mountains and north of the Ohio River and ranges northwestward into Alaska. It is also present in northern Asia and Europe. The muskellunge, *Esox masquinongy* Mitchill, is native to the upper Mississippi drainage, the upper Ohio drainage, the Great Lakes and St. Lawrence area, and the Lake of the Woods drainage. The family is represented in the eastern Atlantic and Gulf states by the chain pickerel, *Esox niger* LeSueur, and the little redfin pickerel, *Esox americanus americanus* Gmelin. The grass pickerel, *Esox americanus vermiculatus* LeSueur, ranges northward through the Mississippi drainage almost to Minnesota. The only species definitely known to occur in Minnesota are the northern pike and the muskellunge. Many different common names have been applied locally to each of these two species.

KEY TO MINNESOTA SPECIES OF FAMILY ESOCIDAE

1. Opercle entirely scaled; body marked with dark wavy crossbars; length usually less than 12 inches; probably not present in Minnesota . . . .
. . . . .Grass pickerel, *Esox americanus vermiculatus* LeSueur
Opercle naked on the lower half; markings variable; lengths up to 3 feet or more 2
2. Cheeks completely scaled; adult body marked with light spots on dark background; mandibular pores 5 or fewer on each side . . . .
. . . . .Northern pike, *Esox lucius* Linnaeus
Cheeks may have lower half naked, partially scaled, or largely scaled; body markings range from dark spots or crossbars on a light background to an almost solid color; mandibular pores more than 5 on each side . . . . .
. . . . .Muskellunge, *Esox masquinongy* Mitchill

Genus *Esox* Linnaeus

This is the only living genus; the characters of the genus are the same as those of the family.

NORTHERN PIKE

Esox lucius Linnaeus

The northern pike (Figure 55) is a more or less elongated fish with a long head which is depressed forward into a pair of large duckbill-like jaws with numerous canine teeth. The depth of the body is contained 5 to 7 times in the length. The dorsal fin is located far back on the body and has 16 to 19 rays.

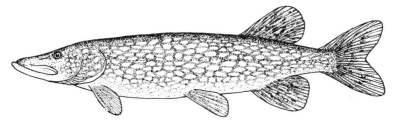

Fig. 55. Northern pike, *Esox lucius* (adult)

The pelvic fins are also far back, a little over halfway between the pectoral fins and the anal fin. The top and front of the head are without scales. The cheeks are entirely scaled, but only the upper half of the opercle is covered with scales. The sum total of sensory pores on the undersides of the lower jaws is never more than 10 (Figure 56).

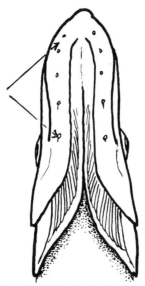

Fig. 56. Northern pike, *Esox lucius*. Sensory pores on lower jaw.

The sides and back are bluish green, and the belly is white or cream. In adults the sides are profusely covered with round or slightly elongated light spots. Some spots or blotches appear on the fins. The juveniles (Figure 57) in their first summer are marked with light bars on a dark background. These bars gradually break up into light spots when the fish is about 6 inches long, but specimens over 12 inches in length have been found still bearing the juvenile bar pattern.

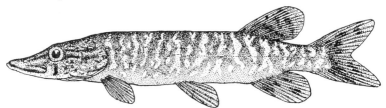

Fig. 57. Northern pike, *Esox lucius* (juvenile)

The northern pike may reach a very large size and weigh from 25 to 30 pounds. Weights of over 50 pounds have been recorded for fish taken in seine hauls. A northern pike weighing 45 pounds, 12 ounces, from Basswood Lake in Lake County, is perhaps the largest specimen caught by an angler in Minnesota. Northern pike grow slowly in the northern lakes, but those living in warmer waters grow to a large size in a few years. They often reach a length of 10 to 12 inches in one year. A 36-inch specimen was found to be nine years old.

Many tales and myths are told by local fishermen about this fish. Some lakes are commonly claimed to have fish so large that no ordinary line will hold them. Although northern pike do indeed grow to great size in many lakes, the characteristically savage rushes displayed by a northern pike of any size take advantage of the frayed line, the loose knot, the cracked guide, and any careless handling of the fish by the angler and tend to give the illusion that a very large fish has been hooked.

In Minnesota and parts of Wisconsin northern pike are often called pickerel, snake pickerel, and many other names. In Canada they are called jackfish. Not too long ago many fishermen and outdoor writers claimed that the large deep-bodied northern pike was a different species from the lean and often smaller young pike which they called snake pickerel. Others have added to the misunderstanding by confusing the juvenile northern pike with the eastern chain pickerel or the southern grass pickerel. The confusion is understandable because there is considerable variation in the size, the markings, and the proportions of the northern pike from various lakes in the state. Years ago we took special pains to examine hundreds of northern pike from throughout the state and from the University of Minnesota collections, and we did not find any differences to indicate the existence of more than one species. We did find one variant, probably a mutant, which will be discussed later.

A myth which is still current is that northern pike do not bite much during the month of August because they shed their teeth and have sore mouths. The loss of teeth and the sore mouth condition was carefully investigated at the University of Michigan by Trautman and Hubbs (1935), who found no basis for this belief. We too have checked hundreds of northern pike during August in Minnesota, and we find no sign that northern pike shed their teeth entirely at one time. Worn-out and broken teeth are replaced as they are lost by new ones which always grow alongside the larger teeth. To our knowledge sore mouths or gums are not related to the loss of teeth. It is known, however, that sore mouths do occur as a result of exposure to the air and injuries from plugs and hooks. It is true that the fish may not bite as well in August, but this can be attributed to the amount of food available. Since food production is at its peak at this time of the year, the pike are well fed and are less likely to take the natural or artificial baits offered by fishermen. It is also a fact that in August the water in many lakes is very turbid with algae, and visibility is so reduced that the lure has to be literally in front of the fish's nose before the fish can see it. The temperature may also be a factor; at this time of the year the large pike seek the deeper and cooler waters. In Lake Vermilion, for example, large northern pike are normally found in the shallows over reefs or along the shores, but in August they seem to desert these preferred habitats for the deeper water off the reefs in the habitat of the walleye. This change in behavior may account for the fact that occasionally very large northern pike are taken by fishermen who are seeking walleyes.

The northern pike is primarily a sight feeder and strikes at anything that moves or excites its curiosity. Generally it lies in wait for its prey within the weed bed or beside a rock or a log and then darts out quickly and seizes the minnow, the perch, or other unwary prey. The body shape of the northern pike is designed for rapid acceleration but not for sustained swimming, hence it lies in wait rather than cruising around like many predacious fish. The unpredictable mad dashes of the hooked northern pike, particularly when the fish first gets a glimpse of the boat, are familiar to most lake fishermen. It is by means of such sudden dashes that it captures its food. The species feeds primarily on living animals, mainly fishes such as perch, small suckers, sunfish, and even on smaller northern pike. Large pike occasionally catch and eat ducklings and small muskrats. In midsummer when large numbers of leeches are present in the shallow waters of northern lakes, the northern pike feed on them almost exclusively. In general we can say that northern pike feed on any living things that are available. They feed in shallow water in the morning during the summer but may exhibit a daily migration to deeper waters beyond the weed margin in the late evening.

Northern pike spawn immediately after the ice melts in April or early May. They ascend small streams or seek flooded grassy margins of lakes where they deposit their eggs at random. Once the spawning is completed, the adults return to the lakes and the rivers. The eggs hatch in about two weeks. A female 26 inches long and weighing about 5 pounds usually has about 60,000 eggs in her ovaries. A large female may deposit over 100,000 eggs. The young pike feed on tiny crustaceans, cladocerans, and copepods for the first two weeks and then switch to larger prey which soon includes small fish fry such as the sucker fry which usually hatch by the thousands at about the same time and in the same place. If food becomes scarce, they quickly resort to cannibalism.

Northern pike are easily stripped, but the results of artificial hatching are poor and cannibalism renders the rearing of fingerlings difficult. The few that are hatched are usually planted as fry in lakes where they are needed, but it is far more efficient to protect their natural spawning areas than to rear them in hatcheries. Until very recently young northern pike occasionally became stranded in the marshes or meadows where they were hatched when the water levels dropped, cutting off their avenue to the lake. Now small dams with control gates are present in many of the important spawning areas; when the young have grown to fingerling size, the gate is opened and the young migrate into the stream, river, or lake. Since wetland areas are also important for waterfowl breeding, every effort should be made to preserve or to restore them.

Forty years ago the silver pike, a striking variant of the northern pike, was noted in several different locations in northern Minnesota. This form has the morphological characters of *Esox lucius* but lacks the spots and other markings on the body. The body is usually dark silver or greenish gray flecked with gold. The fins are finely speckled with black. The opercle is scaled on the upper half only, and the cheek is entirely scaled as in the northern pike. Occasionally specimens are found with faint light spots on the caudal peduncle, very similar to the caudal markings of *E. lucius* but less distinct. The total number of pores on the underside of the jaws is not more than 10, as in the northern pike. Specimens of this variant seldom weigh over 10 pounds.

The fish was first observed in about 1930 in Lake Belletaine, near Nevis, Minnesota, where it was being collected with muskellunge for stripping. The local fishermen reported that it had not appeared in their catches until that year. They regarded it as a form of muskellunge. For several years afterwards this fish was propagated along with true muskellunge at the Nevis hatchery for planting in nearby lakes, and consequently it became fairly widespread. A specimen of this form was collected later from Detroit Lakes, where none had been planted. We took both eggs and fry to the University of Minnesota and reared them, some to three years of age. Apparently the form breeds true, for all offspring were similar to the parents. When crosses between the variant and the northern pike were made, the hybrids had a peculiar black mottling on the body but otherwise the body characteristics resembled those of the northern pike. As proven by the experimental crosses, the type was breeding true in nature; in several lakes near Nevis pure silver-colored individuals of all ages continued to appear and possible hybrid types were uncommon. When the silver variety was crossed with the muskellunge, the hybrids were identical with the hybrids of known northern pike and muskellunge crosses. Sufficient numbers of the silver pike are present in the Park Rapids and Nevis area for Fuller's Tackle Company to recognize it in their annual fishing contest. The fish is apparently a true-breeding mutant of *Esox lucius* which in several lakes has become sexually isolated from the related northern pike and muskellunge. The common name is properly silver pike rather than the earlier name, silver muskellunge, given to it by local fishermen.

The northern pike has an excellent flavor, although the flesh is somewhat bony. The bones encountered are the extra ribs found in many fish which are especially well developed in the northern pike. These ribs are fine Y-shaped bones found just above the larger ribs. With a little knowledge and practice it is possible to remove them as the fish is eaten. A strong fishy flavor may be imparted to the flesh by the slime or mucus present on the skin, but this can be avoided if one carefully skins the fish instead of just scaling it. Forty years ago northern pike were more abundant than at present, and many fishermen considered them as rough or trash fish because of their slimy skin and their voracity. It was not uncommon for fishing clubs and even chambers of commerce to request conservation administrators to remove northern pike from local lakes. It took quite a few years of publicity to promote the northern pike to its present position as one of the most popular game fishes in Minnesota.

Another important but not so obvious feature of the northern pike is its great value as a predator and a natural balancer of fish populations. In the absence of an efficient and voracious predator such as the northern pike, many lakes would be crowded with various panfishes and perch. In fact, the populations would probably be so dense that there would not be enough food for proper growth, and none of the individuals could reach an edible size. Lakes containing stunted fishes usually are found to contain relatively few northern pike or none at all. In lakes where northern pike are present, the pike eat the surplus sunfish, crappies, and perch as well as rough and forage fishes such as minnows and suckers, thus giving the surviving populations room and food to grow to normal size.

The pike's stomach has powerful digestive action; unless the fish is taken immediately after it has eaten, it is difficult to make an analysis of its food habits. Within a few hours after a pike is caught or tangled in a net, the contents of its stomach are digested or regurgitated. For years Eddy tried to determine whether pike consumed quantities of small sunfish; he did not find out until he collected fresh stomachs from hundreds of pike as they were speared through the ice in winter. Each stomach was packed with all manner of small fish, including as many as twenty small bluegills in a single stomach.

Although northern pike are occasionally caught by still-fishing with baited hooks, especially hooks baited with live minnows, they strike best on moving baits, spoons, or plugs. Spoons, large spinners, or plugs trolled slowly along weed beds or cast into the shallows and retrieved bring excellent results. We have taken northern pike on almost every bait imaginable and using almost every fishing technique. In fact, many of the record northern pike taken each year are caught by fishermen who are seeking walleyes, smallmouth bass, or even panfish. Pike take large bass flies at times, but they are usually after larger prey. Many pike fishermen use large suckers (12 inches or longer) for bait, just as the purist muskie fishermen do. The northern pike usually does not mouth the bait or play with it as do many game fishes but aims, hits hard, and usually hooks itself. A wire leader or a very heavy nylon one is required to hold northerns because their sharp canine teeth cut through light leaders with little difficulty. Northerns, particularly large ones, may sulk after taking the hook, and quite often the angler may think his hook is snagged on something until he feels the fish shake its head or begin to move away very slowly. After this initial contact the fish may come rather easily to the boat and then in a tremendous surge take off in the opposite direction. If the angler is not careful, the fish may break what appeared to be a relatively strong line. The next most dangerous period is when the pike appears tired and ready to be landed. In our experience every pike, large or small, saves a bit of energy for one last short run. If the fisherman is not expecting this last surge and attempts to hold the fish, it may be lost at the net. All too often an exhausted northern pike that has finally broken free from its would-be captor will lie temptingly at the surface on its side or finning slowly, only to dash off the minute the net appears. A bout with a northern pike on medium-weight spinning gear leaves the fisherman's arm aching and is an excellent test of his skill as an angler. Despite the feelings of many purist trout or bass fishermen, the northern pike is a tremendous fighter and, pound for pound, must rank near the top of the list for freshwater game fish. And a large northern pike — stuffed, seasoned, and baked — is a gourmet's delight.

The northern pike is also popular for winter spearing in dark houses. Because the fisherman uses a lure to attract the fish, he can select the largest fish to spear. In fact, many of the largest northern pike are taken by spearing. There is a great deal of controversy surrounding this highly selective means of fishing, and Minnesota is one of the few states where it is legal.

Northern pike are caught commercially in a few of the large northern lakes and in many Canadian lakes, and they are usually available, fresh or frozen, in meat markets or at the meat counter of supermarkets.

MUSKELLUNGE

Esox masquinongy Mitchill

The shape of the muskellunge (Figure 58) is very similar to that of the northern pike and many large northern pike have been incorrectly called muskellunge, but the two species are distinctly different. As in the northern pike, the opercle of the muskellunge bears scales only on the upper half while the lower half is naked, and the cheek of the muskellunge usually has scales only on the upper part. However, Minnesota specimens show considerable variation in the presence or absence of scales. The branchiostegals number 16 to 19. The dorsal fin has 19 to 21 rays. The body color is usually silvery, but some muskies from Lake of the Woods and from the Rainy River drainage are dark brown. The markings on the body vary considerably (Figure 58), but when markings are present they always consist of dark spots or bars on a light background. A very good character for identifying the muskellunge is the number of submandibular pores. The number of pores in the muskellunge ranges from 11 to 18, whereas the number in the northern pike is never greater than 10. The lateral line may contain from 130 to 157 scales, usually 147 to 155.

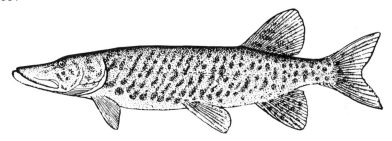

Fig. 58. Muskellunge, *Esox masquinongy*

Three subspecies of muskellunge are recognized in the United States. The subspecies *E. masquinongy immaculatus* (Girard) is the form found in Wisconsin and Minnesota, including Lake of the Woods and the Rainy River. The second subspecies, *E. m. masquinongy* Mitchill, is found in the Great Lakes drainage; although at present it appears to be absent from Lake Superior, it has been reported from the Apostle Islands (Greene, 1935) and in Canadian waters. The third subspecies, *E. m. ohioensis* Kirtland, is found in the Ohio River drainage. The markings of the muskellunge in Minnesota waters are so variable that it is possible to find specimens that fit the markings assigned to all three subspecies.

The muskellunge caught most often in Minnesota has "tiger" markings — broad and irregular bars along the sides of the body and head against a more or less silvery background. The bars are often partially broken up into spots; when they are entirely broken up into spots, they are referred to as "leopard" markings. In very large and old individuals the dark markings may fade and become indiscernible, producing the "silver" type. Juvenile muskellunge are marked with distinct dark bars in their first year. Fish from the brown waters so common to the Arctic drainage are more brownish than silver.

Muskellunge fry exhibit extremely rapid growth, and under optimum conditions in rearing ponds individuals often reach a length of 12 inches in the first four months of life. Under natural conditions the average length at the same age is about 6 inches. Those fish caught by anglers weigh up to 25 or 30 pounds. Perhaps the record fish taken from Minnesota waters by angling is a specimen weighing 56 1/2 pounds which was caught in Lake of the Woods in 1931. The world record is held by a fish weighing 69 pounds, 15 ounces, taken from the St. Lawrence River in 1957. Larger fish have been taken with seines. The maximum age reached by these enormous fish is probably not over fifteen years.

Muskellunge are seldom abundant in any lake where they occur. Perhaps this is because a large area of water is necessary to supply enough food for their voracious appetites. In most lakes where muskellunge occur, northern pike are also abundant, and the pike fry which hatch earlier offer much competition for the newly hatched muskellunge fry. When muskellunge are confined to small lakes, they tend to be smaller in size than their relatives in larger lakes. In Minnesota muskellunge are found in Lake of the Woods, in the Rainy River drainage, in Leech and Cass lakes, and in smaller lakes in the vicinity of Grand Rapids and Park Rapids. We have records of muskellunge in the Mississippi River as far south as Lake Pepin and from St. Anthony Falls north to Brainerd. Muskellunge are propagated at the Park Rapids hatchery for stocking lakes in that area.

Muskellunge are strictly carnivorous, feeding primarily on other fishes such as perch and suckers. They strike at anything that moves, and they have been known to take ducklings and muskrats. Those that we reared in tanks at the University of Minnesota fed on cladocerans and other tiny aquatic organisms for the first week following hatching, but they grew rapidly and thereafter would feed only on newly hatched suckers and other small fish. If they were without food for over an hour, they would start slashing at one another. Almost the only losses that occurred in our rearing experiments were due to cannibalism. On one occasion when we ran out of small food fish, we placed one hundred 2-inch muskellunge in a fish can and rushed them to a rearing pond where there was an abundance of natural food. It was only a twenty-minute ride, but when we counted the fish as we placed them in the pond, we had about fifty well-fed fish. Those in our rearing tanks reached a length of about 6 inches in two months and consumed from ten to fifteen bait-size minnows each day. As noted previously, members of the pike family are capable of tremendous acceleration, and their movements are exceedingly swift. Finning slowly, they stalk their prey, poise, then dart faster than the eye can follow to take their prey and swallow it in one motion. Even if the victim is another muskellunge, one slash is enough to sever the tail of the unlucky relative. During our study we raised several tailless muskellunge, survivors of such attacks.

Muskellunge spawn several weeks later than northern pike, usually during the first part of May. Ordinarily they spawn in tributary streams and shallow lake channels rather than in the flooded marshes and swamps preferred by pike. The eggs are very similar to those of pike and are deposited at random. A female may produce 60,000 to 100,000 eggs, depending on her size. Late-maturing northern pike have been reported as spawning with muskellunge. Further evidence of probable hybridization has been found in the appearance of many specimens which bear muskellunge markings but have only 11 submandibular pores. This makes one suspect that there has been more hybridization than we realize and that many muskellunge are actually northern pike hybrids.

Between 1939 and 1941 a large number of muskellunge eggs were successfully fertilized with northern pike milt at the Nevis hatchery. Northern pike eggs were likewise fertilized with muskellunge milt. Some of the resulting fry were reared in large aquariums and ponds at the University of Minnesota until they were four years old. The experiment indicated that muskellunge hybridize easily with northern pike and apparently can do so easily in nature, particularly where spawning habitats are limited and late-maturing northern pike are common. The hybrids, like many other hybrids, displayed faster growth initially than either the pure northern pike or the pure muskellunge, but after the first year there was little difference in the annual growth of the hybrids and the pure lines. The hybrids also exhibited greater vitality and had a much lower mortality rate than the pure muskellunge and northern pike controls.

A comparison of the known hybrids with thirty-nine muskellunge and over two hundred northern pike showed that the hybrids had some distinctive morphological characters. Ninety-one percent of the hybrids had cheeks that were entirely covered with scales, whereas only 22 percent of the muskellunge had scaled cheeks. It might be noted that the thirty-nine muskellunge included some from north central Minnesota which could have had mixed ancestry. Approximately 75 percent of the hybrids had a total of 10 mandibular pores and the remaining 25 percent had 11 or 12 pores. The number of lateral line scales in the hybrids was usually intermediate to the numbers characteristic of the parents. The muskellunge had 130 to 157 lateral line scales, usually 147 to 155 scales. The hybrids had 129 to 141 scales. The anal fin of the hybrids had 16 to 19 rays, the same range as for the muskellunge but somewhat higher than for the northern pike, which has 14 to 18 rays, usually 14 to 16. The dorsal fin of the hybrids had 18 to 21 rays, the same as for the muskellunge but slightly more than the range for the northern pike, which has 17 to 19 rays. The hybrids had 17 or 18 branchiostegal rays, which is within the range of variation for the muskellunge.

As it seems apparent that a certain degree of hybridization takes place when muskellunge and northern pike are present in the same lake (which is frequently the case), it is difficult to find populations of purebred muskellunge. While conducting a survey of lakes during the period 1934–1940, Eddy found that Shoepack Lake, a small lake between Rainy Lake and Lake Kabetogama, contained a population of muskellunge but no northern pike. The muskellunge from Shoepack Lake all exhibited the pure characters of the muskellunge with no evidence of hybridization. Since Shoepack Lake is a small lake with limited food potential, none of the muskellunge were much over 10 pounds in weight. With the resumption of muskellunge propagation following World War II, Shoepack Lake muskellunge served as a source of fertilized eggs for the Park Rapids hatchery, which still hatches and rears fingerlings for local distribution.

The muskellunge is one of the fishes most sought after by Minnesota anglers and one of the hardest to catch. The fishermen are often purists who fish for no other species and spend years trying to lure an exceptionally large fish from its favorite weed bed or from the protection of sunken logs in flowage areas. Except for rare times when muskellunge go on striking sprees, as they did in Leech Lake several years ago, fishermen can fish for years without hooking one. The muskellunge seems to taunt the fisherman by following the lure closely but not striking, and it may come up close to the boat to stare disdainfully at the excited angler. Its reputation as being the greatest fighter of all the game fishes has made it the greatest prize. Muskellunge are usually caught by trolling or casting outside the weeds using very large or very active spoons. Some fishermen prefer spinners baited with minnows or white suckers; some use white suckers of 12 inches or more in length. The usual procedure is to locate an especially large muskellunge and then to fish for days, weeks, or even years until it finally takes the lure — or until some other lucky angler catches the prize. When fishing in new areas, it is helpful to have a guide who knows the lake and often the home of almost every sizable muskellunge in it. Otherwise one may spend weeks exploring the lake for promising habitats. Usually special rods and reels comparable to surf-casting equipment are used; the rods are heavy, and the reels have a large line capacity. Both casting and heavy-duty spinning tackle are used. It takes patience and luck — with the odds against the fisherman — to hook the wary muskellunge. Landing him once he is hooked requires both luck and great skill.

GRASS PICKEREL

Esox americanus vermiculatus LeSueur

The grass pickerel is rarely more than 12 inches in length. The body is olive green and marked with wavy or wormlike bars. There are about 105 scales in the lateral line. There are usually 11 to 13 branchiostegals.

We are including this fish because it is present in the backwaters of the Mississippi River only a few miles south of the Minnesota-Iowa boundary, and we anticipate that eventually it will be found in extreme southeastern Minnesota. The grass pickerel ranges from Iowa across southern Wisconsin (Greene, 1935) and Michigan into southern Ontario and southward into the Gulf states. Although Surber (1920) reported grass pickerel from Minnesota on the authority of a very early record, we believe the evidence for that record may have been an immature northern pike (*Esox lucius*). No specimens have been reported in Minnesota in the past seventy years, although we have watched all the University of Minnesota's numerous survey collections in the hope of finding one. The species is too small to have value as a panfish or a game fish.

Family CYPRINIDAE
The Minnow Family

The minnows are usually of small size, although the carp, which is not native, may reach a weight well over 50 pounds. Several American species reach a weight of several pounds and a length of 18 inches, but many species have a maximum size of about 2 inches. Over 2,000 species are known. Jordan, Evermann, and Clark (1930) list 307 species from North and Central America. With the exception of one Japanese species, all minnows are strictly freshwater fishes. The minnow family is represented in Minnesota and the neighboring states by more individuals and species than any other family of fish. Hubbs and Cooper (1936) state that the number of minnows in Michigan waters probably runs into many hundred millions. They attribute this abundance to several factors. First, minnows as a group occupy a great variety of habitats and eat many types of food. Second, most species require a relatively short time to reach sexual maturity. Third, a large number of minnows can occupy a small space and find sufficient food and shelter because the individuals are usually small.

Many species are so similar externally that it is difficult to distinguish one from another. Consequently this family is extremely difficult to study. In addition the name "minnow" is often applied locally without discrimination to any small fish. To complicate matters still further, there are a number of small fishes with similar names (for instance, the topminnow and the mudminnow) which belong to other families.

In the spring the male minnow often develops tubercles on the top of the head, on the pectoral fins, and along the sides of the body. Shape, position, size, and number of tubercles are useful in species identification. In some species bright colors, particularly red, orange, and yellow, appear on the fins and in streaks along the body of the male. Breeding males are strikingly different in appearance from nonbreeding males, and it is difficult for the beginner to identify them from the standard keys (which usually describe nonbreeding adults). Young individuals are usually more slender than adults of the same species, and the eyes of young individuals are always much larger. The young fish often show a black lateral stripe and a caudal spot not possessed by the adults, although these marks are also common in the adults of many species.

In all members of this family the head is naked in the nonbreeding state. One dorsal fin is present, but spines are absent in all Minnesota species except in the introduced carp and goldfish. Fewer than 10 soft dorsal rays are present in native minnows, but this number is exceeded in carp and goldfish. No teeth are present on the jaws. The pharyngeal teeth are well developed and form one of the most important characters for identification. The teeth are arranged in not more than two rows on each posterior branchial arch in all local species except the carp. (The carp has three rows.) The outer row contains 1 or 2 teeth, and the inner or main row contains 4 or 5 teeth.

In order to be observed the teeth must be carefully dissected out by turning back the opercle and exposing the last gill arch, which bears the teeth. The arch lies against and inside the shoulder girdle supporting the pectoral fins. The arch must be carefully separated from the girdle by cutting on each side of it, and then it can be removed by cutting each end. The tissue must be dissected away from the teeth with needles, taking care not to injure the fragile teeth. The pharyngeal arches bearing the teeth are most easily removed from fresh specimens; after removal they should be placed in a vial of water to allow the tissue to decompose. If teeth are missing, their position is marked by an empty socket which can be seen easily with the aid of a dissecting microscope or a 10X hand lens. Pharyngeal teeth are deciduous and are constantly being lost and replaced during the life of the individual. They vary from sharp hooked types for piercing to flat molarlike teeth for grinding.

The various species of the minnow family show considerable differences in the selection of food from the general supply available to them. The minnows of Minnesota and neighboring states are mainly carnivorous, although they seldom eat fish or other large aquatic organisms. The principal diet of most species consists of insects and entomostracans. A few species eat mostly vegetation, and a few others feed almost wholly on the organic mud at the bottom of ponds and streams. Forbes and Richardson (1908) made the following observations:

In the general scheme of aquatic life, the native members of this family, taken together as a group, play a multiple role. They operate, to some extent, as a check on the increase of the aquatic insects, from which they draw a large part of their food supply; they make indirectly available, as food for their own most destructive enemies, these aquatic insects, many terrestrial insects also, which fall into the water and are greedily devoured by them, and the mere mud and slime and confervoid algae gathered up from the bottom of the waters they inhabit; and they rival the young of all larger fishes, their own worst enemy included, by living continuously, to a great degree, on the *Entomostraca* and insect life which these fishes must have, at one period of their lives, in order to get their growth. They also offer a considerable means of subsistence to certain aquatic birds, such as kingfishers, and members of the heron family; and, through their contributions to the support of the best of food fishes, they form an important link in the chain of agencies by which our waters are made productive in the interest of man. . . .

From the standpoint of the predaceous species, minnows are young fishes which never grow up, and thus keep the supply of edible fishes of a size to make them available to the smaller carnivorous kinds when the young of the larger species have grown too large to be captured or eaten. . . . Moreover, by their great numbers, by their various adaptations and correspondingly general ecological distribution, and by their permanently small size, the minnows must distract in great measure the attention of carnivorous fishes from the young of the larger species, upon which, without them, the adults of these larger species would fall with the full force of their voracious appetites. By offering themselves, no doubt as unconscious, but sufficient, substitutes, they thus help to preserve — for their own future destruction, however, be it noticed — the young of many species which would otherwise be forced to feed on each other's progeny. It is not too much to say, consequently, that the number of game fishes which any waters can maintain is largely conditioned upon its permanent stock of minnows.

Faced with such facts we should take steps to control and to supplement, where possible, nature's effort to preserve a proper balance of game and forage fishes. At present there are hundreds of bait-minnow dealers scattered over the northern states, and most of their stock is procured from public waters, in nearly every instance at the expense of game fishes. Several years ago certain streams and lakes in Minnesota had to be closed entirely to the taking of minnows for commercial purposes, and conditions have now reached an acute stage in which the natural food supply is so reduced as to curtail the game fish capacity of certain lakes and streams. Minnows have sometimes been hauled over two hundred miles in an effort to supply the demand for live bait. When a dealer, without boasting, informs you that he has marketed over 100,000 dozen minnows in a single season, the magnitude of the industry and its effect upon fish life are manifest. And this is not the worst of it by any means, for it is safe to assert that for every minnow marketed by the dealer at least five others have been destroyed, either through careless handling when they were seined, sorted, or transported to the dealer's holding vats or through improper facilities for their care at the place of sale. Many minnow dealers have their own rearing ponds and no longer depend on seining for their bait supplies. There are also minnow wholesalers with large and expensive rearing facilities from which to supply stocks of minnows to the small bait dealers. The rearing ponds produce stocks that are uniform and can be easily graded for the angling market. The vast majority of minnows native to Minnesota waters are not good bait fish. They are not hardy enough to survive crowding and handling, and they die quickly when placed on the hook.

Some species of this family have played an important economic role in addition to being bait and food for other fishes. Many of the larger species such as the carp are important food fishes, particularly in Europe. The important European species of the minnow family include tench, roach, bleak, and bream. The crystalline coloring matter of various cyprinids is said to have been employed for ornamental purposes by the Chinese for hundreds of years. The important artificial pearl industry in France and Germany utilizes the scales of the bleak.

KEY TO MINNESOTA SPECIES OF FAMILY CYPRINIDAE

1. Dorsal fin with a long base and more than 11 soft rays; dorsal and anal fins each with a strong spinous ray 2
   Dorsal fin with a short base and fewer than 10 soft rays; no spinous ray in dorsal or anal fin 3
2. Upper jaw with 2 barbels on each side; lateral line with more than 32 scales (except in mirror carp and leather carp) . . . .
   . . . . .Carp, *Cyprinus carpio* Linnaeus
   No barbels; lateral line with fewer than 30 scales . . . .
   . . . . .Goldfish, *Carassius auratus* (Linnaeus)
3. Cartilaginous ridge of lower jaw prominent, separated by definite groove from lower lip; intestine spirally wound around air bladder . . . .
   . . . . .Stoneroller, *Campostoma anomalum* (Rafinesque)
   Cartilaginous ridge of lower jaw hardly evident, not separated from lower lip; intestine not wound around air bladder 4
4. Premaxillaries nonprotractile; upper lip connected with skin of snout by a bridge of tissue which the premaxillary groove does not cross 5
   Premaxillaries protractile; upper lip separated from skin of snout by a deep groove continuous across the midline 6
5. Snout projecting far beyond the horizontal mouth; eyes superolateral . .
   . . . . .Longnose dace, *Rhinichthys cataractae* (Valenciennes)
   Snout scarcely projecting beyond the somewhat oblique mouth; eyes lateral . . . . .Blacknose dace, *Rhinichthys atratulus* (Hermann)
6. Maxillary with a barbel (usually small and often hidden in the groove on the upper jaw); barbel occasionally obsolete in *Semotilus* 7
   Maxillary without a barbel (a barbellike swelling occurs at the end of the maxillary in the breeding males of *Pimephales notatus*) 13
7. Barbel at or near end of maxillary and always slender; teeth in main row always 4–4 8
   Barbel on lower edge of maxillary, well in advance of posterior end (usually concealed in groove between maxillary and premaxillary; often flaplike or obsolescent); teeth in main row typically 5–4 12
8. Scales more than 55 in lateral line . . . .
   . . . . Lake chub, *Couesius plumbeus* (Agassiz)
   Scales fewer than 45 in lateral line 9
9. Blotches present on sides along lateral band 10
   Blotches not present on sides along lateral band 11
10. Barbel as long or longer than diameter of pupil of eye; sides of body rather heavily sprinkled with black dots . . . .
    .Speckled chub, *Hybopsis aestivalis* (Girard)
    Barbel shorter than diameter of pupil of eye; sides and back marked with scattered X-shaped spots . . . .
    . . . . .Gravel chub, *Hybopsis x-punctata* Hubbs and Crowe
11. Mouth somewhat oblique and slightly inferior, upper lip scarcely over-

hung by snout; eye shorter than upper jaw; least suborbital width less than half postorbital length of head (about half postorbital length of head in largest adults); spot at caudal base round and blackish; caudal fin red in live juveniles; teeth typically 1,4–4,1 . . . .
. . . . .Hornyhead chub, *Nocomis biguttatus* (Kirtland)
Mouth horizontal and strictly inferior, upper lip considerably overhung by snout; eye longer than upper jaw; body without definite spots (beware of parasite specks); teeth typically 1,4–4,1; color silvery, without dark lateral band; adults 4 to 10 inches in length; dorsal fin inserted distinctly in advance of pelvic fin . . . .
. . . . .Silver chub, *Hybopsis storeriana* (Kirtland)
12. Black spot on dorsal fin near front of base, indistinct in young; mouth large, upper jaw extending at least to below front of eye; sides not mottled by specialized dark scales; scales in lateral line fewer than 60.
. . . . .Creek chub, *Semotilus atromaculatus* (Mitchill)
No black spot on dorsal fin; mouth small, upper jaw not extending to below front of eye; sides mottled by specialized dark scales; scales in lateral line 65 to 75 . . . . .Pearl dace, *Semotilus margarita* (Cope)
13. Lateral line scales more than 60 14
Lateral line scales fewer than 55 18
14. Intestine short, with a single main loop, and less than twice as long as body; body with a single dusky lateral band; teeth in main row typically 5–4, sometimes 5–5, 4–5, or 4–4 15
Intestine elongate, with two crosswise coils in addition to primary loops, and more than twice as long as body; body with two black lateral bands; teeth 5–5 or 5–4 17
15. Peritoneum black; lateral line incomplete; scales minute, more than 80 in lateral line, each with radii on all fields . . . .
. . . . .Finescale dace, *Chrosomus neogaeus* (Cope)
Peritoneum pale; lateral line complete except in young of *Semotilus margarita*; scales fewer than 80 in lateral line, with radii only on exposed fields 16
16. Head narrow; gape very wide, upper jaw extending to front of eye; nuptial tubercles small but numerous, developed on head and often also on nape; snout sharp . . . .
. . . . .Redside dace, *Clinostomus elongatus* (Kirtland)
Head width moderate; gape relatively small, upper jaw not extending to front of eye; nuptial tubercles minute or undeveloped; snout blunt . .
. . . .*Semotilus margarita* (see 12)
17. Mouth strongly oblique and curved; length of upper jaw less than one-fourth length of head; distance from tip of snout to back of eye usually about equal to rest of head . . . .
. . . . .Northern redbelly dace, *Chrosomus eos* Cope
Mouth somewhat oblique and curved; length of upper jaw more than one-fourth length of head; distance from tip of snout to back of eye distinctly

longer than rest of head . . . .
. . . . .Southern redbelly dace, *Chrosomus erythrogaster* Rafinesque
18. Abdomen behind pelvic fins with a fleshy keel not covered with scales; lateral line much decurved; anal fin falcate . . . .
. . . . .Golden shiner, *Notemigonus crysoleucas* (Mitchill) Abdomen behind pelvic fins rounded over and scaled; lateral line not greatly decurved; anal fin scarcely falcate 19
19. First dorsal ray more or less thickened, separated by membrane from first well-developed ray, and with a thick coating of adipose tissue; a dark spot, faint in young and in some females, at front of dorsal fin near but not at base; back flattened; preceding characters conspicuous only in adults 20
First dorsal ray a thin splint, closely attached to first well-developed ray, and with a thin covering of adipose tissue; no dark spot at front of dorsal fin near base (but a dark spot is present at the very base in *Notropis umbratilis*); back little flattened 22
20. Peritoneum silvery; intestine short (S-shaped) . . . .
. . . . .Bullhead minnow, *Pimephales vigilax* (Baird and Girard) Peritoneum blackish or black; intestine somewhat elongated, with at least one short extra coil 21
21. Mouth terminal and oblique; caudal spot faint; lateral line very short (in Great Lakes subspecies) . . . .
. . . . .Fathead minnow, *Pimephales promelas* Rafinesque Mouth inferior and horizontal; caudal spot conspicuous; lateral line complete . . . . .Bluntnose minnow, *Pimephales notatus* (Rafinesque)
22. Mouth extremely small and nearly vertical; dorsal rays typically 9; teeth in main row 5–5 or 5–4, strongly serrate . . . .
. . . . .Pugnose minnow, *Opsopoeodus emiliae* Hay Mouth large and oblique to horizontal except in *Notropis anogenus*; dorsal rays typically 8; teeth in main row 4–4 23
23. Lower lip restricted to rather prominent lateral lobes . . . .
. . . . .Suckermouth minnow, *Phenacobius mirabilis* (Girard) Lower lip normal, not restricted to lateral lobes 24
24. Anal fin with 9 to 12 rays, rarely 8; teeth 2,4–4,2 25
Anal fin with usually 7 or 8 rays, rarely 9; teeth in outer row usually 0 or 1, but often 2 in *Notropis heterodon, N. texanus*, and *N. hudsonius* . .
. 28
25. Origin of dorsal fin directly above or slightly anterior to insertion of pelvic fins . . . . Common shiner, *Notropis cornutus* (Mitchill) Origin of dorsal fin distinctly behind insertion of pelvic fins 26
26. Body deep, depth typically more than head length in adults or equal to head length in young; exposed portions of scales deeper than long; nuptial tubercles large; breeding males with much red over entire body and fins; dorsal fin with prominent black spot at extreme anterior base .
. . . . .Redfin shiner, *Notropis umbratilis* (Girard)

Body slender, depth much less than head length; exposed portions of scales not deeper than long; nuptial tubercles minute; breeding males with little or no red or with red confined to head region; dorsal fin lacks prominent black spot at anterior base 27

27. Snout short and blunt, length less than two-thirds distance from posterior margin of eye to posterior end of head; body rather sharply compressed; form of body elliptical, deepest near middle of length ....Emerald shiner, *Notropis atherinoides* Rafinesque
Snout produced and sharp, length more than two-thirds distance from posterior margin of eye to posterior end of head; body thicker and heavier; form of body somewhat ovate, deepest anteriorly ....
...................Rosyface shiner, *Notropis rubellus* (Agassiz)

28. Intestine greatly elongated, usually more than twice standard length; peritoneum black 29
Intestine short; S-shaped, much less than twice standard length; peritoneum usually silvery or flecked with black pigment 31

29. Body with dusky lateral band; mouth U-shaped ....
......................Ozark minnow, *Dionda nubila* (Forbes)
Body silvery or brassy; mouth not U-shaped 30

30. Dorsal fin rounded; body brassy; scales with focus less eccentric and with about 20 radii in adults ....
.................Brassy minnow, *Hybognathus hankinsoni* Hubbs
Dorsal fin somewhat falcate; body silvery; scales with focus near basal edge and with about 10 radii in adults ....
.................Silvery minnow, *Hybognathus nuchalis* Agassiz

31. Eye small, less than one-fourth length of head in adults; muzzle conical, head subtriangular in outline; dorsal fin subquadrate in outline, last rays in adults much more than half as long as the longest rays 32
Eye large, more than one-fourth length of head in adults; muzzle bluntly rounded, head not triangular in outline; dorsal fin subtriangular in outline, last rays less than half as long as longest ray 33

32. Anal fin with usually 8 rays; dorsal fin with black blotch on membranes between posterior rays; teeth usually 1,4–4,1 ....
......................Spotfin shiner, *Notropis spilopterus* (Cope)
Anal fin with usually 9 rays; dorsal fin without black blotch; teeth usually 4–4 .... Red shiner, *Notropis lutrensis* (Baird and Girard)

33. Large, conspicuous, and well-defined black spot on base of caudal fin; commonly more than 3 inches in total length ....
...................Spottail shiner, *Notropis hudsonius* (Clinton)
No conspicuous black spot on base of caudal fin (if developed, not sharply set off from lateral band); maximum total length about 3 inches
....34

34. Lateral band blackish, sometimes very indistinct in life, continued forward through eye and around muzzle; lateral line incomplete except

in *Notropis anogenus* 35
Lateral band dusky or obsolete, not definitely continued forward through eye and around muzzle; lateral line complete 38

35. Mouth extremely small, almost vertical; upper jaw extending only to below anterior nostril; teeth of inner row lacking; lateral line nearly complete or complete; peritoneum blackish . . . .
. . . . .Pugnose shiner, *Notropis anogenus* Forbes
Mouth rather large, moderately oblique; upper jaw extending beyond anterior nostril almost to below eye; teeth of inner row frequently developed; lateral line incomplete; peritoneum silvery 36

36. Lateral band surrounding muzzle confined to chin and premaxillaries; mouth oblique, making angle of less than 60 degrees from horizontal; teeth of outer row 1 or 2, usually developed; blackened borders of lateral line pores not expanded into crescentic bars 37
Lateral band surrounding muzzle encroaching on snout above premaxillaries but not on chin; chin not black; mouth oblique, making angle of much less than 60 degrees from horizontal; teeth of outer row lacking; dark borders to lateral line pores expanded to form prominent crescent-shaped black crossbars . . . .
. . .Blacknose shiner, *Notropis heterolepis* Eigenmann and Eigenmann

37. Mouth oblique, making angle of decidedly less than 60 degrees from horizontal; jaws equal or nearly so; snout sharp; dark bars on scales of next row above lateral line alternating with black marks on lateral line scales, producing a zigzag appearance; anal fin with 8 rays . . . . . .
. . . . .Blackchin shiner, *Notropis heterodon* (Cope)
Mouth oblique, making angle of less than 60 degrees from horizontal; lower jaw distinctly included; snout rather blunt; scales of next row above lateral line without definite dark bars; anal fin with 7 rays . . . . .
. . . . .Weed shiner, *Notropis texanus* (Girard)

38. Anal fin almost always with 7 rays 39
Anal fin almost always with 8 rays 41

39. Body deep; prominent lateral band terminates in a small caudal spot; usually less than 2 inches long . . . .
. . . . .Topeka shiner, *Notropis topeka* Gilbert
Body elongate; no prominent lateral band or caudal spot; more than 2 inches long 40

40. Teeth usually 1,4–4,1; middorsal stripe not expanded at front of dorsal fin but surrounds base . . . . . . .River shiner, *Notropis blennius* (Girard)
Teeth 4–4; middorsal stripe expanded in front of dorsal fin and interrupted at front of base . . . .Sand shiner, *Notropis stramineus* (Cope)

41. Snout blunt, overhanging; mandible shorter than upper jaw; angle of jaw considerably anterior to posterior tip of maxillary; dorsal fin high, length almost equal to distance from occiput to origin . . . .
. . . . .Pallid shiner, *Notropis amnis* Hubbs and Greene
Mouth terminal or snout just slightly overhanging; mandible equal

to or almost equal to length of upper jaw; dorsal fin not high, length much less than distance from occiput to origin 42
42. Mouth small; length of upper jaw about equal to diameter of eye; exposed surface of anterior lateral line scales elevated, more than twice as high as long; teeth 4–4 ..Mimic shiner, *Notropis volucellus* (Cope)
Mouth large; upper jaw longer than eye; exposed surface of lateral line scales not elevated and with usual shape; teeth 1,4–4,1 ....
....................Bigmouth shiner, *Notropis dorsalis* (Agassiz)

Genus *Cyprinus* Linnaeus

This genus contains the carp, which is well known in both Europe and North America. The carp is native to eastern Asia, but it has been widely introduced elsewhere. Only one species, *Cyprinus carpio* Linnaeus, occurs in Minnesota, and the characters for this species will serve to distinguish the genus. Several species occur in the Old World.

CARP
Cyprinus carpio Linnaeus

The carp (Figure 59) is the largest of the minnows in this country, often reaching a weight of over 20 pounds and a length of more than 2 feet. There are records of carp weighing over 50 pounds. Carp have been regarded as one of the most important freshwater fishes in the world, furnishing high-protein food for millions of people in the Orient and in central Europe. They have been domesticated and reared in ponds in China and nearby countries for many centuries, and a number of breeds or strains have been produced. We are not certain when they were introduced into Europe, but they probably arrived in the eleventh or twelfth century along with the gradual spread of pond culture westward from China. Pond culture later became highly de-

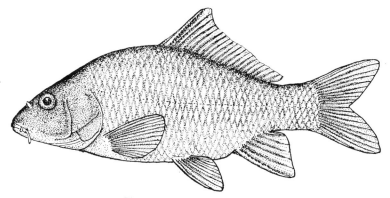

Fig. 59. Carp, *Cyprinus carpio*

veloped throughout central Europe. Carp were introduced into England shortly before 1500 and became very popular. Izaak Walton (1653) called the carp the "queen of the rivers." Since carp are among the most adaptable of all fishes, they flourished wherever they were introduced except in the far north.

In the United States German immigrants in the middle 1800s yearned for fat carp, and to satisfy them the carp was introduced into this country. At least one private attempt was made to introduce the species before 1850, but it was not successful. In 1872 carp were successfully introduced into California, and in 1877 the United States Fish Commission secured some carp and maintained them in ponds in Washington, D.C. These fish were considered to be so valuable that the ponds had to be guarded. In a few years the offspring of these carp were released into rivers of the Mississippi drainage where they spread rapidly. The actual stocking of Minnesota waters was not undertaken until 1883, although carp were already moving up from the lower Mississippi River.

Carp can be distinguished from native North American minnows by the long dorsal fin with more than 11 soft rays and an anterior stout spine with serrations on its posterior margin. The anal fin has a similar spine. Carp also differ in having three rows of pharyngeal teeth, 1,1,3–3,1,1, which are molar-like, and two pairs of barbels at the angle of the upper jaw. The lateral line contains 33 to 40 scales. The scales are large and more or less golden brown.

Carp have spread through most of the stream systems of the United States. They prefer relatively warm waters, and in Minnesota they thrive in shallow mud-bottom lakes and large streams in the southern and central parts of the state. They seem to avoid the swift rocky streams, and they are usually not common in trout streams. We have not found them in the Lake of the Woods drainage. Moore and Braem (1965) collected carp in the St. Louis River, in 1971 one specimen was caught off the Grand Marais breakwater in Lake Superior, and there is a record from Thunder Bay in Canada. In 1920 there were no carp in the Mississippi River above St. Anthony Falls, but by 1935 the carp had extended their range up to Little Falls. They did not appear in the upper St. Croix River above Taylors Falls until recently. Undoubtedly the spread of the species northward despite natural barriers has been facilitated to some extent by the occasional release of small carp along with other minnows which are discarded from fishermen's bait pails. In recent years carp have invaded the Red River drainage and have extended their range northward. McCrimmon (1968) has described the invasion and dispersal of the species in Canada. Carp first appeared in Saskatchewan in 1929 and in Manitoba in 1938, and by 1967 they were present far north in the Nelson River. At least some of these moved northward by way of the Red River. It was long thought that the cold waters would prevent them from spreading northward, but it seems evident that they are so adaptable that they can adjust to more extreme environments than we formerly thought possible.

In Europe and Asia many different varieties of carp have been selected for breeding. Recently European fishery biologists have undertaken an intensive study of carp culture to supplement the meat supply. Part of their program consists of research on the hereditary characters of the carp, and they have been successful in producing strains with faster growth, higher efficiency in food utilization, and different spawning periods.

The three varieties of carp originally introduced into Minnesota were the scale carp, the mirror carp, and the leather carp. These three types differ markedly in their phenotypes: the scale carp is completely covered with scales and probably represents the original wild strain, the leather carp lacks scales, and the mirror carp has only a few large scales. The mirror carp is the variety most widely used in pond culture in the Old World. A study of the inheritance of these types has been made by Wohlfarth and Lahman (1963). In their study they recognize a phenotypic line carrying a lethal gene N which causes the death of all progeny homozygous for the gene (NN). The mode of inheritance of scalation is controlled by two independent genes, S and N, as follows: If we cross a homozygous scale carp (genotype SS) with a mirror carp (genotype ss), the offspring are all scale carp (Ss). If we then cross two of the first generation individuals, the genetic inheritance of their offspring will result in one mirror carp (ss) for every three scale carp (SS, Ss, and Ss).

Line carp have the genotype $NnSs$, and if we cross two line carp we get six line carp ($NnSS$ and $NnSs$), three scale carp ($nnSS$ and $nnSs$), two leather carp ($Nnss$), and one mirror carp ($nnss$); the deviation from the 9:3:3:1 ratio characteristic of dihybrid crosses is the lethal effect of the homozygous NN condition.

There is more than an academic reason for including this bit of genetics in our discussion of the carp. When the species first appeared in Minnesota waters, three types were commonly seen — the leather carp, the mirror carp, and the scale carp. The fourth type, the line carp, was simply not recognized by either commercial fishermen or fisheries biologists. Eddy and Surber (1947) mention the presence of leather carp, although it was rare at that time. Recent conversations with John Moyle of the Minnesota Department of Natural Resources and with various commercial fishermen indicate that leather carp are no longer present or at least are exceedingly rare. Mirror carp appear occasionally, but they are rare enough to evoke comment when they are seen. The original stocks from which the present carp populations arose must have carried the gene N in the heterozygous condition, and some were of the line type. Since the homozygous condition NN is lethal, selection will operate to increase the frequency of the recessive gene n. The fact that leather carp were present years ago but are not present today indicates that selection has in fact favored the recessive gene and that the dominant gene may have been eliminated from Minnesota carp populations. Scale carp are most frequent in large samples of fish, far out of proportion to the 3:1 ratio we might expect. Unfortunately, we have not made the counts necessary in order to estimate the frequency of S and s genes, but it appears that the s gene has been selected against. The two types of selection are quite different, for N acts as a lethal factor when homozygous, but the s gene, while selected against in the homozygous condition, can be preserved in the population in the heterozygous condition Ss. The main point is that the carp population has undergone evolution in the relatively short time since its introduction into the United States less than a century ago.

Carp are highly prolific; females weighing from 15 to 20 pounds may produce over 2,000,000 eggs. They spawn at random in late April or May, crowding into shallow bays or moving upstream into headwater sloughs. The scene at the spawning bed is quite spectacular as hundreds if not thousands of carp swarm into the shallows, often with their bodies half out of water, to spawn with much splashing, which can be heard for some distance. The eggs hatch in ten to twenty days, depending on the temperature. The newly hatched carp grow very rapidly, reaching a length of 8 inches or more in their first year.

Carp are omnivorous, feeding on both vegetation and animal matter. They do not seem to feed directly off the bottom; instead they uproot the vegetation and then feed eagerly on the tender shoots and roots as they settle to the bottom. As the carp move along the weeds near shore, the water plants drop as if they were being mowed. When the fish have stirred up a cloud of mud, debris, and plants, they back off and then swim through the mass, sucking up whatever is edible. (Lakes heavily infested with carp can be recognized by the turbid waters.) They do the same when confined in aquariums. When they are fed corn, they wait until it settles to the bottom; then they root up the corn and silt and swim through the debris, sucking out the corn. Their ability to eat rough food makes them one of the most efficient fishes in the utilization of food produced in Minnesota lakes. There are records of very fertile lakes supporting 1,000 pounds of carp per acre, which is at least three times the best poundage of panfish and game fish the lakes can support. Carp are very abundant in some of the shallow lakes which are subject to frequent winter-kills, but the species, especially the larger individuals, seems to have little tolerance for low oxygen conditions and in bad winters hundreds of tons of carp have suffocated.

Carp are not very popular in Minnesota because they destroy the native vegetation, ruining the spawning and feeding beds of the native fishes. They render the ordinarily clear water of many lakes turbid, and they are not as desirable for eating as many native fishes. But it seems to be impossible to eradicate them completely so we must try to keep them under control and to prevent them from getting into waters where they do not now occur.

The rough fish removal programs are mainly designed to reduce carp populations by seining or trapping. Poisoning is impractical except in very small lakes. State fishermen and contract commercial fishermen, usually seining under the ice in late winter, remove thousands of pounds of carp annually. These are sold to wholesalers who hold them in ponds or cribs and feed them until the market prices are suitable and then ship them to Chicago and New York markets. Nevertheless, the demand for carp in these markets appears to be declining.

Seining carp is not easy because the fish are extremely wary and any noise or disturbance will send them fleeing to deep water. We have tried to get a seine around carp concentrated on a spawning bed, but the moment we put out the seine they all dashed for deep water. When making ordinary seine hauls in survey work, we find that carp are experts at jumping over the corkline or diving under the leadline as soon as they realize they are surrounded. Because of this, trapping seems to be more practical. Carp are caught readily in traps set in the streams through which they try to move into the lakes to spawn. Dams with screens at the top of the apron are used to keep them out of such lakes; carp are so persistent in their migrations that they wriggle up the aprons of these dams when only a fraction of an inch of water is flowing over the apron.

In commercial operations, Minnesota has sold many millions of dollars worth of carp, far more than any other species of commercial fish, but this does not compensate for the damage to the lakes and to the recreational value of native fishes. During World War II a commercial firm at Mankato canned carp and sold the product to the army under the name "lake fish." The canned carp was suitable for use in hot dishes and salads. After the war the company was required to label their product as carp, and there was little further demand for it. Smoked carp has an excellent flavor, and it probably would find a good market if it were available commercially. The flavor of carp can be improved by cutting out the so-called mud line, a dark streak in the flesh on each side of the fish. The flesh is coarse and has a somewhat muddy flavor, and panfrying does not make them very palatable. In Europe they are seasoned with all kinds of herbs and spices and then baked, broiled, or boiled, making an excellent dish which is quite popular.

Izaak Walton gives the following recipe for carp in *The Compleat Angler* (1653): "Put him with his blood and liver, which you must save when you open him, into a small pot or kettle; then take sweet marjorum, thyme, and parsley, of each a handful; a sprig of rosemary, and another of savory; bind them into two or three small bundles, and put them in your carp, with four or five whole onions, twenty pickled oysters, and three anchovies. Then pour upon your carp as much claret wine as will only cover him; and season your claret well with salt, cloves, and mace, and the rinds of oranges and lemons. Then cover your pot and set it on a quick fire till it be sufficiently boiled. Then take the carp, and lay it, with the broth, into a dish; and pour upon it a quarter of a pound of the best fresh butter, melted, two or three eggs, and some herbs shred; garnish your dish with lemons and so serve it up." This elaborate recipe leaves little doubt that carp was considered a delicacy in that famous angler's day — and in view of the ingredients there was hardly any need for concern about a faintly muddy flavor!

Genus *Carassius* Nilsson

The species of this genus are native to the Old World, but two species which have been domesticated have been introduced into the United States.

These are the goldfish, *Carassius auratus* (Linnaeus), and the crucian carp, *Carassius carassius* (Linnaeus); both are closely related to the carp but lack barbels. Only the goldfish is found in Minnesota waters.

GOLDFISH

Carassius auratus (Linnaeus)

The goldfish (Figure 60) is easily distinguished from the carp by its dentition (the pharyngeal teeth are in one row, 4–4) and by the absence of barbels on the upper jaw. The species is native to Japan and China and has relatives in Europe. In the wild state, goldfish are olivaceous in color or melanistic. Goldfish and carp are the only Minnesota fishes which have descended from domesticated fish. In very early times goldfish were domesticated by the Chinese, and many genetic varieties, some quite bizarre and grotesque, were selected for display as aquarium fishes or in formal gardens. Almost every household in the United States has had goldfish at some time or other.

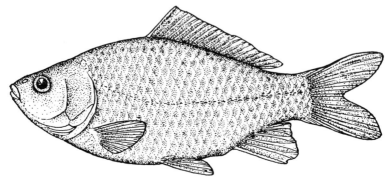

Fig. 60. Goldfish, *Carassius auratus*

Goldfish have been introduced into several lakes in the St. Paul-Minneapolis metropolitan area. They are known from Lake Calhoun, Como Lake, and Silver Lake. Eddy and Surber (1947) reported that goldfish were found occasionally in Lake Minnetonka, but no specimens were collected by Phillips in his intensive survey of the lake in the summer of 1969. Small lakes in central and southern Minnesota have at various times supported populations of goldfish, and occasional individuals have been taken by fishermen from the sloughs along the Minnesota River below Fort Snelling (Eddy and Surber, 1947). Some of these records may be the results of accidental introductions, but most undoubtedly were made by tenderhearted individuals who wished to dispose of their pet goldfish. Fortunately, to date goldfish have not shown the hardiness to cold and the adaptability of the carp or they too might represent a serious management problem in Minnesota as they do in some eastern states.

Contrary to popular belief, goldfish are not small fish; when they are released from the confinement of a fish bowl into a lake or a stream, they may grow to a weight of several pounds. In 1941 members of a fish survey crew from the Minnesota Department of Conservation seined Como Lake in St. Paul and took several goldfish that weighed over 2 pounds. Like certain other Old World minnows, goldfish and carp appear to be more tolerant of waters that have been enriched or polluted than are their New World relatives. Perhaps the domesticated fishes have become more adapted to man and his uses or abuses of land and water than the relatively wild North American fishes.

Genus *Campostoma* Agassiz

Only one species in this genus is found in Minnesota. The species is characterized by a cartilaginous ridge which is confined to the lower jaw; the intestine is wrapped many times around the gas bladder.

STONEROLLER

Campostoma anomalum (Rafinesque)

The stoneroller (Figure 61) reaches a maximum size of 8 to 10 inches. The body is brownish and more or less mottled. The dorsal and anal fins each have a dark crossbar at one-third or one-half the height of the fin. The peritoneum is black and can usually be seen through the belly wall. The upper lip of the mouth is thick and fleshy; the lower lip has a prominent inside cartilaginous ridge which serves as a distinctive character for the identification of the species. The intestine is coiled several times around the gas bladder. The dorsal fin has 8 rays, and the anal fin has 7 rays. The lateral line has 49 to 55 scales. The pharyngeal tooth formula is 0,4–4,0.

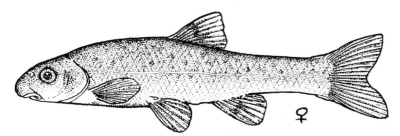

Fig. 61. Stoneroller, *Campostoma anomalum* (female)

The stoneroller and its several subspecies range from Minnesota over the Great Plains area to Texas and eastward to the Atlantic coast. The only subspecies in Minnesota is the central stoneroller, *Campostoma anomalum pullum* Agassiz, which prefers creeks and small rivers rather than lakes or very large rivers. We find the stoneroller in all the small rivers and creeks of the Mississippi River drainage in Minnesota, but it is absent from the Lake Superior drainage and the border lakes region. It is present but not very common in the Red River drainage and in the Mississippi River north of St. Anthony Falls.

Stonerollers spawn in June or early July when they are two or three years old. The male develops large tubercles on the head, the back, and the dorsal fin (Figure 62). Both the dorsal fin and the anal fin develop reddish brown or orange bands on each side of a dark crossbar. The female develops less intense but similar colors and lacks the tubercles. The male has a definite dark spot at the base of the caudal fin. A more diffuse spot is displayed by the female.

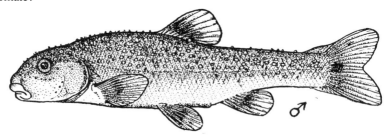

Fig. 62. Stoneroller, *Campostoma anomalum* (breeding male)

The male prepares a nest or site for the eggs. He carries pebbles up to 1/2 inch in diameter and builds a pile on a clean gravel area in a creek or a small stream. Usually the pile is less than 2 feet in diameter. Cahn (1927) reported that some piles contain about half a bushel of pebbles and that several males probably cooperated to make such large piles. As the female deposits her eggs in the pile of pebbles and gravel, the male fertilizes them and the eggs settle into the protective crevices.

The structure of the stoneroller's mouth makes it easy for the species to feed off the bottom. In the stomachs we have examined, we have found very little animal food but much plant material, including not only filamentous algae but microscopic diatoms from the bottom sediments. Some stomachs were filled with mud.

The stoneroller has little value as a bait minnow, and it is not an important forage fish. Small boys catch quite a few stonerollers on worms and proudly carry them home. To this group of anglers these minnows are rather important and provide much recreation.

Genus *Rhinichthys* Agassiz

These fishes are of moderate size. The small mouth is terminal or subinferior; the upper jaw is nonprotractile, and a small barbel is usually present at the end of the maxillary. Five species are known, two of which are found in Minnesota.

BLACKNOSE DACE

Rhinichthys atratulus (Hermann)

The blacknose dace (Figure 63) rarely exceeds a length of 4 inches. The upper part of the body is dark brown or brownish black and is spotted with numerous black blotches; the lower part of the body is silvery and is speckled with small black spots. Breeding males have a dusky red lateral band. A small barbel is usually present on the end of each maxillary; although the barbel is frequently quite prominent, we occasionally find individuals with reduced or undeveloped barbels. The mouth is terminal, and the jaws are of equal length. The scales are small; the lateral line contains 62 to 71 scales. The dorsal fin has 7 or 8 rays, and the anal fin has 7 rays. The pharyngeal tooth formula is 2,4–4,2. The males can be distinguished from the females by their longer pectoral, pelvic, and anal fins.

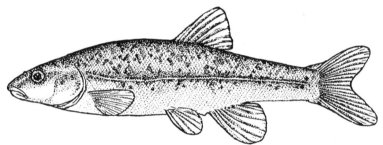

Fig. 63. Blacknose dace, *Rhinichthys atratulus*

The blacknose dace and its several subspecies range from Manitoba and North Dakota to Nova Scotia and southward to North Carolina and Nebraska. The subspecies *Rhinichthys atratulus meleagris* Agassiz, the western black-nose dace, is common in most of the streams of Minnesota. Although sometimes present in lakes, it seems to prefer small streams.

The blacknose dace spawns in riffles over gravel and rubble, in water often only 2 or 3 inches deep. Phillips (1967) observed the spawning habits of dace in the headwaters of the Mississippi River at Lake Itasca. They spawned from mid-June until the first week in July, which is one month later than the spawning dates in Michigan (Hubbs and Cooper, 1936). Hubbs and Cooper also reported that dace do not reach maturity until their third summer. The male and the female make a nest of small pebbles in which the female deposits the eggs. No further care is given to the eggs.

The blacknose dace feeds on all kinds of aquatic insects, worms, and amphipods, on some large algae, and on other plant material. This minnow is sometimes used for bait; it is quite hardy, but it is apparently not very popular.

LONGNOSE DACE
Rhinichthys cataractae (Valenciennes)

The longnose dace (Figure 64) is usually small, but we have occasionally taken individuals up to 6 inches in length. It is similar in many respects to the blacknose dace but is easily identified by its elongated snout. The snout projects far anteriorly over the subterminal mouth. The upper jaw is longer than the lower jaw. This dace is evenly pigmented and is usually soft brown in color, sometimes almost black, on the upper part of the body and dusky silver below. It lacks the prominent black blotching characteristic of the blacknose dace. The longnose dace is more elongate than the blacknose dace. Breeding males have dusky reddish pigmentation on their sides. The scales are small; the lateral line contains 63 to 70 scales. The dorsal fin has 7 or 8 rays, and the anal fin usually has 7 rays. The pharyngeal tooth formula is 2,4–4,2, although a few individuals have 1,4–4,2.

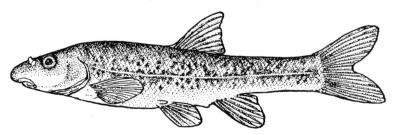

Fig. 64. Longnose dace, *Rhinichthys cataractae*

The longnose dace is one of the most widely distributed minnows. With its many subspecies it is found in northwestern Canada and over most of the United States with the exception of the southeastern coastal region and Alaska. The populations in Minnesota are represented by the Great Lakes subspecies, *Rhinichthys cataractae cataractae* (Valenciennes). Longnose dace are common in the small streams of southeastern Minnesota, in the St. Croix River, and in the drainages of Lake Superior and the border lakes. We have taken them in the Rum River and other tributaries of the Mississippi River above St. Anthony Falls and in several parts of the Red River drainage. Cox (1897) reported their presence in the Pomme de Terre River at Appleton in the Minnesota River drainage, but we have obtained no specimens there despite intensive seining in the habitats normally preferred by this species.

Both species of *Rhinichthys* often occur in the same stream, but the longnose dace lives in much swifter water than does the blacknose dace. Longnose dace are able to live in rapids where the current is so swift that it is difficult for the collector to maintain his footing. Close observations show that they take shelter beneath or between the rocks and boulders and are out of the full force of the current. When they leave a sheltered area, they protect themselves from the current by swimming near the bottom or along the surface of boulders, where the velocity of the current is lowest. The gas bladder of the longnose dace is much reduced in size, giving the fish greater density and less buoyancy and enabling it to sink to the bottom. Thus the dace is able to thrive in a habitat where most species cannot survive. The species is common along the shores of Lake Superior and the large rocky border lakes where the pounding waves create current conditions similar to those of swift streams.

The immature insects characteristic of rapid water make up the major part of the dace's food. Kuehn (1949) studied the food habits of longnose dace from Thompson Creek, a tributary of the Root River, and found that the larvae of Diptera (midges and blackflies) and mayfly nymphs comprised 65 percent and 26 percent, respectively, of their diet while algae accounted for less than 1 percent.

Longnose dace spawn in swift water over gravel-rubble bottoms. They usually spawn in May in southern Minnesota, but in northern Minnesota they spawn into July. They spawn in riffles in streams and on similar bottom substrates along the shores of large lakes.

Genus *Couesius* Jordan

The genus *Couesius* is represented by one species and is characterized by the description of the species.

LAKE CHUB

Couesius plumbeus (Agassiz)

The lake chub (Figure 65) reaches a length of more than 5 inches. The long and rather stout body is dark olive above, blending to dusky white below. The mouth is terminal and not very large. A slender barbel is present near the tip of the maxillary but not at the very tip as in *Hybopsis* and *Nocomis*. The scales are small and are usually crowded anteriorly; the lateral line contains 50 to 80 scales. A dark lateral band extends from the base of the caudal fin to the snout. No strong caudal spot is present, although a vague blotch may be found occasionally on the caudal base. The dorsal fin has 8 rays, and the anal fin has 7 or 8 rays. The pharyngeal tooth formula is usually 2,4–4,2 (2,4–4,3 in one

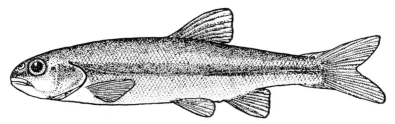

Fig. 65. Lake chub, *Couesius plumbeus*

specimen) in our material, but McPhail and Lindsey (1970) list 0,4–4,0 and 2,4–5,2 for specimens from northwestern Canada. Superficially the body shape of the lake chub resembles the creek chub, *Semotilus atromaculatus*, but the lake chub can be distinguished by the presence of a maxillary barbel and the absence of the dark caudal spot and the spot at the base of the dorsal fin found in the creek chub. The breeding males are blotched with reddish orange on the sides anteriorly and have dark pigment on the paired fins. Males in western Canada develop fine tubercles on the head, on the scales just posterior to the head, and on the dorsal surface of the pectoral fin (McPhail and Lindsey, 1970), but we have not observed these turbercles in Minnesota specimens.

The lake chub is widely distributed throughout northern North America from the Yukon in Alaska to the Fraser River and eastward through Canada to Nova Scotia. It occurs in part of the Great Lakes, in Hudson Bay, and in the upper Missouri River drainage of Wyoming, South Dakota, and Nebraska. An isolated population, perhaps a relict of a southern Pleistocene range, is known from northeastern Iowa (Bailey, 1969). In Minnesota we find this chub in lakes and streams including Lake Superior and its tributaries and from the border lakes westward to Lake of the Woods. We have treated the species as monotypic because the several subspecies ranging from Lake Superior westward seem to be of uncertain systematic status, differing in the number of lateral line scales and in fin structure.

The lake chub usually spawns on gravel or sand bottoms in lakes and streams from mid-June into July. It feeds mostly on small aquatic insects, but it may also feed occasionally on planktonic organisms. In some places in the north the species is used as a bait minnow, but it is probably more important as a forage fish.

Genus *Nocomis* Girard

The genus *Nocomis* has recently been resurrected (Lachner and Jenkins, 1967) and removed from the genus *Hybopsis*. *Nocomis* includes six species, but only one species occurs in Minnesota. The mouth is terminal and lacks the overhanging snout characteristic of *Hybopsis*. A barbel is present at the end of the maxillary.

HORNYHEAD CHUB
Nocomis biguttatus (Kirtland)

The hornyhead chub (Figure 66) reaches a length of nearly 12 inches. The stout body is dark olive brown above and is dusky silver or silvery on the sides. A dark lateral band is present, and there is a prominent black spot on the caudal base. A distinct barbel is on the tip of the maxillary. The lateral line usually contains 41 to 45 scales. The origin of the dorsal fin is over or slightly behind the origin of the pelvic fins. The dorsal fin has 8 rays, and the anal fin has 7 rays. The pharyngeal tooth formula is usually 1,4–4,1, but we have found individuals with 2,5–4,2 and Eddy and Surber (1947) have reported variants with 1,4–4,0 and 0,4–4,0.

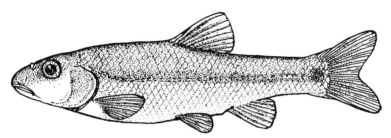

Fig. 66. Hornyhead chub, *Nocomis biguttatus*

During the breeding season the males develop numerous large spiny tubercles on their heads, a pronounced red spot posterior to the eye, and reddish orange pigment on the fins. The females remain quite drab and lack tubercles. They spawn in late May in southern Minnesota and in late June in northern Minnesota. The males construct nests in riffles, usually in water less than 20 inches deep. They create small depressions either by piling up pebbles or by sweeping out a cavity in the debris and silt with their tails. During nest-building the male attracts one or two gravid females to his site. As the females deposit eggs in the nest, the male continues to add more stones. When the spawning has been completed, the nest is a conspicuous pile of stones and gravel. The fertilized eggs are lodged in the crevices between the stones, where they are fairly safe from predators (usually other minnows). Hubbs and Cooper (1936) reported nests up to 3 feet in diameter and from 2 to 6 inches deep.

During the spawning period large numbers of other species of minnows gather around the chub's nest. They feed on eggs swept away from the nest by the current or attempt to snatch eggs out of the nest. After spawning has been completed, the nests are abandoned by the hornyhead chub; several other species, such as the rosyface shiner and the common shiner, may then appropriate the piles of stones and pebbles for their own spawning sites. Our general observations indicate that at times the spawning of a number of different species of minnows may coincide or overlap and may take place in the same pool or riffle. Under these conditions the eggs of one species may be accidentally fertilized by the male of another species, resulting in various hybrid combinations. Even intergeneric hybrids are not uncommon in certain streams in southeastern Minnesota. We have only seen specimens of first generation hybrids in our collections.

The hornyhead chub ranges from Wyoming and the Dakotas to the Hudson River and southward through the northern Ohio River drainage to northeastern Oklahoma. It is distributed all over Minnesota, but it is primarily an inhabitant of small or medium-sized streams. It is not common in lakes or large rivers but is taken occasionally near the mouths of small tributary streams.

This species feeds on all sorts of small aquatic animals, on some plant material, and on terrestrial insects which fall into the water. It is sometimes sold by dealers as a bait minnow but is not as hardy as the more common bait minnows.

Genus *Hybopsis* Agassiz

The genus *Hybopsis* comprises a large group of barbeled minnows found throughout North America. All the species have distinctive long barbels located on the tips of the maxillaries and subterminal mouths with prominent overhanging snouts. Three species of *Hybopsis* are known from Minnesota waters.

SILVER CHUB
Hybopsis storeriana (Kirtland)

The silver chub (Figure 67) reaches a maximum length of 10 inches. It has a greenish iridescent back but is otherwise silvery except for a pale dusky lateral band. The snout is bulging and overhangs the subterminal or inferior mouth. The maxillaries bear long slender barbels at the posterior tips. The lateral line contains 35 to 40 scales, usually about 38. The pharyngeal tooth formula is 1,4–4,1, 1,5–4,1, or 1,4–4,0. The dorsal fin has 8 rays, and the anal fin has 8 rays. The origin of the dorsal fin is distinctly in front of the origin of the pelvic fins.

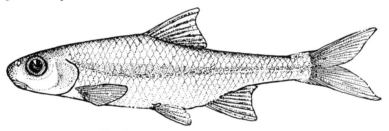

Fig. 67. Silver chub, *Hybopsis storeriana*

The silver chub ranges from eastern North Dakota to New York and south to northern Alabama and Oklahoma. It prefers large rivers and river lakes and is rarely collected in small rivers. The species is quite common in the Minnesota River, in the Mississippi River below St. Anthony Falls, and in the St. Croix River up to Taylors Falls. We have taken silver chubs from several places on the Red River and from the Red Lake River at Crookston. Cox

(1897) reported the silver chub from the Otter Tail River at Breckenridge, but we have not found it in recent collections from the same river. Trawling operations by the Department of Conservation in Lake St. Croix indicate that the silver chub is quite abundant there in waters deeper than 10 feet. One reason we have not taken large samples of this chub is that undoubtedly we did not adequately seine the deeper waters of the large rivers; we relied on minnow seines which seldom reached depths greater than 6 feet. We occasionally take silver chubs when seining off the slopes of sandbars in the Mississippi River in Lake Pepin and from Frontenac southward but never in large numbers.

The silver chub spawns in May and June, but we know little about its spawning habits or its diet.

GRAVEL CHUB

Hybopsis x-punctata Hubbs and Crowe

The gravel chub (Figure 68) is usually less than 4 inches in total length. The body is pale silver with a faint lateral stripe, and the sides are profusely marked with small X-shaped spots. Some light pigmentation is evident on the dorsal and caudal fins. A prominent barbel is on the end of the maxillary, and the pointed snout protrudes slightly beyond the upper jaw. The dorsal fin has 8 rays, and the anal fin has 7 rays. The lateral line contains 39 to 43 scales.

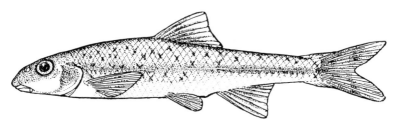

Fig. 68. Gravel chub, *Hybopsis x-punctata*

For many years this fish was without a scientific name; it was referred to as "*Hybopsis sp.*" in many papers or was placed with the species it most closely resembled. Eddy and Surber (1947) placed it under *Erimystax dissimilis* (Kirtland) as the gravel chub. It was not until 1956 that Hubbs and Crowe gave it a scientific name. The genus *Erimystax* is now regarded as a subgenus within the genus *Hybopsis*. *Hybopsis dissimilis* (Kirtland), the Ohio River chub, was formerly confused with the gravel chub.

The gravel chub is represented by two subspecies. The eastern subspecies ranges from southern Minnesota to Ohio and southward to Arkansas and Oklahoma. We have only a few records of this species from Minnesota, one from the upper Iowa River just east of Granger in Fillmore County and others from five stations on the Root River, also in Fillmore County. Hubbs and

Lagler (1964) and Bailey (1969) have noted the rarity of this attractive little chub and suggest that it may become extinct. The preferred habitat seems to be shallow riffles over pea-sized limestone gravel. The destruction of such habitats by erosion and siltation from intensive agricultural practices may be the reason for the scarcity of this species.

The gravel chub reportedly spawns in the spring, but we know nothing more about its spawning habits or its diet.

SPECKLED CHUB

Hybopsis aestivalis (Girard)

The speckled chub (Figure 69) is a slender minnow that reaches a length of about 2 1/2 inches. The body is pale silver speckled or flecked with small black dots above the lateral line. There is a prominent barbel at the posterior end of each maxillary. The snout is rounded and projects distinctly over the inferior mouth. The lateral line contains about 37 scales. The dorsal and anal fins have 8 rays. The pharyngeal tooth formula is 0,4–4,0.

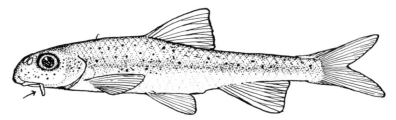

Fig. 69. Speckled chub, *Hybopsis aestivalis*

The speckled chub and its several subspecies range from the upper Missouri drainage in Iowa to southern Minnesota and southward to Texas and western Florida. Until about 1960 we thought this chub was rare in Minnesota, but recently we have taken it in many places in the southern half of the state. We have specimens from the Minnesota River above Mankato, the St. Croix River between Taylors Falls and O'Brien State Park, the Mississippi River below Red Wing, and the Cannon and Zumbro rivers. The reason we were not aware of the true abundance of the speckled chub was that we had not seined in its preferred habitat. The species lives in fast water over shifting sand bottoms, and it was not until 1960 that we really explored this apparently barren habitat. The shifting sand is so loose that it is difficult to seine, and the little chub apparently dives into the sand when disturbed. Another problem is that the fish is so small that it easily passes through the 1/4-inch-mesh seines we commonly use. Finally, when the fish is freshly caught, it is almost translucent and is easily overlooked in a seine unless it happens to wiggle and attract the eye. The western sand darter, *Ammocrypta clara*, is a common associate of the speckled chub, and if we take one we can usually take the other with a little more effort.

We know little about the speckled chub's spawning or feeding habits except that it spawns in May or early June.

Genus *Semotilus* Rafinesque

This genus is made up of medium-sized to large minnows characterized by a small inconspicuous barbel just in front of the end of the maxillary, often concealed in a groove between the maxillary and the premaxillary. The pharyngeal teeth are in two rows, either 2,5–4,2 or 2,4–5,2. Two species are found in Minnesota waters.

CREEK CHUB
Semotilus atromaculatus (Mitchill)

The creek chub (Figure 70) reaches a length of 12 inches in six or seven years. The body is dusky silver with a dark lateral band and a prominent black spot at the anterior base of the dorsal fin, located on the membranes between the first and third rays. A small barbel is located in a groove a short distance anterior to the tip of the maxillary. A small black spot is often present on the base of the caudal fin. The pharyngeal tooth formula is 2,5–4,2. The teeth are strongly hooked. The lateral line contains 50 to 60 scales; the scales are crowded anteriorly. Immature creek chubs, up to a length of 2 or 3 inches, resemble the young of several other minnows. They are especially difficult to distinguish from young pearl dace.

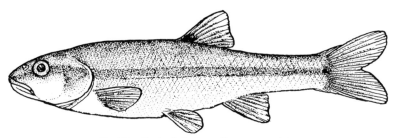

Fig. 70. Creek chub, *Semotilus atromaculatus*

The creek chub ranges from Montana to the Gaspé Peninsula and southward into the Gulf states. Two subspecies have been described; in the southeastern United States a slightly different subspecies, *Semotilus atromaculatus thoreauianus* Jordan, takes the place of the Minnesota subspecies, *Semotilus atromaculatus atromaculatus* (Mitchill). The creek chub prefers small streams and rivers and is found only occasionally in lakes and large rivers.

The species spawns in the spring and early summer in clear streams, generally over a bottom of pea-sized gravel and rubble at the head of swift water. The breeding males have coarse tubercles on their heads and have brightly colored orange, blue, and purple sides. The male constructs a nest that consists of a ridge of gravel and pebbles parallel to the current, either carrying the pebbles in his mouth or pushing them along the bottom. All the pebbles are transported upstream, and a ridge is formed with a concavity on the downstream side. During the preparation of the nest the male fiercely defends his nest site against other creek chubs, large and small. Encounters with other males may be quite vigorous, or they make take the form of ritualized combat which Reighard (1910) terms "deferred combat." The owner of the nest usually wins, even when the challenger is larger. The male patrols his nest area and permits the female, when ripe and ready to spawn, to approach the nest. Deposition and fertilization of the eggs takes only a few seconds, and the fertilized eggs become lodged in the crevices between the pebbles where they are well protected from predation.

During the spawning of the creek chub, other species of minnows gather around the margins of the nest to eat any eggs that drift out of it. Subsequently other species such as the hornyhead chub, the common shiner, and the blacknose dace may use the same riffle site for their own nest construction and spawning. Many nests and their contents probably are disturbed or destroyed by the activities of these late-spawning minnows.

The spawning activities of the creek chub can be observed in almost every small stream in the state. It requires a little patience and a pair of polarized sunglasses to cut down the glare of the sunlight reflected from the water. The small piles of clean stones in and at the head of the shallow riffles and small rapids are quite conspicuous, and often the fish can be observed darting around and away from the observer as they are frightened from the nest.

Creek chubs are quite common in beaver dam pools and may compete with trout for food. They feed on all kinds of aquatic and terrestrial insects, amphipods, bits of vegetation, and even on small fish. Barber and Minckley (1971) noted that aquatic insect larvae and pupae, fish, and mollusks make up 95 percent of the food of creek chubs taken in the headwaters of the Mississippi River in Itasca State Park during the summer months. Barber and Minckley found that they feed most intensively in the early evening and least in the morning. As the fish grow, their diet shifts from the larvae of small Ephemeroptera and small Diptera to the larvae of caddis flies and larger Diptera and eventually to fish. Barber and Minckley also found that the quantity of a food item in the chub's diet is proportional to the availability of the food in the stream.

Creek chubs will bite on baited hooks and small spinners. The trout fisherman finds them particularly annoying when they steal his bait or rise to his fly or even take his lure before a trout gets a chance at it. They are occasionally used for bait.

PEARL DACE

Semotilus margarita (Cope)

The pearl dace (Figure 71) is smaller than the creek chub, usually under 6 inches long, with small scales and a mottled appearance. The lateral line contains 62 to 75 scales, usually about 70. The pearl dace differs from the creek chub in the absence of a black spot at the anterior base of the dorsal fin, and it has a smaller mouth. The posterior margin of the mouth does not extend back of a line drawn vertically along the anterior margin of the eye and the sides of the body. Breeding males have a light crimson or pink band; the females do not have this pigmentation. The pectoral fin of the male is significantly longer than that of the female.

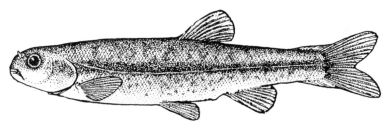

Fig. 71. Pearl dace, *Semotilus margarita*

Three subspecies have been described; one of them, *Semotilus margarita nachtriebi* (Cox), is found in Minnesota. The original description was based on specimens collected in Mille Lacs and in several lakes in the Park Rapids area. The pearl dace is found in streams throughout Minnesota except those in the southwestern part that drain into the Missouri River. The species is common in the streams tributary to Lake Superior and the Rainy River, in the small streams draining into Mille Lacs, and in several small tributaries of the upper St. Croix River east of Hinckley and Askov. It is also quite abundant in small tributaries of the Cedar River south of Austin and in the Park Rapids area where Cox collected his specimens. We have taken specimens from the tributaries of the Mississippi River south of the Twin Cities and in several small tributaries of the Minnesota River, but the species is not common there. Our largest collections have come from the Kawishiwi River drainage in the border lakes region.

Genus *Clinostomus* Girard

Minnows in this genus are of medium size. They are characterized by a broad black band, a long and pointed head, and a very large mouth. One species in the genus is found in Minnesota.

REDSIDE DACE

Clinostomus elongatus (Kirtland)

The redside dace (Figure 72) reaches a length of about 5 inches. The body is dark blue mottled with silver on the belly. It has an indistinct dusky band with a slight interspace between the band and the dark back; the band is very prominent in preserved specimens. The dorsal fin has 8 rays, and the anal fin has either 8 or 9 rays. The mouth is large and very wide with a projecting lower jaw. The snout is sharp. The lateral line is complete and has from 58 to 71 scales; in Minnesota specimens the average number of scales in the lateral line is 65. The pharyngeal tooth formula is usually 2,5–4,2, but we have seen a few individuals with a 2,4–4,2 formula.

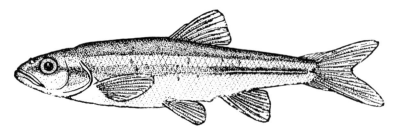

Fig. 72. Redside dace, *Clinostomus elongatus*

The redside dace exhibits marked sexual dimorphism during the breeding season. The breeding males have a bright crimson or reddish orange band shaped like a parallelogram on their sides anteriorly. The female is brownish gray with an indistinct black band. Koster (1939) found females with red sides, but we have not observed any females with red pigmentation. Both males and females in breeding condition develop small tubercles or pearl organs over most of their bodies, although those of the female are smaller. The males have significantly longer pectoral fins than the females.

This species ranges from southern Minnesota eastward through the southern part of the eastern Great Lakes drainage and the Ohio River drainage and south into northeastern Oklahoma. It is restricted in Minnesota to the smaller tributaries of the Cannon, Zumbro, and Root rivers in southeastern Minnesota. Greene (1935) believed that the species was in the process of becoming extinct in Wisconsin, and Harlan and Speaker (1969) stated that it was probably no longer present in Iowa. We thought until recently that it was rare in Minnesota, but we have found fairly large populations apparently reproducing successfully in the middle fork of the Zumbro River. The species is usually associated with the southern redbelly dace and the Ozark minnow.

The reduction in numbers or apparent rarity of the redside dace in other parts of its former range may be due to disturbances caused by modern agricultural practices. In Minnesota it is found in small streams where limestone bedrock is on or near the surface of the ground and where the surrounding land has been left in woodlots or is used for light pasturage. In these small streams where the habitat is relatively undisturbed, we find relicts of the preagricultural fish fauna of the state. These streams are rarely subject to flash floods or rapid fluctuations in water level and are spring-fed. Many streams in which the redside dace may have been present in preagricultural times are now filled with silt deposits, dry one day and a raging torrent the next, and only the hardiest species with the widest tolerances manage to survive in them.

Koster (1939) and Greene (1935) noted hybrids between the redside dace and the common shiner and the creek chub, respectively, but in a study of the life history of the redside dace Koster did not report any crossmatings. He thought that since the three species spawn in the same riffles at the same time accidental cross-fertilization would be possible. To our knowledge no back-crosses have been observed or reported.

Genus *Chrosomus* Rafinesque

The genus *Chrosomus* has recently been reported to be synonymous with the Old World genus *Phoxinus* Rafinesque by Banarescu (1964) in a monograph on the fishes of Romania. However, there is no documentation for this proposal except page precedent (that is, *Phoxinus* is used earlier in the text than *Chrosomus*) in Rafinesque (1820), and no specimens of New World *Chrosomus* were examined by Banarescu. We support the opinion of McPhail and Lindsey (1970) that the genus *Chrosomus* should be retained until a revision involving all the species of *Phoxinus* and *Chrosomus* is published. There seems to be ample argument for a conservative approach at least for the present, and little damage is done by retaining the genus *Chrosomus*. We treat *Pfrille* as a synonym for *Chrosomus*, based in part on the numerous hybrids between *C. eos* and *C. neogaeus* (New, 1962; Legendre, 1970), but McPhail and Lindsey retain the genus *Pfrille*. The zoogeographic implications of Banarescu's proposal are quite profound, especially with respect to the origin of the New World Cyprinidae, because *Phoxinus* would thus represent the only species of an Old World genus of minnows that is native to North America (see McPhail and Lindsey, 1970). Our translation of Banarescu (1964) does not differ significantly from the translation of Berg (1949), except that Banarescu was apparently correct in attributing the genus *Phoxinus* to Rafinesque rather than to Agassiz. We retain the genus *Chrosomus* in this book, but the genus *Phoxinus* is already appearing in the literature. We hope that someone will undertake a study of all the species in the genus so that a more objective decision eventually will be possible.

Legendre (1970) has recommended placing the pearl dace, *Semotilus margarita*, in the genus *Phoxinus*, based on intergeneric hybrids between *Chrosomus* (= *Phoxinus* of Legendre) and *Semotilus*, but we do not find the evidence compelling. Intergeneric hybrids between cyprinids and between genera of other families are not uncommon. We would argue that what is needed is a better understanding of the biology of the species before the significance of hybrids can be evaluated.

SOUTHERN REDBELLY DACE

Chrosomus erythrogaster Rafinesque

The southern redbelly dace (Figure 73) is one of the most colorful minnows. It reaches a length of about 3 inches. The back is dark greenish with dark blotches, and the belly is silvery or yellowish in nonbreeding specimens. The sides are distinctly marked with two dark lateral bands and an interspace ranging from red to cream in color. In breeding males the flanks, the lower parts of the body, and the ventral fins are bright crimson. The red color may be so vivid that the fish may appear to be bleeding, although there is considerable variation in the amount and intensity of the red pigment. Breeding females are yellow or amber rather than red; we have never seen a female with red pigmentation.

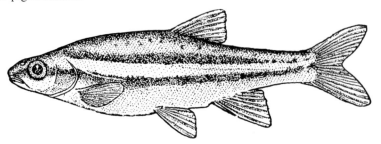

Fig. 73. Southern redbelly dace, *Chrosomus erythrogaster*

The scales of the dace are small, numbering about 85 rows along the body; the lateral line is very short or incomplete. The dorsal fin has 8 rays, and the anal fin has 7 to 9 rays, usually 8. The pharyngeal tooth formula is 0,5–5,0 or 0,5–4,0; the latter formula occurs in about 2 percent of Minnesota specimens (Eastman, 1970). Immature individuals of the southern and northern redbelly dace may be difficult to distinguish. The most useful character for differentiating the two species is the angle of the mouth (Figure 74), which is 48° to 50° from the horizontal in *Chrosomus erythrogaster* and 57° to 61° from the horizontal in *C. eos* (Phillips, 1969b). In mature male southern redbelly dace (those more than 2 inches in standard length), the pectoral, dorsal, and anal fins are longer than those of the females.

Phillips prepared a very detailed analysis of the variation in Minnesota southern and northern redbelly dace and determined the distribution of the two species within the state. The southern redbelly dace is restricted to the tributaries of the Mississippi River from the Cannon River just north of Red Wing southward to the Missouri River drainage in southwestern Minnesota. The southern redbelly dace spawns from late May until the middle of June.

Phillips (1969c) estimated the fecundity of the species by counting the eggs in ten females ranging in length from 59 to 80 mm; these females contained 5,708 to 18,888 eggs.

Phillips (1969a) found diatoms to be part of the diet of the southern redbelly dace. Cahn (1927) reported that the species feeds on algae, other small vegetation, and occasionally *Hyalella*. These little fishes survive well in aquariums. If the day length is controlled, they retain their brilliant red pigmentation for a long period of time. In our estimation they rival in attractiveness many of the exotic aquarium fishes and of course are not as temperature sensitive as many of the exotic species.

NORTHERN REDBELLY DACE
Chrosomus eos Cope

The northern redbelly dace is seldom over 2 inches in length. The body is marked on the sides with two broad lateral bands; the interspace is cream or reddish. The dorsal fin has 7 or 8 rays, usually 8, and the anal fin has 7 to 9 rays, usually 8. The species is similar to the southern redbelly dace except for its more oblique mouth (Figure 74) and its smaller size. Breeding males are sometimes reddish in color but more often are yellowish orange. They are not quite so colorful as the southern redbelly dace.

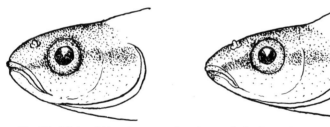

Fig. 74. Distinguishing characters of northern redbelly dace (*Chrosomus eos*) and southern redbelly dace (*C. erythrogaster*). *Left*, head of *Chrosomus eos*; *right*, head of *C. erythrogaster*.

The northern redbelly dace is found from British Columbia to the Hudson Bay drainage and eastward to Nova Scotia and from Montana, Colorado, and central Minnesota eastward to Pennsylvania. There is an isolated population in northwestern Nebraska. In Minnesota it is found throughout the Red River drainage, the drainage of the Mississippi River above St. Anthony Falls, the border lakes region, and the Lake Superior drainage. Its range overlaps that of the southern redbelly dace in southeastern Minnesota (Phillips, 1969b). It is found in habitats ranging from small streams to bog lakes.

Slastenenko (1958) reports that northern redbelly dace spawn during the summer, scattering their eggs over filamentous plants, and that the eggs hatch in eight to ten days. He further reports that the species feeds on plants, small insects, and zooplankton. The actual spawning has not been observed, but Hubbs and Cooper (1936) reported that in Michigan waters these dace use filamentous algal mats as spawning beds. The species has spawned successfully in the aquariums at the University of Minnesota, using a synthetic fiber mat as a site for egg deposition, and the resulting fry were raised to maturity.

The northern redbelly dace hybridizes with the finescale dace (New, 1962). Hybrids are rare in Minnesota populations where the two species are sympatric; they have been found only in the St. Croix drainage east of Hinckley. Both the southern and northern redbelly dace are tolerant of temperatures ranging from 34° to 90° F and thrive on dried aquarium foods. Hubbs and Cooper (1936) have described the biology of the northern redbelly dace in detail and have noted that it can be reared in bog ponds for bait. It is often used as a bait minnow in northern Minnesota (Dobie, Meehan, and Washburn, 1948).

FINESCALE DACE

Chrosomus neogaeus (Cope)

The finescale dace (Figure 75) is usually 2 or 3 inches long but occasionally reaches a length of 4 inches. It is a robust minnow which slightly resembles the northern redbelly dace. The two species are frequently found together in bog ponds and old beaver ponds, but the finescale dace is less common in

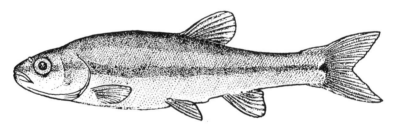

Fig. 75. Finescale dace, *Chrosomus neogaeus*

streams than the northern redbelly dace. The finescale dace has only a single broad dusky lateral band, but occasionally there is a second dark band above an iridescent gold band. The northern redbelly dace almost invariably has two dark lateral bands with a light interspace. The intestine of the finescale dace has a single loop and that of the northern redbelly dace has a double loop. Both the dorsal and anal fins of the finescale dace have 8 rays. The scales are small and difficult to count accurately, but there are about 80 rows along the long axis of the body; the lateral line is incomplete. Breeding males display a bright red band on their sides, confined almost entirely to the area below the black band near the pectoral fins; in some specimens there may be flecks of red present above the band, the belly may be yellowish orange, and there may be some pigment on the paired fins.

The finescale dace ranges from northwestern Canada and the Mackenzie River to New Brunswick (Mcphail and Lindsey, 1970) and south into Minnesota, Maine, and Vermont. Relict populations south of the main range of the species are known from the lower Mississippi River in Wisconsin and from Colorado, Nebraska, and South Dakota (Bailey and Allum, 1962). In Minnesota this species is found in the Lake Superior and border lakes drainages and in the Red River drainage. It is abundant locally in the headwaters of the Mississippi River near Itasca State Park (Stasiak, 1972). McPhail and Lindsey (1970) have noted that the finescale dace, which they place in the genus *Pfrille* as *P. neogaea* (Cope), more closely resembles the Old World genus *Phoxinus* than do any members of the New World genus *Chrosomus*.

The finescale dace is an excellent bait minnow because it survives crowding and is extremely hardy. Many bog lakes and ponds in northern and northeastern Minnesota that do not have fish populations provide excellent rearing ponds for this hardy little fish. It is a common bait minnow in northern Minnesota and is marketed under the name "rainbow chub," but bait dealers are rather reluctant to divulge their sources of supply. Until very recently our knowledge of the distribution of this species was fragmentary because our surveys seldom covered bog ponds and lakes.

The finescale dace spawns in April and May, very shortly after the ice has melted in the lake or pond (Stasiak, 1972). Stasiak was able to rear two generations of dace in the tanks at the University of Minnesota; the adults used the underside of a fiber mat as a spawning site. Dobie, Meehan, Snieszko, and Washburn (1956) report that dace feed largely on phytoplankton, although some individuals eat quantities of zooplankton, amphipods, and aquatic insects. Stasiak notes that finescale dace feed in large part on mollusks, particularly members of the fingernail clam family Sphaeridae.

Genus *Phenacobius* Cope

The genus *Phenacobius* contains the suckermouth minnows. These minnows are 4 to 5 inches in total length and have a dark lateral stripe and a suckerlike mouth. Five species are known from North America, but only one species occurs in Minnesota.

SUCKERMOUTH MINNOW

Phenacobius mirabilis (Girard)

The suckermouth minnow (Figure 76) is usually 3 or 4 inches in total length and has a cylindrical body. It is distinctly characterized by its suckerlike mouth. The upper lip is fleshy, and the lower lip has fleshy side lobes but is not completely fleshy as in the true suckers (Figure 77). The 8 rays in the dorsal fin differentiate this species from members of the sucker family. The upper part of the body is iridescent olive green, and the lower part (below the lateral line) is dusky silver. A dark lateral band about the width of the eye

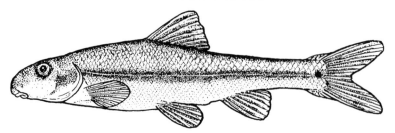

Fig. 76. Suckermouth minnow, *Phenacobius mirabilis*

extends from the tip of the snout along the lateral line to the base of the caudal fin where it ends in a prominent black spot (Figure 76). The dorsal fin has 8 or 9 rays, usually 8. The anal fin has 6 to 8 rays, usually 7. The lateral line has 41 to 50 scales and averages about 45 scales in our specimens. There are no scales on the breast. The pharyngeal tooth formula is 0,4–4,0.

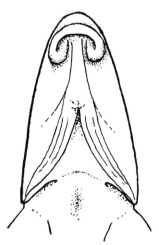

Fig. 77. Suckermouth minnow, *Phenacobius mirabilis*. Ventral view of mouth showing fleshy side lobe of lower lip.

The suckermouth minnow ranges from Colorado and South Dakota to western Ohio and southward to Louisiana and Texas. Eddy and Surber (1947) stated that the suckermouth minnow is rare in Minnesota and is restricted to the southeastern counties. We have found this species to be widespread in the Cannon River and the southern tributaries of the Mississippi River. However, it is never abundant, and we have rarely collected more than four or five individuals at a single station. We find it most often in small streams and rivers such as the lower Zumbro River below Zumbro Falls. It is widely distributed throughout Iowa (Harlan and Speaker, 1969), but in Wisconsin it is restricted to the southwestern part of the state below LaCrosse (Greene, 1935).

Suckermouth minnows spawn in the late spring; gravid females have been taken in late May and early June. Breeding males are heavily covered with small tubercles and are brightly covered with an iridescent blue and silver pigmentation.

The food of suckermouth minnows is largely aquatic dipteran larvae and caddis fly larvae. Little if any plant material is consumed except when it is accidentally ingested along with insect food.

Genus *Notemigonus* Rafinesque

One species is known from eastern North America and is represented by several subspecies. The western form, *Notemigonus crysoleucas auratus* Rafinesque, is native to Minnesota.

GOLDEN SHINER

Notemigonus crysoleucas (Mitchill)

The golden shiner (Figure 78) is a deep-bodied minnow which reaches a total length of more than 8 inches in Minnesota and as much as 12 inches in the southeastern states. The body has a translucent golden tinge that fades rapidly when the fish is removed from the water. The lateral line contains 45 to 52 scales; it has a distinct downward curve. The margin of the belly is sharply keeled behind the pelvic fins. The dorsal fin has 8 rays, and the anal fin has 10 to 15 rays, usually about 12 in Minnesota specimens. The gill rakers are fine and numerous.

The golden shiner and its four subspecies range from Saskatchewan to Quebec and southward to Florida and north central Texas. They have been so widely distributed by the bait industry that it is difficult to determine what the native range may have been. The western golden shiner, *Notemigonus*

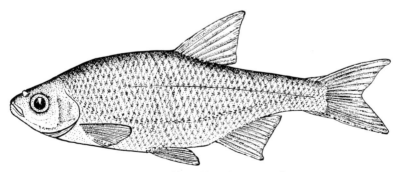

Fig. 78. Golden shiner, *Notemigonus crysoleucas*

crysoleucas auratus Rafinesque, is the subspecies originally native to Minnesota. The southern and eastern forms have been introduced by bait dealers, and now we have a problem in certain areas of the state in ascertaining which subspecies we actually have.

Recent surveys of Lake Minnetonka show that the golden shiner has become more abundant than it was when surveys were made ten or twenty years ago. The golden shiner is primarily a lake species in Minnesota, although we have collected it occasionally in rivers close to the outlets and inlets of lakes in the central and western parts of the state. Eddy and Surber (1947) pointed out that this shiner is very hardy and tolerant of very low oxygen concentrations in both summer and winter. Superficial observations indicate that it is also tolerant of very highly eutrophic conditions. The golden shiner has been able to adapt itself to the oligotrophic (low nutrition) conditions in the northeastern lakes as well as to the eutrophic (high nutrition) conditions of the south central lakes.

Golden shiners spawn in the summer, scattering their adhesive eggs over the aquatic vegetation at random. They feed mainly on entomostracans and algal material strained from the water by means of their fine gill rakers, but they also eat aquatic insects, small leeches, and *Hyalella*.

Large golden shiners will take artificial flies and may provide some sport on light tackle. They are popular as bait minnows, and they have some commercial importance because they are marketed locally and in other states. Many are reared in ponds to supply the bait industry, and the species has been widely distributed by bait dealers.

Genus *Pimephales* Rafinesque

In these small to medium-sized minnows, the first rudimentary dorsal ray is more or less thickened and is distinctly separated from the first well-developed ray by a membrane. Several species are distributed throughout North America, but only three of these species are known to be present in Minnesota.

BULLHEAD MINNOW

Pimephales vigilax (Baird and Girard)

The bullhead minnow (Figure 79) reaches a length of 3 inches. It has a rather stout body and a blunt head. The snout is rounded and is about as long as the diameter of the eye. The mouth is terminal. The body is dusky yellow above and silvery below with a lateral band which may be somewhat diffuse. There is a small black spot at the base of the caudal fin and another spot just above the anterior base of the dorsal fin. The lateral line is complete and has 39 to 44 scales. The anterior scales on the nape and on the anterior lateral region are crowded and small. The dorsal fin has 8 or 9 rays, and the first short undeveloped ray is separated by a membrane from the first fully developed ray. The anal fin has 7 rays. The pharyngeal tooth formula is 0,4–4,0. In many ways the bullhead minnow is similar in appearance to the bluntnose minnow, but it differs in having a rounded snout, a terminal mouth, a silvery peritoneum (instead of black), and a short intestine which is S-shaped with no coils, similar to the intestine of the genus *Notropis*.

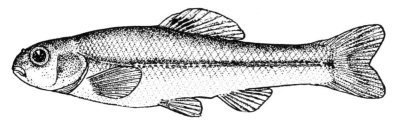

Fig. 79. Bullhead minnow, *Pimephales vigilax*

The bullhead minnow and its several subspecies are distributed from southern Minnesota to West Virginia and south to northern Alabama and to the Rio Grande Basin in Mexico. Raymond E. Johnson, former director of the Research Section of the Minnesota Department of Conservation, identified this species in collections made by the Minnesota Department of Conservation from the Blue Earth River near Mankato. We have not been able to find additional specimens from that area despite intensive collecting. The most northern area from which we have taken specimens is Lake Pepin near Lake City. The bullhead minnow is common in the Zumbro and Root rivers and in major tributaries of the Mississippi River south of Lake Pepin, but we have not collected it from similar habitats in the mouth of the Cannon River. Forbes and Richardson (1908) report that it prefers clear streams and that it is seldom found in lakes.

We have not observed the spawning of the bullhead minnow in Minnesota. They are reported to spawn in late spring and early summer. The spawning males develop blackish heads, dark backs, a row of 5 tubercles just above the upper lip, and a row of 4 tubercles between and above the nostrils. Parker (1964) has described the spawning habits of bullhead minnows in Oklahoma. The male selects and prepares a nesting space on the underside of a board, a stick, a stone, or a tile. After the spawning is completed, the male guards the eggs until they hatch.

The bullhead minnow feeds extensively on algae and other vegetation but may also feed on small snails, *Hyalella*, and other small bottom-dwelling animals.

BLUNTNOSE MINNOW

Pimephales notatus (Rafinesque)

The bluntnose minnow (Figure 80) reaches a length of about 3 inches. It has an elongated body with a blunt snout that is slightly longer than the diameter of the eye. The snout extends over the upper jaw, making the mouth subterminal. The body is olivaceous with a prominent dark lateral stripe that extends to the tip of the snout. The peritoneum is black. There is a black spot at the base of the caudal fin and a prominent dark spot just above the anterior base of the dorsal fin. The lateral line is complete and has 41 to 45 scales. The scales are crowded anteriorly; the crowding is most pronounced on the back just posterior to the head. The dorsal fin has 8 rays; the first short rudimentary ray is separated from the first well-developed ray by a distinct membrane. The anal fin has 7 rays. The pharyngeal tooth formula is 0,4–4,0.

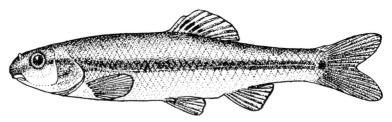

Fig. 80. Bluntnose minnow, *Pimephales notatus*

The bluntnose minnow is distributed from North Dakota and Manitoba through the Great Lakes and southward to Oklahoma, northern Alabama, and Virginia. It is common in Minnesota lakes and streams but is not very abundant in large rivers. We have collected it from all drainage basins in the state.

The spawning habits of bluntnose minnows are similar to those of fathead minnows. They usually start to spawn in the late spring and continue to spawn through much of the summer. The spawning males are pale olivaceous and develop three rows of prominent tubercles across the snout. They also develop a small barbellike structure in each corner of the mouth. The tubercles and barbels disappear after spawning. Breeding males are so different from non-breeding males that their identification may be difficult. The females are drab in color and lack both barbels and tubercles when in breeding condition. The male prepares a nest under almost any object — a rock, a stick, a log, an old tin can, or a piece of broken crockery. He is not discriminating and seems ready to make good use of the refuse that has accumulated in many streams. He excavates a cavity beneath his chosen shelter, using his tail to sweep out the mud and debris. Then he entices a female to deposit her adhesive eggs on the ceiling of the nest. He remains to guard the nest and to agitate the water under the eggs until they hatch in one or two weeks, depending on the temperature. The female may produce more than 1,000 eggs during the summer.

The bluntnose minnow feeds to a large extent on unicellular and filamentous algae but will eat all kinds of small animal life. The adults grub up many chironomid larvae from the muddy bottoms; at times these make up a large part of their diet.

Bluntnose minnows are not as hardy as fathead minnows and are not as popular for bait.

FATHEAD MINNOW

Pimephales promelas Rafinesque

The fathead minnow is usually 2 or 3 inches in length. The dorsal fin is marked with a horizontal black bar across the middle and has 8 or 9 rays; the first ray is short and separated from the long second ray by a distinct membrane. The anal fin has 7 rays. A lateral stripe is present, but the anterior half is diffuse. The lateral line is incomplete; the scale rows on the body number 42 to 48 and are crowded anteriorly. The pharyngeal tooth formula is 0,4–4,0. The peritoneum is black.

The fathead minnow and its subspecies are distributed east of the Rocky Mountains from northwestern Canada to Quebec and Maine, south to the Susquehanna River, through the Ohio River system, and southwestward into Mexico. They have been so widely distributed in the southwestern United States by bait transportation that it is difficult to determine their original range. They are very common in Minnesota waters, thriving in shallow lakes, ponds, and ditches where there is less predation than in the larger lakes.

The fathead minnow spawns in the spring when the water temperature reaches 67° or 68° F and continues to spawn through most of the summer. The breeding male develops a conspicuous gray pad of spongy tubercles on the back anterior to the dorsal fin and two rows of strong tubercles across the snout (Figure 81). The sides of the body become almost black except for two

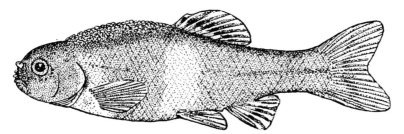

Fig. 81. Fathead minnow, *Pimephales promelas* (breeding male)

wide vertical bars which are light in color. The female remains quite drab (Figure 82). We find their nests on the underside of sticks, boards, and rocks, usually in water from 3 to 12 inches deep. The male sweeps out a slight depression under the nest if the object is too close to the bottom. By some manner of gymnastics the female manages to deposit her adhesive eggs on the underside of the object, and the male fertilizes them. The male guards the nest and strokes the eggs constantly with the pad of tubercles on his back. Often every available site is used for a nest, and sometimes the nests are crowded

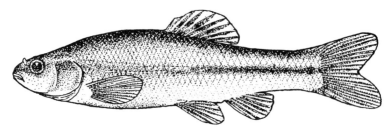

Fig. 82. Fathead minnow, *Pimephales promelas* (female)

together. All manner of objects are used for nest sites. We observed a most unusual nest on a bryozoan colony attached to a boom log protecting a causeway across a small lake in western Minnesota. The submerged surface of the log was completely covered with a colony of the bryozoan *Plumatella*, and the fathead minnows had made small depressions in the zoothecae resembling inverted saucers, each of which contained eggs just about to hatch. Isaak (1961) noted that mature females contain eggs in all stages of development and that they spawn repeatedly as the eggs mature; consequently, eggs in several stages of development are observed within a single nest. He concluded that spawning continues all summer until the females have spawned their entire egg complement. Markus (1934) observed that a single female deposited eggs on twelve different dates between May 16 and July 23, each time in the same nest. He was of the opinion that the primary function of the male, aside from fertilizing the eggs and guarding the nest, is to agitate the water and to remove the diffusion gradients that may be established by the high metabolism of the developing eggs. When Markus brought eggs into the laboratory without the attendant male, the eggs died, but they hatched if the water was agitated constantly. Apparently part of the male's duty is to clean and to aerate the eggs. Isaak found that the nests in his study area averaged about 600 eggs per nest, but some nests contained as many as 6,000 eggs while others contained only a few eggs. He noted that large leeches and painted turtles preyed on the eggs and destroyed many nests. The male's attempts to ward off these predators were futile.

The fathead minnow is one of the hardiest and most tenacious of life of all the bait minnows. If the minnow is hooked through the lips or the tail or under the dorsal fin, it will stay alive for over a day, which makes the species a favorite with many fishermen. A very important and valuable bait industry has been developed in Minnesota in the past thirty-five years, and a major part of this industry is the production and marketing of the fathead minnow. At present there are over 3,000 retail dealers in the state and over 350 wholesale dealers. It is estimated that many hundreds of thousands of dollars worth of fathead minnows are sold to local dealers and to out-of-state customers as far away as Florida and New Mexico.

A few bait dealers have private ponds for rearing their own stocks of minnows. Others stock any suitable ditch or natural pond and later harvest the minnows as they need them. Practically all dealers seine as many wild minnows as they can from local ditches, ponds, and shallow lakes. Because the fathead minnow can withstand extremely low oxygen conditions, it is adapted to live where few other fish species can survive. Harlan and Speaker (1969) state that 300 pounds per acre can be produced from the best ponds in Iowa. The fathead minnow spawns in its second year of life and rarely survives to the third year, which makes it more desirable for bait rearing than other popular bait fishes; golden shiners and common suckers grow rapidly and live longer, and consequently they become too large to use for bait.

The fathead minnow has been used in Minnesota recently for mosquito control. The Metropolitan Mosquito Control District has abandoned insecticides and has stocked these minnows in the sloughs, ponds, and ditches where mosquitoes breed. The minnows have been successful in reducing the populations of larval mosquitoes in these areas to a satisfactory abatement level. Because the shallow depth of many ponds results in frequent winterkills, those ponds will require continued stocking, but the cost will probably be less than that for chemical controls and will eliminate any possible side effects from insecticides. The program provides us with a good example of a biological pest control.

The fathead minnow is primarily herbivorous. The young fish feed on small algae of the plankton and later on filamentous algae. The adults feed on the bottom algae, aquatic insects, worms, entomostracans, and other animals. Their stomachs often contain large quantities of mud and detritus probably taken in along with the food organisms.

Genus *Dionda* Girard

These small minnows have a U-shaped mouth and a prominent black lateral band on the body. Two species are known from North America, but only one is present in Minnesota.

OZARK MINNOW

Dionda nubila (Forbes)

The Ozark minnow (Figure 83) is about 3 inches long and resembles a shiner. It has a pronounced dark lateral band that terminates in a dark caudal spot. Anteriorly the band passes around the snout and encroaches on the chin. The body is silvery black above and fades to silver or bronze below. The margins of the caudal fin and the lower fins may be tinged with a faint yellow-orange pigment. The snout is slightly pointed and extends just beyond the mouth. The dorsal and anal fins usually have 8 rays. There are usually 34 to 38 scales in the lateral line. The pharyngeal tooth formula is 0,4–4,0.

The Ozark minnow is distributed from Wyoming to Illinois and south to the Ozarks. We did not take this minnow in Minnesota before 1950. We included it in the Minnesota fish fauna (Eddy and Surber, 1947) at the suggestion of

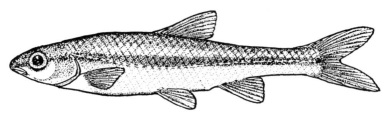

Fig. 83. Ozark minnow, *Dionda nubila*

Carl L. Hubbs, who had identified the minnow from the Cedar River. Underhill (1957) collected specimens from the Cedar River, and Phillips and Underhill (1967) found the species to be present in the south and middle forks of the Zumbro River in Dodge and Olmsted counties. It is locally abundant in small headwater streams, and from our records and those of Harlan and Speaker (1969) it seems to prefer small limestone creeks. With one exception Greene (1935) found it only in the southwestern driftless area of Wisconsin. Attempts to locate the specimens reported by Greene from the St. Croix River have been unsuccessful to date, and we have failed to collect any from the St. Croix River drainage in Minnesota. Four of the six records for this minnow in Illinois (Forbes and Richardson, 1908) are from the driftless area. Based on present distribution and local abundance, we concur with the suggestion of Harlan and Speaker that the Ozark minnow's occurrence may be determined by some geological requirement met only in the driftless area which was not covered by ice of Iowan age. The present populations of the species in Minnesota and Iowa are isolated from each other by intervening land and river systems.

We know little about the spawning habits of the species other than that it spawns in late spring.

Genus *Opsopoeodus* Hay

This genus is monotypic, and the description of the species serves to characterize the genus. Recently Gilbert and Bailey (1972) suggested that *Opsopoeodus* be regarded as synonymous with the genus *Notropis*, but we prefer to retain the genus *Opsopoeodus*.

PUGNOSE MINNOW

Opsopoeodus emiliae Hay

The pugnose minnow (Figure 84) rarely reaches a maximum length of 4 inches. The body is yellowish to silver with a dark lateral band and a dark spot at the base of the caudal fin. The head is short and blunt with a small upturned mouth which is almost vertical. The lateral line contains 37 to 40 scales. The breast is without scales. The dorsal fin has 7 to 10 rays, usually 9. The anal fin has either 8 or 9 rays. The pharyngeal teeth vary, but the typical formula is 0,5–5,0.

The pugnose minnow is distributed from southern Minnesota east to Michigan and southward to Texas and western Florida. Until ten years ago, we had no specimens from Minnesota in our collections. We have since collected specimens from several localities along the Mississippi River south of Red Wing and from the Zumbro and Root rivers. We have examined specimens from the Wisconsin side of the Mississippi River which had been deposited in the University of Michigan Museum of Zoology. The scarcity of specimens from Minnesota is probably because we have not collected extensively in the sloughs and backwaters of the Mississippi River below the Twin Cities. We suspect that this minnow is more common in southeastern Minnesota than was previously thought.

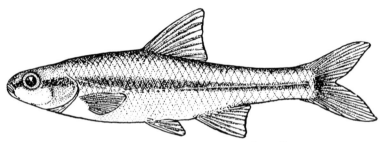

Fig. 84. Pugnose minnow, *Opsopoeodus emiliae*

We know nothing about its spawning habits. It feeds on small immature aquatic insects, entomostracans, and *Hyalella*.

Genus *Notropis* Rafinesque

This genus contains more than a hundred species of generally small minnows which are distributed throughout eastern North America. We have collected seventeen species in Minnesota waters, the largest number of species in any of the fish genera known from the state. The genus is not well defined and is usually divided up into a number of subgenera to give an indication of the degree of relationship within the large genus. Species of this genus are among the most difficult for untrained workers to identify, and several species have been confused in the past by eminent ichthyologists. Members of the genus are often referred to simply as shiners.

PALLID SHINER

Notropis amnis Hubbs and Greene

The pallid shiner (Figure 85) reaches a maximum length of 2 1/2 inches in length. The body is silvery with a thin lateral stripe extending onto the head.

The species is readily recognized by the blunt overhanging snout which extends far beyond the upper lip. The mandible is shorter than the upper jaw, and the angle of the jaw is considerably anterior to the posterior tip of the maxillary. The mouth and the snout resemble those of the silver chub, but the pallid shiner lacks the chub's characteristic barbel. Both the dorsal fin and the anal fin have 8 rays. The dorsal fin is rather high; its length is almost equal to the distance between the occiput and the dorsal origin. The lateral line has 34 to 36 scales. The pharyngeal tooth formula is 1,4–4,1.

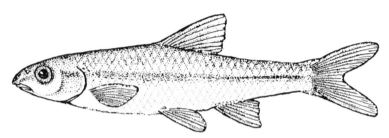

Fig. 85. Pallid shiner, *Notropis amnis*

The pallid shiner is found from southern Minnesota to Indiana and southward to eastern Texas. It prefers running water in large rivers and occurs near the sandbars in the Mississippi River below Lake Pepin; it seldom enters the mouths of tributary streams. It is a rare species in Minnesota, and we have collected it on only a few occasions. All specimens reported by Greene (1935) from Wisconsin and by Harlan and Speaker (1969) from Iowa came from the Mississippi River. A specimen in the University of Michigan Museum of Zoology was collected above Nevers Dam on the St. Croix River north of Taylors Falls, but our intensive collecting from this section of the river has failed to yield further specimens. We have several specimens taken by survey crews from the lower part of the Root River in Houston County (Johnson and Moyle, 1949). Hubbs (1951) reported a specimen from the Minnesota River near Fort Snelling. Four specimens were collected from the Mississippi River below the effluent from a military dredging operation at Brownsville (Phillips and Underhill, 1967).

We know nothing about the spawning or feeding habits of this shiner.

PUGNOSE SHINER

Notropis anogenus Forbes

The pugnose shiner (Figure 86) is moderately stout and reaches a maximum length of about 2 inches. The body is silvery with a dusky back and silvery sides. A dark lateral band extends from the snout through the eye to the base of the caudal fin. The chin is pigmented, and the peritoneum is black. The terminal mouth is small and curves sharply upward at an oblique angle of more than 60° from the horizontal; it extends back about half way to the eye. The lateral line has 34 to 37 scales. The pharyngeal tooth formula is 0,4–4,0. The dorsal fin has 8 rays, and the anal fin has 7 or 8 rays.

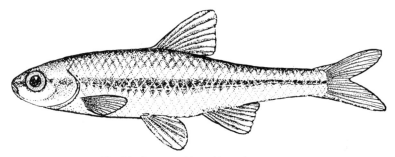

Fig. 86. Pugnose shiner, *Notropis anogenus*

The pugnose shiner is one of the rarest shiners. Bailey (1959) stated that "recent collecting has failed to take *Notropis anogenus* in some areas where it occurred in the past, for example, Illinois . . . and Ohio." Changes by man in streams, rivers, and lakes have been responsible for the disappearance of this minnow. We know little about its life history and habits, but our experience in collecting it indicates that it prefers weedy waters in streams and lakes. The recent tendency to clean out aquatic plants from the shallow margins of many lakes to create swimming beaches will probably eliminate the species in the near future.

The pugnose shiner ranged originally from North Dakota eastward through northern Illinois, Indiana, and Ohio to the St. Lawrence drainage, but now it occurs only in parts of Michigan, Wisconsin, and Minnesota. We found it in some of the lakes within the Twin Cities area forty years ago, but it is no longer present there except in a few parts of Lake Minnetonka (Phillips, personal communication). It is still present in many undisturbed lakes in all Minnesota drainages except the Lake Superior drainage, and it is perhaps better represented in Minnesota than in the other states where it is still extant. There is a single doubtful record from the St. Louis River. Bailey (1959) made a very detailed study of the distribution of the species and its present status.

EMERALD SHINER

Notropis atherinoides Rafinesque

The emerald shiner (Figure 87) usually reaches a length of about 4 inches, but occasionally we have taken specimens up to 5 inches in total length. The slender elliptical body is translucent green above and silvery below. A faint lateral band may be present. The eye is large; its diameter is about equal to the length of the snout. The maxillary reaches to about the front margin of the eye. The dorsal fin has 8 rays, and the anal fin has 9 to 14 rays, usually 10 or 11. The lateral line has 35 to 41 scales, usually 38 or 39.

The emerald shiner and its subspecies range from northwestern Canada to Lake Champlain and southward to Texas and Virginia. The subspecies found in Minnesota is probably *Notropis atherinoides atherinoides* Rafinesque, commonly known as the river emerald shiner, although it is possible that this subspecies may intergrade with the lake emerald shiner in Lake Superior. The emerald shiner is distributed throughout Minnesota, and we have collected it from all the drainage systems in the state. It is most common in lakes and large rivers, but it enters the mouths of tributary streams in the fall. On a number of occasions we have taken several thousand in a single seine haul in Belle Creek, a small tributary of the Cannon River near Welch, Minnesota. When present in such large numbers, they shimmer and sparkle as the sun strikes their emerald dorsal surfaces and their silvery sides. The dense schools of minnows which fishermen see circling their boats in open lake waters are usually this species. Smelt fishermen seining the shores of Lake Superior near Duluth often take these minnows along with smelt and trout-perch. They often swarm in large schools around docks in many lakes, and they usually stay close to the surface.

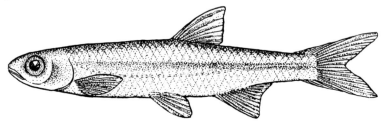

Fig. 87. Emerald shiner, *Notropis atherinoides*

Emerald shiners feed largely on plankton and occasionally on insects at the surface. They spawn in the spring in shallow water over reefs or near the shore. They are important forage fish and may at times be used for bait, but they are not very hardy and die quickly when confined in a minnow pail.

RIVER SHINER

Notropis blennius (Girard)

The river shiner (Figure 88) reaches a length of 2 1/2 inches or slightly more. It has a pale olive back and silvery sides; a middorsal streak passes around each side at the base of the dorsal fin. A silvery lateral band is present on each side. The dorsal fin has 8 rays, and the anal fin usually has 7 rays, occasionally 8. The pharyngeal tooth formula is usually 2,4–4,2, but it varies in about 7 percent of our specimens.

The river shiner is distributed from Alberta and Wyoming east to Pennsylvania and south to Texas and Tennessee. It is frequently present in large rivers but rarely occurs in lakes. It is very abundant in the Mississippi River from Lake Pepin southward and in the Rainy River. We have not collected it from the St. Croix River above Taylors Falls or from the Lake Superior drainage, although there is an authentic record for the species from Lake Winnebago in the Lake Michigan drainage in Wisconsin (Greene, 1935). In Minnesota we have collected it mostly from the mouths of tributaries to the Mississippi and Rainy rivers and off sandbars in both the Mississippi and St. Croix rivers.

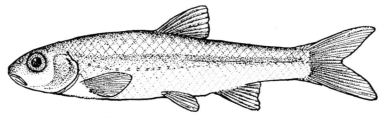

Fig. 88. River shiner, *Notropis blennius*

The river shiner and the silvery minnow (*Hybognathus nuchalis*) often occur together, and the young are superficially similar and may be confused. The length of the intestine and the number of rays in the anal fin are characters which are useful in distinguishing the two species. The intestine of the river shiner is shorter than the length of the body, whereas the intestine of the silvery minnow is at least three times as long as the body. The anal fin of the river shiner typically has 7 rays, and the anal fin of the silvery minnow typically has 8 rays.

The river shiner spawns throughout the summer over gravel bottoms and sandbars (Trautman, 1957).

MIMIC SHINER

Notropis volucellus (Cope)

The mimic shiner (Figure 89) reaches a maximum length of about 2 1/2 inches. The body is silvery with a dusky back. It has a faint and rather diffuse

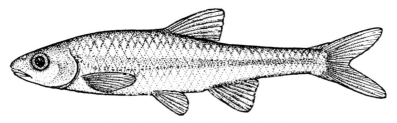

Fig. 89. Mimic shiner, *Notropis volucellus*

lateral band that is restricted to the body and does not encroach on the head. The lateral line is complete and has 32 to 38 scales (34, 35, or 36 scales are about equally frequent in our collections). The dorsal fin has 8 rays. The number of rays in the anal fin varies from 7 to 9 but is usually 8. The pharyngeal tooth formula is typically 0,4–4,0. The mimic shiner resembles the sand shiner in some ways but can be distinguished by its U-shaped head when viewed from above. Characters useful in distinguishing the mimic shiner, the sand shiner, and the big mouth shiner are presented in Table 1.

Table 1. Characters useful in distinguishing the bigmouth shiner (*Notropis dorsalis*), the sand shiner (*N. stramineus*), and the mimic shiner (*N. volucellus*).

Character	Bigmouth shiner	Sand shiner	Mimic shiner
Anal fin rays	Eight	Seven (rarely eight)	Eight (rarely seven or nine)
Pharyngeal tooth formula*	1,4–4,1	0,4–4,0	0,4–4,0
Eyes	Supralateral	Lateral	Lateral
Predorsal scales	Irregular in size and pattern	Regular in pattern and uniform in size	Regular in pattern and uniform in size
Snout shape, dorsal view	V-shaped	V-shaped	U-shaped
Pigment near anal margin	Absent	Absent or faint	Present and dark

*Eastman (1970)

The mimic shiner with its several subspecies ranges from Lake of the Woods through southern Canada to the upper St. Lawrence drainage and south through Minnesota to Alabama and central Texas. We have collected it in all but the Missouri River drainage in Minnesota. It is most abundant in the lake regions of the state but is locally abundant in the St. Croix River just below Taylors Falls.

Mimic shiners are usually pelagic during the day and move into the littoral region at night, avoiding areas with heavy vegetation. Seining at night on beaches may yield thousands of individuals in a single seine haul while similar hauls during the day may yield only a few individuals or none. During the day they form large schools and at times swim about in the shadow of a boat in open water; the schools contain thousands of individuals, usually all of one size. These shiners are important forage fish for walleyes in many northern lakes. Probably most walleye fishermen have seen small fish jumping out of the water and creating great swirls at the surface; usually this is caused by a school of perch or by walleyes which are feeding on mimic shiners. A cast with a small spinner or spoon will quickly tell you what the predators are; if they are walleyes, you can probably increase your catch by following the school of minnows. On dark nights walleyes sometimes follow the shiners into the shallows, and at such times shoreline casting may be productive.

Mimic shiners feed largely on dipteran pupae, mayfly adults, and amphipods during the evening and on *Daphnia pulex* during the early morning (Moyle, 1969). In Moyle's very detailed study of the mimic shiner he reported that marked changes took place in the diurnal feeding habits of the species. He was unable to observe spawning, but from examination of the gonads of fish at weekly intervals he determined that spawning in Long Lake in Clearwater County took place during the last week in July and the first two weeks in August.

BIGMOUTH SHINER

Notropis dorsalis (Agassiz)

The bigmouth shiner (Figure 90) reaches a maximum length of about 3 1/2 inches. The body is olivaceous above with a thin middorsal stripe; the sides are silvery with a diffuse lateral band. Both the dorsal and anal fins have 8 rays. The lateral line has about 35 scales, but the numbers may vary from 32 to 40. The pharyngeal tooth formula is typically 1,4–4,1, but occasionally a

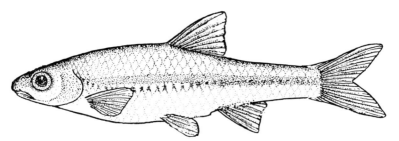

Fig. 90. Bigmouth shiner, *Notropis dorsalis*

tooth of the minor row may be lacking. The bigmouth shiner is more variable in the number of fin rays and the number of scales than any other species of *Notropis* found in Minnesota (Underhill and Merrell, 1959; Underhill, 1960). The bigmouth shiner, the sand shiner, and sometimes the mimic shiner may be collected together, particularly in the fall near the mouths of tributary streams. Since these species are somewhat similar in general appearance, they are difficult to identify. Table 1 compares the characters which distinguish these minnows.

The bigmouth shiner, represented by several subspecies, is distributed from Wyoming and Colorado to the Dakotas and Missouri and eastward through the southern Great Lakes region to New York and Pennsylvania. We find the bigmouth shiner to be one of the most common minnows in Minnesota, occurring in all drainages except the Lake Superior drainage. It prefers small streams with sand and silt bottoms and is not very abundant in large rivers or in most lakes, although it may be locally abundant at the mouths of streams over sandbars.

Sometimes the bigmouth shiner is used as a bait minnow, but it does not live very long in a minnow pail. We know almost nothing about its spawning habits.

SAND SHINER

Notropis stramineus (Cope)

The sand shiner (Figure 91) reaches a maximum length of about 3 inches. It is a silvery minnow with a pale olivaceous back. It has a dorsal stripe continuous with a black patch at the center base of the dorsal fin. The dorsal fin has 8 rays, and the anal fin has 7 or 8 rays, usually 7. The snout is quite blunt. The lateral line has 32 to 37 scales, usually 34 or 35. A vague lateral band is present but is very diffuse anteriorly. The pharyngeal tooth formula is 0,4–4,0.

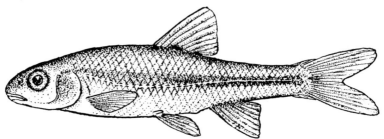

Fig. 91. Sand shiner, *Notropis stramineus*

The sand shiner, including several subspecies, is distributed from North Dakota to the St. Lawrence and Ohio River drainages and south to Mexico. The Minnesota sand shiner, probably the subspecies *Notropis stramineus stramineus* (Cope), is common throughout the St. Croix River, in the tributaries of the Minnesota River, and in the Mississippi River south of St. Anthony Falls. It is known north of St. Anthony Falls but is not as common there as it is farther south. We have not collected it from the Lake Superior drainage in Minnesota, although Greene (1935) found it in Wisconsin tributaries, and Taylor (1954) recorded it from tributaries in the Upper Peninsula of Michigan. We find the sand shiner in both the Red River and Hudson Bay drainages of Minnesota, but it is not abundant.

The sand shiner prefers streams with moderate or strong currents and sandy gravel bottoms. Trautman (1957) compared the distribution of this shiner prior to 1935 with his more recent collections and found that it was no longer present where silt had covered the gravel and sand riffles. In heavily populated areas the sand shiner may not be able to adjust to increased erosion and siltation.

Sand shiners are commonly associated with bigmouth shiners (*N. dorsalis*), but usually only one of the species is abundant. The sand shiner is more common in rivers and large streams, but the bigmouth shiner is more common in small headwater streams. The sand shiner is also found in association with the mimic shiner (*N. volucellus*) in the St. Croix River from Taylors Falls to Marine. Both species seem to be abundant near sandbars in swift waters. Table 1 compares the characters which differentiate the sand shiner, the bigmouth shiner, and the mimic shiner.

The sand shiner is of importance as a forage fish and may be used occasionally as a bait minnow, but it is not particularly hardy. It feeds on small insects, crustaceans, and some algae.

COMMON SHINER

Notropis cornutus (Mitchill)

The common shiner (Figure 92), a rather stout minnow, is usually 3 to 5 inches in length but may reach a length of 12 inches. It has a silvery iridescent body with a dark middorsal streak but no distinct lateral stripe. The lateral line contains 36 to 41 scales, usually 39 or 40, which are distinctly elongated vertically. In adults the lateral line scales have a peculiar shaggy appearance. The dorsal fin has 8 rays; the anal fin usually has 9 rays but occasionally has 8 or 10. The origin of the dorsal fin is distinctly anterior to a line drawn vertically from the origin of the pelvic fins. The pharyngeal tooth formula is typically 2,4–4,2.

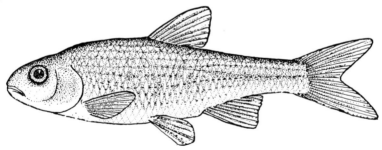

Fig. 92. Common shiner, *Notropis cornutus*

The common shiner, represented by several subspecies, is distributed from Saskatchewan to Quebec and south to Colorado, Kansas, and the Gulf coast drainage. It ranges southward along the Atlantic coast to Virginia. It is one of Minnesota's most abundant minnows and is found throughout the state in waters ranging from intermittent streams to large rivers and lakes.

The common shiner exhibits considerable variation in characters such as the number of scales in the lateral line, the number of caudal peduncle scales, and the number of pectoral fin rays (Underhill, 1961). Populations of common shiners from the Lake Superior drainage have significantly more scales in the lateral line than other populations from Minnesota waters. On the other hand common shiners from the Lake Superior drainage have significantly fewer pectoral fin rays than other shiner populations. A long-term study is presently under way in an effort to determine the significance of the variability in this species.

The common shiner spawns in late May in southern Minnesota and usually a week or two later in northern Minnesota. The spawning males develop rosy pigmentation on their bellies and on the paired fins and acquire large deciduous tubercles on their heads. The males pile up small pebbles and gravel for a nest at the heads of riffles, or they may appropriate nests already constructed by the hornyhead chub or the creek chub. At the height of the spawning season there is great activity as each male attempts to hold his territory against other males and at the same time to attend to the females that enter his territory to deposit eggs. The male is aggressive toward other males of his own species but not toward the females or toward any males of different species that may intrude into his territory. We do not know how they are able to distinguish spawning competitors. Raney (1940) and Miller (1964) have described the breeding activities of the common shiner in detail.

Common shiners have some value as bait fish and as forage fish for game species. They are not very hardy when used as bait, but it is possible to preserve them with salt so that they can be used for bait when it is difficult to carry live minnows. Large common shiners will readily take live bait, flies, small spinners, and spoons. The trout fisherman especially finds this shiner to be a nuisance when one of them takes his lure just as a trout is ready to strike. Large individuals taken on a fly rod or with ultralight spinning gear can put up quite a fight and provide some sport. Small boys who catch these shiners at the old swimming hole or beneath a bridge will attest to the fact that they are good to eat.

WEED SHINER

Notropis texanus (Girard)

The weed shiner (Figure 93) seldom exceeds a length of 2 1/2 inches. It resembles the blackchin shiner and the pugnose shiner and has been confused on occasion with these species. We have compared the distinguishing characters of the three species in Table 2. The weed shiner is olivaceous with a slight brassy tinge above and silvery on the sides. It has a dark and rather diffuse lateral band which extends over the head and touches the chin. A small detached spot is present at the base of the caudal fin. The lateral line has 31 to 37 scales, usually 34 or 35; the lateral line is incomplete in about 90 percent of the specimens from Minnesota. The dorsal fin has 8 rays, and the anal fin has

Table 2. Characters useful in distinguishing the weed shiner (*Notropis texanus*), the blackchin shiner (*N. heterodon*), and the pugnose shiner (*N. anogenus*).

Character	Weed shiner	Blackchin shiner	Pugnose shiner
Peritoneum	Silvery	Silvery	Black
Anal fin rays	Seven, rarely eight	Eight, rarely seven	Seven or eight
Lateral line	Usually incomplete	Incomplete	Complete
Lateral stripe	Diffuse	Prominent; gives the appearance of a zig-zag line in fresh specimens	Prominent
Mouth	Small, nearly horizontal	Large and oblique; reaches anterior margin of eye	Small, not reaching the eye; oblique angle greater than 60° from horizontal
Snout	Blunt	Sharp	Blunt
Pharyngeal tooth formula*	Typically 2,4–4,2; occasionally 1,4–4,2, 0,4–4,2, 2,5–5,2, 2,4–4,1, or 2,4–4,0	Typically 1,4–4,1	Typically 0,4–4,0

*Eastman (1970)

7 rays, rarely 8. The pharyngeal tooth formula is variable but slightly more than 90 percent of the specimens we have examined have a formula of 2,4–4,2.

The weed shiner is distributed from Minnesota to Michigan and southward to Texas and western Florida. Two subspecies are recognized within this range; the Minnesota form is the northern weed shiner, *Notropis texanus richardsoni* Hubbs and Greene, which is more slender than its southern relative.

The common name of this shiner comes from its preference for weedy

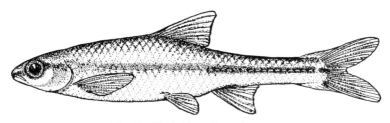

Fig. 93. Weed shiner, *Notropis texanus*

zones in large rivers and streams. We have collections from the lower Mississippi River below St. Anthony Falls, the St. Croix River below Taylors Falls, and the Otter Tail River in the Red River drainage. Hubbs and Greene (1928) and Greene (1935) reported the species from the St. Croix River above Taylors Falls, but we have not taken any specimens from that area in the past twenty years. Although we have a large series of specimens from the Otter Tail River, we have not collected any from other tributaries of the Red River. We commonly find the weed shiner and the blackchin shiner together and equally abundant in running water. The Otter Tail River where the weed shiner is very abundant is actually a series of lakes connected by short stretches of running water. The distribution pattern we have observed in Minnesota indicates that the weed shiner has rather narrow and restricted preferences for rivers rather than lakes. We think the weed shiner probably migrated up the glacial River Warren (the precursor of the Minnesota River) and entered glacial Lake Agassiz but survived only in the Otter Tail River. The absence of suitable habitats in the present Minnesota River may explain why we have not collected it from that river or its tributaries.

We know little about the spawning habits or the feeding habits of the weed shiner.

TOPEKA SHINER

Notropis topeka Gilbert

The Topeka shiner (Figure 94) seldom reaches a total length of 2 inches. The deep body is dusky silvery olive in color with a prominent lateral band that terminates in a small black caudal spot. The lateral band is diffuse anteriorly but quite distinct on the posterior half of the body. The snout is blunt, and the mouth is rather oblique. The dorsal fin has 8 rays, and the anal fin has 7 rays. The lateral line has about 35 scales.

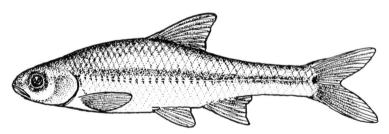

Fig. 94. Topeka shiner, *Notropis topeka*

We have collected the Topeka shiner only twice in Minnesota from the Rock River (Rock County) in the Missouri River drainage. This attractive little minnow has a very restricted range which includes South Dakota, Iowa, Nebraska, Kansas, Missouri, and southwestern Minnesota. No other fish has such a distribution pattern (Minckley and Cross, 1959). Minckley and Cross have noted shifts in the abundance and the distribution of the Topeka shiner in Nebraska over several decades. It is now less common in the prairie streams, probably because of changes in the climate and agricultural development. The Topeka shiner was common in the unditched portions of the Vermillion River in South Dakota and in several of its small tributary streams (Underhill, 1959). Eddy and Surber (1947) included the species in the Minnesota fish fauna on the basis of specimens identified by Carl L. Hubbs in a collection taken by Meek from the Cedar River near Austin in 1890. Intensive collecting in this drainage over the past twenty years has failed to produce additional specimens, and we must assume that the species has disappeared from the drainage. It has been reported as rare in the upper Des Moines River (Harrison, 1949), the upper Iowa River, and the Cedar River (Cleary, 1953) and absent from the Wapsipinicon River (Cleary, 1952) in Iowa.

We know nothing about its spawning or feeding habits.

ROSYFACE SHINER

Notropis rubellus (Agassiz)

The rosyface shiner (Figure 95) reaches a length of 4 or 5 inches. The elliptical body is olivaceous above and silvery below with a distinct lateral stripe. The stripe is more evident in preserved specimens and may not be apparent in live fish. The snout is pointed and slightly longer than the diame-

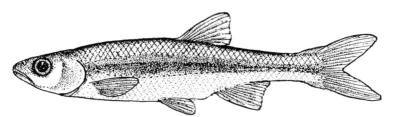

Fig. 95. Rosyface shiner, *Notropis rubellus*

ter of the eye. The origin of the dorsal fin is distinctly behind the origin of the pelvic fins. The dorsal fin has 7 to 9 rays, usually 8. The anal fin has 8 to 12 rays, usually 9 to 11. The lateral line has 33 to 41 scales, usually 37 to 39. The pharyngeal tooth formula is usually 2,4–4,2, but occasionally one tooth is lacking in one or both outer minor rows. The rosyface shiner resembles the emerald shiner but can be distinguished by its sharper and longer snout; it also has a more prominent middorsal streak.

The rosyface shiner ranges from North Dakota and Manitoba to the St. Lawrence and Hudson rivers, southward to Virginia, and through most of the Ohio River drainage. We find it in the tributaries of the Mississippi River south of St. Anthony Falls, in the Minnesota River, and in the Red River. We have not found it in the St. Croix River, in the Mississippi River above St. Anthony Falls, or in the Lake Superior drainage. Specimens taken and identified by Evermann and Latimer (1910) from Lake of the Woods were later proven to be emerald shiners (Hubbs, 1945).

The breeding males have blood-red ventral fins and a dark red stripe that extends ventrolaterally from the opercle to the origin of the pelvic fins. The red pigmentation gives the males the appearance of being wounded. The females may be slightly tinged with pink, but they are never bright red. In southeastern Minnesota spawning generally takes place over gravel rubble or limestone shingle bottoms in small pools below riffles during late May or early June. Pfeiffer (1955) made a detailed study of the life history of the rosyface shiner in New York.

Hybrids between the rosyface shiner and the common shiner appear quite frequently in collections from the streams of southeastern Minnesota, but we have not found hybrids in collections from the Minnesota and Red river drainages. Both species spawn at about the same time and in the same habitat. The common shiner constructs a nest or uses the nest of the hornyhead chub or the creek chub, while large aggregations of rosyface shiners spawn over nearby gravel rubble or limestone shingle bottoms. Accidental hybridization can occur when milt of the rosyface shiner is carried by the current into the nest of the common shiner. The eggs of the rosyface shiner can also be accidentally fertilized by sperm of the common shiner. Detailed studies of hybridization between these two species may be found in several papers (Raney, 1940; Reed, 1957; Rudolph J. Miller, 1963, 1964).

SPOTFIN SHINER

Notropis spilopterus (Cope)

The spotfin shiner (Figure 96) may reach a length of 4 inches. The body is steel blue with a spot formed by dark pigment on the membranes between the last three rays of the dorsal fin. The spot may be obscure or faint in very small individuals. There is a prominent dusky vertical bar just posterior to the opercle; in breeding males the bar becomes very prominent. The breeding males are profusely covered with small tubercles and have dull yellow pig-

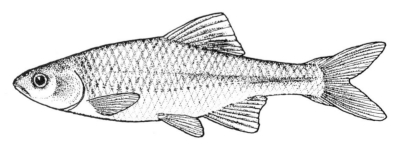

Fig. 96. Spotfin shiner, *Notropis spilopterus*

mentation on their ventral fins. The body is rather deep and has only a faint hint of a lateral stripe posterior to the dorsal fin. The dorsal fin usually has 8 rays, occasionally 9. The anal fin has 7 to 9 rays, usually 8. The lateral line has 33 to 39 scales, usually 36 or 37. The pharyngeal tooth formula is 1,4–4,1.

The spotfin shiner is distributed from North Dakota and Missouri eastward to Lake Champlain and Virginia. It prefers large rivers with sandy silt bottoms. In Minnesota it is common in the St. Croix and Minnesota rivers and in the Mississippi River above and below St. Anthony Falls. We have not collected the spotfin shiner in the Lake Superior drainage. Both Woolman (1895) and Hankinson (1929) reported specimens from the Sheyenne River, a medium-sized tributary of the Red River in North Dakota. We have not found the species in any Minnesota tributaries of the Red River.

The spotfin shiner has some value as bait but is seldom used by Minnesota anglers. It feeds on small insects but may also consume some entomostracans and algae. It spawns in the summer, depositing its eggs in crevices near logs and rocks.

RED SHINER

Notropis lutrensis (Baird and Girard)

The red shiner (Figure 97) reaches a maximum length of about 3 inches. The very deep body is steel blue above and silvery below. A faint lateral stripe extends posteriorly from the dorsal fin. The fins are distinctly reddish. The dorsal fin has 8 rays, and the anal fin has 8 to 10 rays, usually 9. The

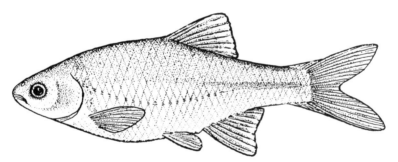

Fig. 97. Red shiner, *Notropis lutrensis*

lateral line has 31 to 37 scales, usually 33 or 34. The pharyngeal tooth formula is 0,4–4,0 or 0,4–4,1. The red shiner superficially resembles the spotfin shiner but can be distinguished by its deeper body, blunter snout, and the absence of a spot on the membranes of the dorsal fin. The breeding males have bright orange-red ventral fins and a very dark vertical bar on the sides just posterior to the opercle. They are profusely covered with fine tubercles which give their bodies the texture of sandpaper. By late June the colors fade and by early August the tubercles disappear.

The red shiner and its several subspecies range from Wyoming to southern Minnesota, through Iowa and Illinois, and southward to Mexico. The species appears to be restricted to the Missouri drainage in Minnesota; we have taken it only in the Rock River, a tributary of the Big Sioux River in Rock County, just south of Luverne, and from the Little Sioux River, also in Rock County. In Iowa it is common in the Missouri River drainage and in the southeastern part of the state (Harlan and Speaker, 1969). It has not been reported from Wisconsin or from the Great Lakes drainage. It has been introduced (probably by bait dealers, since the species is used as a bait minnow) in the southwestern waters of the Colorado River in Arizona and California. It is also possible that it appears by such introduction in parts of Minnesota.

REDFIN SHINER
Notropis umbratilis (Girard)

The redfin shiner (Figure 98) reaches a maximum length of about 3 1/2 inches. It is a deep-bodied minnow with a blunt snout. The body is steel blue above with silvery underparts. A lateral band on the sides becomes diffuse anteriorly. A dark splotch is present at the anterior base of the dorsal fin. The lateral line scales average about 50 and are crowded anteriorly. The dorsal fin has 8 rays and the anal fin has 9 to 11 rays, usually 10. The pharyngeal tooth formula is 2,4–4,2.

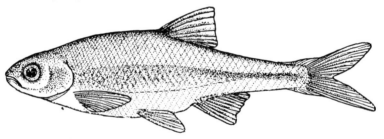

Fig. 98. Redfin shiner, *Notropis umbratilis*

Breeding males of the species are quite spectacular with their iridescent steel blue bodies, dusky red fins, and fine tubercles covering most of the body and the paired fins. Eddy and Surber (1947) refer to them as ''a perfect gem of a minnow.'' The females remain rather drab but may display a few tubercles. Immature redfin shiners may be confused with immature common shiners, but the young redfin shiners can be distinguished by the black spot at the anterior base of the dorsal fin and by the origin of the dorsal fin posterior to the origin of the pelvic fins rather than over or before the origin of the pelvic fins.

The redfin shiner and its several subspecies are distributed from southern

Minnesota and eastern Kansas through the Great Lakes drainage southward to eastern Texas, Kentucky, and West Virginia. The subspecies found in Minnesota is *Notropis umbratilis cyanocephalus* (Copeland), the northern redfin shiner. We have found the redfin shiner only in southeastern Minnesota. It is quite common in the south branch of the Zumbro River, west of Rochester, and it is also present in other branches of the Zumbro River. Eddy and Surber (1947) reported it from Dobbins Creek, a tributary of the Cedar River east of Austin. We have collected a large series of specimens from several other tributaries of the Cedar River, including Rose Creek, Otter Creek, and Woodbury Creek, and the species is also common in the headwaters of the Cedar River near Lansing. Evermann and Latimer (1910) reported the redfin shiner from the Red River and from Lake of the Woods, but Hubbs (1945) checked their specimens and found that they were specimens of the bluntnose minnow (*Pimephales notatus*) and the common shiner (*Notropis cornutus*). We have never found the redfin shiner in the Lake Superior drainage, the Mississippi River above St. Anthony Falls, the St. Croix River, or the Minnesota River.

We know little about the spawning habits of the redfin shiner. The condition of the gravid females we have taken in our sampling indicates that the species spawns from late May to late June.

This shiner feeds on aquatic and terrestrial insects and on other small animal life that may be available. At times it seems to feed extensively on filamentous algae and bits of higher plants.

SPOTTAIL SHINER

Notropis hudsonius (Clinton)

The spottail shiner (Figure 99) sometimes reaches a total length of 4 inches. It is silvery with a prominent dark caudal spot. In preserved specimens a dark lateral band can be seen, but in living specimens no band is evident. The

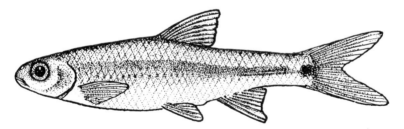

Fig. 99. Spottail shiner, *Notropis hudsonius*

lateral line contains about 39 scales. The dorsal fin has 8 rays, and the anal fin has 7 or 8 rays, usually 8. The pharyngeal tooth formula is usually 2,4–4,2, but of all native Minnesota minnows the spottail shiner shows the most variation in the arrangement of the pharyngeal teeth. Only 51 percent of the fish examined by Eastman (1970) had the so-called normal arrangement. He found nineteen different arrangements in 49 percent of 1,635 fish he examined. These variations were not confined to any single population or to any local area.

The spottail shiner and its many subspecies range from the Northwest Territories of Canada to North Dakota and Kansas, east to the Hudson River, southeastward through Iowa, Illinois, and the northern Ohio drainage, and southward in the coastal region to Georgia. It is found in all drainage systems in Minnesota and is most common in large rivers and lakes. It is very common in Lake of the Woods, Lake St. Croix, and Lake Pepin. Eddy and Surber (1947) discussed the subspecific status of the Minnesota forms and noted that all their specimens belonged to the nominal subspecies, *Notropis hudsonius hudsonius* (Clinton). Increased pollution and siltation from industry and agriculture may have had an influence on the abundance of the spottail shiner, especially immediately south of the Twin Cities and in the Minnesota River drainage. Trautman (1957) noted that the spottail shiner is intolerant of silt-laden and polluted waters.

Spottail shiners spawn in late June and early July, scattering their eggs in sand and gravel beds. They feed on entomostracans, amphipods, immature insects, and some algae.

BLACKNOSE SHINER

Notropis heterolepis Eigenmann and Eigenmann

The blacknose shiner (Figure 100) reaches a length of about 2 1/2 inches. The body is silvery or brassy and has a lateral band that extends forward

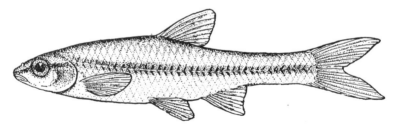

Fig. 100. Blacknose shiner, *Notropis heterolepis*

through the eye and around the snout but does not touch the chin. The lateral band has a row of crescent-shaped marks formed by the dark edges of the lateral line scales. The lateral line is more or less incomplete, sometimes extending beyond the posterior margin of the dorsal fin. The lateral line to the caudal base contains 32 to 39 scales, usually 34 or 35. The dorsal fin has 8 rays, and the anal fin usually has 8 rays, occasionally 7. The pharyngeal tooth formula is 0,4–4,0. The blacknose shiner resembles superficially the black-chin shiner but can usually be distinguished from it by the absence of pigment on the chin and the presence of crescent-shaped marks in the lateral band.

The blacknose shiner ranges from Saskatchewan to Nova Scotia, south to Iowa, and eastward through the northern Ohio River drainage. It is found in the glacial lakes of Minnesota and is abundant in the northern part of the state, but it is not common in the southern part (Eddy and Surber, 1947; Underhill, 1957). It seems to prefer clean weedy lakes and streams. The present trend for the elimination of higher aquatic plants from bathing beaches and from private lake fronts may result in the scarcity or disappearance of this pretty little minnow. Trautman (1957) noted that since 1950 the blacknose shiner in Ohio was rapidly disappearing from many waters where it had formerly been abundant. In Iowa this species was thought to be extinct because none had been collected since 1890, but it was found in Trumbull Lake, Clay County, in 1955 (Harlan and Speaker, 1969). Harlan and Speaker note that clear water with vegetation is now rare in Iowa and that the scarcity of such habitats may have caused the disappearance of the blacknose shiner.

The blacknose shiner spawns in early summer. It feeds largely on small aquatic insects, crustaceans, and algae.

BLACKCHIN SHINER

Notropis heterodon (Cope)

The blackchin shiner (Figure 101) seldom exceeds a length of 2 1/2 inches. The body is bronze to olive yellow above with silvery sides. A rather diffuse dusky lateral stripe extends over the head and onto the chin. The dark edges of

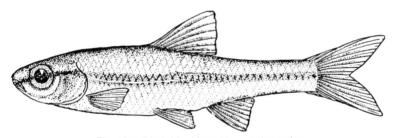

Fig. 101. Blackchin shiner, *Notropis heterodon*

the scales in the lateral line and the row above alternate, producing a zigzag effect. The lateral line has 31 to 38 scales and is incomplete. The dorsal fin has 8 rays, and the anal fin has 7 or 8 rays, usually 8. The pharyngeal tooth formula is typically 1,4–4,1. The characters in Table 2 will help to distinguish the blackchin shiner from similar small striped shiners.

The blackchin shiner is distributed from North Dakota to Quebec and south to Iowa and New York. Hubbs and Lagler (1964) state that it is found in the glacial lake districts of North and South Dakota, Minnesota, Wisconsin, northern Illinois, Michigan, southern Ontario, western Pennsylvania, and New York. It was formerly present in Iowa and northern Ohio. We find the blackchin shiner most abundant in the lake region of the northern half of Minnesota and have taken it only occasionally in the Mississippi River drainage south of the Twin Cities. It seems to prefer lakes, but it is common in the upper Mississippi River between the source and Bemidji and in the Otter Tail River of the Red River drainage. In many places the species has vanished, probably as a result of increased siltation and the accompanying turbidity; these factors may also explain its disappearance from Iowa (Harlan and Speaker, 1969) and from Ohio (Trautman, 1957). It has been observed that blackchin shiners may be abundant in Lake Itasca for several years and then become rare for several years before becoming abundant again. These fluctuations seem to correlate with the rising and lowering of the water levels caused by shifts in annual rainfall. High and stable water levels are followed by population increases. The factors involved are complex but may be related to spawning conditions.

Blackchin shiners feed primarily on entomostracans, small amphipods, small immature aquatic insects, and some algae. They spawn in late May and early June.

Genus *Hybognathus* Agassiz

This genus includes small to medium-sized minnows characterized by a black peritoneum and a long intestine, usually three to ten times the length of the body. Two species belonging to the genus are found in Minnesota lakes and streams.

BRASSY MINNOW

Hybognathus hankinsoni Hubbs

The brassy minnow (Figure 102) reaches a length of 3 or 4 inches. The body is yellowish and quite brassy or golden on the sides. A very faint lateral band is present posterior to the dorsal fin. The snout is blunt and is about as long as the diameter of the eye. The dorsal and anal fins each have 8 rays. The

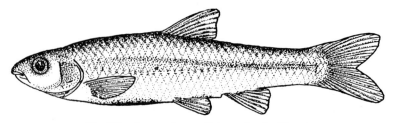

Fig. 102. Brassy minnow, *Hybognathus hankinsoni*

lateral line has about 35 scales. Each scale has about 20 faint radii, which is the best character for distinguishing the brassy minnow from the silvery minnow.

The brassy minnow is very common in small streams throughout all the drainages of Minnesota. It ranges from Montana and eastern British Columbia eastward to Lake Champlain and south to Colorado, Nebraska, and Missouri. It is very frequently used as a bait minnow in the Great Lakes region (Dobie, Meehan, Snieszko, and Washburn, 1956), but we find from experience that it is less hardy than the fathead minnow and is not among the top bait minnows in Minnesota. Slastenenko (1958) lists it as occurring in creeks and lakes and often in bog waters; in our experience it is ubiquitous.

The brassy minnow spawns in quiet water in the early spring. It appears to be primarily herbivorous and feeds largely on algae.

SILVERY MINNOW

Hybognathus nuchalis Agassiz

The silvery minnow (Figure 103) reaches a length of more than 5 inches. It resembles the brassy minnow but differs in a number of characters. It is more silvery in color and has a longer and more pointed snout; the dorsal fin is longer and more pointed, and the scales have only 10 or 12 radii. The lateral line has 35 to 39 scales. The dorsal fin and the anal fin each usually have 8 rays, sometimes 7. The pharyngeal tooth formula is 0,4–4,0.

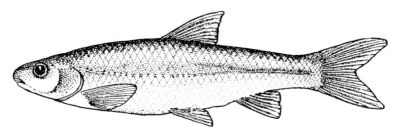

Fig. 103. Silvery minnow, *Hybognathus nuchalis*

The silvery minnow and its several subspecies are distributed from the Missouri River drainage of Montana to the Connecticut River system and southward to the Gulf drainage, but the species is not present in all parts of the upper Great Lakes drainage. Eddy and Surber (1947) reported it from small lakes and streams in Minnesota, but it is mostly restricted to large rivers and the mouths of the larger tributaries of the Mississippi River south of St. Anthony Falls and the Minnesota River. We find it also in the backwaters and the floodplain lakes of the Mississippi River valley south of Hastings.

Silvery minnows spawn in May and June. Breeding males may have some yellow on their sides and develop tubercles on their heads, bodies, and fins.

Occasionally females in breeding condition also develop a few tubercles. The eggs are deposited in quiet shallow water, often on muddy bottoms.

The silvery minnow feeds largely on algae, diatoms, and other plant material and may also eat a few entomostracans. Forbes and Richardson (1908) reported quantities of mud in the stomachs of some specimens. Silvery minnows have value as bait fish, but they do not survive for long in a minnow pail without aeration.

Family CATOSTOMIDAE
The Sucker Family

The members of the sucker family vary greatly in shape. Some species are elongated and cylindrical, others have thin and strongly compressed bodies, and still others have deep thick bodies. The trunk is covered with cycloid scales, but the head is scaleless. The lips are thick and fleshy; the lower lip may be plicate or finely grooved and is often partially or wholly papillose. The size of the mouth varies in different species but is always more or less extensible (protractile), enabling the fish to suck food from the bottom. No teeth are present, but there are structures somewhat like teeth on the bones of the last pharyngeal arch located in the posterior part of the pharynx. These "teeth" are in a single row resembling a comb. In the river redhorse (*Moxostoma carinatum*) the pharyngeal teeth are heavy and molarlike. In other suckers they are finer, but all suckers use them to grind up their food. Suckers have no spiny fin rays; the dorsal fin contains 10 or more soft rays. The pelvic fins are inserted far back on the abdomen. The gas bladder is large and is divided into two or three chambers. The gill membranes are united to the isthmus.

The species of the family Catostomidae are all strictly freshwater fishes. The only species found outside North America is *Myxocyprinus asiaticus* from China. This relict species is similar in form to members of the genus *Carpiodes*. A subspecies of the longnose sucker, *Catostomus catostomus*, is found in Siberia. Seven genera and at least seventeen species have been reported from Minnesota, where they form a very important element of the fish fauna. Most of them are not considered by anglers as game fish, but they play an essential role in water ecology by converting rough vegetation and waste material into food for other fishes and for higher animals and by helping to clean up the lakes and streams. A few species bite readily on a baited hook, but most are rarely caught by anglers. Some species (buffalo and carpsuckers) are seined by commercial fishermen or are caught in traps. A few species are used for food, but as all suckers have accessory ribs, usually a pair for each vertebrae from head to tail, they are bony and not popular for food. Some species are processed for pet and other animal foods.

The abundance and distribution of many species of the sucker family in Minnesota have changed greatly during the past thirty-five years. Pollution and siltation are probably the causes for many of these changes. Also many of the early records are misleading as a result of inaccurate identification

273

and incomplete collecting. Sight records in the absence of specimens are always subject to question despite the reputation of the observer, and a careful perusal of the literature dealing with fish distribution patterns will reveal some astounding blunders based on sight records by competent ichthyologists and early naturalists. The safest and in the end the only solution to this continuing dilemma is to deposit at least one specimen of the fish in question in a natural history museum. If in the past specimens of suckers, especially *Carpiodes*, had been preserved for subsequent study, there would be less speculation today about their relative abundance and about the distribution of various species. Our present knowledge is based on more extensive collecting and on careful identification. The distribution of the suckers in Minnesota has been summarized by Phillips and Underhill (1971), and the sucker key is drawn from their report.

Eddy and Surber (1947) listed the black buffalo, *Ictiobus niger* (Rafinesque), from the Mississippi River, but their specimens from Minnesota have been lost. Phillips and Underhill (1971) were unable to locate specimens from Minnesota in either the United States National Museum or the University of Michigan Museum of Zoology. There is a single specimen in the Minnesota collection from the Mississippi River at Guttenberg, Iowa. Phillips surveyed commercial fishermen in southeastern Minnesota in 1968, but they were unable to supply any specimens. The species could easily be confused with *I. bubalus*, as noted by Eddy and Surber. Until definite records are found, we believe that the species should be regarded as *probably* present in the extreme southeastern portion of the state.

The western lake chubsucker, *Erimyzon sucetta kennerli* (Girard), was also included in the fish fauna of Minnesota by Eddy and Surber (1947): "Although no records of the western lake chubsucker . . . are known from Minnesota, it has been reported from southern Wisconsin (Greene, 1935) and may occur in southeastern Minnesota." Hubbs and Lagler (1964) listed the species as formerly present in Iowa, and Harlan and Speaker (1969) agreed that it was no longer present in Iowa waters. We have never collected it and know of no specimens from Minnesota; consequently we believe that it does not exist at present in Minnesota.

The related creek chubsucker, *E. oblongus* (Mitchill), was also included in the Minnesota fish fauna (Eddy and Surber, 1947), but there are no specimens extant and all reports are sight records. Until evidence to the contrary becomes available, we recommend removal of the creek chubsucker from the Minnesota fish faunal list.

KEY TO MINNESOTA SPECIES OF FAMILY CATOSTOMIDAE

1. Dorsal fin rays more than 20 2
   Dorsal fin rays fewer than 20 8
2. Lateral line scales more than 50; body relatively elongate, depth contained more than 4 times in standard length . . . .

...................Blue sucker, *Cycleptus elongatus* (LeSueur)
Lateral line scales fewer than 50; body relatively stout, depth contained fewer than 4 times in standard length 3

3. Distance from eye to posteroventral angle of preopercle about three-fourths distance from eye to upper gill cleft; subopercle evenly curved, broadest at middle 4
Distance from eye to posteroventral angle of preopercle approximately equal to distance from eye to upper gill cleft; subopercle angularly curved, broadest below middle 6

4. Mouth terminal, oblique, large; anterior tip of upper lip nearly level with lower margin of eye ....
.............Bigmouth buffalo, *Ictiobus cyprinellus* (Valenciennes)
Mouth subterminal, nearly horizontal; anterior tip of upper lip far below lower margin of eye 5

5. Body depth contained 2.2 to 2.8 times in standard length; back arched and ridgelike; distance from front of mandibles to posterior tip of maxilla less than diameter of eye in young, approximately equal to diameter of eye in adults ....
...............Smallmouth buffalo, *Ictiobus bubalus* (Rafinesque)
Body depth contained 2.6 to 3.2 times in standard length, back moderately arched; distance from front of mandibles to posterior tip of maxilla approximately equal to diameter of eye in young, about twice diameter of eye in adults ...*Black buffalo, *Ictiobus niger* (Rafinesque)

6. Lateral line scales typically 36 to 38 (extremes 35 to 39); nostrils in subadults and adults situated above posterior one-third of lower jaw or behind it; snout relatively long in subadults and adults, contained 3.5 times or less in head length ....
......................Quillback, *Carpiodes cyprinus* (LeSueur)
Lateral line scales typically 34 or 35 (extremes 33 to 37); nostrils situated above anterior two-thirds of lower jaw; snout relatively blunt throughout life, contained 3.5 times or more in head length 7

7. Anterior dorsal fin rays short throughout life, the longest ray typically less than two-thirds length of dorsal fin base; body depth in adults typically contained 2.6 times or more in standard length ....
.................River carpsucker, *Carpiodes carpio* (Rafinesque)
Unbroken anterior dorsal fin rays in adults longer than dorsal fin base; body depth in adults contained 2.6 times or less in standard length; not readily distinguishable from *Carpiodes carpio* when specimens are under 4 inches in total length ....
.............Highfin carpsucker, *Carpiodes velifer* (Rafinesque)

8. Lateral line typically obsolescent in adults; series of longitudinal stripe-like rows of dark spots along body in adults, not strongly developed in young; air bladder divided into two parts ....
.................Spotted sucker, *Minytrema melanops* (Rafinesque)

Lateral line fully developed in adults; no rows of spots present along body; air bladder divided into two or three parts 9
9. Lateral line scales 55 or more; scales crowded anteriorly 10
   Lateral line scales fewer than 55; scales not crowded anteriorly.
  11
10. Lateral line scales 55 to 75 ....
   ....White sucker, *Catostomus commersoni* (Lacépède)
   Lateral line scales more than 90 ....
   ....*Longnose sucker, *Catostomus catostomus* (Forster)
11. Head depressed dorsally, concave between eyes; body with 4 to 6 darkly pigmented saddles; air bladder divided into two parts ....
   ....Northern hog sucker, *Hypentelium nigricans* (LeSueur)
   Head convex dorsally between eyes; body lacking distinct dark saddles; air bladder divided into three parts 12
12. Scale rows around caudal peduncle 16; dark spots at bases of dorso-lateral scales ......Greater redhorse, *Moxostoma valenciennesi* Jordan
   Scale rows around caudal peduncle 12 to 15, usually 12 (16 rows in 2 of 310 specimens identified as *M. macrolepidotum*); dark spots at bases of dorsolateral scales present or absent 13
13. Pharyngeal teeth heavy and molariform ....
   ....River redhorse, *Moxostoma carinatum* (Cope)
   Pharyngeal teeth fragile, compressed, and comblike 14
14. Dorsal fin rays typically 15, occasionally 14; lower lips meeting medially at sharp angle; plicae of lips broken into papillalike elements by transverse folds; distance from dorsal fin to occiput approximately equal to length of dorsal fin base ....
   ....Silver redhorse, *Moxostoma anisurum* (Rafinesque)
   Dorsal fin rays typically 12 to 14; plicae of lips not appearing papillose, although transverse folds are frequently present; distance from dorsal fin to occiput distinctly greater than length of dorsal fin base 15
15. Lower lips meeting in a straight line posteriorly (meeting at obtuse angle in 40 percent of observed specimens under 3 inches in total length); mouth relatively small (Figure 104); spots at bases of dorso-

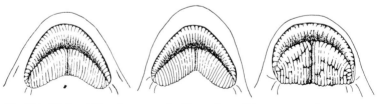

Fig. 104. Distinguishing characters of golden redhorse (*Moxostoma erythrurum*), black redhorse (*M. duquesnei*), and northern redhorse (*M. macrolepidotum*). *Left,* lips of *M. erythrurum*; *center,* lips of *M. duquesnei*; *right,* lips of *M. macrolepidotum.*

lateral scales ....
..........Northern redhorse, *Moxostoma macrolepidotum* (LeSueur)
Lower lips meeting at obtuse angle posteriorly (meeting in straight
line in 6 percent of observed specimens); mouth relatively large (Figure
104); no distinct dark spots at bases of dorsolateral scales 16
16. Lateral line scales 42 to 49, typically 44 to 48; pelvic fin rays 9, frequently 10; caudal peduncle slim, contained 10.7 or more times in
standard length .....Black redhorse, *Moxostoma duquesnei* (LeSueur)
Lateral line scales 38 to 44, typically 39 to 42; pelvic fin rays typically 9, rarely 10; caudal peduncle deeper, contained fewer than 10.7
times in standard length ....
............Golden redhorse, *Moxostoma erythrurum* (Rafinesque)

Genus *Ictiobus* Rafinesque

Members of this genus are characterized by a long dorsal fin with 23 to 31
rays. They may be confused with the carpsuckers which also have a long
dorsal fin, but in adult buffalo the distance from the eye to the free angle of the
preopercle is equal to or slightly less than the distance from the eye to the
dorsal margin of the gill cleft. The free margin of the subopercle forms a
smooth and even curve and is broadest at its middle. The anterior fontanelle in
the roof of the skull is either closed or reduced in size and the posterior
fontanelle is open.

BIGMOUTH BUFFALO

Ictiobus cyprinellus (Valenciennes)

The bigmouth buffalo (Figure 105) has a robust elliptical body. It is the
largest Minnesota sucker, weighing up to 50 pounds. Harlan and Speaker
(1969) record specimens from Iowa weighing as much as 80 pounds. The
body is olive brown, coppery along the back fading to dull olive green on the
sides and belly. The head is large with a blunt and broadly rounded snout. The
mouth is terminal, more so than in any other Minnesota sucker species; it is
very large and oblique and is protractile forward. The upper lip is almost on a
level with the lower margin of the orbit. The scales are very large. An
extended series of specimens taken recently from Lake St. Croix at Bayport
had 35 to 39 scales in the lateral line with an average of 37. The dorsal fin is
very long and has 23 to 31 rays with an average of 27.

The bigmouth buffalo ranges from North Dakota to Lake Erie and southward to Alabama and Texas. This species is apparently the most common and
the most widely distributed buffalo in Minnesota. It is common in the St.
Croix River and in the Mississippi River drainage below St. Anthony Falls. It
is not present in the Lake Superior drainage. From early accounts it is apparent that the bigmouth buffalo was formerly even more abundant and more
widely distributed in the state than it is at present. Seventy-five years ago it

was reported in the Mississippi River above St. Anthony Falls, near Grand Rapids (Cox, 1897) and Brainerd (Eddy and Surber, 1947). The drought of the early 1930s and the excavation of drainage ditches in southern and especially south central Minnesota have eliminated many lakes that formerly supported large populations of the species. It is not common in the Red River drainage, although it is present in the Qu'Appelle River drainage of Saskatchewan, a tributary of the Assiniboine River which joins the Red River at Winnipeg, Manitoba. The buffalo is apparently no longer present in southern Manitoba (R. P. Johnson, 1963).

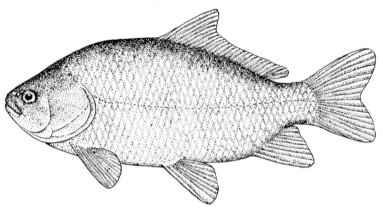

Fig. 105. Bigmouth buffalo, *Ictiobus cyprinellus*

Despite habitat changes and pollution the bigmouth buffalo seems to be holding its own in the Mississippi, Minnesota, and St. Croix rivers and in some of their tributary lakes. It is apparently a very hardy fish and more tolerant of pollution and high turbidity than other suckers. In some respects it is like the introduced carp; it thrives in the same waters where the carp has become abundant, but fortunately it lacks the obnoxious habits of the carp.

Buffalo prefer warm and shallow sluggish waters where they feed largely on small mollusks, aquatic insect larvae, and vegetation. They move into shallow bays and sometimes up small tributary streams into sloughs to spawn during the latter part of April and through May. They deposit their eggs in the dead vegetation and debris on the bottom; the eggs adhere to the vegetation until they hatch in about ten days at a temperature of 62° F.

Tremendous numbers of buffalo are taken by commercial fishermen in Lake St. Croix in the summer and in the Mississippi River near Winona in the winter. Jordan and Evermann (1902) described spawning runs in central and southern Minnesota; the flooded marshes and the lake inlets were so congested with fish that farmers were able to slaughter vast numbers with clubs and pitchforks. Such runs still occur, but they are not as common as in the past. Large numbers of buffalo are also taken in carp traps during the spawning migration. Traps set at the outlets of Lake Washington and Lake Jefferson near Mankato during the spring of 1953 were so full of carp and buffalo that one could almost walk across on their bodies without getting wet.

Buffalo seldom bite on baited hooks but occasionally can be taken on setlines baited with doughballs. They are bony and occasionally have a muddy flavor, but those from clean waters are excellent when properly cooked. The flesh is sometimes smoked.

SMALLMOUTH BUFFALO

Ictiobus bubalus (Rafinesque)

The mouth of this buffalo is small and subterminal; it is only slightly oblique and is protractile downward. The tip of the lower lip is far below the lower margin of the eye, about halfway between the lower margin of the eye and the chin. The body is compressed, and the back is elevated. The head is short; its length is slightly more than one-fourth the standard length. The lips are rather coarsely plicate or striated and quite thick. The long dorsal fin has 24 to 29 rays, usually 26 or 27. There are 35 to 38 scales in the lateral line, usually about 36.

The smallmouth buffalo ranges from southern Minnesota to southern Michigan, throughout the Ohio River drainage, and southward to Alabama and Mexico. In Minnesota the species is restricted to the Mississippi River below St. Anthony Falls and Lake St. Croix. Phillips and Underhill (1971) examined forty-two specimens from Lake St. Croix taken during the summer of 1968. The largest specimen weighed 7 pounds, but there are reports from commercial fishermen of individuals weighing up to 15 pounds. Eddy and Surber (1947) pointed out that commercial fishermen recognize the differences between the smallmouth buffalo and bigmouth buffalo but that they do not distinguish between them when marketing the fish.

The feeding and spawning habits of the smallmouth buffalo are similar to those of the bigmouth buffalo.

Genus *Cycleptus* Rafinesque

This genus differs from *Carpiodes* and *Ictiobus* (which are the only North American genera having a long dorsal fin) in that it lacks a fontanelle or soft spot in the head and has a long slender body and a relatively small head. The genus *Cycleptus* is monotypic and is restricted in its distribution to the Mississippi River drainage basin.

BLUE SUCKER

Cycleptus elongatus (LeSueur)

The blue sucker (Figure 106) reaches a length of more than 2 feet. The body is elongate and slightly compressed. The color ranges from dusky blue to bluish black. The head is very small and slender, tapering to a fleshy snout with a bluntly pointed muzzle. The mouth is inferior. The protractile lips are rather thick and are directed downward. Each lip has five or six rows of tuberclelike papillae. The lower lip is incised posteriorly. The long dorsal fin is elevated anteriorly and has 30 to 32 rays. The anal fin has 7 or 8 rays. The scales are rather small with 55 to 58 scales in the lateral line.

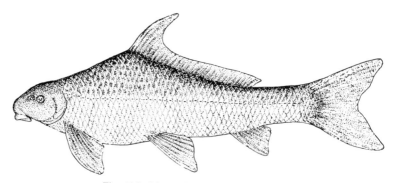

Fig. 106. Blue sucker, *Cycleptus elongatus*

The blue sucker ranges from Minnesota and Wisconsin southward into Tennessee and northeastern Mexico. It is common in the Missouri River and in reservoirs in South Dakota. Blue suckers appear to be one of Minnesota's rarest suckers. We have specimens from the St. Croix River and the Mississippi River south of St. Paul. Like many native fish species, this sucker is not tolerant of pollution; while it was never abundant, its numbers have been further reduced in the past seventy-five years. Cox (1897) reported that blue suckers were taken in Minneapolis in 1880.

The blue sucker is highly esteemed as a food fish. The flesh is firm and flaky and has a good flavor.

Genus *Carpiodes* Rafinesque

The genus consists of silvery deep-bodied fishes with long dorsal fins. In many species the anterior rays of the dorsal fin are more or less elongated. The dorsal fin has 23 to 30 rays. If the fin rays (particularly the anterior rays) have been broken, it is almost impossible at times to identify an individual specimen. Recently Eastman (1970) prepared a key to the pharyngeal teeth of Minnesota suckers which is very useful in the identification of damaged specimens. The subopercle is broadest below the middle, and the posterior margin is triangular in appearance. Both anterior and posterior fontanelles are open. The other characteristics of the carpsuckers are quite variable.

The common name of the genus is generally abbreviated to carp, and members of the genus are often called American carp, carpsuckers, or river carp by the river fishermen. Commercial fishermen usually call them all silver carp. These fishes are not in any way related to the introduced European carp.

The species in this genus are all bottom feeders; they are indiscriminate in their food habits, eating almost any animal or plant material they encounter. The flesh is soft and very bony, even for suckers, and more often than not has a muddy flavor. They are of little value as food fish and are often discarded.

RIVER CARPSUCKER

Carpiodes carpio (Rafinesque)

The river carpsucker (Figure 107) can be distinguished from the quillback by the presence of a knob on the tip of the lower jaw. The anterior rays of the dorsal fin are usually less than two-thirds the length of the base of the fin. The nostrils are slightly posterior to the tip of the lower lip.

The river carpsucker is one of Minnesota's problematic species. There are literature accounts indicating that it is common in the Mississippi and Minnesota rivers in Minnesota (Cox, 1897; Surber, 1920; and Eddy and Surber, 1947), but Phillips and Underhill (1971) were unable to find any specimens in Minnesota waters. Greene (1935) reported the river carpsucker as "not uncommon" in the Mississippi River in Wisconsin, and Becker (1966) collected it in southwestern Wisconsin. We suspect that the species is present in the Mississippi River in southeastern Minnesota but that specimens of the quillback (*Carpiodes cyprinus*) have been confused with the river carpsucker (*C. carpio*) and that this may explain some of the previous records of the river carpsucker.

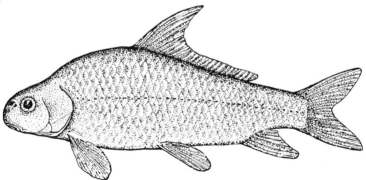

Fig. 107. River carpsucker, *Carpiodes carpio*

HIGHFIN CARPSUCKER

Carpiodes velifer (Rafinesque)

The highfin carpsucker is usually 9 to 13 inches long and weighs less than 1 1/2 pounds. It resembles the quillback, *Carpiodes cyprinus*, in having the back elevated. It also closely resembles the quillback in body conformation, color, and the character of the dorsal fin. The anterior rays of the dorsal fin are elongated; sometimes their length is greater than the length of the base of the fin. If the anterior rays are unbroken, they are the longest dorsal rays of any of the carpsuckers. There is a small knob on the tip of the lower jaw, prominent in adults but less well developed in young fish. The anterior nostril is usually just above or just slightly posterior to the tip of the lower jaw.

The highfin carpsucker ranges from southern Minnesota and Iowa east to the Ohio River drainage, south through Tennessee to the Gulf coast drainage of Alabama, and from Mississippi to eastern Texas and north through the Missouri River drainage to Nebraska. The species is known in Minnesota from the Mississippi River below St. Anthony Falls, the Minnesota River, and the St. Croix River. Eddy and Surber (1947) reported that the species was rather common in the lower Mississippi River and its small tributaries in southern Minnesota, but since then there has been a decline in the populations of this species. Only a single specimen was taken in Lake St. Croix in a four-year period by Howard Krosch, a state fisheries biologist. Two specimens taken from Garman Lake, LeSueur County, in 1952 are in the University of Minnesota collections.

QUILLBACK

Carpiodes cyprinus (LeSueur)

The quillback (Figure 108) has an ovate or oblong body, somewhat compressed, with an elevated back. The body is light olive above, silvery on the sides, and pale on the fins. The anterior rays of the dorsal fin are long, nearly equal to the length of the base of the fin. The lips are full, thick, and flesh-colored in life, and the halves of the lower lip meet at an acute angle. The snout is about one-third the length of the head and is bluntly pointed. The nostrils are posterior to the tip of the lower jaw. Minnesota specimens have 25 to 31 dorsal rays, usually 27 to 29. The lateral line contains 35 to 39 scales, usually 37.

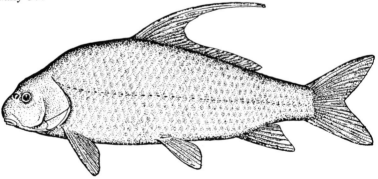

Fig. 108. Quillback, *Carpiodes cyprinus*

The quillback ranges from Lake of the Woods throughout the Great Lakes (except Lake Superior) and southward to Alabama and Kansas. It is present in the Missouri River drainage of Iowa. There are specimens in the University of Minnesota collection from Lake of the Woods, Lake St. Croix, and the southern third of Minnesota. It has been reported from Red Lake (Surber, 1920) and the Mississippi River near Wolf Lake in Beltrami and Hubbard counties (north of St. Anthony Falls), but there are no specimens extant. As Eddy and Surber (1947) pointed out, it is so difficult to distinguish the various species of carpsuckers that it is almost impossible to know whether the quillback is really common or whether casual observers have confused it with the river carpsucker (*Carpiodes carpio*) or even one of the other species of *Carpiodes*.

Genus *Minytrema* Jordan

This genus is monotypic, and the characteristics of the species serve to describe the genus.

SPOTTED SUCKER

Minytrema melanops (Rafinesque)

The spotted sucker (Figure 109) is dusky in coloration, ranging from coppery gray to somber gray. Each scale has a dark spot at the base, giving the fish its spotted appearance. In live fish the spots are barely visible because of the dark background pigmentation and become obvious only after the speci-

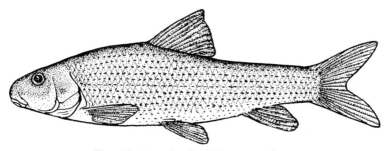

Fig. 109. Spotted sucker, *Minytrema melanops*

men is preserved. The spots give the appearance of longitudinal stripes in adults. Young spotted suckers are easily confused with several other species of suckers if one depends on the pigmentation pattern for identification. The lateral line is obsolescent in adult fish. The dorsal fin has 11 or 12 rays. The lateral line contains 43 to 47 scales. The lips are very thin and striated.

The spotted sucker ranges from Minnesota to Pennsylvania and southward to Florida, Kansas, and Texas. In Minnesota it is found in the St. Croix River below Taylors Falls. Personnel of the Minnesota Department of Natural

Resources netted sixteen adult fish of both sexes in swift shallow water just below Taylors Falls in 1968. The fish were taken in May while spawning was in progress; eggs and milt were stripped easily from the fish (Krosch, personal communication). These specimens were returned to the water. To our knowledge the species has not been recorded above Taylors Falls in the St. Croix River drainage. Spotted suckers are fairly common in the Mississippi River from Lake Pepin southward. A single specimen in the University of Minnesota collections was taken in 1899 from the Minnesota River near Belle Plaine. We have seined the Minnesota River and its tributaries rather intensively in the past twenty years, but no further specimens have been taken. Our records indicate that the spotted sucker prefers large rivers or river-lake habitats; we have only one specimen from a tributary of the Mississippi River (Phillips and Underhill, 1971).

Genus *Hypentelium* Rafinesque

This genus is monotypic. Its range is limited to the eastern section of the United States.

NORTHERN HOG SUCKER

Hypentelium nigricans (LeSueur)

The northern hog sucker (Figure 110) varies in color from steel gray to soft brown on the back and sides; the ventral surface is white. It has a large head and dark cross-shaped blotches. (A description of this species is superfluous for any boy who has ever fished in southern or east central Minnesota.) The

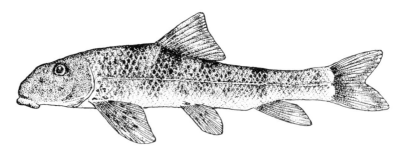

Fig. 110. Northern hog sucker, *Hypentelium nigricans*

head has a concavity between the eyes. The eyes are dorsally located and posterior to the middle of the head. The lateral line contains 48 to 55 scales. Northern hog suckers inhabit small streams and rivers in fast water over gravel-rubble bottoms.

Forbes and Richardson (1908) alluded to the similarity of this sucker and the darters in habits, habitat, and behavior. If one sits quietly beside a small riffle and watches closely, he may be rewarded by seeing a northern hog sucker dart from one spot to another. The moment the fish stops, it is lost to sight for its coloration allows it to melt into the background. The black bars on the sides and across the back break up the body outline, the elongate head resembles a small oblong stone, and the large pectoral fins look very much like flat pebbles. We have taken colored movies of a northern hog sucker in a riffle, and the protective value of the pigment pattern is evident. The viewer can distinguish the fish from its background only when the camera "zooms" in on it. The fish literally disappears again when the camera "zooms" out. The fish was in water less than 6 inches deep and did not move until we approached within a foot of it. Very often when we seine riffles the presence of the northern hog sucker is betrayed only by the wake of the disturbed fish.

The northern hog sucker ranges from Minnesota eastward to New York and southward to northern Alabama and Oklahoma. In Minnesota it is common in the St. Croix River and in the tributaries of the Minnesota River from Mankato to the headwaters. The species is also common in all tributaries of the Mississippi River south of Hastings. Along certain of the tributaries of the Minnesota River in western Minnesota drainage practices have so altered the river habitat in the past two decades that the northern hog sucker is now rare or absent. We have never taken this sucker in heavily polluted agricultural or industrial waters, but it is present in waters with moderate agricultural enrichment.

Northern hog suckers spawn in shallow riffles, and in late spring many individuals congregate in such habitats. During the spawning period the usually quiet and secretive behavior of the suckers gives way to chasing, splashing, and what appears to be very frenzied activity. In extreme examples individuals may strand themselves temporarily on the shore. The breeding females are larger than the males; in Minnesota the females range in total length from 14 to 20 inches and the males from 11 to 16 inches. In most instances a single female is attended by two males, and the chasing occurs as the males defend their roles as spawning partners. An interloper may be chased by one or both of the attending males, and the chase generally stops when the intruder reaches a pool downstream from the spawning riffle. The female in the meantime appears oblivious to all the activity and usually retains her position in the riffle. Once spawning has occurred, the suckers return to their shy and retiring behavior pattern.

Genus *Moxostoma* Rafinesque

These are suckers of large size with coarse scales (usually fewer than 55 in the lateral series) and bright coloration. They frequent clear streams and lakes and are among the first fishes to succumb when the water becomes polluted or continuously turbid. This susceptibility may account for their disappearance from many lakes and streams in southeastern Minnesota. Phillips and Underhill (1971) have presented a detailed critical study of the members of this genus in Minnesota waters.

Redhorses are important commercially because their flesh is very palatable. Large quantities were served in restaurants during World War II under the name of "mullet."

NORTHERN REDHORSE

Moxostoma macrolepidotum (LeSueur)

The northern redhorse (Figure 111) is superficially similar to the silver redhorse, *Moxostoma anisurum*, but it is easily distinguished by its smaller dorsal fin, reddish caudal fin, and smaller mouth. The head is contained in the standard length about 5 times (range 4.0 to 5.5). The lateral line contains 41 to 47 scales, usually 42. There are 11 to 15 scale rows above the lateral line,

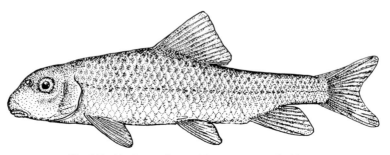

Fig. 111. Northern redhorse, *Moxostoma macrolepidotum*

15 to 19 scale rows below the lateral line, 12 to 14 scales around the caudal peduncle, and 4 to 7 scales below the lateral line. The dorsal fin has 11 to 14 soft rays, usually about 13. The anal fin has 6 to 8 rays, usually 7. The pectoral fins have 14 to 18 rays, usually 16. The pelvic fins have 8 to 10 rays, usually 9. The mouth is small, and the lower lips meet in a straight line in fish more than 3 inches long but may form an obtuse angle in specimens under 3 inches (Figure 104).

The northern redhorse is the most common species of *Moxostoma* in Minnesota and is found in all drainage basins in the state. It ranges from the Mackenzie River basin east of the Rocky Mountains to the Hudson Bay drainage and Quebec, south through New York to the Ohio River drainage, and west to Arkansas, Kansas, and Montana; it is common throughout the Great Lakes drainage. The species inhabits streams and rivers and is fairly common in lakes in Minnesota. In Lake of the Woods it constitutes a considerable portion of the commercial catch in the pound-net fishery.

Northern redhorses spawn somewhat later than most suckers. In the upper

Mississippi River spawning occurs in late May and early June, about three weeks after the common white suckers have spawned.

Of all the catostomids the northern redhorse is probably the "cleanest" feeder. It feeds to a large extent on living insects and other animal life and less on bottom vegetable matter than the other suckers.

The northern redhorse is the only Minnesota redhorse that bites readily on a baited hook and may on occasion take a wet fly or a plug. Northern redhorses are good sport when taken on a fly rod, particularly in fast water. Angleworms or night crawlers are excellent bait if a few split shot are used to make the bait drift close to the bottom. A 2-pound redhorse in fast water will provide even the trout purist with an exciting battle. Another virtue of redhorse fishing is that there is no wait between bites. Fishing in rapids below dams is particularly productive when the fish are on their spawning run. The white and flaky flesh of this sucker is considered by many to be the very best of all suckers. Baked or smoked, it is a real delicacy.

SILVER REDHORSE

Moxostoma anisurum (Rafinesque)

The silver redhorse (Figure 112) reaches a maximum length of about 2 feet and a weight of 7 or 8 pounds. In contrast to the other species of *Moxostoma* it is pale gray or silver gray in color, and the caudal fin is smoky gray rather than reddish. The upper lobe of the caudal fin is notably longer than the lower lobe

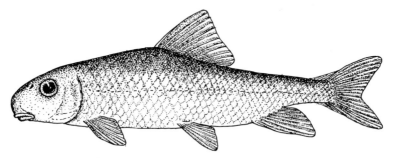

Fig. 112. Silver redhorse, *Moxostoma anisurum*

when the fin is depressed. The head is large and is contained 3 to 5 times in the standard length, usually 3 or 4 times. The depressed dorsal fin is longer than that of other redhorse species; its length is approximately one-third the standard length. The dorsal fin has a greater number of rays (14 to 16, usually 15) than any other Minnesota redhorse. The eye is large, about one-third the length of the snout and one-sixth to one-seventh the length of the head. There are 38 to 46 scales, usually 41, in the lateral line, 13 to 15 scale rows above the lateral line, 17 to 20 scale rows below the lateral line, 12 to 14 scale rows around the caudal peduncle, and 4 to 6 scales below the lateral line. The pectoral fins have 15 to 18 rays, usually 17. The pelvic fins have 8 to 10 rays, usually 9. The lips are full and are broken up into papillae; the halves of the lower lip meet at an acute angle.

The silver redhorse ranges from the Hudson Bay drainage of Manitoba to Quebec and southward to northern Alabama and Missouri. Minnesota records of the silver redhorse include the St. Croix and Zumbro rivers and Lake of the Woods. Despite the fact that there are many literature records (Eddy and Surber, 1947; Phillips and Underhill, 1971), there are few specimens extant. We would like to encourage fishermen and others who obtain redhorses to send them to us if they have doubts about the identity of their specimens. Sight and field records have led to much confusion about the distribution of the redhorse species and certain other fishes. Carlander (1942) observed that one out of thirty redhorses taken by commercial fishermen in Lake of the Woods was a silver redhorse (*Moxostoma anisurum*) and that the northern redhorse (*M. macrolepidotum*) made up the major portion of the catch. His observations are in marked contrast to those of Evermann and Latimer (1910), who reported the silver redhorse as "not uncommon." It is possible that this species has been affected by recent changes in the stream and lake habitats and in environmental conditions.

RIVER REDHORSE

Moxostoma carinatum (Cope)

The river redhorse is the largest Minnesota redhorse; specimens over 2 feet long and weighing up to 15 pounds have been collected from Lake St. Croix. The most characteristic feature is the heavy and thick pharyngeal arch bearing large molariform teeth; all other Minnesota species have slender and fragile pharyngeal arches with fine comblike teeth. The head is large, over one-fourth the standard length; it is also very deep, about one-fifth the standard length. There are 40 to 44 scales (usually 42 or 43) in the lateral line, 13 to 15 scale rows above the lateral line, 16 to 19 scale rows below the lateral line, and 12 to 15 scale rows (usually 12 or 13) around the caudal peduncle. The dorsal fin has 12 to 14 rays, usually 13. The anal fin has 7 to 9 rays, usually 7. The pectoral fins have 15 to 18 rays, usually 17. The pelvic fins have 8 to 10 rays, usually 9. Breeding males are tuberculate and have significantly longer anal fins than do mature females. The river redhorse exhibits less sexual dimorphism than most Minnesota species (Phillips and Underhill, 1971).

The river redhorse is aptly named for it is restricted to large rivers and river lakes in the Mississippi River drainage, including the Ohio River and the Missouri River to Sioux City, Iowa. The species is now rare in the Ohio River (Trautman, 1957) and has not been found in the Missouri River since the late 1800s. It is found in the St. Lawrence River basin in Quebec and formerly was common in Lake Erie. It is also found in northern Alabama and Georgia west to the Ozark region. The species is a recent addition to the list of

Minnesota fishes (Phillips and Underhill, 1967), although it is remarkable that a fish as distinctive and as common as the river redhorse could have been overlooked for such a long period. At first we thought it might be a recent migrant into Minnesota waters, but a careful examination by Phillips of all *Moxostoma* in the University of Minnesota collections and in the collections housed in other institutions revealed the presence of four specimens of the river redhorse taken in the Minnesota River near Jordan and Belle Plaine in 1899. These specimens, which were originally collected by survey crews of the Minnesota Natural History Survey, had been incorrectly identified, three as *M. aureolum* (= *M. macrolepidotum*) and one as *M. anisurum*.

The species has been taken each year since 1966 from Lake St. Croix by personnel of the Minnesota Department of Natural Resources. The skeleton of a river redhorse was collected from a sandbar at the mouth of the Sunrise River (Chisago County) on the St. Croix River north of Taylors Falls. We have specimens of the river redhorse from the Minnesota River between Jordan and Belle Plaine, but none from the Mississippi River south of St. Paul. The species was taken in the 1890s in Iowa, but Harlan and Speaker (1969) reported that it had possibly become extinct since then in the Mississippi River. The river redhorse may have been eliminated from all but the relatively clear waters of Lake St. Croix and the St. Croix River.

GOLDEN REDHORSE

Moxostoma erythrurum (Rafinesque)

The golden redhorse is similar to the silver redhorse and the black redhorse. Coloration varies from dark gray to bronze olive, depending on the habitat from which the fish is taken. The halves of the lower lip are striated and meet at a very sharp angle (Figure 104). The dorsal fin and the caudal fin are gray to light slate in color. The eye is small; its length is just slightly more than one-seventh the head length in the adult. The length of the depressed dorsal fin is about equal to the distance between the origin of the dorsal fin and the occiput. There are 38 to 42 scales (usually 41) in the lateral line, 11 to 14 scale rows (usually 13) above the lateral line, 15 to 17 scale rows (usually 16) below the lateral line, and 12 or 13 scale rows around the caudal peduncle. The dorsal fin has 12 to 15 soft rays, usually 13. The anal fin has 7 or 8 rays, usually 7. The pectoral fin has 15 to 18 rays, usually 17. The pelvic fin has 8 to 10 rays, usually 9.

The golden redhorse has been collected from all the drainage systems in Minnesota except the Lake Superior basin. It occurs in streams, rivers, and lakes, but recent collections indicate that it is most abundant in southeastern Minnesota and the tributaries of the St. Croix River. This species ranges from Minnesota east through the Great Lakes to Lake Erie (exclusive of Lake Superior) and the Ohio River drainage and from northern Alabama and Georgia into Oklahoma and north to Iowa.

The golden redhorse spawns in late May or early June. We have observed spawning in Rock Creek, a tributary of the St. Croix River in Chisago and Pine counties, just east of Rock Creek, Minnesota. Spawning occurred in early June in riffles less than 6 inches deep. The backs of the breeding fish were exposed, and there was a great deal of chasing, presumably by the males. We were able to collect forty-five individuals; eggs and milt flowed freely from the fish even when they were handled very gently. The males had tubercles on the snout and on the anal and caudal fins. The females were slightly larger than the males. Anyone who has observed the spawning activities of the redhorse — with all the splashing, chasing, and "galloping" through the water in addition to the reddish color of the fins — already knows how the species acquired its common name. If one exercises a little imagination, the fish seem to resemble horses cavorting in a pasture.

GREATER REDHORSE

Moxostoma valenciennesi Jordan

The greater redhorse has 16 scale rows around the caudal peduncle. This character has been considered to be diagnostic of the species, but we have found specimens of the northern redhorse (*Moxostoma macrolepidotum*) with 16 scale rows around the caudal peduncle. The greater redhorse resembles the river redhorse in appearance but has comblike pharyngeal teeth. The individual teeth are not as compressed as in other redhorses; Trautman (1957) described them as "squarish." The lower lips meet at an angle.

The range of the greater redhorse (Hubbs and Lagler, 1964) is from Wisconsin and Illinois through the Great Lakes basin to the St. Lawrence River and Lake Champlain, but we have no records of the species from Lake Superior. Trautman (1957) indicates that the species is an inhabitant of clear lakes and streams; it has been driven from some of its former range by increased turbidity resulting from soil erosion and chemical pollutants. The presence of the greater redhorse in Minnesota is doubtful (Phillips and Underhill, 1971), but there is one specimen from the Mississippi River at La-Crosse, Wisconsin, in the University of Michigan Museum of Zoology. We include the species in the Minnesota fauna on the basis of that specimen. Eddy and Surber (1947) discussed the species as *Moxostoma rubreques*.

BLACK REDHORSE

Moxostoma duquesnei (LeSueur)

The black redhorse is reported to reach a length of 2 feet, but all Minnesota specimens have been less than 15 inches in total length. It is the smallest of the Minnesota redhorses. Phillips and Underhill (1971) have examined the Minnesota material and have presented detailed measurements of these specimens. The black redhorse has 42 to 49 scales (usually 46) in the lateral line, 14 or 15 scale rows (usually 14) above the lateral line, 18 or 19 scale rows below the lateral line, and 12 to 14 scale rows (usually 12) around the caudal peduncle. The dorsal fin has 12 to 14 rays, usually 13. The anal fin has

7 rays. The pectoral fins have 15 to 17 rays, usually 16. The pelvic fins have 9 or 10 rays. (The pelvic fins of this species contain 10 rays with greater frequency than those of other Minnesota redhorses; the other species typically have 9 rays.) The eye is small; its diameter is slightly more than two-fifths the length of the snout in adults. The caudal peduncle is slender and is contained more than 10.7 times in the standard length. The distance from the dorsal fin to the occiput is distinctly greater than the length of the base of the dorsal fin. The mouth is relatively large, and the lower lips meet at an obtuse angle posteriorly (Figure 104). The black redhorse is similar in many respects to the golden redhorse (*Moxostoma erythrurum*) but may be distinguished from it by the slender caudal peduncle.

The black redhorse ranges from southeastern Minnesota, northern Iowa, and southern Wisconsin to eastern Ontario and the St. Lawrence River drainage, south to northern Alabama, and west to Arkansas and Oklahoma. It is present in the Zumbro and Root rivers in southeastern Minnesota. Johnson and Moyle (1949) identified specimens taken from the Root River in 1945 by survey crews of the Department of Conservation. Fifteen specimens were collected by Underhill in the Zumbro River in Dodge and Olmstead counties in 1967. The largest sample included eleven individuals (six males and five females) which were taken on May 16; all were mature fish and apparently were about to spawn. From these limited records it would appear that the black redhorse inhabits relatively small clear streams that have not been subject to much erosion or siltation.

Genus *Catostomus* LeSueur

Members of this genus have fine scales and short dorsal fins with fewer than 20 rays. Many species and subspecies are found in North America, but only two species occur in Minnesota and the neighboring states.

WHITE SUCKER

Catostomus commersoni (Lacépède)

The white sucker (Figure 113), probably the most common species of sucker in Minnesota waters, reaches a length of 20 inches or more, but the average total length of Minnesota specimens ranges from 12 to 17 inches. It has a slender cylindrical body and a rather blunt snout. The upper lip is thin and has two or three rows of papillae. The scales are much smaller than those of the preceding species, numbering approximately 70 scales (within a range of 60 to 80 scales) in the lateral line. White suckers are quite variable in coloration; during the spawning season they may be jet black and sometimes they are referred to by spear fishermen as black suckers. The breeding males have a well-marked black lateral band; below this there is a salmon-colored or rosy band. The latter is not as prominent as the red band in the longnose sucker. The two species are often together on spawning runs but are easily distinguished from one another. The white sucker, like many species of fish, is at its most handsome during the breeding season, after which it returns to its drab grayish white color. The moment when the color change takes place is highly dramatic; a breeding sucker can change from its striking rosy-black bands to a light color in a matter of minutes. Other species of fish display changes in pigmentation, but usually the transformation takes hours rather than minutes. On several occasions when we took breeding suckers in the seines, we called the students over to see how colorful the fish were, but by the time the students arrived the coloration had changed — and the students had reason to question silently the visual acuity of the instructors.

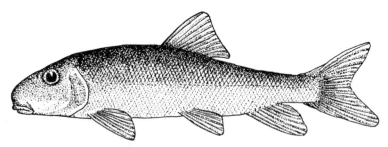

Fig. 113. White sucker, *Catostomus commersoni* (adult)

As mentioned earlier, this is the most common and the most widely distributed sucker in the Minnesota fauna. The species is found in almost every permanent body of fresh water from small streams to large lakes. In North America it occurs from the Mackenzie River basin in the Northwest Territories to eastern Canada and southward to the Gulf states.

White suckers spawn in late April in southern Minnesota to mid-May in the more northern waters of the state. The fish usually run up the small tributary streams until they encounter an impassable barrier, but many spawn in the shallow margins of almost all Minnesota lakes. The exact time of spawning varies from year to year and is dependent on the spring thaw and the spring rains, so it is difficult to predict with any certainty when these spectacular migrations will occur. Within a few weeks after spawning has been completed, the adults all migrate back downstream, and millions of small golden-eyed fry appear in the streams. These fry also soon disappear, many contributing to the diet of hungry game fish fry and fingerlings.

In the spring of 1917 white suckers spawned in extraordinary numbers in the long series of rapids in the Mississippi River below the power plant at Bemidji; at one place in an eddy the eggs accumulated to a depth of 18 to 24 inches over an area estimated to be 1,500 square feet. Suckers, especially white suckers, have a tremendous reproductive potential and produce thousands of eggs per individual. One 20-inch white sucker we examined contained almost 140,000 eggs; depending on the size of the female, egg production may average from 36,000 to 130,000 eggs per mature female. One would expect the lakes and streams to be filled with white suckers, but over many years there is little evidence, except under very special conditions, that marked shifts have occurred in the sizes of sucker populations; one must conclude that the mortality among the progeny of each female must be very high. In a detailed study of the white sucker population of Many Point Lake in Becker County, Olson (1963) reports that although white suckers are common in the lake they are of little forage value to the predacious fishes present. He further suggests that his findings may be related to the capability of this species to avoid capture rather than to the deliberate selection of other species for food by predatory fishes. The evidence indicates that the highest mortality from all causes must occur very early in the life cycle of the species. The fact that the survival rate of suckers reared in ponds is much higher than that of suckers reared in lakes and streams supports the argument that the highest mortality tends to occur during the earliest stages, probably as a result of predation.

It is interesting to speculate on the possibility that selective sport fishing has altered the balance between the large predacious species such as the northern pike and the walleye and the forage species such as the sucker, but there is little concrete evidence to support such speculation. Nevertheless, there is evidence that the nonaggressive sucker can compete successfully with the more desirable game fish. When a number of small trout lakes in northeastern Minnesota were poisoned, they were found to contain large populations of white suckers and longnose suckers. Subsequent stocking of these lakes with trout and restrictions on the use of live minnows and suckers for bait have resulted in excellent yields of trout for the sport fishery. Here we see another illustration that competition between species is rather subtle and not necessarily the "tooth and claw" phenomenon that it was assumed to be until quite recently. Although young trout and young suckers compete for the same food resources, the reproductive potential of the sucker is vastly greater than that of the trout and the suckers grow more rapidly and soon are too large to serve as prey for even the adult trout.

Young white suckers up to 6 inches long differ quite strikingly from their older brethren. They have three very prominent spots about 1/4 inch in diameter on their sides (Figure 114). As they mature, the spots fade and eventually disappear. The size at which the spots disappear varies considerably; we have taken individuals 10 inches in total length that still displayed prominent spots. None of the other Minnesota sucker species have this pattern. Young redhorses have quite different pigmentation patterns that form diagonal bands on a gold background.

Suckers seldom bite on a baited hook but are frequently taken in nets and seines. Most are caught during the spawning migrations when they crowd into shallow water. At this time they are extremely vulnerable and they can be taken very easily with dip nets and can even be captured by hand. There are records of as much as two tons of white suckers being caught in one night in pound nets set to take walleyes for spawn (Eddy and Surber, 1947). White suckers are highly esteemed as food fish, and many are smoked, salted, or pickled. They may also be used to make fish soup, a favorite Finnish dish. Although the flesh is quite bony, it is firm, flaky, and very sweet and has considerable commercial value.

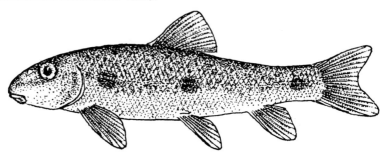

Fig. 114. White sucker, *Catostomus commersoni* (juvenile). Prominent spots on side of body.

Anglers, particularly trout fishermen, have accused suckers of destroying large quantities of trout spawn, but there is no evidence to support such allegations. Suckers may compete with young stream trout, but young suckers in turn are food for the large piscivorous brown trout. It is not uncommon for the bait fisherman to take trout and white suckers on worms from the same spot when fishing in beaver dam ponds. In fact, a 2-pound sucker on a fly rod can give a trout fisherman visions of a sizable prize and also quite a tussle before the not-so-exciting fish is landed.

White suckers are subject to summerkills in many Minnesota lakes and may accumulate in such numbers on beaches that they become a serious nuisance and must be cleared away. (One of us at age twelve was introduced to this phenomenon at Eagle Lake near Cromwell, Minnesota — and has never again volunteered for an unknown task since that time.) The cause of death is not known, but it may be simply old age. Lake Itasca experiences an annual die-off in late summer. We have examined fish at the surface which were still alive but which displayed peculiar respiratory opercular movements and were unable to swim or to orient themselves. The fish were large, 15 to 20 inches in total length, and there was no evidence of an external cause of death. The ospreys and the bald eagles have an easy time in capturing prey when a die-off occurs. Casual observations indicate that the ospreys take only those suckers that are still capable of some directed swimming and ignore dead fish or those in the last throes.

Suckers are among the most easily managed of all species under the usual methods of artificial production. The hatching rate is about 95 percent under normal conditions, and in ponds the fry grow to a length of 4 inches or more in their first summer. They are probably the most important bait fish now handled by minnow dealers. Suckers of 10 to 12 inches in length are very much in demand by anglers who seek trophy walleyes or northern pike on the assumption that big fish require big bait. Whether a hungry fish is very discriminating about the size of a potential meal is impossible to know, but a large bait may discourage an ax-handle-sized predator while a more modest bait may be inviting to it. Once again it appears that the confidence of the fisherman is what really counts. Some muskie fishermen swear by large suckers to lure the big one out of his favorite weed bed.

LONGNOSE SUCKER

Catostomus catostomus (Forster)

The longnose sucker (Figure 115), as the common name implies, is characterized by a long pointed snout that extends considerably beyond the mouth. The scales are small and crowded anteriorly; the lateral line contains 95 to 114 scales. The coloration varies considerably, but the body is generally dark gray or black on the dorsal surface and white on the ventral surface. Specimens from very clear waters such as Lake Superior may have a silvery sheen. Breeding males are heavily tuberculate and have a wide crimson band on the lateral body surface. The band fades after breeding is completed and returns again in the very late fall. Females lack the rosy band and the tubercles.

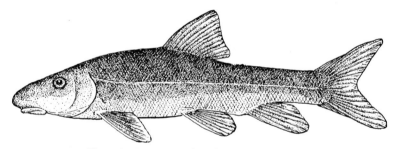

Fig. 115. Longnose sucker, *Catostomus catostomus*

The longnose sucker ranges from the St. Lawrence River and Great Lakes basin west to the Rocky Mountains and northward into the Hudson Bay, Mackenzie, and Yukon drainages of Canada. It is present in Alaskan lakes and rivers. The species of sucker found in Siberia is recognized as a subspecies of the longnose sucker and is thought to have migrated westward by way of freshwater streams on the Bering land bridge during the late Pleistocene. In Minnesota the longnose sucker is common in Lake Superior, Lake of the Woods, the Rainy River and its tributaries, Lake Vermilion, and other lakes in the Hudson Bay and Lake Superior drainage basins. It is also common in all the streams tributary to Lake Superior from the St. Louis River north to the Pigeon River. At times, longnose suckers may be very abundant in the mouths of streams and may be mistaken for trout, and like trout they are difficult to catch on hook and line. These suckers are very common in the St. Louis River up to the power dam above Fond du Lac, west of Duluth. Greene (1935) reported them from both Lake Superior and Lake Michigan in Wisconsin. Commercial fishermen take longnose suckers occasionally at depths of over 600 feet but say that they are usually found in shallower water.

Longnose suckers are lake fish and are usually observed only during the spring spawning runs. The spawning runs are determined in large part by the time of the spring thaw, but in northeastern Minnesota they generally occur in late May or early June. The spawning runs of the longnose sucker and the white sucker often take place in company. Large runs formerly occurred between Kimball Lake and Mink Lake, just east of the Gunflint Trail north of Grand Marais. At the outlet of Mink Lake there is a culvert, and in 1947 the pool below the culvert was literally packed with longnose suckers. That year the water levels were low, and the spawning suckers found themselves trapped in the pool, where they provided a feast for gulls, ravens, crows, and various animals. On another occasion at the same site, the low water levels forced the migrating fish to swim with their backs out of the water.

The flesh of this sucker is firm and of good flavor, but it is quite bony. It is delicious when smoked, and even the most discriminating gourmet would have difficulty distinguishing it from more exotic smoked fish. Only the bones give it away. Longnose suckers are seldom taken on hook and line, appearing to ignore baited hooks. Occasionally they can be snagged; most of those caught by anglers have been accidentally hooked. Spearing, especially during the spring spawning run, is the common method of taking this species.

Family ICTALURIDAE
The Catfish Family

The catfishes are easily recognized by their scaleless bodies, adipose fins, stout spines in the dorsal and pectoral fins, and the presence of barbels on the upper and lower jaws. All members of this family have four long barbels on the underside of the lower jaw, a short barbel near each nostril, and a very long barbel at the end of each maxillary. They have broad heads and wide mouths in which the upper jaw is formed anteriorly by the premaxillaries. They have pads of bristlelike teeth in the upper jaw. Some catfish species are among the largest freshwater fishes, and among native Minnesota fishes they are surpassed in size only by the sturgeon.

Five genera are recognized in the catfish family, and three of them occur in Minnesota. The species in this family are strictly freshwater fishes. Their distribution is restricted to North America exclusive of the Pacific (where they have been introduced). The closely related family Siluridae includes several species of European and Asian catfish, such as the great wels, *Siluris glanis*, of the Danube River, which reaches a length of 13 feet. Other closely related families include the sea catfishes of the Atlantic coast, the South and Central American catfishes, and the electric catfishes of Africa.

The larger species of catfish are all important food fishes. They keep well in cold storage and may be shipped alive for great distances if they are packed in ice. We have kept them alive all day in wet burlap sacks; when placed in a tank at the University, none appeared to have any adverse effects from their long sojourn out of water. River fishermen may keep catfish in the bottom of the boat all day, put them on a stringer when they get back to the dock, and find that the fish still try to swim away. They are as tenacious of life as the archaic gars and bowfins. Commercial fishermen keep live catfish in stock tanks. The buyer can pick out the individual he desires, the merchant dips it out, and the fisherman can support his "story" with a fish.

The smaller species of catfish make excellent aquarium fish; they are quite attractive, and they are scavengers which help to keep the aquarium clean. It is surprising that these little fish have not caught the fancy of the tropical fish enthusiasts. Perhaps they are not exotic enough, but it seems more probable that most fish fanciers are not aware of the existence of these species. Several of our associates have aquariums with small bullheads and other species of fish native to Minnesota, and their tanks rival any that we have seen with more

297

expensive and less hardy exotic species. All species of catfish are extremely hardy, require little attention, and eat almost anything they are offered. At present we are feeding the catfish in the University of Minnesota aquariums dog food, and they seem to thrive just as well as those in the Mississippi River that are feeding on minnows, crayfish, mollusks, and vegetable matter — in fact, on virtually anything edible. Before the development of the pet food industry our catfish did very well on a diet of rolled oats, supplemented occasionally with live minnows.

Most of the species in the family are nocturnal, and the best fishing occurs between sunset and sunrise.

KEY TO MINNESOTA SPECIES OF FAMILY ICTALURIDAE

1. Caudal fin deeply forked . . . .
   . . . . .Channel catfish, *Ictalurus punctatus* (Rafinesque)
   Caudal fin not deeply forked, generally rounded 2
2. Adipose fin free, not connected to caudal fin 3
   Adipose fin connected or partially connected to caudal fin 6
3. Anal fin rays fewer than 16, usually 13 . . . .
   . . . . .Flathead catfish, *Pylodictis olivaris* (Rafinesque)
   Anal fin rays more than 16 4
4. Anal fin rays 17 to 24; barbels under jaw gray to black 5
   Anal fin rays 23 to 27, usually 23 to 25; barbels under jaw whitish . . .
   .Yellow bullhead, *Ictalurus natalis* (LeSueur)
5. Anal fin rays 21 to 24; pectoral spines with strong barbs on posterior edge; belly in adults usually whitish . . . .
   . . . . .Brown bullhead, *Ictalurus nebulosus* (LeSueur)
   Anal fin rays 17 to 21; pectoral spines not strongly barbed on posterior edge; belly in adults usually yellowish . . . .
   .Black bullhead, *Ictalurus melas* (Rafinesque)
6. Band of teeth on premaxillary without backward lateral extensions . . 7
   Band of teeth on premaxillary with distinct backward lateral extensions
   . . . . .Stonecat, *Noturus flavus* Rafinesque
7. Pectoral spines with fine teeth or serrae on posterior edge; notch between caudal and adipose fins more or less acute . . . .
   . . . . .Slender madtom, *Noturus exilis* Nelson
   Pectoral spines smooth on posterior margin but with a longitudinal groove; no notch between caudal and adipose fins . . . .
   .Tadpole madtom, *Noturus gyrinus* (Mitchill)

Genus *Ictalurus* Rafinesque

This genus contains medium-sized to large catfishes with forked or rounded caudal fins. The four species found in Minnesota waters include one catfish and three bullheads.

CHANNEL CATFISH

Ictalurus punctatus (Rafinesque)

The channel catfish (Figure 116) has a rather slender body and a large, deeply forked caudal fin that fits this game fish well for life in the swift waters where it usually lives. The mouth is small in comparison with the mouths of other catfishes. The barbels surrounding the mouth are very long. In color the channel catfish ranges from light bluish olive to gunmetal gray and is dark anteriorly and light on the posterior flanks. The body is sparsely sprinkled with blackish spots. Old males become dark in color and tend to lose their spots. The anal fin has 24 to 29 rays. The channel catfish is one of two species in the genus that have a continuous bony ridge from the supraoccipital bone in the skull to a small bone extending forward from the base of the dorsal fin.

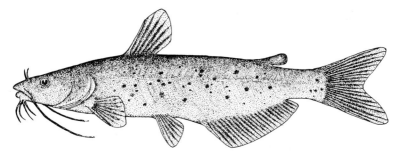

Fig. 116. Channel catfish, *Ictalurus punctatus*

The channel catfish is known to attain a length of 3 feet and a weight of more than 25 pounds, but most specimens taken in Minnesota weigh only 3 or 4 pounds, and an individual weighing 10 to 15 pounds is an unusual fish. Unfortunately we cannot find any authentic records for the largest channel catfish caught in Minnesota.

The channel catfish ranges from Montana to the Ohio Valley and southward through the Mississippi Valley to the Gulf of Mexico and into Florida. In Minnesota it is common in most of the large swift-water tributaries of the Mississippi River (for instance, the St. Croix and Minnesota rivers). It prefers clean rivers and is not common in lakes except the river lakes such as Lake St. Croix and Lake Pepin. Populations are found in the Minnesota River, and several very nice specimens have been taken from the tributaries of the Blue Earth River above Mankato. Large specimens are taken in the vicinity of the Black Dog Power Plant near Savage on the Minnesota River. The species is also present in the Red River and several of its larger tributaries such as the Red Lake and Otter Tail rivers. We have not taken channel catfish from the Mississippi River above St. Anthony Falls. Individuals less than 12 inches long are found very commonly in small tributaries some distance from a large river; they may migrate downstream into the river as they grow older.

We have collected the channel catfish from the St. Louis River, a major tributary of western Lake Superior, but it is not known elsewhere in the Lake Superior drainage (Greene, 1935). The distribution of the channel catfish indicates that it reached the St. Louis River by way of an early St. Croix River connection to Lake Duluth, the Pleistocene precursor of Lake Superior. There is also the possibility that early plantings by the United States Bureau of Fisheries may be responsible for the presence of the disjunct population of channel catfish, but there is no evidence to support this contention.

We know very little about the spawning habits of the channel catfish in Minnesota, but it appears to spawn in swift water, usually in early spring. The channel catfish is now raised successfully in ponds and flooded rice fields as a commercial fish in Arkansas, Louisiana, Missouri, and Oklahoma, and fingerlings are available for stocking ponds. A large industry has already developed, and the fish are sold to restaurants throughout the South. The fish are marketed at lengths of 12 to 15 inches. The United States Fish and Wildlife Service has carried out breeding experiments in the course of which they have developed a true albino strain.

The channel catfish, like other catfish, is omnivorous, but it feeds primarily on small fish, clams, and snails. Consequently minnows, crayfish, and worms are good baits. Stink baits such as strong cheese and sour chicken entrails are perhaps the best. Each bait has its advocates, and the merits of each are defended with the same vigor as the merits of the gray hackle or the fan-wing royal coachman among trout enthusiasts. Channel catfish are known to take plugs and small spinners, and the smallmouth bass fisherman is occasionally surprised to find a channel catfish on his hook. On occasion this catfish will rise to a fly. While the catfish may not be such a spectacular fighter as the smallmouth bass, if you happen to hook one with a fly rod, it will require much skill to land it.

During periods of high water catfish move into the flooded mouths of small streams and backwaters, apparently for forage. Their presence is usually evidenced by streams of small bubbles rising to the surface. Sometimes by watching these bubbles the fisherman can cast his bait so it will be in the path of the feeding fish, and he will be rewarded with some really good sport, especially if he is using light spinning tackle or a fly rod. When the main river is out of its banks and is practically unfishable, these flooded stream mouths should be investigated. Although catfish can be caught at almost any hour, they are nocturnal in their habits and most catfish fishing takes place at night. At the catfish holes along the Minnesota, Mississippi, and St. Croix rivers, life begins after dark. The banks which are deserted during the day become populated by the most delightful philosophers you will ever hope to meet. "Cat" fishermen are a breed unto themselves, and not to have known them is to have had a very incomplete experience as a fisherman. As mentioned previously, there are as many catfish baits as there are flies in the book of the dry-fly purist or lures in the box of the confirmed muskie angler. Fishing for catfish is a serious business, but it is a kind of fishing that involves companionship, yarns, and a sharing that is rare among fishermen except on opening day. Some warm summer night, try your luck and enjoy a little of what may be Minnesota's most popular kind of fishing.

Setlines or trot lines for catfish are often used by commercial fishermen. The fish are kept alive in tanks until they can be marketed. Along the lower Mississippi and Missouri rivers it is possible to pick a catfish for dinner, just as one might pick out a lobster at some seacoast restaurant. The flesh of channel catfish is white and fine and has an excellent flavor. It can be fried, baked, and even smoked. If you have never sampled catfish, you have missed a treat.

BROWN BULLHEAD

Ictalurus nebulosus (LeSueur)

The brown bullhead (Figure 117) reaches a length of 18 inches and a weight of 3 or 4 pounds, but the majority of those taken by sport fishermen rarely exceed 12 inches. The body is more elongate than that of the black bullhead, and specimens from the northern portion of the brown bullhead's range are more robust than their southern relatives. The anal fin is moderately

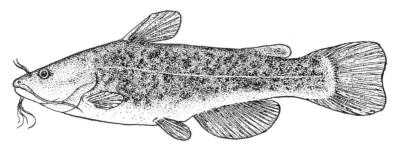

Fig. 117. Brown bullhead, *Ictalurus nebulosus*

long and has 17 to 24 rays (counting the rudimentary rays), usually 18 to 21. The anal fin base is about one-half the standard length. The barbels under the jaw range from gray to black. The body shows a wide range of coloration from yellowish to black, but in Minnesota specimens the color is usually a dark yellowish brown mottled with dark green. The brown bullhead can be distinguished from the black bullhead, *Ictalurus melas*, by the yellow coloration of the ventral surface, the absence of a light bar at the base of the caudal fin, and the presence of strong barbs or serrations on the posterior margin of the pectoral spines (Figure 118). The latter character is generally useful in identifying the two species, but in large brown bullheads the spines may be worn down and dull.

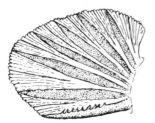

Fig. 118. Distinguishing characters of brown bullhead (*Ictalurus nebulosus*) and
black bullhead (*I. melas*). *Left*, pectoral fin of brown bullhead showing barbs
on pectoral spine; *right*, pectoral fin of black bullhead.

The range of the brown bullhead is from North Dakota into New England, southward to the northern part of the Ohio Valley, and along the Atlantic coast to Virginia. Although present in the Great Lakes drainage, the species is not known from the Minnesota drainage of Lake Superior; there are records of it from the streams tributary to Lake Superior in Wisconsin and Michigan (Moore and Braem, 1965). Of the three species of bullheads found in Minnesota waters the brown bullhead is probably the most common. It is an inhabitant of lakes and quiet streams and rivers. Brown bullheads are abundant in the backwaters of the Mississippi River south of St. Paul and in the Minnesota River from its headwaters at Big Stone Lake to Fort Snelling. The large tributaries of the Minnesota, Blue Earth, Chippewa, Cottonwood, and Lac Qui Parle rivers also support sizable populations. The species is common in the Mississippi River from St. Anthony Falls north to the headwaters at Lake Itasca. It is present but not abundant in the Red River and its tributaries and in the upper St. Croix River and its tributaries.

Spawning occurs in early April in southern Minnesota and in late June in the northern lakes. In the summer great schools of jet-black young are often seen in warm stagnant pools, sloughs, and lake margins, swimming at the surface. Both parents usually guard the young by patrolling the margins of the school. In many northern lakes this is the only indication that bullheads are present. Cabin and resort owners are often surprised to hear that there are bullheads in their walleye lake. In walleye lakes the populations of bullheads are usually very small, and the chances of catching a bullhead are rather slim. Brown bullheads build nests about 6 inches deep on sand or mud bottoms in water up to 2 feet deep, according to Forbes and Richardson (1908). Sometimes they use the mouths of muskrat burrows or natural depressions as nest sites. The cream-colored eggs are deposited in masses and are guarded by the males. Females between 11 and 13 inches long have from 6,000 to 13,000 eggs in their ovaries.

Like its relatives, the brown bullhead is a delicious food fish and can be prepared in the same manner as the black bullhead. There are no records to attest to the bullhead's popularity and the species is not generally categorized as a sport fish, but we would guess that there are more bullhead anglers than all other fishermen combined.

BLACK BULLHEAD

Ictalurus melas (Rafinesque)

The black bullhead (Figure 119) is the smallest bullhead species in Minnesota. It rarely reaches a length of 15 inches and is usually only 6 to 10 inches in total length when mature. The black bullhead has a stouter build than the brown bullhead. The pectoral spines are relatively smooth on the posterior edge, and no strong barbs are present. The caudal fin is slightly emarginate.

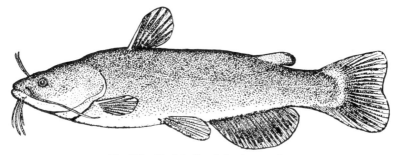

Fig. 119. Black bullhead, *Ictalurus melas*

The anal fin is short and deep and has 17 to 22 rays, usually 17 to 20; the length of its base is nearly one-fifth the standard length. The rays are pale in color and stand out in contrast to the black of the membranes between them. The barbels under the jaws are light gray or black. The body varies in color from greenish brown to black on the upper body surface, the sides have a green or gold luster, and the underside of the head and body as far back as the anal fin is greenish, plumbeous, yellowish, or bright yellow (but never satiny white). The light bar across the base of the caudal fin is a useful distinguishing character in adults. The bullheads are all very similar in appearance, and adults as well as immature individuals can be difficult to identify.

At least two subspecies of the black bullhead have been recognized. The subspecies present in Minnesota is the northern black bullhead, *Ictalurus melas melas* (Rafinesque). The northern black bullhead ranges from North Dakota to northern New York and southward into Kentucky and Iowa, where it may intergrade with another subspecies. This bullhead is quite common in shallow lakes and muddy streams over most of southern and central Minnesota. It has not been taken in the Lake of the Woods drainage, but it is present in the St. Louis River in the Lake Superior basin. In the past the black bullhead was abundant in the Red River; it is now restricted to the tributaries of that river. It is also common in the Rock River in the Missouri River drainage of southwestern Minnesota.

In Minnesota tremendous numbers of black bullheads may be found below the small dams that were designed to regulate lake levels. On one occasion the numbers of fish were so great that it was difficult to believe there was any water present. Individual fish on the margins of the pool were forced onto the beach until they could flop back into the milling mass of fish. A dip net sample showed that both black and brown bullheads were present.

Black bullheads, like the other bullheads, are gregarious and travel in large schools which at times contain all three species native to the state. Like the other two species, black bullheads are omnivorous and feed on large quantities of vegetable and animal matter. Under confined conditions they will feed on smaller fish, but stomach samples from hundreds of bullheads from various Minnesota lakes indicate that fish are not important in their diets. Bullheads are not fast swimmers, and probably most healthy fish would have very little difficulty in escaping from them. The stomach contents of 80 percent of the bullheads we examined contained vegetable matter, and 70 percent contained insect remains. Entomostracans occurred in 43 percent of the stomachs, and in several stomachs entomostracan remains made up such a large proportion of the contents that it is doubtful that they were ingested accidentally. The remains of minnows were found in 12 percent of the stomachs, unidentified fish in 5 percent, sunfish in 4 percent, and perch in 3 percent. A very small percentage of the stomachs contained frogs, leeches, crayfish, and amphipods. From these and other studies it is apparent that bullheads are opportunistic, eating whatever food (including carrion) is available. The vegetation found in bullhead stomachs may have been taken in accidentally while they were feeding on organisms living on stems or leaves or in the decaying vegetation on the bottom of the lake or stream. In a study of the food habits of bullheads Cable (1928) found that they prefer animal food but are able to digest plant material and will eat vegetation or decayed material when it is the only food available to them. Bullheads in the University of Minnesota aquarium eat almost anything from oatmeal to live fathead minnows.

The Minnesota black bullhead, like the other bullheads, spawns from late April to early June. It makes a nest in shallow water on a sand or mud bottom or may use natural depressions or even muskrat burrows as nest sites. The young remain together in dense schools guarded by the male. These schools gradually break up and merge with other schools of young bullheads.

Bullheads are regarded by many Minnesotans as rough fish, and they are seldom sought by anglers. In Iowa, however, they are very popular, and we have known Iowa fishermen to return home from a Minnesota vacation highly satisfied with their large strings of bullheads.

All species of bullheads are delicious. Their flesh is reddish or pink in contrast to the white flesh of other catfish. To prepare a bullhead for the pan, cut off the pectoral spines and the head; then grasp the skin with a pair of pliers and pull it off the body. The fish can be rolled in cornmeal, flour, or bread or cracker crumbs and deep-fried, baked, or made into fish cakes. Some people like to dip them in a special batter. Connoisseurs of bullheads compare the flavor to that of chicken. The bullhead's appearance is distasteful to some, but one should not let appearances obscure the fact that the flesh is excellent.

YELLOW BULLHEAD

Ictalurus natalis (LeSueur)

The yellow bullhead reaches a length of 12 to 18 inches. The body is usually bright yellow mottled with darker pigmentation. The body is short and heavy, the head is short and quite broad, and the mouth is wide. The long anal fin has 23 to 27 rays, usually 23 to 25, counting all the rudimentary rays. The length of the base of the anal fin is usually more than one-fourth the body length. The caudal fin is more rounded than that of the black bullhead or the brown bullhead. The barbels on the lower jaw are whitish, and this character is one of the most useful ones in distinguishing the yellow bullhead from the other bullheads.

The yellow bullhead ranges from North Dakota to New York, southward along the Atlantic coast, and westward to Tennessee and Texas. Although it is present in the lower Great Lakes drainage in some abundance, there are only four records of the species in Lake Superior, and all of them are from large streams in Wisconsin (Moore and Braem, 1965, Figure 36). Many of the shallow lakes tributary to the Mississippi River south of the Twin Cities support populations of yellow bullheads in company with both black and brown bullheads. Yellow bullheads also may be locally common in the sluggish streams of southern Minnesota. They are not present in the Red River drainage or in the lakes of the northern one-third of the state. Of the three species of bullheads in Minnesota, the yellow bullhead is the least common. In fact, taking a specimen of the yellow bullhead in the course of our surveys is an occasion for comment. The species is common in Iowa and in southern waters.

The spawning habits of the yellow bullhead are similar to those of the bullhead species discussed earlier in this chapter. Egg counts from a few females, all 10 or 11 inches long, disclosed an average of 4,000 eggs per fish. The eggs are deposited in May or June, and until the young attain a total length of about 2 inches they are guarded closely and vigorously by the male parent. Schools of several hundred young bullheads may occur in quiet water. The school is compact, sometimes forming an almost perfect circle. Some of the young fish may break off from the main group and then return, or the main group may follow the "explorers," forming a rectangular school. Close observation reveals the parent nearby, circling its progeny or following slightly behind the school. Often two adults are present; in instances where we have captured the adults, one was found to be a female and the other a male. In some cases it appears that both parents attend the school. If the young are approached by other fish, the guardian appears to challenge the intruder while the young swim rapidly away.

Like other catfishes, this species is best described as a scavenger because it eats almost anything, dead or alive, that it finds in the water — minnows, crayfish, insects, snails, and aquatic worms. Aquatic plants may also form an important part of the diet, but availability seems to be the most important factor in determining what will be eaten. The young feed primarily on entomostracans, insect larvae, and aquatic worms. Despite their coarse food habits, yellow bullheads are excellent food fish; the flesh is fine in texture, firm, and delicious. With the exception of trout the catfishes are the easiest fish to prepare, and — best of all — they have few bones to contend with. Of the three species of bullheads the yellow bullhead is the most difficult to prepare because the skin is thin and tears more easily than that of the other species.

Genus *Pylodictis* Rafinesque

These are large catfishes with slender bodies and flat heads. The lower jaw projects markedly beyond the upper jaw. The pad of teeth in the upper jaw has backward extensions at each end. A monotypic genus, its range includes the entire Mississippi River drainage system.

FLATHEAD CATFISH

Pylodictis olivaris (Rafinesque)

The flathead catfish (Figure 120) varies considerably in color but is usually yellowish mottled with brown or sometimes grayish mottled with dark brown. It is characterized by a slender body, much depressed anteriorly. The head is very large, broad, and much depressed, with the lower jaw projecting. The barbels are short. The dorsal spine is weak, and the dorsal fin has 6 rays. The adipose fin forms a high rounded flap, free at the posterior end; its length is slightly less than the length of the anal fin. The pectoral spines are strong and serrated on both edges. The pelvic fin has 9 or 10 rays, and the anal fin has 12 to 15 rays. The caudal fin is almost rounded and is scarcely emarginate. The lower tip of the caudal fin is white in young individuals.

This catfish is common in Lake St. Croix, in the Minnesota River, and in the Mississippi River southward from St. Anthony Falls. It is not known from

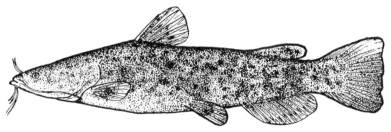

Fig. 120. Flathead catfish, *Pylodictis olivaris*

the Mississippi River north of St. Anthony Falls or from the St. Croix River above Taylors Falls. The power dam at Taylors Falls prevents the upstream migration of fish at present, but before the construction of the dam there was a series of rapids in the river that extended from the Dalles of the St. Croix a distance of approximately six miles upstream to the site of Nevers Dam, and it is probable that the fish could pass upstream. The absence of the species above the falls is best explained on the basis of lack of suitable habitat. It appears to prefer large sluggish rivers and rarely is found in any but the large low-gradient tributaries of the Mississippi River and the connected backwaters. Young individuals are taken occasionally during seining operations on the faces of the old wing dams, but the adults occur in deeper waters below the dams. The Minnesota Department of Natural Resources fisheries crews have taken huge specimens in their trawls in both Lake St. Croix and Lake Pepin in recent years. Richard Sternberg, a fisheries biologist, has also taken large specimens in trap nets in the Mississippi River south of Lake Pepin. The best localities for the species are found below the wing dams or the navigation dams.

Flathead catfish seem to be less common than channel catfish and are much larger. Weights of 40 pounds are not uncommon for fish in Minnesota waters, and specimens weighing 90 to 100 pounds have been recorded from the Missouri River. The world's record for a flathead catfish taken by an angler is held by a fish weighing slightly less than 100 pounds which was caught in the Missouri River below Yankton, South Dakota.

Flatheads are taken commercially on setlines, in seines, or in trap nets. "Jugging" is another fishing method sometimes used by commercial fishermen on the Missouri and lower Mississippi rivers. A gallon jug is used as a float, and heavy cutty hunk or nylon line is attached to the jug along with a cement block for a sinker. A very large hook, sometimes hand-forged, is attached several feet from the cement block, and a small carp is used as bait. Since flathead catfish like to live in log jams among old deadheads, the jug and the carp are tossed into the midst of such an area. The next day the jug is checked, and the reward is, often enough, a big catfish. Fishing in such places is certainly hazardous and requires strong terminal tackle.

The best angling is below the lock and dams on the Mississippi River south of Lake Pepin. Live minnows, stonecats or "willow cats" (*Noturus flavus*), and crayfish are said to be good baits, with stonecats preferred by Minnesotans. When a catfish takes the bait the first time, the novice catfish fisherman is usually certain that his line is snagged; after the fish begins to move, the chances are fairly good that it will continue to move unless the line is very strong indeed.

Another technique used for catching catfish is called "tickling." (This method involves capturing the fish by hand, but the approach is somewhat different from that used for "tickling" trout.) In the spring when the water is high, flathead catfish occasionally enter flooded backwaters where they become landlocked as the water levels return to normal. The fish that have been stranded in this manner can be caught by "tickling." As a boy, Eddy and his young companions used to probe in hollow logs and under stumps in flooded areas with their hands, sticks, or pitchforks, often dislodging and capturing large flatheads. On one occasion, one of the boys stuck his bare foot under a stump — right into the mouth of a flathead catfish. The boy lost most of the skin from the top of his foot, but he took home a 60-pound catfish.

Flathead catfish eat mostly fish, but they are not averse to any kind of animal food, fresh or carrion. At times their diet includes seeds, crayfish, mollusks, and garbage.

This species spawns in June and July. The male cleans out a place for the nest under a log, a stump, or a brush pile in quiet water. After the eggs are spawned, the male guards them until they hatch. The young leave the nest in dense schools and are usually tended by the male until the school breaks up.

Genus *Noturus* Rafinesque

The stonecat and the madtom formerly were placed in the genera *Noturus* and *Schilbeodes*, respectively. In a monograph dealing with these small catfishes, Taylor (1969) presents evidence indicating that the differences between the two are not sufficiently great to warrant generic separation and recommends that they be placed in the single genus *Noturus*. We are following his recommendation in our discussion of these ictalurids. The members of this genus are small fishes. The adipose fin is keellike and continuous with the dorsal fin, except for a shallow notch. There is a well-developed poison gland beneath the epidermis surrounding the base of each pectoral and dorsal spine. A small prick from a spine can be exceedingly painful, more so than a similar prick from any of the other catfishes.

STONECAT
Noturus flavus Rafinesque

The stonecat (Figure 121) has a moderately elongate body, broad and flat in front of the dorsal fin and cylindrical behind. It is yellowish brown to slate gray in color, and the belly is white. The caudal fin has a white margin, and a small oval yellowish spot is present at the posterior end of the dorsal fin.

This species is easily distinguished from the bullheads and the young of *Pylodictis* by the fact that the long and low adipose fin is continuous with the caudal fin. The round caudal fin and the broad flat head distinguish the stonecat from the young of *Ictalurus*, which have either a forked fin or a more round head. The premaxillary band of teeth has projections extending posteriorly from the corners.

The stonecat is distributed from Montana through the Great Lakes area to Lake Champlain and south to Oklahoma and Alabama. The species inhabits swift water and lives in the crevices between rocks or beneath logs. It is common in the St. Croix River and its tributaries and in the streams tributary to the Minnesota and Mississippi rivers south of St. Anthony Falls. We have taken it on the steep faces of wing dams below Taylors Falls but not in the main channel over shifting sand or in the slower portions of the main river. Perhaps the most unique habitat was the discarded trunk door of a 1947 Chevrolet. A total of seven stonecats were taken from the cavities in the trunk door in a seine haul from a branch of the Zumbro River near Concord, Minnesota. At that point the stream served as a dump for all kinds of solid waste. The stream bottom was heavily silted and the former gravel-riffle habitats were buried, but the trunk door provided an adequate substitute habitat for the fish. (We have noticed that stonecats generally disappear from sections of streams subject to heavy enrichment and the siltation associated with erosion.) We have no records of the stonecat from the Red River drainage in Minnesota, but biologists at the University of Manitoba have taken specimens from the Red River near Winnipeg (Stewart and Lindsey, 1970). The stonecat is also present in the Lake Superior drainage of Wisconsin (Moore and Braem, 1965). Moore and Braem took specimens in Douglas County, Wisconsin, from the Nemadji River, which has its headwaters in Carlton County, Minnesota.

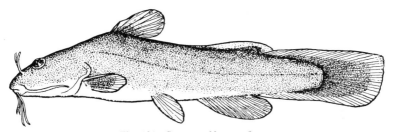

Fig. 121. Stonecat, *Noturus flavus*

The stonecat spawns under rocks, logs, or large sticks, where the female deposits a jellylike egg mass. The male and probably the female guard the nest until the eggs hatch and the young are ready to leave.

The diet of the stonecat includes quantities of larval aquatic insects, small snails, other aquatic animals, and occasionally some vegetation.

The stonecat is considered to be an excellent bait by river fishermen from Lake Pepin southward, where the species is called the willow cat. It is a very hardy little fish, and its bottom-dwelling habits make it an ideal bait fish for saugers and walleyes and for its larger relatives, the channel catfish and the flathead catfish.

TADPOLE MADTOM

Noturus gyrinus (Mitchill)

The tadpole madtom (Figure 122) rarely exceeds a length of 4 inches. The body is purplish olive to dark brown, without noticeable speckling. Three dark shadowlike streaks may be present on the sides. The body is robust and short; it is deepest just anterior to the origin of the dorsal fin. The adipose fin is continuous with the caudal fin. The mouth is terminal, and the jaws are subequal. The premaxillary bands of teeth are truncate laterally and lack backward extensions. The pectoral spines are deeply grooved and lack serrations. The pectoral fin has 6 to 9 soft rays, usually 7.

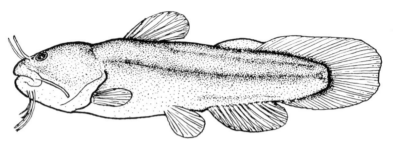

Fig. 122. Tadpole madtom, *Noturus gyrinus*

The tadpole madtom is found in quiet or slow-moving water and is the only madtom found in Minnesota lakes. It appears to prefer soft silt bottoms or the heavy debris of the lake margin. In Lake Itasca it is quite common in the loose accumulation of star-duckweed (*Lemna trisulca*) that develops along the windward shoreline in late summer. Seining success is greatest at night; specimens are rarely taken during the daylight hours except in the debris. We have taken hundreds of madtoms from the weed beds of small streams.

Tadpole madtoms are widely distributed from North Dakota to Quebec and southward to Florida and eastern Texas. They are found throughout Minnesota from the St. Louis River in the Lake Superior drainage to the Red River in the west. They are often mistaken for young bullheads. There are reports that they are good bait fish, but they seem to be used less often than stonecats by river fishermen.

The species has poison glands just beneath the epidermis surrounding the spines of the pectoral and dorsal fins. The secretions from these ductless glands are released when the epidermis is torn. The wound produced by a spine is usually less painful than the sting of a bee, but a former graduate student who accidentally pressed his hand down on a madtom displayed a more traumatic reaction. The spine penetrated his index finger, and shortly thereafter his finger became numb. By midnight he reported numbness in his hand. A day later he still showed a slight reaction to the wound. As is the case with reactions to insect stings, individual reactions to the madtom's poison vary, but since some people may be unusually sensitive to the poison madtom wounds should not be treated lightly. There has not been any research on the nature of the venom.

Tadpole madtoms feed largely on *Hyalella*, dipteran larvae, large entomostracans, and some algae. They spawn in late spring or early summer, but we know nothing about their spawning habits.

SLENDER MADTOM

Noturus exilis Nelson

The slender madtom (Figure 123) is more slender than the stonecat (*Noturus flavus*) and has a terminal or subterminal mouth. The pectoral spine is short, straight, and serrate; the serrae are long and straight and usually number 5 to 8 per spine. The pectoral fin has 8 to 10 soft rays, usually 9. The body coloration varies from yellowish brown to black; the dorsal, anal, and caudal fins have black margins. An obscure black spot is usually present just anterior to the dorsal fin. Coloration and degree of pigmentation vary considerably throughout the range of the species (Taylor, 1969).

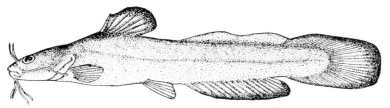

Fig. 123. Slender madtom, *Noturus exilis*

Eddy and Surber (1947) originally included the slender madtom in the Minnesota fish fauna on the basis of a report (Cox, 1897) of its presence in the Blue Earth River. In 1954 three specimens were collected by a survey crew of the Minnesota Department of Conservation from Otter Creek, a tributary of the Cedar River in Mower County, not far from the town of Lyle (Eddy and Underhill, 1959). Extensive collecting in other streams in the same area has failed to reveal further specimens of this handsome madtom. We feel that Cox's record from the Blue Earth River is questionable because it is from an entirely different stream system. We suspect that his record was based on a specimen of the stonecat, a species which is still found in the Blue Earth River and throughout the Minnesota drainage. The slender madtom has a disjunct range including Minnesota, Iowa, Illinois, Kansas, Missouri, and Arkansas and a separate population in the Tennessee and Cumberland basins (Taylor, 1969). Taylor states that the species inhabits small streams, where it lives in riffles containing limestone slabs, rubble, or gravel.

Family ANGUILLIDAE
The Eel Family

Many related families of eels, mostly marine, are found in the warmer parts of the world. All are distinguished by long slender bodies. The family is represented by many species found in Europe, northern Africa, Asia, and the Philippines and other islands and in the streams draining into the Indian Ocean. The only freshwater eel in North America is a species of the genus *Anguilla* which is restricted to streams draining into the Gulf of Mexico and the Atlantic Ocean. Freshwater eels are not found in the Pacific drainage of the United States.

Genus *Anguilla* (Shaw)

The only species of this genus found in the United States is the American eel, *Anguilla rostrata* (LeSueur). A very similar species is found in the streams of Europe and northern Africa. The American species is found only in streams east of the Rocky Mountains.

AMERICAN EEL
Anguilla rostrata (LeSueur)

The American eel (Figure 124) has a very long cylindrical body with a rather compressed tail. The body varies slightly in color but is dark brown above and yellowish below with an off-white belly. Male eels never reach a large size; the adult females may reach a length of 4 feet, although they are more often 2 or 3 feet in length. The apparently smooth skin has abundant mucus glands which make it slimy and slippery. The scales are minute and embedded and can only be distinguished on close examination. They are arranged in a pattern of blocks with the scales of each block at right angles to the adjacent blocks. The lateral line is well developed. The head is small and elongated; the eyes are small and placed over the angle of the jaws. The lower jaw projects beyond the upper jaw. The bones of the head are modified, and no maxillaries are present. The pectoral fins are well developed, but pelvic fins are absent. The dorsal and anal fins are elongated and have numerous fin rays; they are both confluent with the caudal fin. Small slitlike opercular openings are present. The only fishes which could be confused with the eel in Minnesota are the lamprey species. Although their shape is the same, the lampreys lack pectoral fins and jaws and have seven pairs of gill pores.

312

Eels were at one time fairly common in Minnesota in the Mississippi River and its tributaries as far north as St. Anthony Falls, but they have declined during the past fifty years. The numerous dams along the river have prevented the easy migration of eels from the sea, and pollution may have rendered some sections of the river impassable. Nevertheless, a few eels manage to get through the locks and around the obstacles into the upper waters. Fishermen still occasionally catch eels in the Minnesota River near Savage and in Lake Pepin and Lake St. Croix, but it is doubtful that eels will ever return to their former abundance. Recently they have appeared in Lake Superior. Hollie Collins of the University of Minnesota, Duluth, has provided us with records of seven specimens which were taken from Lake Superior between 1966 and 1971. Professor Collins is planning to examine the otoliths to determine the age of the specimens in his charge. These specimens are the first records from the Lake Superior drainage in Minnesota. The eel was not native to the Great Lakes above Niagara Falls but was widely introduced (Hubbs and Lagler, 1964), and apparently the recent appearance of the species in Lake Superior was made possible by the completion of the St. Lawrence Seaway.

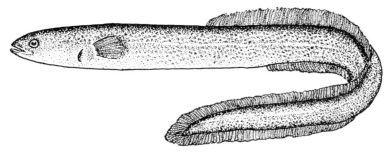

Fig. 124. American eel, *Anguilla rostrata*

The presence of eels in Minnesota waters is remarkable because of their complicated life history and the many hazards they encounter in the course of it, even within their usual range. American eels are catadromous, reproducing in the sea and entering fresh water to grow to adult size but returning to the Sargasso Sea area of the Atlantic to spawn. Only the females reach Minnesota. The males, which are smaller, remain near the mouths of the rivers until the females move to the sea. The females produce from 10 million to 20 million eggs. Apparently the adults die; they are never seen again. The eggs hatch into leaflike larvae which bear little resemblance to adult eels. For years the larvae were thought to be a peculiar species unrelated to the eel and were given the name of *Leptocephalus*. The semitransparent larvae feed near the surface and grow rapidly as they drift with the ocean currents along the coast of North America and into the Gulf of Mexico. When they reach an estuary or the mouth of a river such as the Mississippi River, the larvae metamorphose into the tiny eels known as elvers. When their metamorphosis is complete, they enter the river. Only the females ascend the river, traveling mostly at night; the males remain near the mouth of the river. Obstacles such as low dams, waterfalls, and rapids do not deter the females in their upstream migration. On moist nights they crawl around dams and waterfalls with relative ease. They seek large quiet pools in the stream and remain in them from four to seven years until they reach sexual maturity. They are voracious and feed on any animal matter, dead or alive. In the salmon streams of Scotland and Scandinavia they are regarded as serious predators.

Eels are nocturnal and usually spend the day hidden under rocks or logs or buried in the mud. We have known them to leave the water at night and crawl to swampy places to feed on frogs and similar prey. Captive eels in the University of Minnesota aquariums have occasionally escaped from their tanks and remained out of water for twenty-four hours without any apparent injury. Once four of our eels disappeared from a 500-gallon aquarium. We assumed that they had escaped or that they had died and had been eaten by other fishes. Two years later we had some unexpected visitors and turned on the lights at about midnight to exhibit our fishes. To our surprise the four eels were swimming about the aquarium, but in thirty seconds they had hidden themselves under the debris and silt. We transferred them later to a clean aquarium; since they no longer could hide, they spent the day lying quietly on the bottom, sometimes upside down — which on occasion sent excited students to the office to report ''dead'' eels.

Eels have been highly regarded as food for many centuries. The flesh is white and has a good flavor. After eels have been skinned, they can be cooked, pickled, smoked, or jellied. They command a high price on the eastern markets in the United States. A few years ago one restaurant in the Lake Pepin area occasionally offered eel on the menu. Many special gourmet items featuring eel are imported from Europe. Eels are usually caught commercially in traps and weirs in the rivers along the Atlantic coast, but pollution and commercial use of the rivers has greatly reduced the catch in the United States and in Europe. Many years ago the skin of the eel was used in the production of fine bookbindings, buggy and riding whips, and other items.

Family PERCOPSIDAE
The Trout-perch Family

The trout-perch resembles both a trout and a perch. An adipose fin is present, a characteristic shared with the trout and several other families. The overall appearance is superficially similar to that of a small perch. The body is elongate, heavy anteriorly, and compressed posteriorly. The bones of the head are cavernous. The head is somewhat pointed, the mouth is small, and the maxillary bones are small. The premaxillaries border the protractile upper jaw. The jaws have weak teeth. The gill membranes are free from the isthmus; the pseudobranchiae are developed. A lateral line is present. The trout-perch is the only species of fish in Minnesota waters with ctenoid scales and an adipose fin. It is restricted in its distribution to the fresh waters of North America. A single genus, *Percopsis*, is recognized.

Genus *Percopsis* Agassiz

This genus contains two species. The trout-perch, *Percopsis omiscomaycus* (Walbaum), is found in eastern North America. The second species, *P. transmontana* (Eigenmann and Eigenmann), is found in the Columbia River basin.

TROUT-PERCH
Percopsis omiscomaycus (Walbaum)

The trout-perch (Figure 125) reaches a maximum length of 8 inches, but most Minnesota specimens are 3 to 5 inches in total length. As has already been noted, this fish bears a superficial resemblance to a perch or a small walleye but may be distinguished from these species by the presence of an adipose fin similar to that of a trout or a whitefish. When fresh from the water, the trout-perch has a peculiar translucent appearance, and its body is mottled with light and dark color. The color varies from pale yellow to white with a series of dark spots along the middorsal stripe and along the lateral line; one or two additional spots may be present between the middorsal stripe and the lateral line. The head is conical and lacks scales. The head length and the body depth are contained in the standard length 3.2 and 4.4 times, respectively. The dorsal fin origin is slightly anterior to the middle of the body and has 1 or 2 splintlike spines and usually 10 or 11 soft rays. The spines are quite variable; in some individuals they may be prominent in all fins, while in others

315

they may be found only by dissection with the aid of a microscope. In some cases the spines may be visible in one or more fins but barely discernible in another fin. The anal fin has 1 or 2 spines and 6 or 7 soft rays. The pelvic fin has 1 very weak spine and 8 soft rays. The lateral line contains 40 to 51 scales, usually 45.

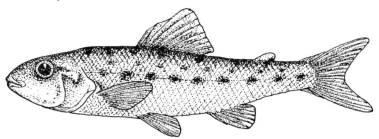

Fig. 125. Trout-perch, *Percopsis omiscomaycus*

The trout-perch is found from Alberta to Quebec and southward into Kansas, Missouri, and Virginia. It is abundant in the St. Croix River, the Mississippi River both above and below St. Anthony Falls, the Rainy River, and most of the deep clear lakes of the state. Personnel of the Minnesota Department of Natural Resources have taken large numbers while trawling in Lake St. Croix. Trout-perch are rare in small streams, but on one occasion we took a large sample from the Nemadji River in Carlton County.

Trout-perch spawn from late May to mid-June. They usually select sandbars in lakes for this purpose but may also ascend rivers and spawn on sand or gravel bottoms. They appear to be temperature sensitive; summer die-offs occur with some regularity in lakes such as Mille Lacs and are usually of great concern to fishermen (in part because they mistake the small trout-perch for young walleyes). Lake Vermilion also has die-offs, and the phenomenon seems to be associated with higher than average temperatures. Generally trout-perch prefer deep water, but the results of shoreline seining in lakes indicate that at times large numbers of them move into shallow water at night. Trautman (1957) made a similar observation in Lake Erie.

Family APHREDODERIDAE
The Pirate Perch Family

The body of the pirate perch is compressed, and the back is somewhat flattened dorsally. The mouth is of medium size and oblique. The lower jaw projects beyond the upper jaw; the upper jaw is not protractile. The jaws and the vomer, palatine, and pterygoid bones bear teeth; the maxillary bones are well developed. The margins of the preopercle and the preorbital are serrated. There is a prominent spine on the opercle. No pseudobranchiae are present. There are 6 branchiostegal rays. No lateral line is present. In adults the vent is located just posterior to the lower jaw. The air bladder is simple; there are 12 pyloric ceca. The family is represented by a single species and is limited in its distribution to eastern North America.

Genus *Aphredoderus* LeSueur

The genus is monotypic and is found from southern Minnesota eastward to New York and south to Texas. The form found in the Atlantic drainage is the nominal subspecies, *Aphredoderus sayanus sayanus* (Gilliams). The western subspecies, *A. s. gibbosus* LeSueur, is present in the Mississippi River drainage.

PIRATE PERCH
Aphredoderus sayanus (Gilliams)

The pirate perch (Figure 126) reaches a maximum length of about 5 inches. The body is very dark purple or slaty olive dorsally and white ventrally. There is a dark vertical bar (similar to that of the mudminnow) on the caudal peduncle and a dark vertical band at the base of the caudal fin. The two bars are separated by a lighter bar. During the spring spawning season mature individuals become somewhat iridescent, and the ventral surface takes on a yellowish hue. The body is oblong, heavy anteriorly, and compressed posteriorly. The back is somewhat elevated in the region of the dorsal fin. The dorsal fin is high and has 2 or 3 spines and 6 soft rays. The anal fin has 2 spines, and the pelvic fins have 1 spine; these spines are short and often difficult to find with the unaided eye. The head length and the body depth are contained 3 times in the standard length. The scales are strongly ctenoid; there are from 45 to 60 scales in a direct line from the margin of the opercle to the base of the caudal fin. An interesting anatomical feature of this fish is the

317

position of the anal opening. In adults it is on the isthmus under the throat and anterior to the pectoral fins, but in young fish under 1 1/2 inches in length it is usually posterior to the pelvic origin and between the pelvic fins. As the fish mature, the anal opening moves anteriorly until it is jugular in position, but even in young fish it is more anterior than in any other species. Forbes and Richardson (1920) atrribute the common name to Charles C. Abbott, a pioneer ichthyologist, who observed that a specimen he had in an aquarium ate only other fish.

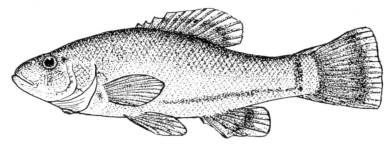

Fig. 126. Pirate perch, *Aphredoderus sayanus*

The pirate perch is a southern species and ranges north in the Mississippi River into southern Minnesota. Our collections contain only specimens collected from sloughs near Winona and La Crescent. Greene (1935) listed this species from five localities in southwestern Wisconsin, and Becker (1966) collected five individuals at four sites on the Wisconsin River and its tributaries in the same general area.

This species prefers oxbow lakes, sloughs, overflow ponds, marshes associated with streams of very low gradient, and similar habitats where the bottom types are soft mud, muck, and debris. Such habitats usually support a luxuriant growth of aquatic plants, and the pirate perch lives within the protection of the vegetation, mud, and debris. Over the past decade we have collected from many such habitats in the Mississippi River floodplain south of Lake Pepin but have failed to take additional specimens. It is a difficult fish to collect because it lives in sloughs where the soft muddy bottoms hinder seining. Several sloughs which had been poisoned yielded large numbers of pirate perch. Trautman (1957) notes that dredging, ditching, siltation, and draining can easily destroy the habitat of the pirate perch. He believes that these operations may explain the changes in the abundance of the species in streams tributary to western Lake Erie in Ohio.

The pirate perch is predacious and feeds on small aquatic insects and other organisms including small fish. We know very little about its spawning habits except that it is a spring spawner. It builds a nest, and both the male and the female are reported to guard the eggs.

Family GADIDAE
The Codfish Family

The members of the codfish family have rather slender bodies which are heavy anteriorly but compressed posteriorly. They have small scales of the cycloid type. The long dorsal fin extends almost the entire length of the back; in some species it is divided into two parts and in others into three parts. No spines are present in any of the fins. The caudal fin is rounded. The anal fin is elongated and inserted far back. The pelvic fins are jugular in position, located in front of the pectoral fins. Four pairs of gills are present, and there is a slit behind the fourth pair. No pseudobranchiae are present. Pyloric ceca are numerous in some species. The gas bladder is usually well developed.

This well-known marine family contains the cod, the haddock, and many other important species. It is represented in Minnesota by one species. The tomcod, an anadromous species occurring along the Atlantic coast from Virginia northward, is the only freshwater species in North America.

Genus *Lota* (Cuvier)

This genus includes only one species that is found in northern North America; several subspecies are found in northern Europe and Asia. The characters for the genus are the same as for the following species.

BURBOT

Lota lota (Linnaeus)

The burbot (Figure 127), often called the lawyer (in Minnesota) or the eelpout (in the East), is the only strictly freshwater member of the codfish family found in North America. In Minnesota burbot seldom exceed a length of 30 inches or a weight of 10 pounds, although weights up to 75 pounds have been reported elsewhere. The body is dark olive with darker markings on the back and the sides, which gives the fish a somewhat reptilian appearance. The body is elongated and slender, compressed posteriorly but deep-bellied anteriorly. The head is small, broad, and depressed. There is a small barbel at each of the nostril apertures and a small median barbel under the tip of the lower jaw. The eyes are very small. The head is contained about 4.6 times in the length, and the body depth is contained about 6 times in the length. The mouth is rather broad; the maxillary extends to below the posterior margin of the eye. The jaws are set with numerous teeth arranged in

319

bands. There is a crescent band of small vomerine teeth in the roof of the mouth. The skin appears smooth, but close examination will reveal tiny embedded cycloid scales. No spines are present in any of the fins. The elongated dorsal fin is divided; the anterior portion has 13 soft rays, and the posterior portion has 76 soft rays. The elongated anal fin has about 68 rays. The pelvic fins are slender and jugular in position, extending below and slightly in front of the pectoral fins. The rounded caudal fin and the dorsal fins are more or less mottled.

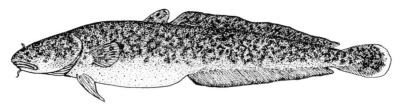

Fig. 127. Burbot, *Lota lota*

The burbot is a cold-water species that ranges from New England and Pennsylvania to the Columbia River and northward to the Arctic Ocean and into Alaska, where it intergrades with the Siberian subspecies. It occurs in the headwaters of the Missouri River and in most of the large lakes and streams of Minnesota from Mille Lacs northward. Occasional specimens have been taken as far south as Lake Pepin and the Whitewater River. It is present in Lake Superior and in Lake of the Woods, where Evermann and Latimer (1910) reported it as one of the most abundant fishes.

The burbot is voracious and feeds on all sorts of fish. We have seen a burbot attack and attempt to swallow a fish nearly its own size. The species has been accused of being destructive to game and valuable food fishes. The burbot examined by us contained mostly perch, suckers, whitefish, and ciscoes, but they are known to feed heavily on the eggs of many species when these are available. They often gorge themselves until their distended stomachs give them a grotesque appearance. We do not know whether the burbot's depredations are extensive enough to render it a nuisance, but it probably is not any more destructive than many game fishes such as northern pike and muskellunge. At any rate this fish is fairly secure from extinction because it lives in deep water in the summer and seldom bites except when it comes into shallow water in the winter. We often catch burbot in nets set for lake trout at depths of over 400 feet in Lake Superior. In the winter they may be speared or caught with hook and line through the ice.

This species spawns in shallow water in lakes and streams before the ice melts. Spent females are often found in the first part of February, indicating that spawning takes place in midwinter. They have been observed spawning in the swift open water of tributary streams as early as January. They spawn at random and are very prolific, producing as many as 1 million eggs per female.

The burbot is a cousin of the highly esteemed codfish and its flesh is equally good, but in northern Minnesota it has acquired the name "dogfish" because it is regarded as fit only for dog food. A few years ago a commercial venture was undertaken for the extraction of oil from burbot livers. The venture did not succeed, partly because the supply was limited to the burbot which were discarded by local commercial fishermen. The prejudice against eating this fish has developed largely because of its unprepossessing appearance. With a shape somewhat like a eel, a bulging potbelly, a smooth skin, and reptilian markings, it does not appeal to the average fisherman, but these are qualities which in no way affect its food value. Nevertheless, hundreds of burbot are discarded by ice fishermen on lakes such as Mille Lacs. The species is carnivorous, as are many prized game fishes, and its diet is not much different from the diet of the walleye and the northern pike. The flesh is white and firm and is not as bony as that of the northern pike. In flavor the flesh is the equal of many game fishes; when properly cooked, it should appeal to the most discriminating appetite. In northern Europe burbot has been eaten and enjoyed for centuries. The next time you catch a burbot, do not throw it away. Skin it, and then bake, fry, or broil it, as you prefer, and you will be pleasantly surprised by its palatability. If you know how, you can even make it into lutefisk.

Family CYPRINODONTIDAE
The Killifish Family

The fishes in this family are all warm-water fishes, and most of them are small. They possess rather large cycloid scales and have an imperfect or poorly developed lateral line. The head is rather flattened, and the mouth is small. The lower jaw is more or less projecting, and the upper jaw is protractile. Teeth are present on the jaws and sometimes on the vomer in the roof of the mouth. The gill membranes are free from the isthmus, and the gill rakers are short. Only 4 to 6 branchiostegal rays are present. A single dorsal fin with soft rays is usually inserted far back. The caudal fin is either rounded or square but not forked. Many genera and species (including the topminnows) are known from brackish and fresh waters of the southern states, the Atlantic coast, Mexico, and Central America, but only one genus is found in Minnesota.

Genus *Fundulus* Lacépède

This genus includes many species commonly known as killifishes. They have elongated bodies, and the sexes are sometimes marked quite differently. The genus contains many southern and eastern species, some of which live in brackish water. One species is found in Minnesota; three others have been reported from Iowa (Harlan and Speaker, 1969).

BANDED KILLIFISH
Fundulus diaphanus (LeSueur)

The banded killifish (Figure 128) found in Minnesota is often called the western banded killifish; it differs slightly from the eastern banded killifish. The western banded killifish is usually 2 or 3 inches long, but we have occasionally found specimens up to 4 inches in length. The body is olivaceous with silver sides and olive-black and silver crossbars; the back is sometimes lightly spotted. The fins are rather plain except in breeding males, in which the dorsal fin is strongly marked with one or two irregular stripes. The head is contained 4 times in the length, and the depth is contained 4.8 times. The lower jaw projects strongly beyond the upper jaw, although the mouth is small. The western banded killifish has from 43 to 45 rows of scales on the side, whereas the eastern banded killifish usually has more. The dorsal fin has 13 soft rays, and the origin of the dorsal fin is before or over the origin of the

322

anal fin. The anal fin has 11 rays. The western banded killifish has 14 to 16 crossbars on each side, whereas the eastern banded killifish has up to 20 crossbars.

The banded killifish ranges from Manitoba, eastern North Dakota, and Iowa eastward through northern Illinois, Indiana, and Ohio to Quebec and southward to South Carolina. It is reported to be fond of muddy brooks and ponds where there is vegetation. We have found it to be very common in the shallow water of most central and southern Minnesota lakes, particularly over sandy bottoms. We have found it throughout Minnesota except in the north-eastern corner of the state. It does not occur in the swift cold waters of trout streams or in the deep cold-water lakes.

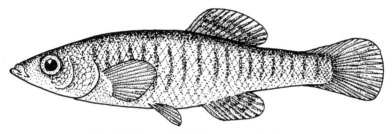

Fig. 128. Banded killifish, *Fundulus diaphanus*

The mouth of the killifish is well developed for skimming the surface of the water, and the species feeds largely on algae, entomostracans, and small terrestrial and aquatic insects which are present near the surface.

We do not know much about the spawning habits of the killifish except that it spawns at random in shallow water, usually over sandy bottoms where some vegetation is present. Since we find ripe females with large mature eggs in midsummer, we know that the species spawns through the summer months.

The banded killifish has little value as a bait fish because it cannot with-stand handling and confinement in a minnow pail. Specimens which we have collected while seining for minnows died soon after being placed in a live-box or a holding tank. The banded killifish is preyed upon by game fishes, but to our knowledge it is not utilized by them as a major food item.

Family POECILIIDAE
The Livebearer Family

Members of this family resemble superficially those of the killifish family, Cyprinodontidae, but the livebearer males can be distinguished by the presence of a modified anal fin. The anal fin is modified as an intromittent organ in the male and is used to transfer sperm to the female during breeding. The eggs are fertilized in the oviduct of the female, and the eggs develop within the oviduct. The guppies, well known to most tropical fish fanciers, belong to this family. Many of the other members of the family are also popular aquarium fishes. A vast majority of the species in this family are tropical or subtropical in their distribution.

One species, *Gambusia affinis* (Baird and Girard), often known as the mosquitofish, was introduced into Minnesota from Ohio for use in mosquito control in the Metropolitan Mosquito Control District in 1958. Successive introductions were made in 1959 and 1960, but no further stockings were made after 1961 (A. W. Buzicky, personal communication). Records made available to us indicate that the introductions were not successful in establishing breeding populations and that continued annual stockings would be required if the mosquitofish were to be useful as a biological control. In 1958, 1,180 fish were stocked in 14 ponds located in Anoka, Hennepin, Ramsey, Scott, and Washington counties, and in 1959 approximately 6,000 fish were stocked in 18 ponds in the five-county area. Some of the fish in the initial stockings survived and reproduced, and there were indications that where the species survived the winter the mosquito populations were significantly reduced. The initial success led to further introductions in 1960 from locally produced stock. Over 52,000 fish were stocked in 128 different sites, but sampling in 1961 revealed that the fish had survived in only 19 ponds.

There is evidence that in many of the ponds the oxygen was exhausted during the winter, resulting in a winterkill. Other winter environmental conditions affecting the success of several populations were the depth of the water, the time and the depth of various snowfalls, and the thickness of the ice. In general many ponds where mosquitoes breed have high water levels in the spring and early summer but may have very low water levels by late fall and may freeze to the bottom in the winter. Some ponds and small lakes not subject to annual or regular winterkills already support fish populations which may prey on the mosquitofish and prevent them from getting established. Under favorable conditions and in the absence of predatory fishes, however,

324

the mosquitofish apparently can survive and reproduce in Minnesota. At present the fathead minnow (*Pimephales promelas*) is being used as a biological control for mosquitoes. It tolerates severe environmental conditions better than almost any other Minnesota fish with the possible exception of the mudminnow (*Umbra limi*).

Genus *Gambusia* Poey

At least six species have been assigned to this genus, and additional species may occur in Mexico.

MOSQUITOFISH
Gambusia affinis (Baird and Girard)

The mosquitofish (Figure 129) is rarely more than 1 inch in total length. The body is light olive brown, and each scale has a dark edge. Some individuals have a bar near the eye. There is evidence of a faint lateral streak, but there

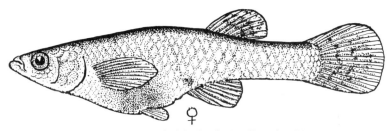

Fig. 129. Mosquitofish, *Gambusia affinis* (female)

is no lateral line. There are 20 to 32 scale rows in the lateral series. The dorsal fin has 7 to 9 rays. The anal fin of the female has 8 to 10 rays; the anal fin of the male is thin and elongate and the rays are modified (Figure 130). Males are not as abundant as females and are smaller in size.

The various subspecies of the mosquitofish range from Florida northward

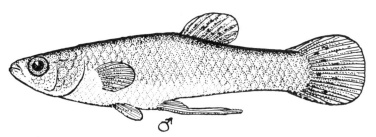

Fig. 130. Mosquitofish, *Gambusia affinis* (male). Modified anal fin.

to New Jersey and westward to southern Illinois. The mosquitofish introduced into Minnesota came from the Toledo Area Sanitary District and was undoubtedly one of the two most common forms of *Gambusia affinis* — *G. a. affinis* or *G. a. holbrooki* — found on the Atlantic coast, but we do not know which one it was. Trautman (1957) notes that in the Toledo Area Sanitary District it was *G. a. affinis* that survived and flourished in tests where both subspecies were stocked in adjacent ponds. No subspecific determinations were made by the staff of the Minnesota Department of Conservation, and unfortunately we were unaware of the introductions until 1967.

Because of their very small size, mosquitofish may be overlooked in seine hauls, and they find it easy to escape through an ordinary minnow seine. They breed continuously throughout the summer, producing broods at intervals of two or three weeks. A single female may produce over three hundred offspring during a single summer. Mosquitofish are surface feeders and hence are very efficient predators on mosquito larvae.

Family GASTEROSTEIDAE
The Stickleback Family

The members of this family are mostly marine, but several species are able to enter fresh water and one species lives exclusively in fresh water. Another species lives equally well in fresh water and in brackish water along the seacoasts.

The sticklebacks are small fish with slender fusiform bodies and very slender caudal peduncles. The body is either naked or covered with bony plates. No scales are present. The anterior portion of the dorsal fin consists of stout spines, each with a small membrane but not attached to the adjacent spines. Posteriorly the dorsal fin is fully developed with soft rays. The mouth is well developed with oblique or slightly upturned jaws; the jaws are set with sharp teeth. The premaxillaries are protractile. The pelvic fins are abdominal and consist of a stout sharp spine and several rudimentary rays. The pubic bones tend to form longitudinal plates under the skin at the base of the pelvic fins. The anal fin has 1 spine and 8 to 10 soft rays. Two genera, each with a single species, occur in Minnesota.

KEY TO MINNESOTA SPECIES OF FAMILY GASTEROSTEIDAE

No lateral keel on peduncle; peduncle deeper than wide; caudal fin rounded; dorsal spines 4 to 7, usually 5 . . . .
. . . . .Brook stickleback, *Culaea inconstans* (Kirtland)
Sharp lateral keels on caudal peduncle; peduncle much wider than deep; caudal fin lunate or slightly forked; dorsal spines 6 to 12, usually 9 . . . . . .
. . . . .Ninespine stickleback, *Pungitius pungitius* (Linnaeus)

Genus *Culaea* Whitley

This genus contains only one species and is exclusively a freshwater genus.

BROOK STICKLEBACK
Culaea inconstans (Kirtland)

The brook stickleback (Figure 131) seldom exceeds 3 inches in length. It varies in color from mottled brown to black above and lighter shades below. Breeding males may be reddish or black anteriorly. The skin is without plates or scales. The dorsal fin contains 3 to 7 free spines, usually 5, and 9 to 11 soft rays. The anal fin contains 1 short stout spine and 9 or 10 soft rays. The pelvic fins are located far forward and consist of 1 stout spine followed by 1 or 2 very rudimentary soft rays. The caudal fin is rounded.

The brook stickleback is restricted to cool shallow waters from Kansas to Maine and northward into southern Canada. It has been reported from northeastern New Mexico and other areas where it has probably been introduced with imported bait minnows. The species is quite common in cool ponds, pools, and spring-fed brooks over most of Minnesota.

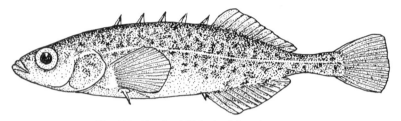

Fig. 131. Brook stickleback, *Culaea inconstans*

In Minnesota brook sticklebacks spawn in early summer in elaborate nests made of vegetable fibers cemented together by a secretion of the male. The nests are usually about the size of a golf ball and have a cavity extending through the center. The eggs are very large for such a small fish; the female deposits 75 to 100 eggs inside the cavity of the nest after considerable urging on the part of the male. The male guards the nest until the eggs hatch. He is very solicitous of the welfare of the eggs; we have one record of a male picking up several eggs which had fallen from the nest and carefully restoring them to the nest. The male is pugnacious and attacks any other fish, regardless of size, which approaches the nest.

Brook sticklebacks are carnivorous and feed on all manner of small aquatic animals. They are of no value for bait but may furnish forage for the few other fishes that frequent their habitat.

Genus *Pungitius* Costa

This genus contains the ninespine stickleback which is found both in salt and fresh water in northern Europe, Asia, and North America. Three other species are known elsewhere.

NINESPINE STICKLEBACK
Pungitius pungitius (Linnaeus)

The ninespine stickleback (Figure 132) seldom reaches a length of more than 3 inches. The body is brownish green above and silver below with rather indistinct vertical bars on the sides. The ninespine stickleback is easily distinguished from the brook stickleback by the 9 dorsal spines (instead of 5) and by many other characters. It is more slender and has a very slender caudal peduncle with strong lateral keels. Although 9 dorsal spines are usually present, there may be anywhere from 8 to 11 of them. The anal fin has a rather stout spine and 8 soft rays. The pelvic fins are represented by a pair of large stout spines located far forward. There are small plates along the bases of the dorsal and anal fins. The caudal fin is slightly forked.

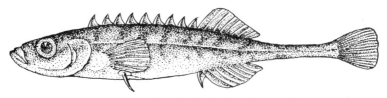

Fig. 132. Ninespine stickleback, *Pungitius pungitius*

The ninespine stickleback is found in the coastal waters and the adjacent stream systems of northern North America, Europe, and Asia. It occurs in Alaska, the Arctic drainage of Canada, the Great Lakes, and in the Atlantic drainage as far south as New Jersey. It is quite common in the shallow waters of Lake Superior along the north shore, where Agassiz (1850) described it as *Gasterosteus nebulosis*. Our first specimens were taken from Lake Superior at Grand Portage in 1879. The species is occasionally found in the Rainy River drainage. In recent years it has been reported from the Mississippi drainage in Indiana (Nelson, 1968) and in Minnesota. Our collection from the Mississippi drainage consists of several specimens taken from Lake Winnibigoshish where the species has recently been introduced either by bait from minnow pails or by floodwater connections with the tributaries of the Rainy River in the Arctic drainage.

The spawning habits of the ninespine stickleback are similar to those of the brook stickleback. The male builds a nest and cares for the eggs and the young. The species is carnivorous and feeds on all manner of small aquatic animals. It has no value as bait but is of some value as forage for other fishes.

Family ATHERINIDAE
The Silverside Family

The silverside family includes a large number of species, most of which are tropical and subtropical in distribution. Only a few are found in temperate zones, and most of these live in the sea and occupy coastal marine or estuarine habitats, although some may enter fresh waters. One strictly freshwater species occurs in Minnesota and the adjacent states.

Genus *Labidesthes* Cope

This genus contains only one species, the brook silverside, *Labidesthes sieculus* (Cope), which ranges from the Great Lakes area southward to Texas and Florida.

BROOK SILVERSIDE
Labidesthes sicculus (Cope)

The brook silverside (Figure 133) in Minnesota usually reaches a length of 2 inches, but occasionally specimens up to 3 1/2 inches are taken. The body is translucent, slender, compressed, and elongate. It is greenish with a prominent and often brilliant silver lateral band. The premaxillary is elongate and

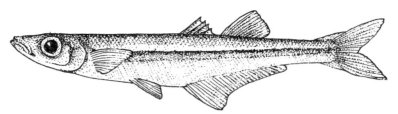

Fig. 133. Brook silverside, *Labidesthes sicculus*

protractile with a concave margin. The mandible extends slightly before the upper jaw, giving the snout a beaklike appearance; it is well adapted for skimming food from the surface of the water. There are two well-separated dorsal fins. The first dorsal fin is small with 3 to 5 weak and very flexible spines. The second dorsal fin has 1 spine and 10 to 12 rays. There are 75 to 79 scales in the lateral series; no lateral line is present. The pectoral fins are inserted high on the body near the upper angle of the gill cleft.

Hubbs (1921) and Cahn (1927) have made detailed studies of the life history of the silverside. The species is gregarious and feeds in schools on or near the surface of lakes and streams. It is very common in most of the clear lakes of central Minnesota, in the Mississippi River above and below St. Anthony Falls, and in the St. Croix River below Taylors Falls. Trautman (1957) reported that the silverside prefers clear waters; it has disappeared from many Ohio streams that have become increasingly turbid since 1900. The species is now restricted in Ohio to clear upland brooks.

Brook silversides feed on entomostracans and small organisms which they skim from the water, and they spend most of their lives less than 2 feet from the water's surface. Because they often skip along the water before a boat, they are sometimes called skipjacks, a common name they share with several other species.

The species spawns in late spring. Each egg has a sticky thread which enables it to float until the thread becomes attached to some object.

The brook silverside is fragile and hardly suitable for bait, but it undoubtedly provides forage for the larger predacious fishes.

Family SCIAENIDAE
The Drum Family

The drum family contains many important marine fishes; only one is a freshwater species. The sea trout, the saltwater drums, and the croakers found off the coasts are important game and commercial fishes. Most members of this family have elongate bodies which are more or less compressed. The lateral line extends over the caudal fin. The caudal fin is usually rounded. The head is large and scaly, and the skull bones are heavy and cavernous. The pharyngeal teeth tend to be large and molariform. Most species in this family have a complicated air bladder with special drumming muscles which are capable of producing audible sounds by vibrating against the air bladder. The ear embedded in the skull contains large otoliths.

Genus *Aplodinotus* Rafinesque

The only species in this genus is the freshwater drum, *Aplodinotus grunniens* Rafinesque. The characters for the genus are the same as for the species.

FRESHWATER DRUM
Aplodinotus grunniens Rafinesque

The freshwater drum (Figure 134), sometimes known locally as the sheepshead, is an elongated and deep-bodied fish weighing usually from 1 to 3 pounds but occasionally as much as 10 pounds. Many years ago there were reports of specimens weighing over 50 pounds, but we have not seen such large ones in recent years. The back is high and compressed anteriorly. The body is mostly silvery gray with a white belly. The snout is blunt and rounded. The subinferior mouth is large and horizontal, with the lower jaw slightly shorter than the upper jaw. Both jaws are covered with weak teeth. The pharyngeal teeth are highly developed; a pair of plates covered with a number of stout molariform teeth grind against a plate in the roof of the pharynx, forming a very efficient chewing apparatus. The lateral line contains 50 to 56 scales and extends posteriorly onto the caudal fin. The anterior portion of the dorsal fin contains 8 or 9 stout spines which can be depressed into a scaly groove. The confluent posterior portion is elongated and contains 25 to 31 soft rays. The anal fin has 2 spines; the first is small, but the second is large and very stout. The soft portion of the anal fin contains 7 or 8 rays. The pelvic fins are thoracic and have threadlike terminal filaments.

The freshwater drum ranges throughout the Mississippi River drainage as far north as St. Anthony Falls, through the Red River drainage into Manitoba and Saskatchewan, and southward into eastern Mexico. It occurs in the eastern drainage of the Great Lakes, but we have no records of it in the cold deep waters of Lake Superior and its drainage. It is a relatively common fish in southern Minnesota and prefers large streams and lakes with shallow mud or sand bottoms.

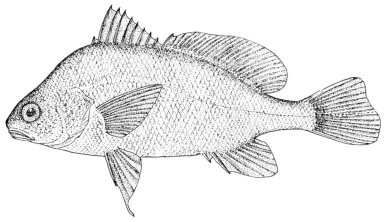

Fig. 134. Freshwater drum, *Aplodinotus grunniens*

The species feeds mostly on small animal life including immature midge larvae, mayflies, leeches, and many other small bottom forms. It has the ability to eat small mollusks, grinding up the shells and digesting the soft bodies. The young drums feed more heavily on large entomostracans and on the amphipod *Hyalella*. The adults spawn in May and June on mud and sand bottoms where there is vegetation, scattering their eggs at random.

The freshwater drum makes a voluntary rumbling sound by vibrating special muscles against the air bladder. The sound can be heard for a considerable distance and is most commonly produced in the evening. When several fish are vibrating simultaneously, the rumbling noise without any apparent source can be quite startling.

The thick skull of the freshwater drum contains an unusual pair of otoliths or ear bones. The otoliths are squarish or roughly J-shaped and are marked with peculiar grooves. They are composed of very dense, ivorylike bone. Anthropologists have dug up large quantities of them from prehistoric Indian food deposits. The otoliths are so hard that they are in perfect condition although most of the other bones have long since disintegrated. Years ago these ear bones were called "lucky stones," and every boy who had any social prestige carried a pair in his pocket. The present generation seems too sophisticated — or too ignorant of their magical qualities — to bother with such trifles!

Drums are seldom caught by anglers, but many are taken by commercial fishermen in seines and traps. Those from weedy water on mud bottoms are not very palatable. Those caught in clean water are edible, although they do not rank with the best commercial fish. The flesh of large drums is rather coarse. In many areas drums are caught and shipped to market in large Midwest cities where they sell quite readily, sometimes under the name "white perch."

Family PERCICHTHYIDAE
The Temperate Bass Family

This family has recently been removed from the sea bass family, Serranidae (Gosline, 1966). It includes freshwater basses of the temperate zone and a few marine species such as the giant sea bass and the striped bass. The striped bass is anadromous and enters fresh water to spawn. Two species are restricted to fresh water, and both of these occur in Minnesota.

Although superficially resembling black bass and crappies (family Centrarchidae), the members of the family Percichthyidae are in no way closely related to them and differ from them in a number of characters. The temperate bass are random spawners; they do not build nests or care for their eggs and young as do most members of the sunfish family. Temperate bass have well-developed pseudobranchiae. There are also a number of small but important differences in the skeleton, particularly in the skull, which distinguish the temperate bass family from the sunfish family.

KEY TO MINNESOTA SPECIES OF FAMILY PERCICHTHYIDAE

Dorsal fins separate; anal fin with 3 spines and 11 to 13 soft rays . . . .
. . . . .White bass, *Morone chrysops* (Rafinesque)
Dorsal fins slightly connected; anal fin with 3 spines and 10 soft rays . . . . .
. . . . .Yellow bass, *Morone mississippiensis* Jordan and Eigenmann

Genus *Morone* Mitchill

This genus contains four species; two of the species are restricted to fresh water and are found in Minnesota.

WHITE BASS
Morone chrysops (Rafinesque)

The white bass (Figure 135) reaches a length of over 18 inches. The deep elliptical body is marked with 9 to 12 longitudinal stripes on a silvery background. The lateral line extends along a stripe with 4 or 5 stripes above it and 5 to 7 stripes below it. The mouth is strong and extends to a point below the middle of the eye. The lower jaw protrudes slightly. The teeth are villiform, arranged in bands on the jaws, on the palatine and vomer bones, and at the base of the tongue. The head is scaled anteriorly to the nostrils. The dorsal fin is completely divided; the anterior portion has 9 strong spines, and the pos-

335

terior portion has 1 spine and 13 or 14 soft rays. The longest dorsal spine is almost half the length of the head. The anal fin has 3 short but very stout graduated spines and 11 or 12 soft rays. The caudal fin is forked. The pelvic fins have 1 spine and 5 rays. The lateral line is complete and contains 55 to 65 scales.

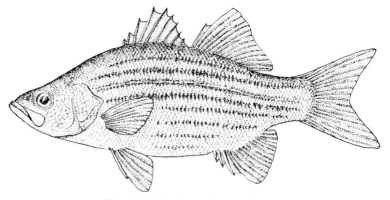

Fig. 135. White bass, *Morone chrysops*

The white bass ranges from southern Minnesota eastward through the lower Great Lakes and St. Lawrence drainages and southward into Texas and northern Alabama. This fish is common in Minnesota in the Mississippi River drainage below St. Anthony Falls. We have records of it in the Minnesota and St. Croix rivers, but it is absent from the Lake Superior and Red River drainages.

White bass usually travel in large schools near the surface of large rivers and the connected lakes, feeding at the surface on aquatic and other insects and small fish, especially small gizzard shad. This can be observed on lakes such as Lake St. Croix and Lake Pepin when the water warms in the spring and large schools of white bass move up the lakes, feeding at the surface and pursuing any schools of gizzard shad in their vicinity.

The white bass spawns in the spring when the temperature is about 60° F. Their spawning migrations are quite spectacular as great numbers of fish move long distances upstream from the rivers into the large lakes connected with them. The eggs are scattered at random on shallow bars and gravelly reefs. The fertility is high, and the eggs hatch in a few days. The growth of the fry is rapid; the young fish may become sexually mature in their second year.

White bass are excellent game fish. They bite readily on minnows, all sorts of artificial plugs, spinners, and flies. Once a school is located, the fisherman can soon catch his limit, especially in the early morning.

YELLOW BASS

Morone mississippiensis Jordan and Eigenmann

The yellow bass (Figure 136) resembles the white bass in many ways. Both species reach a length of about 18 inches, but the yellow bass is more yellowish in color and the longitudinal stripes below the lateral line tend to be broken under the soft dorsal fin. These characters are not always reliable, however, because the color may fade, and we have seen white bass with broken longitudinal stripes. The most reliable characters of the yellow bass are the dorsal fin, in which the anterior and posterior portions are partially connected, and the anal fin, in which the first spine is short and the second and third spines are very long and slender. The dorsal fin usually has only 9 spines and 12 soft rays; the longest ray is about half the length of the head. The anal fin has 9 or 10 soft rays, usually 10. The lateral line has 51 to 55 scales. The base of the tongue lacks teeth.

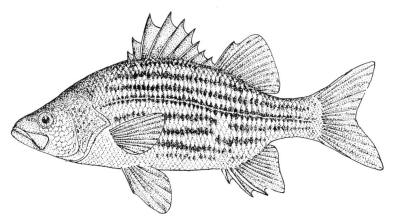

Fig. 136. Yellow bass, *Morone mississippiensis*

The yellow bass seems to be a more southern species than the white bass. It ranges from southern Minnesota to Indiana and south to Texas and Louisiana. It is not common in southern Minnesota but it is known to occur in the Mississippi River and the connected backwaters from Lake Pepin southward. In Iowa it also seems to be restricted to the Mississippi River and its backwaters (Harlan and Speaker, 1969).

The spawning and feeding habits of the yellow bass appear to be similar to those of the white bass. The species is not abundant enough in Minnesota to be of much importance to sport fishermen, but farther south it is regarded as an excellent game fish.

Family CENTRARCHIDAE
The Sunfish Family

The sunfish family is one of the most important families of freshwater panfish and game fish; it contains the sunfishes, the crappies, the rock bass, and the black bass. Approximately thirty species are known, and at least ten of them are more or less common in Minnesota. These are the rock bass, the warmouth, the largemouth bass, the smallmouth bass, two species of crappies, and four species of sunfish. Many common names in addition to these have been applied to various species in the family.

Members of this family superficially resemble the temperate bass family (Percichthyidae), but the Minnesota species of the sunfish family lack the 7 or 8 longitudinal stripes which are characteristic of the temperate bass family. The sunfish species are further characterized by having more or less deep and flattened or compressed bodies. The anterior and posterior portions of the dorsal fin are confluent or joined together. The anterior portion is supported by 5 to 13 sharp spines; the posterior portion is supported by soft rays. The pelvic fins are thoracic in position and have typically 1 spine and 5 soft rays. The anal fin contains 2 to 8 spines.

All the sunfish species are essentially warm-water fishes and prefer, but are not restricted to, fertile lakes of moderate temperatures with abundant rooted vegetation growing in the littoral waters. Some of the species are widely distributed from southern Canada to the Gulf of Mexico. There are more species present in the southern states than in the northern states. The members of this family are all native to North America, but several species (for example, the black bass) have been introduced in Europe, South and Central America, and elsewhere. Only one species is native to an area west of the Rocky Mountains, but others have been introduced into western waters.

All species found in Minnesota are nest builders, although on occasion some species use the nests of other fishes that have already spawned. The male performs the important duties of building the nest and caring for the young. He prepares the nest in shallow water by fanning out a depression in the bottom sediments with his tail fin. He then attracts a female and induces her through courtship activity to lay her eggs in his nest. When the female releases the eggs, the male releases milt to fertilize them as they settle to the floor of the nest. After the egg-laying is completed, the male often chases the female away from the nest site; his behavior is not discriminatory for he chases all intruders away. (An aggressive male may even attempt to nip an inquisitive biologist.) The male remains at the nest until the eggs have hatched and the young fry have dispersed, whereupon he also moves out into new areas.

During the breeding period the male exhibits strong territorial instincts. If he is removed from his nest and is transported several hundred yards away, he swims almost directly back to the nest. Marked fish have been transported several miles and have been recovered again at the nest site in a period so short that random searching was not a reasonable explanation. At Lake Itasca students attached small corks by means of fine monofilament nylon to the dorsal fins of males and were able to observe the almost direct routes of the fish as they returned to their nests. The mechanism by which the sunfishes and other species are able to navigate and return home is discussed in some detail in a delightful book entitled *Underwater Guideposts* (Hasler, 1966).

In Minnesota the sunfish family, with the exception of the crappies, becomes less active and feeds less during the winter than in warmer weather. The reduction of food intake may be due partly to the low temperatures of the water. When we keep bass and sunfish in the University of Minnesota aquariums during the winter and maintain them at low temperatures, we find that they seem to eat less under such conditions.

The sunfishes are the most widespread and abundant members of this family in Minnesota. Four species are found more or less commonly in the state: the bluegill, the pumpkinseed, the green sunfish, and the orangespotted sunfish. The longear sunfish has been reported from the state, but we are not certain that it can be regarded as a Minnesota species. Numerous cases of hybridization involving practically all these species have been noted. Years ago some of the resulting hybrids were described as species, but since then they have been identified as the products of various hybrid combinations. The hybrids show some characteristics of the parent species but lack the pure characters of either. For example, the green sunfish is a relatively small fish, usually less than 5 inches long, with a large mouth; the bluegill is a larger fish with a small mouth. The green bluegill hybrid is rather large and has a big mouth and the colors of both parents. All the sunfishes are more or less brightly colored, and the males are especially colorful during the spawning season.

KEY TO MINNESOTA SPECIES OF FAMILY CENTRARCHIDAE

1. Dorsal fin about equal to length of anal fin 2
   Dorsal fin much longer than anal fin 3
2. Length of dorsal fin much less than distance from origin of dorsal fin to eye; dorsal spines usually but not always 6 ....
   ....White crappie, *Pomoxis annularis* Rafinesque
   Length of dorsal fin about equal to distance from origin of dorsal fin to eye; dorsal spines usually 7 or 8 ....
   ....Black crappie, *Pomoxis nigromaculatus* (LeSueur)

3. Scales large, 53 or fewer in lateral line; body deep and short, the depth usually more than two-fifths the length; dorsal fin not deeply notched between spinous and soft-rayed portions; a black spot usually present on the opercular flap 4
   Scales small, 59 or more in lateral line; body rather long, the depth one-third the length; dorsal fin more or less deeply notched 9
4. Anal fin with usually 6 spines ....
   ....Rock bass, *Ambloplites rupestris* (Rafinesque)
   Anal fin with usually 3 spines 5
5. Teeth present on tongue; maxillary extending almost back to posterior margin of eye ....Warmouth, *Chaenobryttus gulosus* Cuvier
   Teeth absent on tongue; maxillary extending almost to anterior margin of eye 6
6. Pectoral fins of adult short and rounded, about one-fourth standard length
   .... Green sunfish, *Lepomis cyanellus* Rafinesque
   Pectoral fins of adult long and pointed, about one-third standard length . 7
7. Gill rakers short and knoblike ....
   ....Pumpkinseed, *Lepomis gibbosus* (Linnaeus)
   Gill rakers long and slender 8
8. Anal fin with usually 10 to 12 soft rays; distinct black blotch near base of last dorsal rays; lateral line scales more than 40; adults rather large ....
   ....Bluegill, *Lepomis macrochirus* Rafinesque
   Anal fin with 7 to 10 soft rays; no blotch near base of last dorsal rays; lateral line scales fewer than 40; adults small ....
   ....Orangespotted sunfish, *Leopomis humilis* (Girard)
9. Maxillary bone in adult not extending beyond posterior margin of eye; mouth of medium size; scales about 11–74–17; 15 to 18 rows of scales on cheek; spinous dorsal fin low and separated from soft dorsal fin by a moderate notch ....Smallmouth bass, *Micropterus dolomieui* Lacépède
   Maxillary bone in adult extending to or beyond the posterior margin of eye; mouth large; scales about 7–68–16; 10 or 11 rows of scales on cheek; black stripe on sides in juveniles becomes less distinct in large adults; spinous dorsal fin almost separated from soft dorsal fin by a deep notch
   ....Largemouth bass, *Micropterus salmoides* (Lacépède)

Genus *Micropterus* Lacépède

This genus includes six species of black bass, but only two occur in Minnesota. The other four species, including the spotted bass, *Micropterus punctulatus* (Rafinesque), are found only in the southern states.

LARGEMOUTH BASS

Micropterus salmoides (Lacépède)

The largemouth bass (Figure 137) reaches a weight of more than 8 pounds in the northern states; it reaches double this weight in the southern states. It differs from the smallmouth bass in a number of characters. The lower jaw is longer, reaching back to below the posterior margin of the eye. The dorsal fin has 10 spines, occasionally 9, and 12 or 13 soft rays; the spinous portion is higher than in the smallmouth bass and is separated from the soft portion by a deeper notch. The cheeks have 10 or 11 rows of scales. The lateral line has 62 to 68 scales; there are 8 or 9 rows of scales above it. The largemouth bass differs from the smallmouth bass also in the absence of vertical bars and dark mottlings on the sides. A faint dark horizontal stripe may be present on the sides. In fingerlings and young fish this stripe is distinct, but it tends to fade in adults.

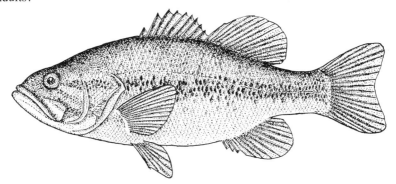

Fig. 137. Largemouth bass, *Micropterus salmoides*

Environmental differences exert an influence on the appearance of the largemouth bass. Those from lakes with clean bottoms are dark green on the sides and silvery below, and the broad blackish band on the sides is almost as distinct as in the young. Adults from mud-bottom lakes may shade from dark olive brown to black with barely discernible markings, and the very young fish may be almost colorless.

The many variations in the largemouth bass caused Lacépède and LeSueur in the early nineteenth century to describe the variants as separate species. Consequently, the largemouth bass has undergone many name changes in recent years. The name assigned to the first proper description, according to the rules of priority, usually becomes the valid scientific name. Forty-five years ago the largemouth bass was known as *Micropterus salmoides* (Lacépède); then it successively became *Aplites salmoides* (Lacépède), *Huro floridana* (LeSueur), *Huro salmoides* (Lacépède), and now it is back to *Micropterus salmoides* (Lacépède).

The largemouth bass was originally found east of the Rockies from Canada southward to Florida and Mexico. It has been widely introduced in other geographic areas. Beyond any question the largemouth bass is one of the most popular game fishes in Minnesota, not because of its fighting ability, which is close to that of the smallmouth bass, but because of its wide distribution in lakes and streams of the state. The species is common in many of the muddy lakes of the southern and central counties and in sloughs and backwaters along the Mississippi River, but it is most abundant in clear-water lakes, particularly in the headwater lakes of the Mississippi and Red river drainages. It also occurs in many small isolated lakes near the Canadian border (how the species comes to be in these lakes, no one knows) and in several lakes in the Quetico Provincial Park north of the Canadian border. It is not common in the Lake Superior drainage and is found in only a few lakes in Cook and Lake counties (as a result of stocking, in most cases). Largemouth bass seem to thrive in small to medium-sized hard-water lakes with clear water, sandy shores, and a substantial growth of marginal weed beds which can produce food for the bass and for the fishes they feed upon.

The spawning of bass is largely controlled by weather conditions. In Minnesota bass spawn from May to July when the water temperature reaches 60° F. A sudden drop of only 10° to 12° below the normal temperature for the spawning season (60° to 65° F) is sufficient to kill the eggs or the newly hatched fry. As a rule, the spawning areas are found in sheltered bays in waters 2 to 6 feet deep. The prevailing winds at this time of year are usually from the south, but if they suddenly shift to the northwest, the temperature usually drops abruptly. If the spawning areas are located on the southern or southeastern side of the lake, a severe loss of eggs or fry or both is likely to occur. The bass desert their nests in short order when the water temperature reaches 48° F. Turbid waters may also disturb the spawning. A light deposit of silt on the eggs causes the bass to desert them. Such an event seldom happens except in lakes in the immediate vicinity of cultivated lands, where the surface soil can be washed into the water over the spawning beds.

The largemouth bass does not always use the same care as the smallmouth bass in selecting nesting sites. Where good beds are available, the largemouth bass uses the same procedure as the smallmouth bass, but sometimes a bottom covered with dead vegetation or an accumulation of roots in shallow water will suffice. The nest is cleaned before the eggs are deposited. A depression 2 to 3 feet in diameter is fanned out by the male. He removes any small pebbles by carrying them away in his mouth. He then seeks a ripe female who deposits eggs as he ejects milt to fertilize them.

Bass are as courageous in defending their nests against all enemies, fancied or real, as are the other members of the family Centrarchidae. From the time the male clears off an area for the nest until the eggs are hatched and the fry leave the nest, every fish (including other bass) appearing within a radius of at least 20 feet is immediately attacked and driven off. Unlike the gregarious sunfishes which nest in colonies, bass build their nests 30 feet or more apart and apparently establish territorial boundaries.

In a defense reaction the males strike at any lure cast near the nest; many are caught at this time, leaving the unprotected nest to the prey of small fishes which soon destroy any eggs or fry. In pond-rearing operations, Surber tried time and again to induce guarding males to take food such as minnows and frogs. They would strike immediately, but after chewing savagely on the minnow or frog for a few seconds they would eject it with considerable force. When a live frog was taken, it was carried some distance away before it was ejected, and immediately afterward the bass resumed his sentry duty. As soon as the newly hatched bass are large enough to leave the nest, they move about in dense schools which usually do not break up until the young fish reach a length of an inch or more. Although at this stage the guardian parent does not defend them as vigorously as he did earlier, he remains as a protector until the school finally scatters.

The largemouth bass is carnivorous and feeds on all manner of animal life. The young fry feed on entomostracans at first but soon begin to eat *Hyalella*, small aquatic insects, and any small minnows they can find in the shallow water. The adults feed on perch, minnows, and small sunfish and eagerly seize crayfish and frogs. Woe to the field mouse that falls in the water — any small animal swimming in the water is prey for the largemouth bass.

Because of the popularity of the largemouth bass as a game fish and because of its ability to thrive in many waters not suitable for trout, walleyes, and other game fishes, there is a demand for fingerling bass for purposes of introduction and stocking. Years ago bass rearing ponds maintained by local sportsmen became popular in many areas. Most of these ponds were artificial and were constructed so that they could be drained to secure the fingerling bass in the fall for planting in local lakes. Bass do not respond to artificial expression and fertilization of the eggs as do walleyes, northern pike, and trout; they must be liberated in ponds and allowed to take care of their own domestic affairs. Consequently, this method of propagation is limited by the number of ponds available and by the size of the ponds (since each male establishes territorial boundaries around his nest). The adult bass often eat their young if the fry are not removed as soon as they are able to take care of themselves. It is possible to increase the number of nesting sites in a given area by building nesting stalls so that the male does not realize how close he is to his neighbors. On the whole this is an expensive and rather impractical method of propagation. It has proven to be much more economical to undertake measures that facilitate reproduction of the species under natural conditions in its home waters. That is, by setting up protected areas where the bass can nest in their own lakes and not be disturbed by humans, the desired results can be secured and at far less effort and expense than is involved in pond propagation.

Largemouth bass have a high reproductive potential. We found that counts of eggs in mature females ranged from 2,000 to 26,000 eggs. A 3-pound female contained nearly 40,000 eggs. Needham (1938) reported that from 2,000 to 7,000 eggs are produced per pound of fish. Except during adverse climatic conditions, the hatch is usually high. Carbine (1939) in Michigan removed the fry from a number of nests and found that the average count was 4,000 fry per nest.

In Minnesota the total catch of largemouth bass by anglers is smaller than the catch of sunfish, crappies, walleyes, or northern pike but is larger than that of smallmouth bass and most trout species. Probably this situation is not because of any scarcity of bass but because most anglers do not fish for bass, although they are the favorite of a relatively small number of anglers who seek them exclusively. The vast majority of the fishermen who swarm to Minnesota lakes are cane-pole fishermen seeking panfish, and unless they use live minnows for bait they rarely hook bass.

Bass fishing requires a special technique. Bass are mostly sight feeders and are least active at midday. In the early morning and the late afternoon they feed in the shallow weedy lake margins. Casting into weed beds with frogs, live minnows, or plugs is the favorite technique of many bass fishermen. Needless to say, the fisherman will save himself a lot of frustration if he uses weedless hooks while fishing in these areas. A bass is not always hooked when it first seizes the lure. Usually it will run some distance with the lure before swallowing it far enough to set the hook. The wise angler lets the fish make the first run, and when it hesitates he sets the hook with a strong but steady pull. When the fight starts, he lets the fish have some line to run with but avoids any slack line that might give the fish an opportunity to shake the hook from its mouth. The fisherman must keep the bass away from snags and logs where the line might become tangled. Bass often try to dive under the boat, so the fisherman should not be completely confident of his catch until the fish is in the landing net. It often requires considerable skill to hook and land a bass.

From a purely epicurean point of view, bass from turbid mud-bottom lakes are rather unpalatable, particularly in the early part of the season before they have had time to lose the muddy flavor which they acquire from the lake bottom where they live during the winter. (It is possible to remove some of the objectionable flavor by soaking the flesh overnight in salt water.) On the other hand, bass taken from clear-water lakes with sand and gravel bottoms have very little of this disagreeable flavor.

SMALLMOUTH BASS

Micropterus dolomieui Lacépède

The smallmouth bass (Figure 138) usually attains a length of more than 12 inches but rarely more than 20 inches. In Minnesota specimens usually weigh up to 4 pounds, but record fish weighing over 11 pounds have been reported in southern states. The smallmouth bass has a mouth of moderate size when compared with that of the largemouth bass, and the maxillary does not extend beyond the eye as it usually does in the largemouth bass. The young are more or less barred and spotted on the sides for the first year or so and never have a black lateral band. The very young fry are jet black; later the caudal fin develops yellow or orange bases, a black center, and a white margin at the tip. The color of the adults varies from dark green flecked with pale gold to pale olive brown with some dark mottling on the back and sides and white on the belly. The markings are pronounced in the live fish but fade quickly when the fish is caught. The eyes are more or less reddish. There are 15 to 18 rows of scales on the cheeks; these are often hard to count. The dorsal fin has 9 or 10 spines and 13 or 14 soft rays. The lateral line contains from 66 to 78 scales. The spinous portion of the dorsal fin is distinctly lower than that of the largemouth bass and is not as deeply notched and separated from the soft rays.

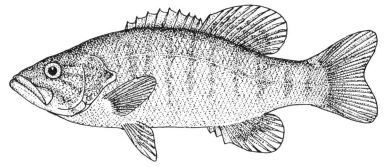

Fig. 138. Smallmouth bass, *Micropterus dolomieui*

In Minnesota lakes and rivers where both smallmouth and largemouth bass occur, fishermen often have difficulty distinguishing adult specimens of the two species. Until the fry are yearlings, however, they are so radically different in their markings that they can be identified at a glance. The markings fade in the older fish, and the length of the maxillaries may be obscured by the angle at which the fish is held in the hand. Although hybridization between the two species is possible, we have no evidence that this has occurred.

The smallmouth bass ranges from the Lake of the Woods region to Quebec and southward to northern Alabama and eastern Oklahoma, and it has been widely introduced elsewhere. It is difficult to determine the original range in Minnesota because unrecorded introductions were made years ago in many lakes, but to the best of our knowledge the species was limited to the Mississippi drainage. It is doubtful that the species occurred in the Red River drainage until it was introduced into some of the headwater lakes where largemouth bass were also present. We find the smallmouth bass in some of the headwater lakes of the Otter Tail and Mississippi rivers. It is quite common in the Mississippi River above Minneapolis, but it is perhaps most abundant in the main channel of the river below Lake Pepin; it seldom occurs in the backwater sloughs of the river. It is common in the St. Croix River above Taylors Falls and in many of its tributaries such as the Kettle River, the Snake River, and Lake Pokegama in Pine County. Although it occurs sporadically in tributaries of the Mississippi River in the southeastern counties, it is more common in the tributaries of the St. Croix. For many years certain lakes in Douglas County, such as Lake Miltona, were probably the most noted smallmouth bass lakes in the United States, but in recent years intensive fishing and other recreational developments have caused the bass population to decline. However, both the smallmouth bass and the largemouth bass are still present in the various lakes of that area.

The smallmouth bass now occurs in the marginal waters of Lake of the Woods and in certain small lakes in Canada. Eddy and Surber (1947) were informed by H. H. Mackay of the Ontario Game and Fisheries Department that smallmouth bass are not native to Lake of the Woods but were introduced by loggers at the turn of the century. He stated that in 1901 and thereafter smallmouth bass were planted in Long Lake (near Kenora), which was separated from Lake of the Woods by a small channel and a dam. The dam was destroyed soon afterward, and the bass escaped into Lake of the Woods. Bass were subsequently planted in other small lakes in that region.

The preferred habitat of the smallmouth bass seems to be clear, moderately cold, swift-flowing streams and medium-sized clear-water lakes with clean gravel or boulder bottoms. Most of the repeated efforts to extend the range of the smallmouth bass in Minnesota waters have had doubtful success, even when adult fish were used for stocking. The records of stocking in the files of the Minnesota Game and Fish Department before 1920 offer little information; the entries list simply "black bass" with no identification of the species. With the aid of more recent records which identify the species, we know that all attempts to stock the coffee-colored northern streams have failed. Efforts to stock the rocky clear-water lakes in the border counties, where all conditions seemed favorable, also have usually ended in failure. In the few northern waters where smallmouth bass were successfully introduced and where they reproduced in large numbers, as in Bear Lake in Lake County, they never exceed 6 inches in length, regardless of age. This may be because lack of predation has resulted in overpopulation and stunting. It seems that the most successful stocking of the border waters resulted from the Canadian introduction.

Referring to the black bass, Henshall (1881) said, "He is plucky, game, brave and unyielding to the last when hooked. He has the arrowy rush of the trout, and the bold leap of the salmon, while he has a system of fighting tactics, peculiarly his own. . . . I consider him *inch for inch* and *pound for pound*, the gamest fish that swims." In many of the clean cold lakes and streams of central Minnesota where the two species intermingle, we doubt that one species can be distinguished from the other on the basis of fighting ability and tactics. Both species are tremendous fighters.

Except when feeding, smallmouth bass frequent deeper water than do largemouth bass. As winter approaches, smallmouth bass retire to the depths where they seem to feed very little; few are caught during the winter. The bulk of their food consists of minnows, small suckers, and even small bullheads. During September they begin to feed on the crayfish which become their main diet during the month of October. Usually smallmouth bass display very little interest in frogs, whereas largemouth bass prefer them at certain seasons.

Smallmouth bass kept in aquariums at the University of Minnesota feed eagerly on live minnows but show no interest in dead ones. Bass of about 3 pounds in weight have an appetite for mice from the janitor's traps, but they do not touch a dead mouse unless someone pulls it through the water by the tail (at the peril of his fingers). The young bass feed largely on entomostracans during the first few weeks of life. Then they are ready for aquatic insects, larger crustaceans, and small minnows. They resort to cannibalism if such food is not available. We have found that young bass grow rapidly and, if they are not crowded, reach a length of 6 inches or more in their first year. In the warmer climates of the south they grow even more rapidly, and in rearing ponds where all conditions are ideal they grow to a larger size than under natural conditions.

Smallmouth bass, like largemouth bass, are not particularly good subjects for artificial propagation. It is possible to strip them and to fertilize the eggs, but generally it seems best to let them spawn naturally. Pond propagation has been found satisfactory for nesting and for rearing the young, but as each male demands considerable space for his own territory and nest, only a limited yield results. If natural spawning is undisturbed, the yield is virtually the same as that produced through pond propagation.

In pond culture operations in early years, a curious phenomenon was repeatedly noted by Surber. Shortly after darkness set in, the fry would spread out over the spawning bed and assume a light gray color which was retained until sunrise the following morning when they resumed the normal jet black color of healthy fry. The same change occurred when the fry were being transported in cans for transplanting during a cold night. Whether the change occurred as a result of the temperature change or as a result of darkness was not definitely determined.

The natural sites selected by the smallmouth bass as spawning grounds are invariably over clean gravel and sand bottoms where there is a decided current. The smallmouth bass spawns at about the same temperature as the largemouth bass — that is, at 60° to 65° F. It is even more sensitive than the largemouth bass to sudden drops in temperature. Consequently, eggs deposited early in the season are often killed, and in this event a second or even a third spawning may occur, sometimes as late as August. The nests are hollow depressions fanned out in the sand by the male. They are usually placed a considerable distance apart because each male establishes his own territory and does not tolerate nearby neighbors. In the care of the nest, the eggs, and the resulting fry the male smallmouth bass shows an attention to duty even stricter than that of the largemouth bass. Any intruding fish is viciously attacked, and at this time even a fisherman's lure is regarded as an intruder. Sticks thrown into the water near the nest may be hit by the fish and knocked into the air.

Although the two species of bass occur in both lakes and streams, the smallmouth bass is found primarily in medium-sized rivers and the largemouth bass is most at home in medium-sized lakes with weedy shores.

The smallmouth bass also seems to flourish in moderately deep rocky lakes and is quite abundant in many headwater lakes of the Red River tributaries.

In some lakes smallmouth bass are heavily parasitized with a number of species of roundworms and tapeworms. Fortunately, these are usually in the viscera and not in the flesh; as far as we know, they are not harmful to man. Bass are frequent victims of a tapeworm in their urogenital organs which renders them sterile and which may be responsible for some of the unsuccessful attempts to establish the species in the border lakes. In 1940 Eddy studied a lake in Mahnomen County where smallmouth bass, the only bass present, were heavily infected. He identified eight different kinds of parasites in their viscera; they were so numerous that the sides of the fish bulged. William Riley of the University of Minnesota found the same condition in this lake in 1920.

Successful bass fishing is an art. True bass fishermen fish for bass only and constitute a small minority of all fishermen. Smallmouth bass are not as widely distributed in Minnesota waters as largemouth bass and must be sought in rivers and lakes where they are known to thrive. It is impossible to give explicit directions for catching bass because only the individual bass knows what it wants and what it will do. Both smallmouth and largemouth bass are capricious, and many fishermen remember the nice big bass that was not interested in any of their fancy lures but that snatched up the worm on the handline of the small boy sitting in the stern of the boat.

Bass feed most actively in the early morning and in the evening. They are mainly sight feeders and usually strike at moving lures. Once in a while they will strike at a bait that is moved gently up and down, but in general the fisherman will have better results with a more vigorously moving lure. Many fishermen cast into the edges of weed beds in lakes or around snags in deep holes in a river and retrieve the lure slowly, just fast enough to keep it from sinking to the bottom. At times fly fishing is successful; bass love a fat grasshopper floating on the surface. All manner of moving lures may be used in casting. Spinners and bright spoons are good, especially if baited with a live minnow, a crayfish, or a hellgrammite. When a bass strikes, it usually hits hard and starts running with the bait, but often it is not hooked and needs a few seconds to orient the bait. Set the hook after the first rush with a gentle pull (a jerk is apt to pull the hook out of the fish's mouth). The excitement begins when the fish starts to clear the water and to try every conceivable escape tactic. Try to maintain a tight line and to keep the fish away from entanglements and snags. Watch out for those final rushes when the bass tries to dive under the boat.

Genus *Ambloplites* Rafinesque

This genus contains several species, only one of which occurs in Minnesota.

ROCK BASS

Ambloplites rupestris (Rafinesque)

The rock bass (Figure 139) reaches a length of 8 to 10 inches. The body is thicker and heavier than that of the sunfish and the crappie. The mouth is large; the maxillary extends to below the middle of the eye. The eye is quite reddish. The dorsal fin has 10 or 11 spines and 10 to 12 soft rays. The anal fin contains 6 spines and 10 or 11 soft rays. The back and sides are ordinarily an olive brown color with a brassy tinge. Each scale is marked with a dark spot. Young rock bass apparently have the ability to change the size of their scale spots, creating a variety of markings. They can produce broad irregular black vertical bars or black blotches on their sides, or they can become almost solid black. They can change quickly from black to pale silver with black splotches.

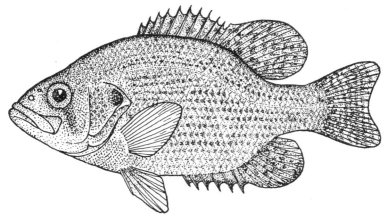

Fig. 139. Rock bass, *Ambloplites rupestris*

The rock bass ranges in southern Canada from Saskatchewan to Quebec and southward to North Carolina and Oklahoma, integrading with the Gulf coast form which extends from Florida to Texas. It is widely distributed in lakes and streams throughout most of Minnesota. It is very common along the weedy margins of small lakes and in the shallow bays of such lakes as Mille Lacs and Lake of the Woods and is least abundant in the Lake Superior drainage. Rock bass are not uncommon in many mud-bottom lakes and creeks.

The male prepares the nest in shallow water among the weeds in May or early June, when the temperature is 60° to 70° F. He guards the eggs and cares for the young fry until they are able to leave the nest. We have counted as many as 12,000 eggs in a large female, but the number usually runs around 5,000.

The food of the rock bass consists mostly of small crayfish, *Hyalella*, aquatic insect larvae, small snails, and small fish. Rock bass have one endearing trait — they will bite on almost any bait and anyone can catch them. They are the favorite fish of small boys who fish from docks. They bite on cut bait, worms, and minnows, and there is nothing they like better than grasshoppers. They seem to travel in schools; once the angler locates a school, he can soon catch his limit. Rock bass are daytime feeders and strike readily on artificial flies, small spinners, and flatfish. We have even caught them on large spoons when trolling in the evening just off the weeds. They love to hang around submerged stumps or snags in water 4 to 8 feet deep. Although the rock bass is of some value as a panfish, it often has a muddy flavor and is not as palatable as the bluegill.

Genus *Chaenobryttus* Gill

This genus contains only one species. The characters of the genus are the same as for the species.

WARMOUTH

Chaenobryttus gulosus (Cuvier)

The warmouth (Figure 140) reaches a length of 8 to 10 inches. It resembles the rock bass in many ways and easily may be mistaken for it. It has a robust body and a large mouth with the maxillary extending back to below the middle of the eye. The back and sides are olivaceous or gray mottled with chocolate and purplish shades, sometimes flecked with gold or green, and with a brassy tinge. Each scale bears a black spot. The belly is pale green or yellow and is speckled with gold or with dark dots. The cheeks and opercle are streaked as in many sunfishes, and the opercle ends in a short black opercular flap. The

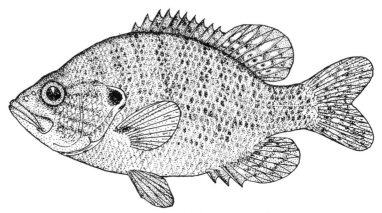

Fig. 140. Warmouth, *Chaenobryttus gulosus*

dorsal fin has 9 to 11 spines, usually 10, and 9 to 11 soft rays. The anal fin of the warmouth has 3 spines and 8 to 10 rays (the anal fin of the rock bass has 6 spines and 10 or 11 soft rays). The lateral line contains 39 to 43 scales. There are 6 or 7 scale rows above the lateral line and 11 or 12 rows below it.

The warmouth ranges from southern Minnesota eastward through the lower Great Lakes region and southward to Florida and the Rio Grande. It seems to prefer shallow mud-bottom lakes and sloughs. We have collected it only from sloughs and backwaters of the Mississippi River from Winona southward; this is probably the northern limit of its range. It may occur in some of the sluggish tributaries of the Mississippi River in southern Minnesota, but we have not taken it except along the river.

Genus *Lepomis* Rafinesque

This genus includes ten species; five species have been reported in Minnesota.

GREEN SUNFISH
Lepomis cyanellus Rafinesque

The green sunfish (Figure 141) reaches a length of 7 inches or more, but Minnesota specimens usually are from 3 to 5 inches in length. The body is

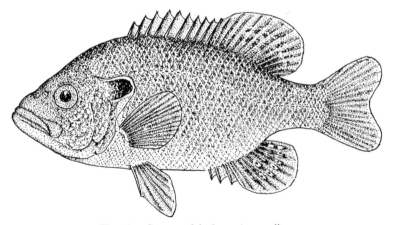

Fig. 141. Green sunfish, *Lepomis cyanellus*

robust but not so deep as that of the bluegill or the pumpkinseed. The green sunfish is the least colorful of all Minnesota sunfishes. The back and sides are olive green, and each scale is flecked with yellow. The belly is yellowish. The opercular lobe is black with a pale border. There is a dark blotch at the posterior base of the dorsal fin. The mouth is large, and the maxillary extends to beneath the anterior margin of the eye. The gill rakers are slender and elongated; their length is about 5 or 6 times their width. The pectoral fins are rounded and short; their length is contained about 4 times in the standard length. The spinous portion of the dorsal fin is rather low, about half the maximum height of the soft-rayed portion. The dorsal fin has 9 or 10 spines and 10 to 12 soft rays. The anal fin has 3 spines and 9 or 10 soft rays.

The green sunfish ranges from South Dakota and Colorado eastward to western New York and south to the Gulf of Mexico and into Mexico. It prefers small shallow lakes and is common in creeks. It is present and sometimes abundant in lakes and small creeks in all parts of Minnesota, but it is not common in all lakes and may be absent from many of them. For example, it is abundant in several small lakes near Ely, although it is absent from nearby lakes. It is abundant in Squaw Lake in Itasca State Park but absent from most of the other lakes in the park. It occurs in many small lakes in the region of the Twin Cities, and it is common in many of the small streams in southern Minnesota as well as in some of the backwaters of the lower Mississippi River.

For some reason this fish never reaches a desirable size in Minnesota waters, although the frequent hybridizations with bluegills and pumpkinseeds produce fish which reach a much larger size. Unfortunately, in the past this fish may have been mistaken for a bluegill and introduced into many lakes where it did not originally occur. Because of its small size and frequent abundance, it is often regarded as a nuisance. When we have investigated reports of lakes containing nothing but stunted sunfish, we have found this species to be the reason for the complaint.

The spawning habits of the green sunfish are about the same as for the other sunfishes. They congregate in shallow sheltered waters with other sunfishes from the middle of May to the middle of June and sometimes again in July for a second spawning. They prefer sandy bottoms in which the males fan out depressions for nests. The females are rather promiscuous, depositing eggs in the nests of several males and sometimes in the nests of other species. The males guard the eggs and watch over the fry until they are able to shift for themselves.

Green sunfish feed on all manner of aquatic insects and also on any flying insects that happen to fall into the water. The amphipod *Hyalella* forms an important part of their food. They bite readily on worms and grasshoppers. Fishermen generally regard them as bait stealers.

ORANGESPOTTED SUNFISH

Lepomis humilis (Girard)

The orangespotted sunfish (Figure 142) may reach a maximum length of 4 inches but is usually only 2 or 3 inches long. It can be recognized by the bright orange spots scattered over its rather slender body. The spawning males are perhaps the most colorful of all sunfishes. The opercular lobe has a large dark spot with a pale margin which may be tinged with red or orange. Longitudinal orange-red streaks are present on the cheeks and the opercles. The belly and the lower fins are more or less red. The pectoral fins are long and pointed; their length is contained slightly more than 3 times in the standard length. The gill rakers are long and slender; their length is about 2 to 3 times their width. The dorsal fin has 9 or 10 spines and 10 or 11 soft rays. The anal fin has 3 spines and about 9 soft rays. The lateral line has fewer than 40 scales.

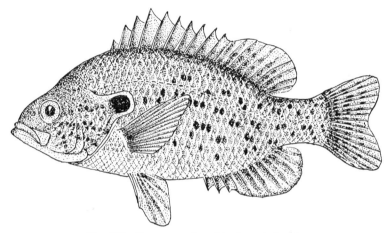

Fig. 142. Orangespotted sunfish, *Lepomis humilis*

The orangespotted sunfish ranges from the Dakotas eastward into Ohio and southward to Texas and northern Alabama. It seems to prefer small sand-bottom streams and lakes. We have found it in some of the small lakes and streams from the area of the Twin Cities southward. Orangespotted sunfish are common in the tributaries of the Minnesota River to its source in Bigstone Lake. They have been taken in the backwaters of the Mississippi River near Hastings and southward where spring-fed bays and inlets are present.

The spawning habits of the orangespotted sunfish are similar to those of the other members of the genus *Lepomis*. They sometimes spawn in areas used by the other lepomid species, and we have a few specimens which may be hybrids. The latter reach a larger size than purebred orangespotted sunfish.

These sunfishes feed on small crustaceans and aquatic insects. Although they will bite on worms and grasshoppers, their small size makes them of little value as panfish.

BLUEGILL

Lepomis macrochirus Rafinesque

The appearance of the bluegill (Figure 143) varies with sex and age and also among individuals of the same sex and age. Commonly the body is light to dark olive with a touch of purple luster in older individuals. Breeding males may have much bright orange and blue on their bodies. The cheeks and opercles are sometimes bright blue; the throat and the belly may be bright yellow. The females and the young bluegills tend to be less colorful than the adult males and are mostly grayish green. The opercular lobe is entirely black; it is rather small in juveniles and females but becomes quite long and prominent in very old males. A dark or black blotch is prominent at the posterior base of the soft dorsal fin. Juveniles and females have 6 to 8 distinct vertical bars on their sides; these bars are less distinct in adult males. The pectoral fins are long and pointed; their length is contained in the standard length about 3 times. The gill rakers are long and slender. The mouth is small; the maxillary barely reaches to the front of the eye. The dorsal fin has 10 spines and 10 to 12 soft rays; the spines are as long as the soft rays or longer. The anal fin has 3 spines and 10 to 12 soft rays. The lateral line has 38 to 45 scales.

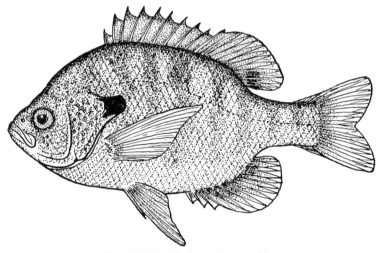

Fig. 143. Bluegill, *Lepomis macrochirus*

The bluegill is one of Minnesota's best known and most widely distributed sunfishes. In the past fifty years it has suffered about as many changes in its scientific names as the largemouth bass has. For many years it was named *Lepomis pallidus* (Mitchill). Then studies of priority led to the successive use of the names *Helioperca incisor* (Cuvier and Valenciennes), *H. macrochirus* (Rafinesque), and finally *Lepomis macrochirus* Rafinesque.

The bluegill and its subspecies are distributed from Minnesota eastward to Lake Champlain, southward into Florida, and southward through Texas into northern Mexico. It is common in all the clear-water lakes and streams of Minnesota except in the cold-water lakes of the northeastern part of the state.

It is rare in the Lake Superior drainage except in a few lakes where it may have been introduced.

The adult bluegills forage in deep weed beds, where they feed on a wide variety of foods. The juveniles feed in shallow water on entomostracans, small aquatic insects, worms, and the amphipod *Hyalella*. As they grow older, they feed more extensively on snails, small crayfish, and all kinds of insects. They may also eat small minnows and some plant material. They are least active during the middle of the day, feeding primarily in the early morning and again in the late afternoon and evening.

Bluegills are very prolific. We have found as many as 67,000 eggs in a single large female. Each of twenty-seven females weighing from 8 to 10 ounces contained 15,000 to 58,000 eggs. Bluegills usually spawn from the last part of May to early July, and we have occasionally found them spawning early in August. They spawn in shallow protected areas, usually in bays where the water is from 3 to 6 feet deep. They choose sandy bottoms for their nests, which the male constructs by sweeping out with his caudal fin a depression 2 to 3 feet in diameter. The nests are often crowded close together, so close that there is no space between them. Sometimes pumpkinseeds and green sunfish join the nesting colony. Each nest is cleared of pebbles and sticks. The male then courts a female to his nest; when she deposits her eggs, he immediately fertilizes them. Once the female has contributed her eggs to the nest, she is chased away, but she may be courted by a neighboring male; if she still has eggs, she may mate with the second male as well. The role of the male is to construct the nest and to guard it and the young fry, but despite his very prominent role in all these activities it is the female that makes the initial choice of the male she will mate with. Once spawning is completed, the male stays by the nest to drive away any intruders. When the eggs hatch and the school of fry leaves the nest, the male may remain with his progeny until they disperse.

Bluegills do not rank as game fish, but they cannot be surpassed as panfish. Their flesh is sweet and very tasty. Some anglers rank bluegills as a boy's fish, but the crowds of boats on many Minnesota lakes on weekends, all still-fishing for bluegills, indicate that bluegills are a favorite with many adult fishermen. A string of 8-ounce bluegills is a nice catch. Most bluegills are caught by still-fishing from a boat in water 6 to 15 feet deep. Often the best place is where there is a drop-off at the edge of a submerged weed bed. The hook should remain several feet above the bottom. Bluegills seem to travel in schools, but probably they also congregate in schools when they sense food in the vicinity. Since they have small mouths, the angler must use small hooks (size 8, 10, or even smaller). They also have the reputation of being nibblers and will soon shred the bait off a large hook. When one starts nibbling at the bait, it will cause the cork to bounce or, if the fisherman is tight-line fishing, will give little tugs at the line. Patience is necessary until the fish actually seizes the baited hook and starts to run with it. In spite of being relatively small, bluegills are quite scrappy and will race in circles as the fisherman attempts to land them. Once a school of bluegills has been located, the action is fast and furious. Worms are the most common bait for bluegills, but grasshoppers seem to be especially appetizing. Bluegills find cut bait less tempting, so it should be resorted to only when nothing else is available. When the midges are emerging in the evening, the bluegills often feed at the surface of the water. At this time they strike at both wet and dry flies and afford great sport for the fly fisherman using light tackle. One of the frustrations of bluegill fishing is that a small perch often steals the bait before the bluegill has a chance at the morsel. On the other hand, the bluegill fisherman may often hook a nice crappie, a rock bass, or on rare occasions a walleye. More than once we have hooked northern pike while using a fly rod for bluegills — the ensuing struggle will always be remembered.

In many lakes the population density of bluegills is so great that the fish are stunted and seldom weigh more than 4 ounces. In lakes which contain a better balance of predators, the bluegills may weigh close to 8 ounces on the average and occasionally up to 2 pounds. The record is held by a fish caught in Alabama which weighed 4 pounds, 12 ounces. Bluegills bite in the winter and provide good sport, but not very many are caught through the ice in Minnesota; walleyes are taken much more frequently by ice fishermen. Nevertheless, in the summer bluegills top the creel censuses of panfish. They are surpassed only by the ubiquitous stunted perch which are seldom included in creel censuses.

PUMPKINSEED
Lepomis gibbosus (Linnaeus)

The pumpkinseed (Figure 144) may reach a length of 9 inches, but the usual range is 6 to 8 inches. It is characterized by a deep compressed body with a bright orange belly. In adults the back is usually raised or humped more than in other species. The outstanding characters useful in distinguishing this sunfish from the bluegill which is often present in the same lake are the bright orange spot below or at the tip of the black spot on the opercular lobe and the absence of a black blotch on the lower posterior margin of the soft dorsal fin. Like young bluegills, young pumpkinseeds have vertical bars on their sides, but the pumpkinseeds have more yellowish bellies. The bars on the sides of adult pumpkinseeds are usually faint or absent, and orange or brown spots usually cover the sides. Breeding males are particularly brightly colored and have wavy bright blue bars on their cheeks and opercles. The mouth is small; the maxillary reaches only a little past the front of the eye. The pectoral fins are long and pointed and are contained fewer than 3 times in the standard length. The dorsal fin has 10 spines and 11 or 12 soft rays. The anal fin has 3 spines and 10 soft rays. The lateral line has 36 to 40 scales. The gill rakers are short and knoblike.

The pumpkinseed ranges from Manitoba and the Dakotas to eastern Canada and southward to North Carolina and Iowa. In Minnesota it is quite widely distributed and is second to the bluegill in popularity as a panfish. It is found throughout the clear lakes of southern and central Minnesota and in many large streams. It occurs along with the bluegill in many lakes in north central Minnesota but is absent from most of the rocky lakes along the Canadian border. It is found in only a few lakes of the Lake Superior drainage, where it has probably been introduced. In many central Minnesota lakes it has hybridized with either the bluegill or the green sunfish to such an extent that it is impossible to determine the species of some individuals.

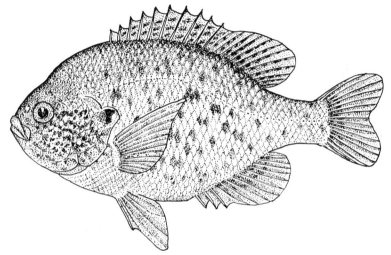

Fig. 144. Pumpkinseed, *Lepomis gibbosus*

The pumpkinseed spawns from late May through June. The fish usually congregate in protected bays in water 3 to 6 feet deep and make their nests on sandy bottoms. Often they join in colonies with bluegills and green sunfish, crowding together so that the nests (usually about 2 feet in diameter) touch. As in other centrarchid species, the males perform the duties of caring for the eggs and the young until they leave the nest.

The pumpkinseed feeds mostly in the deep weed beds or in the deep water just beyond the margin of the weed beds. It eats small minnows and other fishes, aquatic insects, and the amphipod *Hyalella*. It also browses on the stalks of weeds, eating large quantities of small snails. Sometimes, especially in the evening, pumpkinseeds rise to the surface and eat flying insects which chance to be on the surface of the water. Pumpkinseeds are about equal to bluegills in value as panfish. We doubt that anyone can detect any difference in flavor between the two species. The fisherman who catches individuals of both species often does not know the difference between them. Pumpkinseeds bite readily on worms, grasshoppers, and other small natural baits, but they do not seem to be attracted by cut bait. They bite best in the early morning and the late afternoon and appear to be least active at midday. The adults congregate beneath old deadheads and trees that have fallen into the water. In the evening they often rise from the deep water to feed at the surface on insect larvae or on adult insects laying their eggs. At this time fly fishing with small poppers or wet or dry flies can provide tremendous sport. Underhill often catches them on ultralight spinning gear using very small spinners.

LONGEAR SUNFISH

Lepomis megalotis (Rafinesque)

The longear sunfish (Figure 145) reaches a maximum length of 8 inches. The short deep body is colored with brilliant blue and orange spots. The very long and flexible opercular lobe is usually bordered with a red or cream margin. The fins are orange with bluish rays. The cheeks are light olive to orange with prominent wavy streaks or reticulations of emerald blue. The pectoral fins are short and rounded; their length is contained about 4 times in the standard length.

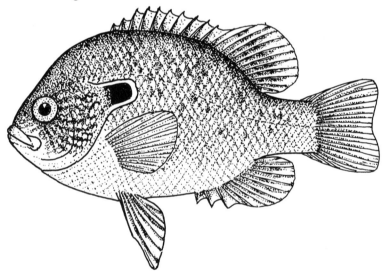

Fig. 145. Longear sunfish, *Lepomis megalotis*

The longear sunfish ranges from Iowa eastward to Quebec and southward to South Carolina, the Gulf states, and Mexico. It is common in Illinois and southern Michigan, and there are records of it in Iowa. Longear sunfish were reported by Cox (1897) from the Pomme de Terre River and from Big Stone Lake. We have never seen any specimens from these areas, although we have examined numerous collections from the same waters, and we doubt the validity of these early records. (Many reports of longear sunfish have resulted from incorrect identifications.) The only record we have accepted is a single specimen collected by the Department of Conservation from Little Rock Lake in Morrison County in 1945. We did not see this specimen, but it was identified by R. E. Johnson, a most competent ichthyologist, and we have no reason to doubt his identification. How this single specimen happened to be in Little Rock Lake, we do not know; no further specimens have been found. An isolated population exists in a small lake north of International Falls in Ontario (Gruchy and Scott, 1966), but we know of no other longear sunfish north of Iowa, where it is considered to be a rare fish (Harlan and Speaker, 1969).

Genus *Pomoxis* Rafinesque

This genus contains only two species, both of which occur in Minnesota. These are deep and thin-bodied fishes. The body is silvery with black or dark greenish mottling or bars. The dorsal and anal fins are large and about equal in length; the anal fin has usually 5 or 6 spines. The scales are large and feebly ctenoid.

WHITE CRAPPIE

Pomoxis annularis Rafinesque

The white crappie (Figure 146) often weighs from 1 to 2 pounds, although specimens weighing up to 4 pounds are reported from the southern states. The shape of the white crappie is about the same as that of the black crappie. Although both species have high backs, the back of the white crappie may be somewhat lower, and the top of the head may be slightly more dished. The dorsal fin and the anal fin have less conspicuous black mottlings than the fins of the black crappie. The body is silvery and more or less mottled with

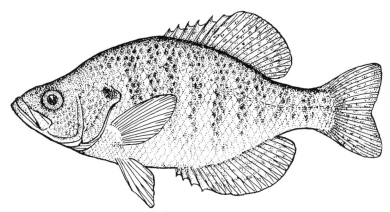

Fig. 146. White crappie, *Pomoxis annularis*

blackish green. Often the mottlings form vertical bars on the sides, particularly in the young fish. In general, the color is lighter than that of the black crappie. The white crappie usually has 5 or 6 dorsal spines, whereas the black crappie usually has 7 or 8 dorsal spines, but this is not an accurate character for distinguishing the species because there are overlapping variations in the number of spines. The best character for separation is in the length of the dorsal fin, which is always shorter in the white crappie; the length of the base is always much less than the distance from the origin of the dorsal fin to the eye.

The white crappie ranges from central Minnesota eastward into southern Ontario and southward to the Gulf of Mexico. It occurs in the Atlantic drainage of Alabama and South Carolina. Central Minnesota is the northern limit of the white crappie's range in the Mississippi River drainage. The species is not common in the area of the Twin Cities, and we have taken it in only a few lakes to the west of this area. However, it is quite common in the Mississippi River below St. Paul, above the dam at Hastings, and in many lakes and large streams of southern Minnesota. It is abundant in the backwaters of the Zumbro River and is not uncommon in parts of the Minnesota River drainage. We have taken a few in some of the tributaries of the Red River, where we think it was probably introduced. The northernmost distribution of the species in Minnesota is in the Red River drainage.

White crappies spawn in the late spring, usually from late May into June. The males prepare the nests, often quite close to other nests. Their habits are about the same as those of the black crappie. The males give parental care to the eggs and the fry.

The feeding habits of the white crappie are also about the same as those of the black crappie. Both feed on a wide variety of small animal life and eat large numbers of minnows and any insect life available.

White crappies are popular game fish and panfish, particularly in the southern parts of their range where they are more common. They can be caught by still-fishing in water 6 to 10 feet deep with live minnows for bait. They will bite on grasshoppers and even on worms, but they do not bite readily on cut bait. In the evening when they feed at the surface, they often strike at artificial flies. Their mouths are tender and it takes skill to land one on a fly rod, but they do not put up much fight. Those caught in clear water are excellent panfish with a fine flavor, but those caught in mud-bottom lakes may have a somewhat muddy taste.

BLACK CRAPPIE

Pomoxis nigromaculatus (LeSueur)

The black crappie (Figure 147) seldom exceeds 12 inches in length, and specimens from Minnesota lakes usually weigh about 8 ounces. The body is elliptical in shape, somewhat elongated, and much compressed laterally. The forehead is somewhat dished but usually not quite as much as in the white crappie. The color is more or less silvery with numerous black or dark green splotches. Juveniles have prominent vertical bars on their sides, but these tend to disappear in the adults. The general coloration of the black crappie is usually darker than that of the white crappie. The black crappie usually has more dorsal spines than the white crappie; the dorsal fin has 7 or 8 spines and 14 or 15 soft rays. The anal fin has 5 to 7 spines (usually 6) and 16 to 18 soft rays. The black crappie can be distinguished from the white crappie by the length of the base of the dorsal fin, which is about equal to the distance from the origin of the fin to the eye (in the white crappie the length of the dorsal fin base is always less than this distance). The black crappie often weighs up to 2 pounds, but occasionally very large ones are caught. The record is held by a 5-pound crappie caught near the mouth of the Vermillion River in 1970.

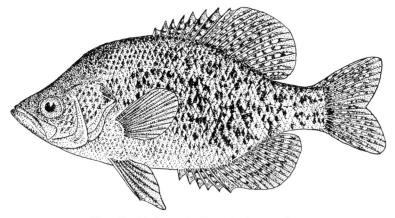

Fig. 147. Black crappie, *Pomoxis nigromaculatus*

The black crappie is more abundant than the white crappie in the northern part of the United States. It is common in lakes and large streams from southern Manitoba eastward to Quebec, over the eastern United States, and south to Florida and Texas. It is abundant in many lakes in Minnesota and is absent only from the deep rocky lakes of the northeastern part of the state, particularly those of the Lake Superior drainage. It prefers large streams and medium-sized lakes and is not common in large lakes.

Crappies mature early, sometimes spawning in the first or second year. They are very prolific; large females weighing from 1 1/2 to 2 pounds may have as many as 140,000 eggs in their ovaries. The average female weighing about 8 ounces contains from 20,000 to 60,000 eggs. In most Minnesota waters crappies spawn in May and June. The nests are often close together in water 3 to 6 feet deep; they are sometimes constructed on bottoms that are softer and muddier than those usually chosen by members of this family. Crappies are easy to propagate in ponds, but they increase just as rapidly in natural lakes if they have a little protection while spawning. In certain Minnesota lakes the species has become overabundant, and these lakes are crowded with stunted crappies. Apparently this condition is partly caused by the absence of large crappies (which may be cannibalistic) and other predacious fishes as a result of selective fishing. The reproductive potential of the crappie is so great that the annual crop needs to be thinned out. This condition also occurs with sunfish and perch in overfished lakes.

Crappies feed on a wide variety of animal life. They eat all kinds of aquatic insects, small crustaceans, minnows, and other small fish. The deep part of weed beds and the outer edges of the beds are their favorite feeding areas. They are probably more active during the winter than any other member of this family, feeding extensively on small fish and aquatic insects throughout the winter. During the late winter and the early spring we often find them gorged with entomostracans, especially *Daphnia* and copepods.

Both species of crappies rank high as game fish and panfish in Minnesota, and they form the major portion of the catch from some lakes. They bite best during the early morning and in the evening. They congregate around submerged treetops and logs just beyond the weeds in water from 6 to 10 feet in depth. They bite best on live minnows, although sometimes they strike eagerly at artificial flies. They are often caught by fishermen trolling with spoons. They do not put up much fight, but their mouths are tender and they must be landed with care. In past creel censuses we have found that next to bluegills more crappies are caught by Minnesota anglers than any other fish. During the winter the black crappie forms about 75 percent of the catch taken by anglers fishing through the ice with hook and line. We have found that in some small lakes more crappies are caught in December than during the entire summer. Live minnows are commonly used for bait. The best fishing is usually where the water is about 10 to 15 feet deep, especially if it is near a drop-off. The best fishing holes can be found by noting the greatest congregation of fishermen.

Years ago some conservationists became concerned about the winter exploitation of the crappies and claimed that females containing the eggs for the next generation far outnumbered males in the catch. In cooperation with the Minnesota Department of Conservation we employed about twenty-five fishermen to angle for crappies and to send them in for sex determination. We found no significant difference in the number of males and females caught. Furthermore, it is possible that we should be more concerned about the number of males caught because they are the ones responsible for preparing the nests and reproduction is governed by the number of nests available. At present we think the crappie's enormous reproductive potential will enable it to hold its own for some time against the fishing pressure exerted by the increasing angling population.

Family PERCIDAE
The Perch Family

The perch family is represented by more species in Minnesota than any other family except the minnow family. It includes the well-known perch, the walleye, and the sauger. It also includes fifteen species of small fishes called darters, which many people think are some kind of minnow. The members of this family are more or less elongate fishes. The lateral line may be complete, incomplete, or obsolete. The mouth is either terminal or inferior. Teeth are present on the jaws and usually on the vomer and palatine bones; sharp pharyngeal teeth are also present. The opercle has a flat spine on its posterior dorsal margin. There are 7 branchiostegals present. The gill membranes are free from the isthmus, and a slit occurs posterior to the fourth gill arch. The gill rakers are slender and serrated. The dorsal fin is completely divided into an anterior fin with usually about 13 spines and a posterior fin with 11 or more soft rays. The anal fin has 1 or 2 spines. The pelvic fins are thoracic and have 1 spine and 5 soft rays.

The larger species found in Minnesota are the common yellow perch (subfamily Percinae), the walleye, and the sauger (subfamily Luciopercinae). The small darters belong to the subfamily Etheostominae and are rather difficult to identify. The subfamily Etheostominae includes fifteen species belonging to three genera: *Ammocrypta*, *Percina*, and *Etheostoma*. Members of the family Percidae, exclusive of the darters, are found in Europe and Asia as well as in North America. They are closely related to the sunfish family but have only 1 or 2 spines in the anal fin instead of 3 or more.

KEY TO MINNESOTA SPECIES OF FAMILY PERCIDAE

1. Six branchiostegal rays; tail not forked or only weakly forked; usually of small size; pseudobranchiae rudimentary or lacking 4
   Seven or rarely 8 branchiostegal rays; tail forked; adults large; pseudobranchiae well developed 2
2. Canine teeth (usually long) present on jaws and palatine bones 3
   No canine teeth present; bars on sides . . . .
   . . . . Yellow perch, *Perca flavescens* (Mitchill)
3. Dorsal fin with about 20 soft rays; a large black spot at base of last 3 dorsal spines; tip of lower lobe of caudal fin usually whitish; no black blotch at base of pectoral fin . . . .
   . . . . Walleye, *Stizostedion vitreum vitreum* (Mitchill)

363

Dorsal fin with about 17 soft rays; no black spot at base of dorsal spines; tip of lower lobe of caudal fin not whitish; distinct black blotch at base of pectoral fin ....Sauger, *Stizostedion canadense* (Smith)

4. Depth of body contained 7 or more times in length; anal fin with 1 spine 5
Depth of body contained fewer than 7 times in length; anal fin with 1 or 2 spines 6

5. Lateral line with 89 to 100 scales; anal fin with 12 to 14 rays ....
.....................Crystal darter, *Ammocrypta asprella* (Jordan)
Lateral line with 65 to 80 scales; anal fin with 10 rays ....
.........Western sand darter, *Ammocrypta clara* (Jordan and Meek)

6. Belly naked except for a row of enlarged scales on the midventral line, or belly more or less scaled with one or more modified scales between pelvic fins; pelvic fins widely separated, space between them usually at least three-fourths the width of the base of either fin; area of anal fin usually as large as area of soft dorsal fin 7
Belly usually scaled, but if naked no midventral row of modified scales present or no modified scales present between pelvic fins; space between pelvic fins less than three-fourths the width of the base of either fin; area of anal fin usually less than area of soft dorsal fin 11

7. Snout extended forward as a small conical protuberance beyond the upper lip; mouth horizontal; anal spines very flexible; crossbars numerous and narrow .... Log perch, *Percina caprodes* (Rafinesque)
Snout not extended beyond upper lip; mouth more or less oblique; anal spines stiff; crossbars either broad or obsolete 8

8. Belly largely scaleless medially but crossed by bridge of scales in front of anus; scales of midline only incipiently modified; premaxillary frenum usually hidden by shallow furrow behind upper lip ....
........................River darter, *Percina shumardi* (Girard)
Belly mostly scaled; scales of midline strongly modified, at least in males; premaxillary frenum usually not hidden by furrow 9

9. Gill membranes united into a broad curve distinctly more distant from tip of snout than is the back of the eye; lateral blotches small; spinous dorsal fin with a submarginal orange band in life ....
....................Slender darter, *Percina phoxocephala* (Nelson)
Gill membranes not united but meeting at a sharp angle and on the midline scarcely farther from tip of snout than is the back of the eye; lateral bars or blotches large; spinous dorsal fin without submarginal orange band 10

10. Lateral line with 52 to 67 scales; cheeks naked; bands broad, large, and squarish; color gilt or bronze in life ....
.................Gilt darter, *Percina evides* (Jordan and Copeland)
Lateral line with 65 to 85 scales; cheeks at least partially scaled; 7 to 9 confluent bars, never forming vertical bands; not gilt or bronze in life
....................Blackside darter, *Percina maculata* (Girard)

11. Premaxillaries protractile, separated from snout by a complete groove
.... 12
Premaxillaries not protractile, not entirely separated from snout by a
groove but connected anteriorly by a fleshy bridge 13
12. Lateral line complete; bar extending forward from eye is broken on
tip of snout ....Johnny darter, *Etheostoma nigrum* Rafinesque
Lateral line incomplete, extending only a short distance; bar extending
forward from eye continuous around snout ....
................Bluntnose darter, *Etheostoma chlorosomum* (Hay)
13. Lateral line obsolete with 8 or fewer pored scales; dorsal fin with usually
6 spines; pectoral fins long and pointed in breeding males; adults usually
under 1 1/2 inches long ....
............Least darter, *Etheostoma microperca* Jordan and Gilbert
Lateral line at least partly developed with more than 10 pored scales;
dorsal fin with usually 8 spines or more; pectoral fins not greatly developed; adults usually over 2 inches long 14
14. Conspicuously marked with longitudinal rows of spots or dashes; head
completely scaleless; males not brightly colored; dorsal spines of
breeding males ending in fleshy knobs ....
.....Striped fantail darter, *Etheostoma flabellare lineolatum* (Agassiz)
Not conspicuously marked with longitudinal rows of spots or dashes;
head partially scaled; males brightly colored; dorsal spines without
fleshy knobs 15
15. Gill membranes very broadly connected; color greenish in life ....
......................Banded darter, *Etheostoma zonale* (Cope)
Gill membranes not broadly connected; not green 16
16. Body slender; depth 5.4 to 6.8 times in length; dorsal fin with 9 to 11 soft
rays, occasionally 12 ....Iowa darter, *Etheostoma exile* (Girard)
Body rather deep; depth 4.5 to 5.4 times in length; dorsal fin with 12
to 14 soft rays 17
17. Cheeks covered with ctenoid scales; opercles scaled ....
.....................Mud darter, *Etheostoma asprigene* (Forbes)
Cheeks scaleless or with a few embedded scales around the eye; opercles
scaled ....Rainbow darter, *Etheostoma caeruleum* Storer

SUBFAMILY PERCINAE

This subfamily contains three species — one in North America, one in
Europe, and one in northern Asia.

Genus *Perca* Linnaeus

There is only one species in this genus in North America. The characteristics of the species serve to describe the genus. A closely allied species, *Perca
fluviatilis* (Linnaeus), is found in southern Europe.

YELLOW PERCH

Perca flavescens (Mitchill)

The yellow perch (Figure 148) may reach a length of 12 to 15 inches and weigh slightly more than a pound. The coloration varies greatly, but usually the sides are golden yellow with 6 to 9 dark crossbars that extend from the back to below the middle of the sides. The dorsal median fins are lightly or heavily pigmented with black; the membranes between the last four spines of the spinous dorsal fin are dusky in adults. The lower fins are tinted with yellowish orange or with bright orange or reddish orange in breeding males. The mouth contains many small teeth but no large canine or tearing teeth; the absence of canine teeth reliably distinguishes young perch from young walleyes and young saugers. Young perch may be distinguished from darters by the presence of large serrations on the preopercular bone.

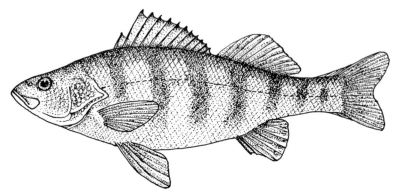

Fig. 148. Yellow perch, *Perca flavescens*

Perch have been widely introduced, intentionally and by accident, throughout the United States, and their original range is difficult to discern. They probably occurred from southern Canada south to Kansas, northern Missouri, Illinois, Indiana, Ohio, and Pennsylvania. Perch are present in the Atlantic drainage from Nova Scotia south to the Carolinas. They are found throughout the lakes and streams of Minnesota that do not experience winterkills, in rivers, and even in the trout streams along the north shore of Lake Superior.

In many lakes perch occur in such immense numbers that they constitute a management problem, the so-called perch-bound lakes filled with stunted perch. Only a few lakes support populations of perch which reach 10 to 12 inches in length and weigh over 8 ounces. When free of parasites, perch make excellent table fish, but unfortunately they are not very popular with the average Minnesota fisherman. They are a delight to children, however, because they bite readily — perch are ''where the action is'' for impatient young fishermen. Large perch caught on light tackle, a fly rod, or ultralight spinning gear are very sporting, and they rival walleyes as food fish.

Perch are harvested commercially in Lower Red Lake by the Chippewa Indians, who operate a cooperative fishery; the perch they harvest command a higher price than walleyes do on the markets in Chicago. The fishery yielded an average of 212,365 pounds of perch per year between 1930 and 1953 (Smith and Krefting, 1953).

Perch are predacious and prefer a diet of minnows, but they also eat aquatic insects, the young of other fishes, crayfish, leeches, and snails. They generally travel in schools composed of individuals of about the same size and age. In the early evening they feed in open water on schools of pelagic minnows such as the mimic shiner (*Notropis volucellus*). During the day they are mostly in the littoral zone where rooted aquatic plants are found. At night they are inactive and usually rest on the bottom among the weeds.

Perch spawn in early May in southern Minnesota and in mid-May or late May in the lakes of central and northern Minnesota. The spawning season lasts from two to four weeks and is regulated by the water temperature. When the water reaches a temperature of 45° to 50° F, spawning activity begins. Perch spawn in open but shallow water, and the eggs settle in heavy adhesive bands on sticks or weeds on sandy bottoms. Spawning generally occurs at night but occasionally takes place during the daylight hours. The eggs are deposited in a gelatinous ribbonlike band that is several inches wide and is folded or pleated. These masses may be several feet or more in length, and the number of eggs in a mass may vary from 10,000 to over 48,000, depending on the size of the female. The egg mass is evidently hydroscopic because it has a volume much greater than the body of the female that laid the eggs. Perch have a high reproductive potential, and if the fry are not eaten by northern pike, walleyes, burbots, and other predacious fish, the species may virtually take over the lake. The only remedy in many instances is to poison the lake and to start over again, attempting to prevent the introduction of undesirable species and to maintain a balance between prey and predator species. Unfortunately, many lakes are too large for such a remedy to be feasible, but the Minnesota Department of Natural Resources has been successful in reclaiming some of the smaller perch-bound lakes and restoring them to their former recreational value.

Perch seem to harbor more parasites than almost any other species of fish found in Minnesota waters. This may be because they feed so extensively on snails and are available in such great numbers for parasitologists to study. In many lakes almost every perch is covered with small black spots; these are the encysted larvae (*Neascus*) or metacercariae of parasitic flatworms or flukes that live as adults in fish-eating birds. Other species of larval flukes living in the perch metamorphose to adults when eaten by the belted kingfisher. A section of perch muscle on close inspection may reveal yellow grubs which are the larval stage of another parasitic flatworm (*Clinostomum*). These parasites are not harmful to man; if the fish is well cooked, the parasites are killed.

Larson (1966) has recorded fifteen species of worm parasites in yellow perch from lakes in the Itasca Park area.

Aside from the parasites, if the perch is large enough, it is an excellent food fish. The flesh is white and firm and equal in flavor to that of the walleye. Perch can be taken throughout the year, and there are no catch limits. They bite readily on almost anything. They are not popular in Minnesota, however, partly because in most lakes they are small and partly because the abundant parasites render them repugnant to many housewives. Those fishermen who disdain perch are missing a tasty morsel indeed. As for the parasites, they simply represent the ecological cycling of perch flesh into fluke flesh, just as walleyes and northern pike represent the cycling of perch flesh plus fluke larvae into walleye or northern pike flesh.

SUBFAMILY LUCIOPERCINAE

This subfamily contains one genus and two species of large predacious fishes. A similar form is found in Europe.

Genus *Stizostedion* Rafinesque

This genus contains two species, the sauger (*S. canadense*) and the walleye (*S. vitreum*), which are found in Minnesota and the neighboring states. Members of this genus are characterized by long and sharp canine teeth on the jaws and on the palatine bones. The body is long and slender, and the head length is greater than the body depth or equal to it. The dorsal fin has more than 15 soft rays, and the anal fin has more than 10 soft rays.

SAUGER

Stizostedion canadense (Smith)

The sauger (Figure 149), often called the sand pike, is a slender fish, usually 12 to 18 inches in total length and commonly weighing 1 or 2 pounds but occasionally as much as 3 pounds. Saugers from the Missouri River reservoirs in South Dakota reach a weight of more than 10 pounds. The body color is blackish or grayish with slight brassy reflections and black mottlings

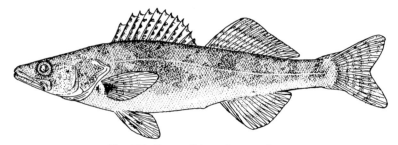

Fig. 149. Sauger, *Stizostedion canadense*

on the sides. The spinous portion of the dorsal fin has black blotches or spots on the membranes between the spines which form oblique rows when the fin is erect. A black blotch is present at the base of the pectoral fin, but it may be obscure in some individuals. The caudal fin is forked. The dorsal fin is separated into two parts; the first part contains 10 to 14 spines, usually 12 or 13, and the second part contains 16 to 20 soft rays. The anal fin has 2 spines and 11 to 13 soft rays. The lateral line has 110 to 130 scales. The pyloric ceca are 4 to 8 in number, and each is shorter than the length of the stomach.

The sauger has a wide distribution throughout the Mississippi River drainage from southern Arkansas to the Missouri and Ohio river basins and the Red River, from the Nelson River basin in Manitoba to New Brunswick, southward to Oklahoma, northern Louisiana, and the Tennessee River drainage, and through the Great Lakes drainage. In Minnesota it is abundant in Lake of the Woods, Rainy Lake, and Lake Kabetogama. It is common in Lake St. Croix, the Minnesota River, and the Mississippi River south of St. Anthony Falls. Cox (1897) reported saugers north of St. Anthony Falls in the Mississippi River drainage, but no specimens have appeared in any collections above the falls during the past three-quarters of a century, and we are inclined to believe the early record was incorrectly identified. Saugers are not present in the western end of Lake Superior or in the St. Louis River.

Spawning occurs in April and May when the saugers migrate upstream into tributaries and headwater lakes. They spawn in shallow water where the eggs are deposited at random by the female accompanied by several males. The female produces from 40,000 to 50,000 eggs. No care is given to the eggs, which hatch in about fourteen days at 50° F. Saugers grow more slowly than walleyes; a 20-year-old sauger may be 18 inches long and weigh only 2 pounds. They are carnivorous and feed on small fish, *Hyalella*, crayfish, and all kinds of aquatic insects.

Saugers are caught and sold commercially from Canadian waters and from Lake of the Woods, but they are not as valuable as walleyes. In Lake of the Woods and Rainy Lake the abundance of saugers may be partly the result of selective commercial fishing for walleyes. Anglers frequently catch saugers when fishing for walleyes in Minnesota waters. Saugers strike readily on artificial lures, live minnows, and worms. As a food fish they are the equal of walleyes, although they are usually smaller.

WALLEYE

Stizostedion vitreum vitreum (Mitchill)

The walleye (Figure 150) ranges in weight from 2 to 8 pounds, but there are records of individuals weighing over 15 pounds. The coloration varies considerably, ranging from dark silver to dark olive brown. Walleyes and saugers are often difficult to distinguish. Freshly caught walleyes may be recognized by the large black spot at the base of the last 3 dorsal spines, whereas saugers have many black blotches forming oblique rows on the membranes of the spinous dorsal fin but lack the large dark spot at the posterior base of the fin. Unfortunately, this pigmentation fades in dead fish and becomes difficult to use as a diagnostic character. The lower lobe of the caudal fin has a wide white margin in the walleye; the caudal fin of the sauger has only a narrow white margin. The walleye has more than 19 soft dorsal rays and fewer than 90 lateral line scales. The eye of the walleye has an opaque appearance which is responsible for the common name. Large canine teeth are present in the walleye.

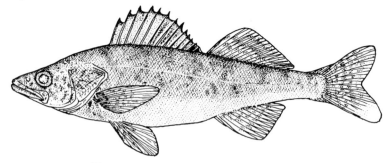

Fig. 150. Walleye, *Stizostedion vitreum vitreum*

The walleye has a much wider distribution than the sauger. It ranges from the Northwest Territories across the Canadian provinces east of the Rocky Mountains into northern Labrador, south along the Atlantic coast to North Carolina, west to northern Arkansas, and north along the Missouri River. The walleye is a desirable game fish and has been widely introduced throughout North America. In the past several decades many impoundments have been stocked with walleyes, especially in the southern and western United States. In Lake Erie another subspecies, the blue walleye (*Stizostedion vitreum glaucum* Hubbs), used to be present, but it is now rare if not actually extinct.

The walleye seems to prefer large lakes which cover thousands of acres, and it thrives in Mille Lacs, Lake Winnibigoshish, Leech Lake, and Otter Tail Lake. In studying the movements of tagged walleyes we have found that some individuals travel over 100 miles in about a month. They prefer clean and cold or moderately warm lakes and rivers and generally retreat to deeper water at or near the thermocline during the months of July and August.

In the spring walleyes make mass migrations up streams and rivers to smaller tributaries and lakes to spawn, usually shortly after the spring thaw. Many spawn on bars and shoals in large lakes. After spawning, the fish remain for about a month before returning to the lake where they disperse. From early June to July they remain in shallow waters over reefs and bars or along the shoreline. With the warming of the surface waters above 72° F they slowly retreat into deeper and cooler waters.

In Minnesota the walleye was native to many lakes and streams throughout the state with the notable exception of the lakes in a limited area of southern Lake County and eastern Cook County where the species was introduced in the 1920s. In more recent years the walleye has declined in numbers or has disappeared from some lakes as a result of man's activities, nutrient enrichment, and pollution, but the large lakes still support sizable populations of this valuable food and game fish, particularly the lakes around the headwaters of the Mississippi River. It is one of the most abundant species in the Upper and Lower Red lakes, and with the exception of the cisco and the sauger the walleye is still the most important fish in Lake of the Woods. Some idea of its former abundance in Rainy Lake can be gained from the results of spawn-gathering operations in the Rat Root River carried on a number of decades ago by the Minnesota Division of Game and Fish. The catch in one night with a single pound net was 36,000 adult fish, with some females weighing as much as 14 pounds. Pollution of the Mississippi River below Minneapolis and St. Paul and in portions of the Minnesota River has drastically reduced the number of walleyes in these rivers. The effects of pollution have been compounded by an increase in the carp and bullhead populations in recent years, and it appears doubtful that the walleye can regain its former abundance. The best we can do is to reduce the pollution and to control the competitors.

Many Minnesota lakes have always had small populations of walleyes. Somehow, despite marginal habitats and few spawning sites, the populations seem to hold their own. In the early days millions of walleye fry were planted in all sorts of lakes, many of which were not suited for walleyes. Fry were dumped at random in lakes where they promptly became food for hungry perch. This promiscuous stocking was considered a panacea for any lake, although there was little if any proof that it increased the walleye population. When the planting was done in lakes suitable for walleyes, it often resulted in the successful introduction of the species. In well-established walleye lakes, however, no increase in the walleye population could be found in years following stocking. In any event man's efforts at propagation are puny compared to natural reproduction of the species in any large walleye lake. In southern Minnesota many large shallow lakes subject to winterkill do not maintain sport fisheries; a heavy stocking of fry in these lakes, where there is an abundance of food and little competition, produces a rapidly growing population of walleyes and excellent fishing until the next unfavorable winter kills off the fish. Many walleyes are now planted as small fingerlings to ensure a better percentage of survival. Rearing ponds are used by many local game and fish clubs in cooperation with the Minnesota Department of Natural Resources. However, walleyes are voracious and require such large quantities of food that they are expensive to rear.

Except in the case of reintroduction and the subsequent maintenance of trout populations in certain lakes, we have little evidence to prove conclusively that stocking is an effective method of creating a sport fishery. Walleyes were introduced into many lakes in Lake, Cook, and St. Louis counties in the early 1920s. In a few years these lakes had the finest walleye fishing in the state. However, in time large numbers of anglers (brought in by seaplanes) and oligotrophic conditions combined to reduce the walleye population to small young fish. Certain of these lakes have been reclaimed as either lake trout or rainbow trout lakes. Each lake must be examined very carefully before final management procedures are established because lack of caution in the past in this respect has created some of the problems of the present.

Lake Minnetonka is known to be the source of large walleyes, particularly during the ice-fishing season. Not too surprisingly, we have not been able to get detailed information on exactly where the fish came from in Lake Minnetonka, but we have seen the fish. The largest was just over 14 pounds. There are a number of other lakes that regularly produce large individual fish but are generally regarded as bass and panfish lakes.

The walleye is the most popular game fish in Minnesota, and the opening of the walleye season is rivaled in popularity only by the opening of the deer season. We have been told that the only time some people go fishing is on opening day, and this is substantiated by the traffic to the walleye lakes on that day. Angling for walleyes is like angling for almost every other game fish — each angler has his own pet methods and lures. The vast majority of anglers fish with minnows; next in popularity are jigs or jigs with minnows or worms attached. Other fishermen troll slowly with a small spinner and a minnow, a modification of the old June bug spinner technique. Still others prefer plugs, spoons, or plain spinners. The recent development of spinning gear, particularly ultralight tackle, has opened up new methods of angling for walleyes as well as for other species. Spinning gear with light line has put a premium on skill and perhaps gives the fish a better chance in the final outcome. A technique that we have found useful during the evening is to move slowly along the shore casting a small spinner into shallow water and retrieving it slowly along the bottom; the hook may get snagged often, but it also catches some nice fish. As a general rule of thumb with this procedure, you are fishing correctly if you hit the shore and lose a few lures. Shoreline fishing may be excellent until early July when the fish move into deeper water. At this time of year casting onto reefs and slowly retrieving the lure may be rewarding. One might also try fishing at night in the shallows, particularly in the dark of the moon, from 11:00 P.M. to 2:00 A.M. Between 5:00 P.M. and 9:00 P.M. walleyes move into shallow water to feed. About sunrise they move out into the deeper waters beyond the weeds. A surface plug (mouse, redhead, wounded minnow, or hula popper) fished parallel to the shoreline will often yield good results on dark nights when the walleyes move inshore to forage on minnows, mudsuckers (horseleeches), and crayfish. Some large walleyes are taken at night in the shallows, even in the winter through the ice.

The depth finder or fathometer is useful in locating fish, especially schools of walleyes when they are in deep water during July and August. The only trouble with these instruments is that they do not tell you the kind of fish or how to catch them. Experts and commercial fishermen use fathometers successfully because from their experience they know the kind of fish most apt to be present. There is little doubt that these electronic units will become more sophisticated as time goes by and may contribute to the success of the angler by reducing proportionately the element of luck. Sport fishing is not believed to be very efficient in harvesting the fish in very large lakes such as Lake of the Woods, and the use of electronic gear by anglers will probably not result in overfishing.

The white flaky meat of fresh walleye provides a treat for anyone who likes fish. Fried, broiled, or stuffed and baked with a touch of lemon or a special sauce, walleye is regarded by many Minnesotans as the best in freshwater fish. It appears on almost every restaurant's menu, often under the name "pike." The walleye is everyman's fish in Minnesota. It does not require expensive tackle or trips to distant lakes. It can be caught by rich and poor alike. Commercial fishing for walleyes is confined to several of the large border lakes and Lower Red Lake. Some of the walleyes sold commercially in Minnesota come from Canadian lakes.

SUBFAMILY ETHEOSTOMINAE

The darters comprising this subfamily are found east of the Rocky Mountains in North America. They presumably evolved on the continent free from competition by members of Old World families that occupy their ecological position. In North America the largest number of species is found in the southeast and south central portions of the United States. The Minnesota darter fauna is rather small in the total number of species, but it represents a very important element of the stream and river community. Minnesota has a total of fifteen species of darters, only three of which are common in lakes. Several species live in weeds and on muddy bottoms, but most species are adapted to live in swift water. The darters forming the subfamily Etheostominae are one of the more colorful and interesting groups of fish found in Minnesota waters. On the origin of the subfamily as a whole, Forbes wrote in 1884 (quoted in Jordan, 1904): "Given a supply of certain kinds of foods nearly inaccessible to the ordinary fish, it is to be expected that some fishes will become especially fitted for its utilization. Thus *Etheostoma* is to be explained by the hypothesis of the progressive adaptation of the young of certain Percinae to a peculiar place of refuge and a peculiarly situated food supply. These are the mountaineers among fishes. Forced from the populous and fertile valleys of the river beds and lake bottoms, they have taken refuge from their enemies in the rocky highlands, where the free waters play in ceaseless torrents, and there they have wrested from stubborn nature a meager living. Although diminished in size by their constant struggle with the elements, they have developed an activity and hardihood, a vigor of life and a glow of high color, almost unknown among the easier livers of the lower lands. Notwithstanding their trivial size, they do not seem to be dwarfed so much as concentrated fishes."

With the exception of two species the darters of Minnesota are less than 5 inches in total length. The least darter, *Etheostoma microperca*, is the smallest fish native to Minnesota. These fishes actually seem to dart rather than swim. They dart through the water and then sink to the bottom only to repeat the performance. When at rest they perch on the bottom or on stones, rocks, or logs, using their pectoral fins as props which form two legs of a tripod with the caudal fin serving as the third leg. One moment they are perching and the next they are gone, making a quick dash with their pectoral fins to a new perch. Their movements are so swift that it is difficult for the eye to follow them. Several species live on sand bottoms where they bury themselves, leaving only the top of the head exposed.

Many of the species we now find to be common were thought to be rare in Minnesota until we improved our collecting techniques and began to sample habitats which had been neglected before. Certain darter species live in the rapids, for instance, and another species is most common at the end of the pool where the water begins to form the head of the rapids. A special technique is required to catch fish in such habitats, particularly with a seine. We learned that it is necessary to hold the seine in the rapids near the foot or lip of the pool, so that when the rocks and boulders are turned over the darters are carried by the current into the seine. We were surprised to find the numbers of fish that live in these apparently inhospitable habitats. Close observation reveals that the darters, like the longnose dace, do not live in the mainstream of the current but in the sheltered spaces between and beneath rocks and boulders. The velocity of the current is lower in these little nooks and crannies, and the fish do not have to expend great amounts of energy in swimming. The buoyancy of a fish which is physically adapted to live in rapids and swift streams is decreased by the reduction in size or the absence of the swim bladder, thus increasing the density of the fish and causing it to sink. The loss or reduction of the swim bladder is not unique to darters or to species living in rapid water, however, but is characteristic of many fishes that are bottom dwellers.

The swift water where many darters live may appear to be a barren and inhospitable habitat, but there are many advantages in being able to live in it. Competitive fishes and enemies are rare. The swift water of the rapids is usually saturated with oxygen. The large surface area of rocks and boulders furnishes a place for the growth of plants, periphyton, and ooze. Small herbivorous insect larvae and nymphs are the most abundant animals living in the rapids, and they form an important portion of the diet of the darters. The darters also feed on the organisms that make up the stream drift. The habitat may seem rigorous, but apparently a few species have become adapted to this portion of the stream.

The Iowa darter, the Johnny darter, and the log perch make excellent aquarium fish, but they require live food in their diets. Other species of darters may be kept in aquariums but only under special conditions. Attempts by several of our associates to keep rainbow darters and fantail darters for extended periods have met with mixed success.

Genus *Ammocrypta* Jordan

The members of this genus are fishes of moderate to large size, with slender elongate bodies. The depth of the body is contained seven or more times in the length. The anal fin has 1 spine. The body is translucent in living specimens.

CRYSTAL DARTER

Ammocrypta asprella (Jordan)

The crystal darter (Figure 151) is usually 4 to 5 inches long. The head is flat, and the snout is rather blunt. The almost translucent body has 3 to 7 saddle marks across the back. There are 4 to 6 blotches on the lateral line. The anal fin has a single spine and 13 or 14 soft rays. The midline of the belly is scaleless. In life the body is yellowish green, but following a few days in preservative the area between the saddle marks becomes white. The lateral line has 90 to 100 scales. The dorsal fin has about 11 spines and 13 to 15 soft rays and is divided into two parts by a wide notch.

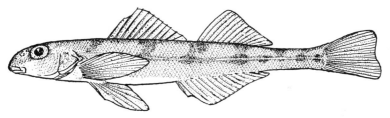

Fig. 151. Crystal darter, *Ammocrypta asprella*

The crystal darter ranges from southern Minnesota to southern Ohio and south to Oklahoma and Alabama. Of all the Minnesota darters the crystal darter is the rarest, and its presence in the Minnesota fish fauna has only recently become apparent. Until 1960 our only record of the crystal darter was from the Mississippi River near Winona. Since that time we have taken several specimens from the Zumbro River near Kellogg. All were collected over shifting sand bottoms from beneath driftwood stuck in the sand and the debris that had accumulated around it in water so swift that it was difficult to hold the seine in place. The seine was held directly downstream as the wood and debris were pulled loose. The fish hiding in the shelter of the obstruction were carried into the seine by the force of the current. We have not taken crystal darters in waters over shifting sand where the western sand darter (*Ammocrypta clara*) and the speckled chub (*Hybopsis aestivalis*) are usually found. No doubt the species is more common than we formerly thought it to be, but its preferred habitat is rather scarce in most of the southeastern portion of the state. We know nothing about its spawning or feeding habits.

WESTERN SAND DARTER

Ammocrypta clara (Jordan and Meek)

The western sand darter (Figure 152) is a slender darter that is almost transparent when alive and is extremely difficult to see in the seine. After preservation a series of small square olive blotches appear along the sides of the fish; these markings are vague in live fish. There are many oblong dark olive spots along the dorsal midline which are also more prominent in preserved material. The head is long and pointed. The lateral line has 67 to 78 scales. The dorsal fin has 10 spines and about 10 soft rays. The anal fin has 1 flexible spine and 8 soft rays. Part of the back and lower sides are scaleless.

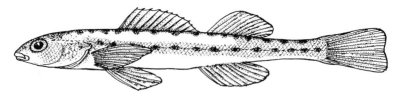

Fig. 152. Western sand darter, *Ammocrypta clara*

The western sand darter and its subspecies range from southern Minnesota to Indiana and south to eastern Texas. The species is common in the Minnesota River, the Mississippi River below St. Paul, and the St. Croix River below Taylors Falls. It is also common in the mouths of the larger tributaries of the Minnesota and Mississippi rivers. This darter is always associated with a shifting sand bottom in a moderate to swift current. It has the habit of burying itself in the soft sand. Eddy and Surber (1947) listed the species from Aitkin and Itasca counties on the basis of a report by Kidd (1927), but since these counties are entirely outside the range for the sand darter, we feel that the records may have been the result of incorrect identification.

The sand darter feeds on small or immature aquatic insects such as mayflies and midge larvae and on *Hyalella*.

Genus *Percina* Haldeman

Fishes belonging to this genus have large anal fins with an area usually as large as the area of the soft dorsal fin. The belly is naked except for a row of enlarged scales on the midventral line or it may be more or less scaled with one or more modified scales between the pelvic fins. The pelvic fins in most species are widely separated, and the space between them is usually three-fourths the width of the pelvic fin base.

LOG PERCH

Percina caprodes (Rafinesque)

The log perch (Figure 153) reaches a length of 6 inches. The body is yellowish brown in life. A variable number of dark crossbars or bands are present on the body; the number of bands ranges from 9 to 19, with 15 or 16 found most commonly. In many populations the bands are vague and appear to form blotches on the posterior third of the body. There is a prominent black spot at the base of the caudal fin. The head is broad with a piglike snout which projects beyond the inferior mouth. The scales are small, and the lateral line contains 68 to 81 scales, usually about 75. The cheeks are completely scaled, the breast is naked, and the nape may be naked, partially scaled, or completely scaled. The belly is naked except for a single median row of enlarged scales and a large modified scale between the pelvic fins. The gill membranes are narrowly connected. The dorsal fin has 13 to 15 spines and 14 to 17 rays, usually 14 spines and 15 rays. The anal fin has 1 or 2 spines and 8 to 12 rays, usually 2 spines and 10 rays. There is no marked difference in coloration between the sexes, but the second dorsal fin and the anal fin are usually slightly larger in the male.

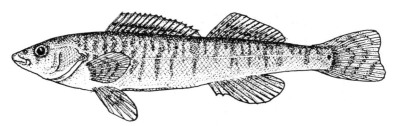

Fig. 153. Log perch, *Percina caprodes*

The Minnesota log perch appears to belong to the subspecies *Percina caprodes semifasciata* (DeKay), which is characterized by a scaleless nape; the presence of specimens with partially or completely scaled napes in the lower Mississippi River and its tributaries may indicate intergradation with *P. c. caprodes* (Rafinesque), which is found farther south. Specimens from the Red River and Rainy River drainages have naked napes and resemble *P. c. semifasciata*. Greene (1935) noted the presence of intergrades in the Milwaukee River, a tributary of Lake Michigan, but not in the Mississippi River drainage of Wisconsin. The log perch, including several subspecies, ranges from Saskatchewan to Quebec and south to Texas, Mississippi, and western Florida. It is found throughout Minnesota in streams, rivers, and lakes and is very abundant. Like the trout-perch, the log perch is often confused by fishermen with small perch or with walleyes.

The log perch spawns in May and June, depositing its eggs at random on shallow sandy bottoms. It feeds on algae, *Hyalella*, all kinds of aquatic insects, and large entomostracans.

GILT DARTER

Percina evides (Jordan and Copeland)

The gilt darter (Figure 154) is a stout compressed fish with a rather blunt snout and a terminal mouth. The body is olivaceous or bronze with 7 or 8 saddle bands across the back; each band is above a deep blue-green lateral bar. The spaces between the bands are yellow with reddish blotches. In breeding males the bands and the bars are confluent and deeper in color, and the head and breast are bright yellowish orange. The dorsal fin, the anal fin, and the pelvic fins are heavily pigmented with bluish black. The females are not so brightly colored. The cheeks and opercles are usually scaleless. The gill covers are only slightly connected at the isthmus. The first part of the dorsal fin has 10 to 13 spines, usually 11 or 12, and the second part has 13 soft rays. The anal fin has 2 spines and 9 to 11 soft rays. There are 52 to 67 scales in the lateral line.

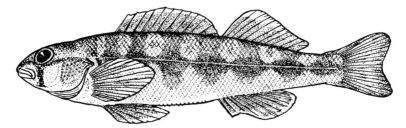

Fig. 154. Gilt darter, *Percina evides*

The gilt darter ranges from eastern Minnesota through the Ohio drainage to New York and south to Oklahoma and northern Georgia. In Minnesota the gilt darter is restricted to the St. Croix River and its tributaries, although we have a few specimens from the mouth of the Cannon River at Red Wing which were taken many years ago. Our intensive collecting recently in the same area has not produced any new specimens, and it is possible that the changes that have occurred in the lower Mississippi River drainage area during the past fifty years have eliminated the clear-water habitat preferred by the species. It is common in the St. Croix River from Taylors Falls south to Lake St. Croix and is very common north of Taylors Falls where Greene (1935) reported the presence of the gilt darter during the period 1925–1928, commenting on the rarity of the species at that time. It was his opinion that "the difficulty of collecting it . . . may explain to some extent the paucity of records." Trautman (1957) notes the apparent disappearance of the gilt darter from Ohio waters. We are of the opinion that in the St. Croix River the gilt darter is a modern relict population which has been isolated in recent times by habitat modification in its former range. We know nothing about its spawning and feeding habits.

BLACKSIDE DARTER

Percina maculata (Girard)

The blackside darter (Figure 155) reaches a length of about 3 inches. The body is greenish yellow with a prominent black band on each side formed by 7 to 9 confluent blotches which vary in size and prominence. The blotches never form vertical bars. The base of the caudal fin has a small black spot, and the

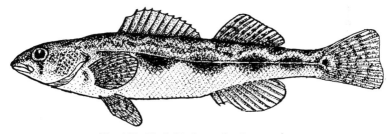

Fig. 155. Blackside darter, *Percina maculata*

back has 6 to 11 dark saddle bands. The cheeks are usually partially covered with scales, the nape may be scaled or naked, and the breast is naked. The dorsal fin contains 12 to 16 spines, usually 13 to 15, and 11 to 14 soft rays. The anal fin has 2 spines and 8 to 11 rays. The lateral line contains 63 to 81 scales, usually 65 to 75. The gill membranes are not connected. The head is pointed but not elongate.

The blackside darter ranges from Saskatchewan and North Dakota to New York and south to Oklahoma and Alabama. It is common in the Red River drainage, including the Rainy River system, the Minnesota River, the St. Croix River below Taylors Falls, and the Mississippi River below St. Anthony Falls. It prefers streams and small rivers such as the Des Moines, Yellow Medicine, Zumbro, and Otter Tail rivers. We know little about its spawning habits. It feeds mainly on small aquatic insects and *Hyalella*.

SLENDERHEAD DARTER

Percina phoxocephala (Nelson)

The slenderhead darter (Figure 156) usually reaches a length of 3 or 4 inches. It is thinner and more elongate than any other Minnesota species of *Percina*. This species has a very slender head and an elongate pointed snout. The gill covers are broadly united by a membrane. The body is yellowish brown with a pattern of dark blotches on the back and sides. There are 10 to 16 narrow dark blotches on each side along the lateral line; usually the blotches are higher than they are long, but they are confluent and give the appearance of a black band. In breeding males the blotches may be broader. A small black spot is present near the base of the caudal fin. The first dorsal fin of the male has a reddish-orange band in the middle and an outer band of pale blue or dark blue on the margin; the colors become very intense in breeding males. The dorsal fin has 11 to 13 spines and usually 12 or 13 soft rays. The lateral line contains 59 to 72 scales, usually 60 to 70 in Minnesota specimens.

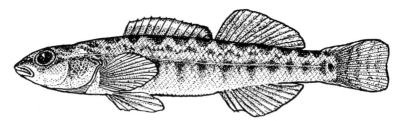

Fig. 156. Slenderhead darter, *Percina phoxocephala*

The slenderhead darter ranges from Minnesota to western Pennsylvania and south to Oklahoma and Tennessee. The species was first collected in Minnesota at the mouth of the Root River in 1943. Since that time we have taken this handsome darter in considerable numbers from the St. Croix River and its tributaries, the tributaries of the Minnesota River to its headwaters, and the Zumbro River, and we have a few individuals from the Root River tributaries of the Mississippi River south of the Twin Cities. We are unable to explain the rarity of the species in some tributaries of the Mississippi River where there appear to be habitats very similar to those occupied by the species in the St. Croix and Minnesota rivers. The failure to collect specimens before 1943 was probably because of inadequate sampling (Underhill, 1959).

RIVER DARTER
Percina shumardi (Girard)

The river darter (Figure 157) reaches a length of about 3 inches. It is most easily distinguished from other *Percina* by the pigmentation pattern on the spinous dorsal fin. There is a black spot on the membrane between the first and second spines, and a black spot appears on each segment of membrane connecting the last three spines. The olivaceous body has 9 to 14 transverse bars (usually 9 or 10) on the sides; the first 4 or 5 bars are narrow and rather vague, and the last 4 or 5 are more prominent and almost square. The last bars may be confluent, giving the appearance of a black band. The bands are most pronounced in breeding males, but they fade after spawning and after death.

There is a very pronounced tear-shaped bar beneath the eye. The cheeks, the opercle, and the nape are scaled; the breast and the belly are usually scaleless, although the belly may be scaled just anterior to the vent. The gill membranes are free from the isthmus and are scarcely connected. The first dorsal fin has 10 or 11 spines, and the second dorsal fin has 13 to 15 soft rays. The anal fin has 2 spines and 10 to 12 soft rays. There are 50 to 56 scales in the lateral line.

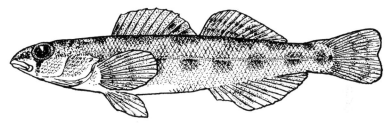

Fig. 157. River darter, *Percina shumardi*

The river darter ranges from Manitoba to Ohio and south to central Texas and Alabama. In Minnesota the species occurs in large rivers and river lakes. There are specimens in our collections from the Rainy River, Lake of the Woods, Lake Pepin, Lake St. Croix, and the Mississippi River south of the Twin Cities. The species is common in the St. Croix River below Taylors Falls, but we have never taken it above the dam, and Greene (1935) did not collect it in Wisconsin. We have many specimens from the mouths of the Cannon and Zumbro rivers and a few specimens from the mouth of Minnehaha Creek in Minneapolis, but we have none from the Minnesota River or the Mississippi River above St. Anthony Falls. There are three records of the river darter from the Red River drainage (Woolman, 1895; Hankinson, 1929), but there are no records of it in the Lake Superior drainage. The river darter in the Hudson Bay drainage is a disjunct population. We know little about its spawning habits except that it spawns in April or May.

Genus *Etheostoma* Rafinesque

In members of this genus the belly is usually scaled, but if the belly is naked there are no enlarged scales on the midventral line and no modified scales between the pelvic fins. The area of the anal fin is usually less than the area of the dorsal fin.

JOHNNY DARTER

Etheostoma nigrum Rafinesque

The Johnny darter (Figure 158) is easily recognized by the W-shaped marks along its sides. Males in breeding color lack these marks and can be difficult to identify. The breeding males are without bright colors but are heavily pigmented with brown; the first dorsal fin is black, and the spines are somewhat enlarged. Brown vertical bands may also be present on the sides of the males, but the presence and development of these bands varies considerably in individuals. The dorsal fin has 13 spines and 10 to 14 soft rays. The anal fin has 1 spine and 6 to 10 soft rays. The lateral line is complete and has 41 to 56 scales. The gill membranes are scarcely connected.

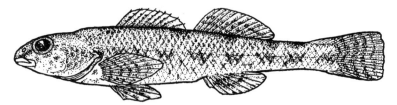

Fig. 158. Johnny darter, *Etheostoma nigrum*

The American pioneer of ichthyology David Starr Jordan wrote about the Johnny darters in 1888: "Any one who has ever been a boy and can remember back to the days of tag-alders, yellow cowslips, and an angleworm on a pin-hook, will recall an experience like this: You tried some time to put your finger on a little fish that was lying, apparently asleep, on the bottom of the stream, half hidden under a stone or leaf, his tail bent around the stone as if for support against the force of the current. You will remember that when your finger came near the spot where he was lying, the bent tail straightened, and you saw the fish resting, head upstream, a few feet away, leaving you puzzled to know whether you had seen the movement or not. You were trying to catch a Johnny darter. Nothing seems easier, but you did not do it." Many readers probably have observed this little fish while sitting on the dock looking down into the shallows or while eating lunch at the river's edge.

The Johnny darter and its several subspecies are distributed from southern Canada, the upper Mississippi Valley, and the Great Lakes drainage to the Atlantic drainage and south to Florida and Arkansas. The Johnny darter is possibly the most abundant darter found in Minnesota, and it certainly has the widest range. It is found in lakes and streams from the Boundary Waters Canoe Area in the northeast to the Missouri River drainage of southwestern Minnesota.

Some workers recognize two subspecies of Johnny darters, *Etheostoma nigrum nigrum* and *E. n. eulepis.* In the first form the cheeks, breast, and nape are naked, and in the second form these areas are covered with scales. We are of the opinion that the two forms are not really worthy of subspecific recognition but are an example of genetic polymorphism since both the naked and scaled forms and intermediate forms are found in many populations of Johnny darters in Minnesota (Underhill, 1963). Intergrades or intermediates are found throughout a large area including Iowa, South Dakota, and Wisconsin, but we have not determined the adaptive value the scaled and naked phenotypes may have. The scaled form is found only in the area of North America that was covered with ice during the Wisconsin glaciation. There has been speculation that the naked form is replacing the scaled form, but it is difficult to find support for this theory because the two forms were not discovered until very recently. Furthermore, the areas occupied by these forms were deglaciated 12,000 years ago, and we have been collecting fish for less than a century; if one form is replacing the other and has not achieved "success" in 12,000 years, it is difficult to imagine that discernible population shifts might occur in less than fifty years. We are carrying on annual sampling in a number of populations throughout the range in Minnesota and hope to find evidence of shifts in the abundance of the two forms, but we have seen no significant changes in the past fifteen years. This may be because the changes wrought by man's interference might be so great as to mask the more subtle natural influences on gene frequencies and as a result on the phenotypes.

The Johnny darter spawns in May and June in nests prepared by the male under sticks and stones. The male guards the eggs but not the young. Entomostracans, some algae, and small immature insects make up the diet of the species.

BLUNTNOSE DARTER

Etheostoma chlorosomum (Hay)

The bluntnose darter (Figure 159) is usually just under 3 inches in length. It is grayish brown with a lateral row of irregular W-shaped blotches. It is very similar to the Johnny darter in appearance but differs in having an incomplete

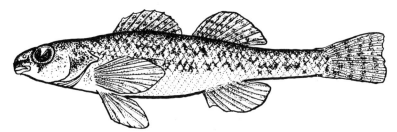

Fig. 159. Bluntnose darter, *Etheostoma chlorosomum*

lateral line which extends only to below the end of the spinous dorsal fin instead of having a complete lateral line. The bar from the eye to the snout does not end at the snout but is continuous around the front of the snout. The snout is blunt; its length is about equal to the diameter of the eye. The gill membranes are scarcely connected.

The bluntnose darter is distributed from southern Minnesota to Indiana and southward to Texas and Alabama. In Minnesota it prefers quiet waters with muddy bottoms and occurs in the sloughs and backwaters south of Wabasha. The only records we have are from extreme southeastern Minnesota. Several specimens were collected by survey crews from the Mississippi River in 1944, from Pine Creek in Houston County, and from an overflow pool of the Root River in 1945. These specimens were examined by Eddy, but they were not deposited in the University of Minnesota collections and their present location is unknown. They may have been lost when the Division of Game and Fish moved into new quarters.

We know nothing about the feeding or spawning habits of the bluntnose darter.

IOWA DARTER

Etheostoma exile (Girard)

The Iowa darter (Figure 160) is a slender fish that reaches a maximum length of about 2 1/2 inches. The male is bright greenish blue with brown blotches and about 11 reddish spots on the sides; the first dorsal fin is bright orange with a dark blue margin. The female is brownish and lacks the bright colors of the male. A prominent black bar extends below the eye. The gill membranes are scarcely connected. The breast is naked. This species is quite variable and is difficult to describe satisfactorily in terms of scale counts and other meristic characters (Carlander, 1941; Eddy and Surber, 1947). The lateral line may be arched or straight, but it is always incomplete, extending to just below the end of the soft dorsal fin. The scales in the lateral line range from 49 to 69 and usually half the scales are unpored, but there is considerable variation in the number of unpored scales. The dorsal fin has 7 to 10 spines, usually 8 or 9, and 9 to 12 soft rays, commonly 10 or 11. The anal fin has 2 spines and 6 to 9 rays.

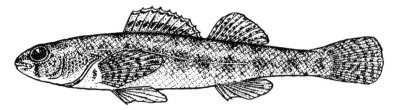

Fig. 160. Iowa darter, *Etheostoma exile*

The Iowa darter is a common lake species but is taken occasionally in streams which are near lakes. It ranges from Saskatchewan to Quebec and south to Colorado, Iowa, Illinois, Indiana, and Ohio. It is present in some streams, floodplain lakes, and sloughs of the Mississippi River south of the Twin Cities, but it is not common.

The Iowa darter is hardy and makes an excellent aquarium fish, but unfortunately the bright colors of the breeding males tend to fade in captivity. Like other species of native fishes, they should be fed fortified dried rations supplemented occasionally with live food.

Iowa darters spawn in May or June in the vegetation of the shallow sand or mud bottoms in lakes or along stream margins, depositing their eggs on rocks or pebbles. They feed on small aquatic insects, crustaceans, and some plankton.

MUD DARTER

Etheostoma asprigene (Forbes)

The mud darter (Figure 161) reaches a length of about 2 1/2 inches. The body is fusiform but stout and compressed. It is brownish in color with greenish crossbars or blotches and with reddish orange between the blotches; the belly is tinged with orange. The spinous dorsal fin has a narrow margin of blue, and the upper half is dotted with reddish orange spots. The soft dorsal fin is mottled with brown. The males are more brightly colored than the females. The dorsal fin has 12 spines and 12 soft rays. The anal fin has 2 spines and 9 soft rays. The scales in the lateral line average about 47; the lateral line is incomplete. The cheeks and opercles are more or less scaled.

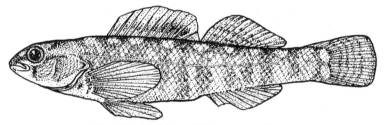

Fig. 161. Mud darter, *Etheostoma asprigene*

The mud darter ranges from Minnesota to Indiana and south to Mississippi and Texas. In Minnesota it is restricted to the Mississippi River and its tributaries south of St. Paul and to the St. Croix River below Taylors Falls. It is common in the mud-bottom sloughs south of Red Wing. Greene (1935) noted its preference for muddy sloughs and river mouths near the Mississippi River and its tributaries. We have taken it often in the mouths of streams near the Mississippi River (Phillips and Underhill, 1967) over gravel rubble in moderate to swift currents. The latter observations agree with those of Forbes and Richardson (1920).

RAINBOW DARTER

Etheostoma caeruleum Storer

The rainbow darter (Figure 162) reaches a length of slightly more than 3 inches. It has a stout body with a large head and large eyes. It is Minnesota's most colorful darter. Breeding males may assume virtually all the colors of the spectrum. The body is brilliantly olivaceous and has blotches of darker olive on the upper body and back. There are 11 or 12 bars of indigo blue that extend downward and backward; the interspaces between the indigo bars are bright orange. The breast is orange, and the cheeks vary from light to intense blue. The median fins have dark blue or bright blue and orange horizontal bars. These colors fade following the breeding season. The female is dull brown in color with a flecking of dark brown pigment. The colors and color pattern exhibited by the male rival or at least equal those of exotic aquarium fishes. The scales in the lateral line range from 40 to 50 in number with an average of about 45. The lateral line is incomplete and usually ends beneath the soft dorsal fin. The cheeks, the nape, and the breast are naked. The gill membranes are scarcely connected. The dorsal fin has 10 to 12 spines, usually 10 or 11, and 12 to 14 soft rays.

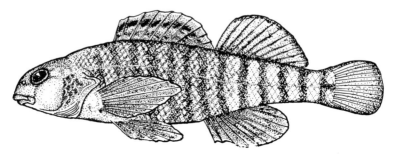

Fig. 162. Rainbow darter, *Etheostoma caeruleum* (male)

The rainbow darter ranges from southern Minnesota to eastern Ontario and south to Arkansas and Alabama. It is very common in the streams tributary to the Mississippi River south of St. Anthony Falls and in the tributaries of the Minnesota River to its headwaters in Big Stone Lake. We have taken specimens from riffles and rapids in the St. Croix River below the dam at Taylors Falls but not above it. We have not found the species in lakes.

The rainbow darter prefers clear rapid water free of domestic pollution but is tolerant of normal agricultural enrichment. It is probably one of the more common species of darters in the small streams of southeastern Minnesota, but early records are lacking because until relatively recently no collections were made in small streams (Eddy and Surber, 1947). Rainbow darters spawn in May, depositing their eggs in pebble or gravel riffles of streams. They feed on all sorts of small aquatic insects, crustaceans, entomostracans, and other animal life common to small streams.

BANDED DARTER

Etheostoma zonale (Cope)

The banded darter (Figure 163) is a slender fish with an obtusely curved snout. It is the only Minnesota darter that has a greenish coloration. There are 6 greenish brown quadrate spots on the back and a greenish or olivaceous lateral band from which 8 narrow dark bands nearly or completely encircle the belly. The dorsal fin of the male is greenish and has a basal bar of dark red pigment; the other fins are yellow-green or light green. The males have more intense coloration than the females. The cheeks and the opercle are scaled; the breast is partially scaled. The gill covers are very broadly connected or joined with the membrane across the isthmus. The dorsal fin has 8 to 10 spines, usually 9, and 10 or 11 soft rays. The anal fin has 2 spines and 7 soft rays. The lateral line is complete and has 42 to 50 scales.

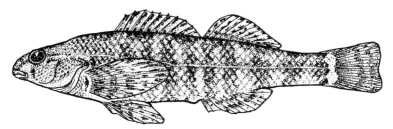

Fig. 163. Banded darter, *Etheostoma zonale*

The banded darter ranges from southern Minnesota to Ohio and western New York and south to Oklahoma, Arkansas, and Alabama. In Minnesota the species has been collected from the tributaries of the Mississippi River below St. Anthony Falls and from many of the tributaries of the Minnesota River. It is not common in any of the streams, and collections of ten or twenty individuals from a single station are unusual; we usually get only four or five. The banded darter seems to prefer the lower lip of pools at the point where the water begins to enter the rapids. The technique we have found to be most successful is to roll rocks across the lip of the pool or to seine obliquely across it. The difficulty of collecting from this rather restricted habitat probably explains the lack of earlier records of the banded darter from all but a few localities in Minnesota (Eddy and Surber, 1947). We know little about its breeding or feeding habits.

STRIPED FANTAIL DARTER

Etheostoma flabellare lineolatum (Agassiz)

The striped fantail darter (Figure 164) reaches a length of 2 1/2 inches. The body is heavy with a long and rather pointed head. It is dark brown, sometimes almost black, with a spot on each scale; the spots give the appearance of a series of lengthwise stripes. The caudal fin is strongly barred. The breeding males are more darkly colored than the females; at the height of the breeding season the spines of the first dorsal fin have little pink or reddish fleshy knobs at their tips. The gill membranes are broadly connected. The dorsal fin has 8 spines and 12 to 14 soft rays. The anal fin has 2 spines and 7 to 9 soft rays. The spinous dorsal fin is much lower than the soft dorsal fin. The lateral line is incomplete, reaching to below the front of the soft dorsal fin; it contains from 40 to 65 scales. The head is naked.

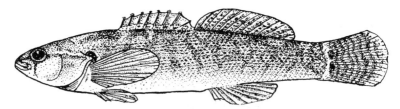

Fig. 164. Striped fantail darter, *Etheostoma flabellare lineolatum*

The fantail darter, including the eastern subspecies, is distributed from Minnesota to Vermont and south to Oklahoma and North Carolina. It is common in the tributaries of the Minnesota River and the Mississippi River south of the Twin Cities. It is rare in the St. Croix River below Taylors Falls. We have not collected it above St. Anthony Falls or above Taylors Falls.

Jordan (1888) referred to fantails as the ''darter of darters'' — the hardiest, wiriest, and wariest of them all and the one most expert in catching other creatures. It is the one that most surely evades your clutch; you can catch a weasel if you can put your finger on one of these fish. Jordan further states that the fantail chooses the coldest and swiftest waters, where, as befits its form, it leads an active predatory life and is the terror of water snails, caddis worms, and mosquito larvae (and, we may add, other small animals). The fantail spawns in May when the male prepares a simple nest among the rocks and pebbles of the stream. The male guards the eggs but not the young.

LEAST DARTER

Etheostoma microperca Jordan and Gilbert

The least darter (Figure 165) holds the distinction of being the smallest fish native to Minnesota waters; it averages 1 to 1 1/2 inches in total length. The mottled olivaceous body is short, moderately deep, and slightly compressed. The males are darker in color than the females. The gill membranes are slightly connected. This darter may be recognized by the absence of a lateral line or by the presence of not more than 8 pored scales in the lateral line series. The pelvic fins reach to the anus and are larger in males. The anal fin has 2 spines and 5 or 6 soft rays. The dorsal fin has 5 to 8 spines and 9 or 10 soft rays. The belly is only partially scaled.

The least darter is usually found in vegetation in the shallow waters of lakes and small streams. Because of its small size, this darter is often missed or overlooked, and it can escape through the common 1/4-inch-mesh seine. A woven nylon seine with 1/8-inch mesh is useful for taking least darters.

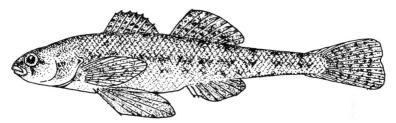

Fig. 165. Least darter, *Etheostoma microperca*

The least darter and its subspecies range from Minnesota to southern Ontario and southward to Kentucky, Arkansas, and Oklahoma. In Minnesota the least darter has a rather peculiar distribution; it is abundant in the Otter Tail River and its tributaries in the Red River drainage, in the Crow Wing River, in the Mississippi River drainage above St. Anthony Falls, and in Otter Creek, a tributary of the Cedar River south of Austin.

The least darter spawns in May, depositing its eggs in vegetation or on stones and sandy bottoms in shallow streams and lakes. It feeds on all sorts of minute aquatic animal life.

Family COTTIDAE
The Sculpin Family

This family contains a number of genera and species, most of which are marine. One genus is restricted to fresh water, but several marine genera have species which sometimes enter fresh water. Sculpins are rather grotesque in appearance. The body is elongate with a very large and depressed head. The eyes are high on the head, almost dorsal in position, and are close together. One or more spinous processes are usually present on the margin of the opercle. Teeth are present on the vomer and palatine bones. The upper jaw is protractile; the maxillary lacks a supplementary bone. The gill rakers are either short and tuberclelike or absent. The body is without scales or may be partially covered with hard prickles. A lateral line is present, but it is incomplete in some species. The pectoral fins are very large and prominent; the pelvic fins are rather small and thoracic, located almost under the pectoral fins. In the fins of many species the soft rays are unbranched and difficult to distinguish from the spines.

Key to Minnesota Species of Family Cottidae

1. Gill membranes free from isthmus; dorsal fins widely separated; second preopercular spine conspicuous; head long; body slender; small but definite slit behind last gill (difficult to see) . . . .
. . . . .Fourhorn sculpin, *Myoxocephalus quadricornis* (Linnaeus)
   Gill membranes not entirely free from isthmus; dorsal fins scarcely separated; second preopercular spine concealed by skin; head broad; body fusiform; no gill slit behind last gill 2
2. Lateral line complete . . . . .Spoonhead sculpin, *Cottus ricei* (Nelson)
   Lateral line incomplete, extending back to region of second dorsal fin . 3
3. Pelvic fin rays typically I,3*; palatine teeth few or absent . . . .
. . . . .Slimy sculpin, *Cottus cognatus* Richardson
   Pelvic fin rays typically I,4*; palatine teeth well developed . . . .
. . . . .Mottled sculpin, *Cottus bairdi* Girard

---

*A sheath encloses the spine with the first soft ray; the spine is not visible without dissection.

Genus *Myoxocephalus* Telesius

These are circumpolar marine sculpins found in the shallow waters of the Arctic Ocean in North America, Europe, and Asia. At least one species has succeeded in invading some freshwater lakes and streams.

FOURHORN SCULPIN

Myoxocephalus quadricornis (Linnaeus)

The fourhorn sculpin (Figures 166 and 167) differs from all the other Minnesota sculpins in that it has a very pale color with only four blotches of pigment on the back. The body is very slender with a long and narrow head

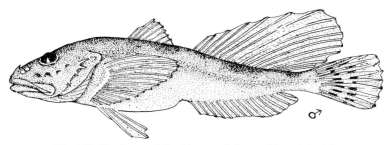

Fig. 166. Fourhorn sculpin, *Myoxocephalus quadricornis* (male)

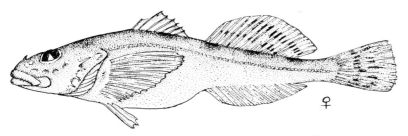

Fig. 167. Fourhorn sculpin, *Myoxocephalus quadricornis* (female)

which is flat and rather cavernous. The preopercle has 4 strong spines. The gill membranes are united and free from the isthmus. The dorsal fin is widely divided with 8 spines in the anterior part and 18 soft rays in the posterior part; the soft rays are greatly elongated in the male. The anal fin has 15 soft rays. The pelvic fins are thoracic and have 1 spine and 3 soft rays.

The fourhorn sculpin, long considered a separate species peculiar to deep lakes in North America such as Lake Superior and to Arctic streams in Canada, originally was known as the deep-water sculpin, *Triglopsis thompsoni* Girard. In the late 1950s it became apparent that this sculpin was not fundamentally different from the Arctic genus *Myoxocephalus* and that it seemed to be a form or subspecies of *M. quadricornis*. The subspecies status is not wholly established, but Hubbs and Lagler (1964) prefer to designate it as *M. quadricornis thompsoni* (Girard).

The fourhorn sculpin is found in freshwater lakes including some of the Great Lakes and some deep lakes of Arctic Canada and the Ottawa drainage of Quebec (Delisle and Van Vliet, 1968). In Minnesota it is usually found in deep water near the bottom of Lake Superior, although it has also been reported in streams in the northern part of the state. We have frequently found specimens entangled in the leadlines of gill nets set for lake trout at depths of about 600 feet off Grand Marais, Beaver Bay, and Isle Royale. Until the development and use of trawls and small-mesh gill nets in the past fifty years, the fourhorn sculpin was known mostly from specimens found in the stomachs of lake trout and siscowets caught at about 600 feet. Recent investigations with trawls have yielded many more specimens.

These sculpins apparently spawn in deep water, although we know little about their habits. The eggs are large; we find females with ripe eggs from late June through July. They are strictly predacious, feeding on *Pontoporeia* and the few species of aquatic insects found on the deep bottoms. Sculpins and their eggs are a significant part of the diet of lake trout and siscowets.

Genus *Cottus* Linnaeus

The many species belonging to this genus are all found in the fresh waters of the Northern Hemisphere. Most of these live in cold streams and lakes. Three species of the genus are found in Minnesota. They are all small, ranging up to about 5 inches in length. They live on the bottom, hiding during the day under rocks and logs in swift streams or along wave-beaten shores of large lakes. Some species are reported to be fall spawners. The males prepare nests and guard the eggs, which are suspended from the underside of rocks and logs. These species are rarely caught in ordinary seining operations. Although we had obtained specimens for our collections by upturning rocks and debris, we had no idea of the abundance of these species until we began to use electric shockers to urge them out of their hiding places. Commercial minnow seiners rarely catch them. Several veteran commercial seiners have brought in specimens of this bizarre fish which they had caught for the first time in many years of minnow seining and which they felt sure was venomous. Despite their appearance, sculpins are harmless.

MOTTLED SCULPIN
Cottus bairdi Girard

The mottled sculpin (Figure 168) reaches a maximum length of about 5 inches in Minnesota. It is gray or brown and distinctly mottled and has a light-colored belly. The body is rather stout and tapers to a narrow tail. The head is flattened and quite wide. The preopercle has a sharp spine which is directed backward and slightly upward; under this are 2 or 3 short spines. The skin is smooth except for the region just posterior to the pectoral fins, where it may be covered with sharp prickles. The lateral line is usually incomplete and has 19 to 26 pores. The first dorsal fin is low and weak with 7 to 10 spines, usually 8; the second dorsal fin is not widely separated from the first and has 16 to 19 rays, usually 18. The pectoral fins are very large and about equal to the head in length. The anal fin has 13 to 15 rays, usually 14. The pelvic fins have 1 spine and 4 rays; the spine is slender and splintlike and can be seen only when dissected with a needle from the first ray to which it is bound.

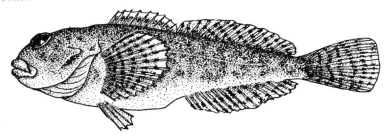

Fig. 168. Mottled sculpin, *Cottus bairdi*

Some investigators have reported that the overlapping of some of these characters makes it difficult to distinguish the mottled sculpin from the slimy sculpin. McAllister (1964) claims that the only reliable character for separating the two species is the postorbital length, which is greater than the length of the caudal peduncle in the mottled sculpin but less than the length of the caudal peduncle in the slimy sculpin. The number of pelvic fin rays may vary. Although we have not examined as many specimens as McAllister has, we have found that the number of pelvic fin rays (4 rays in the mottled sculpin and 3 rays in the slimy sculpin) and a comparison of the postorbital and peduncle lengths are very helpful in distinguishing Minnesota specimens.

The mottled sculpin is distributed from the Pacific drainage eastward across Canada to Quebec and Labrador. In the United States it occurs in streams on the eastern slope of the Rocky Mountains in Colorado and Montana, from Minnesota through the Great Lakes area to New Brunswick, and southward to West Virginia and the mountain streams of Alabama. Scattered populations occur in the mountain drainage of the Ohio River in Kentucky and Tennessee and in the Ozark region.

This is the most common species of sculpin in Minnesota, and it occurs in many small streams of the state. It prefers riffles over gravel, boulder, or limestone shingle bottoms. It is quite common in many large northern lakes with boulder-lined shores. The construction of highways with flooded stone riprap has provided additional habitats for the species.

The mottled sculpin is a bottom feeder and eats all sorts of small aquatic animals, especially *Gammarus* and immature insects. Both the mottled sculpin and the slimy sculpin have been accused of preying on trout eggs, but studies have failed to prove that they eat viable eggs. The studies have shown instead that the trout themselves are cannibalistic and eat their own eggs at times and that the sculpins are an important food item for many Minnesota trout. Occasionally a trout fisherman using worms for bait may hook one of these voracious little fish. They are tenacious, and if they grab the loose end of a worm they may hang on until they are lifted clear of the water; sometimes they do not let go until they are landed.

SLIMY SCULPIN

Cottus cognatus Richardson

The slimy sculpin (Figure 169) is very similar in appearance to the mottled sculpin. It differs mainly in the pelvic fins, which have 1 spine and 3 soft rays, and in the postorbital length, which is always less than the length of the caudal peduncle. The presence of 4 pelvic rays is so rare in Minnesota specimens of the slimy sculpin that this character is very useful in distinguishing the two species. The dorsal fin has 6 to 8 spines, usually 7, and 16 to 18 soft rays. The pectoral fin is large and usually has 13 or 14 rays. The anal fin has 10 to 14 rays, usually 12. The longest anal fin ray of the slimy sculpin is much longer than that of the mottled sculpin and is contained approximately 6 times in the standard length, while the longest anal fin ray of the mottled sculpin is contained about 8 times in the standard length. The male of the slimy sculpin is more colorful than the male of the mottled sculpin and has a rust-orange band on the dorsal fin.

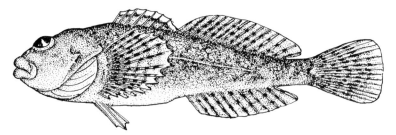

Fig. 169. Slimy sculpin, *Cottus cognatus*

The slimy sculpin ranges from Alaska and northern Canada through the Great Lakes drainage and the area east of the Alleghenies to West Virginia. We find it to be common in the shallow waters of Lake Superior and in practically all the tributary streams. We have taken it from Grand Portage Bay and Grand Portage Creek and from the Temperance, Devil Track, Two Island, Split Rock, Baptism, and Onion rivers on the north shore of Lake Superior. We have taken it in the Little Isabella River in Lake County in the

Hudson Bay drainage. It is also common in Valley Creek near Afton in the St. Croix drainage. Large populations are present in the small streams of southeastern Minnesota which are quite isolated from the general northern range of the species. The species occurs in Garvin Brook (Winona County), Winnebago Creek (Houston County), and the Whitewater and Root rivers and their tributaries. In these streams both the slimy sculpin (*Cottus cognatus*) and the mottled sculpin (*C. bairdi*) may be found, but in all cases the slimy sculpin occurs in the spring-fed headwaters and the mottled sculpin is found farther downstream. The slimy sculpin is often found in association with the brook trout (*Salvelinus fontinalis*) particularly in southeastern Minnesota. We have no records of the slimy sculpin from the Mississippi River drainage above St. Anthony Falls or the Minnesota and Red River drainages. In the Lake Superior drainage both species of sculpin occur in the same streams, but the slimy sculpin seems to prefer a water temperature of about 60.5° F while the mottled sculpin seeks warmer water of about 67.6° F (Smith and Moyle, 1944).

The feeding habits of the slimy sculpin are the same as those of the mottled sculpin. The slimy sculpin may compete with the brook trout for food, but the larger trout feed on the sculpins.

SPOONHEAD SCULPIN

Cottus ricei (Nelson)

The spoonhead sculpin (Figure 170) reaches a maximum length of about 3 inches. The body is stout with a large flat head and a slender tail. The skin is very prickly. The body is olivaceous or gray and is finely speckled and deeply blotched. The dorsal fin is completely divided; the anterior portion contains 7 to 9 spines, usually 8, and the posterior portion contains 15 to 19 soft rays, usually 17. The dorsal spines are quite flexible and resemble unbranched rays. The anal fin has 12 or 13 soft rays. The lateral line is complete. The upper preopercular spine is long and sickle-shaped; below it 2 or 3 small spines extend downward. The spoonhead sculpin can be distinguished from the other species of this genus by the crescent-shaped opercular spine, the complete lateral line, and the prickly skin.

The spoonhead sculpin is found in all the Great Lakes and ranges north-

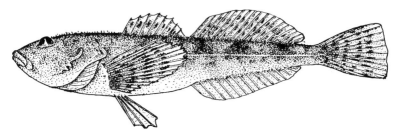

Fig. 170. Spoonhead sculpin, *Cottus ricei*

ward to the Yukon and the Rocky Mountains in Alberta and northward and eastward to Hudson Bay, Quebec, and Labrador. We have specimens which were taken by trawlers off Park Point in the western end of Lake Superior, and Hubbs and Lagler (1964) found specimens off Isle Royale. The species lives in shallow water near the shore but occasionally is found in deeper water. More extensive seining would probably show it to be fairly common.

The spoonhead sculpin spawns in the spring in nests prepared under rocks. We do not know much about its habits. It feeds on entomostracans and small animal life such as worms, aquatic insects, and amphipods.

References and Index

References

Agassiz, L. 1850. *Lake Superior, its physical character, vegetation, and animals compared with those of other and similar regions, with a narrative of the tour by J. E. Cabot.* Boston: Gould, Kendall, and Lincoln.

Alexander, R. M. 1967. *Functional design in fishes.* London: Hutchinson and Co.

Applegate, V. C., and J. W. Moffett. 1955. The sea lamprey. *Sci. Amer.* 192:36–41.

Bailey, R. M. 1959a. Distribution of the American cyprinid fish *Notropis anogenus. Copeia*, pp. 119–23.

———. 1959b. Parasitic lampreys (*Ichthyomyzon*) from the Missouri River, Missouri and South Dakota. *Copeia*, pp. 162–63.

———. 1969. A revised list of the fishes of Iowa, with keys for identification. In *Iowa Fish and Fishing*, ed. J. R. Harlan and E. B. Speaker, pp. 327–77. Iowa Conserv. Comm.

Bailey, R. M., and M. O. Allum. 1962. *The fishes of South Dakota.* Misc. Publ. Mus. Zool. Univ. Mich., no. 119.

Banarescu, P. 1964. *Fauna republicii populare romine. Vol. 13, Pisces-Osteichthyes.* Bucuresti: Acad. Rep. Pop. Rom.

Barber, W. E., and W. L. Minckley. 1971. Summer foods of the cyprinid fish *Semotilus atromaculatus. Trans. Amer. Fish. Soc.* 100:283–89.

Becker, G. C. 1966. Fishes of southwestern Wisconsin. *Trans. Wis. Acad. Sci. Arts Lett.* 55:87–117.

Berg, L. S. 1949. *Freshwater fishes of the USSR and adjacent countries.* Akad. Nauk. SSSR. Vol. 2, Transl. Israel Prog. Sci. Transl., Jerusalem.

Cable, L. A. 1928. *Food of Bullheads.* Rep. U.S. Comm. Fish., pp. 27–41.

Cahn, A. R. 1927. *An ecological study of southern Wisconsin fishes, the brook silverside (Labidesthes sicculus) and the cisco (Leucichthys artedi) in their relations to the region.* Ill. Biol. Monogr., vol. 11.

Carbine, W. F. 1939. Observations on the spawning habits of centrarchid fishes in Deep Lake, Oakland County, Michigan. *Trans. 4th N. Amer. Wildl. Conf.*, pp. 275–87.

Carlander, K. D. 1941. The darters (Etheostominae) of Minnesota. *Proc. Minn. Acad. Sci.* 9:41–48.

———. 1942. *An investigation of Lake of the Woods, Minnesota, with particular reference to commercial fisheries. I. Introduction, limnology, and the fishery.* Minn. Dep. Conserv., Fish. Res. Invest. Rep., no. 42.

Cleary, R. E. 1952. An annotated check-list of the fishes of the Wapsipinicon River drainage in Iowa. *Proc. Iowa Acad. Sci.* 59:435–41.

———. 1953. An annotated check-list of the fishes of the Iowa-Cedar River drainage in Iowa. *Proc. Iowa Acad. Sci.* 60:626–35.

Cox, U. O. 1896. *A report upon the fishes of southwestern Minnesota.* Rep. U.S. Fish Comm. (1894), pp. 605–16.

———. 1897. *A preliminary report on the fishes of Minnesota.* Geol. Natur. Hist. Surv. Minn. Zool. Ser. 3, pp. 1–93.

Cross, F. B., and A. L. Metcalf. 1963. Records of three lampreys (*Ichthyomyzon*) from the Missouri River. *Copeia*, p. 187.

Davis, H. S. 1937. *Care and diseases of trout.* U.S. Bur. Fish. Invest. Rep., no. 35.

Delisle, C., and W. Van Vliet. 1968. First records of the sculpin, *Myoxocephalus thompsonii* and *Cottus ricei*, from the Ottawa Valley, southwestern Quebec. *J. Fish. Res. Board Can.* 24:2733–37.

Dineen, C. E. 1951. A comparative study of the food habits of *Cottus bairdii* and associated species of Salmonidae. *Amer. Midland Natur.* 46:640–45

Dobie, J., O. L. Meehan, S. F. Snieszko, and G. N. Washburn. 1956. 1956. *Raising bait fishes.* U.S. Fish Wildl. Serv. Circ., no. 35.

Dobie, J. R., O. L. Meehan, and G. N. Washburn. 1948. *Propagation of minnows and other bait species.* U.S. Fish Wildl. Circ., no. 12.

Eastman, J. T. 1970. The pharyngeal bones and teeth of Minnesota cyprinid and catostomid fishes: Functional morphology, variation and taxonomic significance. Ph.D. diss., Univ. Minn.

Eddy, S. 1943. Limnological notes on Lake Superior. *Proc. Minn. Acad. Sci.* 11:34–39.

Eddy, S., and K. D. Carlander. 1939. The growth rate of the walleyed pike, *Stizostedion vitreum* (Mitchill), in various lakes of Minnesota. *Proc. Minn. Acad. Sci.* 8:14–19.

———. 1942. *Growth rate studies of Minnesota fishes.* Minn. Dep. Conserv., Fish. Res. Invest. Rep., no. 28.

Eddy, S., and P. H. Simer. 1929. Notes on the food of the paddlefish and the plankton of its habitat. *Trans. Ill. State Acad. Sci.* 21:59–63.

Eddy, S., and T. Surber. 1947. *Northern fishes.* 2d rev. ed. Minneapolis: Univ. Minn. Press.

Eddy, S., and J. C. Underhill. 1959. Recent changes and corrections for the Minnesota fish fauna. *Copeia*, pp. 342–43.

Eschmeyer, P. H., and R. M. Bailey. 1955. The pygmy whitefish, *Coregonus coulteri*, in Lake Superior. *Trans. Amer. Fish. Soc.* 84:161–99.

Evermann, B. W., and H. B. Latimer. 1910. The fishes of the Lake of the Woods and connecting waters. *Proc. U.S. Nat. Mus.* 39:121–36.

Forbes, S. A., and R. E. Richardson. 1908. *The fishes of Illinois.* Natur. Hist. Surv. Ill.

———. 1920. *The fishes of Illinois.* 2d ed. Natur. Hist. Surv. Ill.

Friedrich, G. W. 1933. A catalog of the fishes of central Minnesota. *Copeia*, pp. 27–30.

Frost, W. E., and M. E. Brown. 1967. *The trout.* London: Collins Press.

Gage, S. H. 1893. The lake and brook lampreys of New York, especially those of Cayuga and Seneca lakes. In *Wilder Quarter-Century Book*, Ithaca, pp. 421–93.

———. 1928. The lampreys of New York State — life history and economics. In *A biological survey of the Oswego River system.* Suppl. 17th Ann. Rep. N.Y. State Conserv. Dep. (1927), pp. 158–91.

Gilbert, C. R. 1961. Hybridization versus intergradation: An inquiry into relationships of two cyprinid fishes. *Copeia*, pp. 181–92.

———. 1964. *The American cyprinid fishes of the subgenus Luxilus (genus Notropis).* Bull. Florida State Mus. Biol. Sci. 8:95–194.

Gilbert, C. R., and R. M. Bailey. 1972. *Systematics and zoogeography of the American cyprinid fish Notropis (Opsopoeodus) emilae.* Occas. Pap. Mus. Zool. Univ. Mich., no. 664.

Goldman, C. R. 1966. *Primary productivity in aquatic environments.* Berkeley: Univ. Calif. Press.

Gosline, W. A. 1966. The limits of the fish family Serranidae, with notes on the other lower percoids. *Proc. Calif. Acad. Sci.* 33:91–112.

Graham, J. J. 1956. *Observations on the alewife, Pomolobus pseudoharengus (Wilson), in fresh water.* Univ. Toronto, Ontario Fish. Res. Lab., no. 74.

Greenbank, J. T. 1945. Limnological conditions in ice-covered lakes, especially as related to winter-kill of fish. *Ecol. Monogr.* 15:343–92.

Greene, C. W. 1935. *The distribution of Wisconsin fishes.* Wis. Conserv. Comm.

Grosslein, M. D., and L. L. Smith, Jr. 1959. *The goldeye, Amphiodon alosoides (Rafinesque), in the commercial fishery of Red lakes, Minnesota.* U.S. Fish Wildl. Serv. Fish. Bull. 60, pp. 33–41.

Gruchy, C. G., and W. B. Scott. 1966. *Lepomis megalotis*, the longear sunfish, in western Canada. *J. Fish. Res. Board Can.* 23:1457–59.

Hankinson, T. L. 1929. Fishes of North Dakota. *Pap. Mich. Acad. Sci. Arts Lett.*, vol. 10 (1928), pp. 439–60.

Hansen, M. J., and D. W. Hayne. 1962. Sea lamprey in Ogontz Bay and Ogontz River, Michigan. *J. Wildl. Manage.* 26:237–47.

Harlan, J. R., and E. B. Speaker. 1969. *Iowa fish and fishing.* 4th ed. Iowa Conserv. Comm.

Harrison, H. M. 1949. An annotated list of the fishes of the upper Des Moines River basin in Iowa. *Proc. Iowa Acad. Sci.* 56:333–42.

Hasler, A. D. 1966. *Underwater guideposts.* Madison: Univ. Wis. Press.

Henshall, J. A. 1881. *Book of the black bass.* Cincinnati: Belford Clark and Co.

Heyerdahl, E. G., and L. L. Smith, Jr. 1971. *Annual catch of yellow perch from Red lakes, Minnesota, in relation to growth rate and fishing effort.* Univ. Minn. Agric. Exper. Station Tech. Bull., no. 285.

Hubbs, C. L. 1921. An ecological study of the life-history of the fresh-water atherine fish *Labidesthes sicculus. Ecol.* 2:262–76.

———. 1945. Corrected distributional records for Minnesota fishes. *Copeia*, pp. 13–22.

———. 1951. *Notropis amnis, a new cyprinid fish of the Mississippi fauna, with two subspecies.* Occas. Pap. Mus. Zool. Univ. Mich., no. 530.

———. 1954. Establishment of a forage fish, the red shiner (*Notropis lutrensis*), in the lower Colorado River system. *Calif. Fish Game* 40:287–94.

Hubbs, C. L., and G. P. Cooper. 1936. *Minnows of Michigan.* Cranbrook Inst. Sci. Bull., no. 8.

Hubbs, C. L., and W. R. Crowe. 1956. *Preliminary analysis of the American cyprinid fishes, seven new, referred to the genus Hybopsis, subgenus Erimystax.* Occas. Pap. Mus. Zool. Univ. Mich., no. 578.

Hubbs, C. L., J. R. Greeley, and C. M. Trazwell. 1932. *Methods for the improvement of Michigan trout streams.* Mich. Dep. Conserv., Bull. Inst. Fish. Res., no. 1.

Hubbs, C. L., and C. W. Greene. 1928. Further notes on the fishes of the Great Lakes and tributary waters. *Pap. Mich. Acad. Sci. Arts Lett.* (1927), 7:371–92.

Hubbs, C. L., and K. F. Lagler. 1964. *Fishes of the Great Lakes region.* Cranbrook Inst. Sci. Bull., no. 26.

Hubbs, C. L., and T. E. B. Pope. 1937. The spread of the sea lamprey through the Great Lakes. *Trans. Amer. Fish. Soc.* 66:172–76.

Hubbs, C. L., and M. B. Trautman. 1937. *A revision of the lamprey genus Ichthyomyzon.* Misc. Publ. Mus. Zool. Univ. Mich., no. 35.

Hutchinson, G. E. 1957. *A treatise on limnology. Vol. I. Geography, physics, and chemistry.* New York: John Wiley and Sons.

———. 1969. Eutrophication, past and present. In *Eutrophication: Causes, consequences, correctives*, pp. 17–26. Symp. Nat. Acad. Sci.

Isaak, D. 1961. The ecological life history of the fathead minnow, *Pimephales promelas* (Rafinesque). Ph.D. diss., Univ. Minn.

Johnson, R. E., and J. B. Moyle. 1949. *A biological survey and fishery management plan for the streams of the Root River basin.* Minn. Dep. Conserv., Fish. Res. Invest. Rep., no. 87.

Johnson, R. P. 1963. Studies on the life history and ecology of the bigmouth buffalo, *Ictiobus cyprinellus* (Valenciennes). *J. Fish. Res. Board Can.* 20:1397–429.

Jordan, D. S. 1888. *Science sketches.* Chicago: A. C. McClurg and Co.

———. 1904. *Manual of the vertebrate animals of the northern United States.* 9th ed. Chicago: A. C. McClurg and Co.

Jordan, D. S., and B. W. Evermann. 1902. *American food and game fishes.* New York: Doubleday, Page, and Co.

Jordan, D. S., B. W. Evermann, and H. W. Clark. 1930. *Check list of the fishes and fishlike vertebrates of North and Middle America north of the northern boundary of Venezuela and Columbia.* Pt. 2, Rep. U.S. Comm. Fish. (1928).

Kahn, N. Y., and S. U. Qadri. 1970. Morphological differences in Lake Superior lake char. *J. Fish. Res. Board Can.* 27:161–67.

————. 1971. Intraspecific variations and postglacial distribution of the lake char (*Salvelinus namaycush*). *J. Fish. Res. Board Can.* 28:465–76.

Kidd, P. E. 1927. The food of Minnesota fishes with special reference to the algae. *Trans. Amer. Fish. Soc.* 57:85–91.

Koelz, W. 1931. The coregonid fishes of the northeastern North America. *Pap. Mich. Acad. Sci. Arts Lett.* (1930) 13:303–432.

Koster, W. J. 1939. Some phases of the life history and relationships of the cyprinid, *Clinostomus elongatus* (Kirtland). *Copeia*, pp. 201–8.

Kuehn, J. H. 1949. A study of a population of longnose dace (*Rhinichthys c. cataractae*). *Proc. Minn. Acad. Sci.* 17:81–87.

Lachner, E. A., and R. E. Jenkins. 1967. Systematics, distribution, and evolution of the chub genus *Nocomis* (Cyprinidae) in the southwestern Ohio River basin, with the description of a new species. *Copeia*, pp. 557–80.

Larson, O. R. 1966. Some helminths of Itasca Park fishes. *J. Minn. Acad. Sci.* 33:99–101.

Legendre, P. 1970. The bearing of *Phoxinus* (Cyprinidae) hybridity on the classification of its North American species. *Can. J. Zool.* 48:1167–77.

Lindsey, C. C., and C. S. Woods. 1970. *Biology of the coregonid fishes.* Winnipeg: Univ. Manitoba Press.

McAllister, D. E. 1964. Distinguishing characters for the sculpins *Cottus bairdii* and *C. cognatus* in eastern Canada. *J. Fish. Res. Board Can.* 21:1139–42.

McCrimmon, H. R. 1968. *Carp in Canada.* Fish. Res. Board Can. Bull., no. 165.

McPhail, J. D., and C. C. Lindsey. 1970. *Freshwater fishes of northwestern Canada and Alaska.* Fish. Res. Board Can. Bull., no. 173.

Magnuson, J. J., and L. L. Smith, Jr. 1963. Some phases of the life history of the trout-perch. *Ecol.* 44:83–95.

Markus, H. C. 1934. Life history of the blackhead minnow (*Pimephales promelas*). *Copeia*, pp. 116–22.

Meyer, F. P., and J. H. Stevenson. 1962. Studies on the artificial propagation of the paddlefish. *Progr. Fish-Cult.* 24:65–67.

Miller, R. J. 1963. Comparative morphology of three cyprinid fishes: *Notropis cornutus, Notropis rubellus,* and the hybrid, *Notropis cornutus* X *Notropis rubellus. Amer. Midland Natur.* 69:1–33.

————. 1964. Behavior and ecology of some North American cyprinid fishes. *Amer. Midland Natur.* 72:313–57.

————. 1968. Speciation in the common shiner: An alternative view. *Copeia*, pp. 640–47.

Miller, R. R. 1957. Origin and dispersal of the alewife, *Alosa pseudoharengus*, and the gizzard shad, *Dorosoma cepedianum*, in the Great Lakes. *Trans. Amer. Fish. Soc.* 86:97–111.

Minckley, C. O., and F. B. Cross. 1959. Distribution, habitat, and abundance of the Topeka shiner, *Notropis topeka* (Gilbert), in Kansas. *Amer. Midland Natur.* 61:210–17.

Moore, H. H., and R. A. Braem. 1965. *Distribution of fishes in U.S. streams tributary to Lake Superior.* U.S. Fish Wildl. Serv., Special Sci. Rep., no. 516.

Moyle, P. B. 1969. Ecology of the fishes of a Minnesota lake, with special reference to the Cyprinidae. Ph.D. diss., Univ. Minn.

Needham, P. R. 1938. *Trout streams.* Ithaca: Comstock Pub. Co.

Nelson, D. M. 1970. Ecology of the cisco, *Coregonus artedi*, in two Minnesota lakes. Ph.D. diss., Univ. Minn.

Nelson, J. S. 1968. Deep-water ninespine sticklebacks, *Pungitius pungitius*, in the Mississippi drainage, Crooked Lake, Indiana. *Copeia*, pp. 326–34.

New, J. G. 1962. Hybridization between two cyprinids, *Chrosomus eos* and *Chrosomus neogaeus. Copeia*, pp. 147–52.

Olson, D. E. 1963. Role of the white sucker in Minnesota waters. *Proc. Minn. Acad. Sci.* 31:68–73.

Parker, H. J. 1964. Natural history of *Pimephales vigilax* (Cyprinidae). *Southwest. Natur.* 8:228–35.

Peterka, J. J., and L. L. Smith, Jr. 1970. Lake whitefish in the commercial fishery of Red lakes, Minnesota. *Trans. Amer. Fish. Soc.* 99:28–43.

Pfeiffer, R. A. 1955. Studies on the life history of the rosyface shiner, *Notropis rubellus. Copeia*, pp. 95–106.

Phillips, G. L. 1967. Sexual dimorphism in the western blacknose dace, *Rhinichthys atratulus meleagris. J. Minn. Acad. Sci.* 34:11–13.

———. 1969a. Diet of minnow *Chrosomus erythrogaster* (Cyprinidae) in a Minnesota stream. *Amer. Midland Natur.* 82:99–109.

———. 1969b. Morphology and variation of the American cyprinid fishes *Chrosomus erythrogaster* and *Chrosomus eos. Copeia*, pp. 501–9.

———. 1969c. Accuracy of fecundity estimates for the minnow *Chrosomus erythrogaster* (Cyprinidae). *Trans. Amer. Fish. Soc.* 98:524–26.

Phillips, G. L., and J. C. Underhill. 1967. Revised distribution records of some Minnesota fishes, with addition of two species to the faunal list. *J. Minn. Acad. Sci.* 34:177–80.

———. 1971. *Distribution and variation of the Catostomidae of Minnesota.* Occas. Pap. Bell Mus. Natur. Hist., Univ. Minn., no. 10.

Purkett, C. A., Jr. 1961. Reproduction and early development of the paddlefish. *Trans. Amer. Fish. Soc.* 90:125–29.

Pycha, R. L., and L. L. Smith, Jr. 1955. Early life history of the yellow perch, *Perca flavescens* (Mitchill), in Red lakes, Minnesota. *Trans. Amer. Fish. Soc.* 84:249–60.

Rafinesque, C. S. 1820. *Ichthyologia ohiensis, of natural history of the fishes inhabiting the river and its tributary streams.* Lexington: W. G. Hunt.

Raney, E. C. 1940a. Breeding habits of the common shiner. *Zoologica* (New York) 25:1–14.

———. 1940b. Reproductive activities of a hybrid minnow, *Notropis cornutus* X *Notropis rubellus. Zoologica* (New York) 25:361–67.

Reed, R. J. 1957. The prolonged spawning of the rosyface shiner, *Notropis rubellus* (Agassiz) in northwestern Pennsylvania. *Copeia*, p. 250.

Reid, G. K. 1961. *Ecology of inland waters and estuaries.* New York: Reinhold Pub. Corp.

Reighard, J. 1910. *Methods of studying the habits of fishes with an account of the breeding habits of the horned dace.* Bull. U.S. Bur. Fish., vol. 28, pp. 1113–36.

Ruttner, F. 1963. *Fundamentals of limnology.* 3d ed. Toronto: Univ. Toronto Press.

Slastenenko, E. P. 1958. *The freshwater fishes of Canada.* Toronto: Kiev Printers.

Smith, L. L., Jr., and R. L. Butler. 1952. Movements of marked walleyes, *Stizostedion vitreum vitreum* (Mitchill), in the fishery of the Red lakes, Minnesota. *Trans. Amer. Fish. Soc.* 81:179–96.

Smith, L. L., Jr., and R. H. Kramer. 1964. The spottail shiner in Lower Red Lake, Minnesota. *Trans. Amer. Fish. Soc.* 93:35–45.

Smith, L. L., Jr., and L. W. Krefting. 1953. Fluctuations in production and abundance of commercial species in the Red lakes, Minnesota, with special reference to changes in the walleye population. *Trans. Amer. Fish. Soc.* 83:131–60.

Smith, L. L., Jr., and J. B. Moyle. 1944. *A biological survey and fishery management plan for the streams of the Lake Superior north shore watershed.* Minn. Dep. Conserv., Tech. Bull., no. 1.

Smith, L. L., Jr., and R. L. Pycha. 1960. First year growth of the walleye, *Stizostedion vitreum vitreum* (Mitchill), and associated factors in the Red lakes, Minnesota. *Limnol. Oceanogr.* 5:281–90.

Smith, S. H. 1968. Species succession and fishery exploitation in the Great Lakes. *J. Fish. Res. Board Can.* 14:667–93.

Stasiak, R. H. 1972. The morphology and life history of the finescale dace, *Pfrille neogaea*, in Itasca State Park, Minnesota. Ph.D. diss., Univ. Minn.

Stewart, K. W., and C. C. Lindsey. 1970. First specimens of the stonecat, *Noturus flavus*, from the Hudson Bay drainage. *J. Fish. Res. Board Can.* 27:170–72.

Surber, T. 1913. *Notes on the natural history of fresh-water mussels.* Bull. U.S. Bur. Fish., vol. 32, pp. 101–16.

————. 1920. *A preliminary catalogue of the fishes and fish-like vertebrates of Minnesota.* Appendix, Bienn. Rep. Minn. Game Fish Comm.

Taylor, W. R. 1954. *Records of fishes in the John Lowe collections from the Upper Peninsula of Michigan.* Misc. Publ. Mus. Zool. Univ. Mich., no. 87.

————. 1969. *A revision of the catfish genus Noturus Rafinesque with an analysis of higher groups of Ictaluridae.* Bull. U.S. Nat. Mus., no. 282.

Thompson, D. H. 1933. The finding of a very young *Polyodon. Copeia*, pp. 31–33.

Thurston, C. E. 1962. Physical characteristics and chemical composition of two subspecies of lake trout. *J. Fish. Res. Board Can.* 19:39–44.

Trautman, M. B. 1957. *Fishes of Ohio.* Columbus: Ohio State Univ. Press.

Trautman, M. B., and C. L. Hubbs. 1935. When do pike shed their teeth? *Trans. Amer. Fish. Soc.* 65:261–66.

Underhill, J. C. 1957. *The distribution of Minnesota minnows and darters.* Occas. Pap. Minn. Mus. Natur. Hist., no. 7.

————. 1959. Fishes of the Vermillion River, South Dakota. *Proc. S.D. Acad. Sci.* 38:96–102.

————. 1960. Variation in the red shiner, *Notropis lutrensis* (Baird and Girard). *Proc. Minn. Acad. Sci.* 28:78–80.

————. 1961. Infra-specific variation in the common shiner, *Notropis cornutus frontalis* (Agassiz) from Minnesota and South Dakota. *Proc. Minn. Acad. Sci.* 29:259–66.

————. 1963. Distribution in Minnesota of the subspecies of the percid fish *Etheostoma nigrum* and of their intergrades. *Amer. Midland Natur.* 70:470–78.

Underhill, J. C., and G. A. Cole. 1967. The summer standing crop, growth, and distribution of *Chironomus plumosus*, in Lake Itasca, Minnesota. *J. Minn. Acad. Sci.* 34:181–86.

Underhill, J. C., and D. J. Merrell. 1959. Intra-specific variation in the bigmouth shiner (*Notropis dorsalis*). *Amer. Midland Natur.* 61:133–47.

Walton, I. 1653. *The compleat angler.* New York: E. P. Dutton and Co. (Everyman's Library, 1906).

Welch, P. S. 1952. *Limnology.* New York: McGraw-Hill Book Co.

Wiebe, A. H. 1930. *Investigations on the plankton production in fish ponds.* Bull. U.S. Bur. Fish., vol. 46, pp. 137–76.

Wohlfarth, G., and M. Lahman. 1963. Genetic improvement of carp. IV. Leather and line carp in fish ponds of Israel. *Bamidgeh* 15:3–8.

Woolman, A. J. 1895. *A report upon ichthyological investigations in western Minnesota and eastern North Dakota.* Rep. U.S. Fish Comm. (1893), pp. 343–73.

Wynne-Edwards, V. C. 1933. The breeding habits of the black-headed minnow (*Pimephales promelas* Raf.). *Trans. Amer. Fish. Soc.* 62:382–83.

Zumberge, J. H. 1952. *The lakes of Minnesota: Their origin and classification.* Minn. Geol. Surv. Bull., no. 35.

Index